KILLING
FOR
COUNTRY

REG UHR OF THE NATIVE POLICE

KILLING FOR COUNTRY

A FAMILY STORY

DAVID MARR

Published by Black Inc.,
an imprint of Schwartz Books Pty Ltd
Wurundjeri Country
22–24 Northumberland Street
Collingwood VIC 3066, Australia
enquiries@blackincbooks.com
www.blackincbooks.com

9781760642730 (paperback)
9781743823309 (ebook)

 A catalogue record for this
book is available from the
National Library of Australia

Cover design by Mary Callahan
Text design and typesetting by Beau Lowenstern
Cover image: Thomas Coward, Subinspector of Police, 1871.
State Library of Queensland.

To those who told the truth

I did not work alone.

This book is the result of a deep collaboration
over four years with my partner,
Sebastian Tesoriero.

CONTENTS

A NOTE

I remember my great-grandmother. She had a crumpled face and faded away when I was too young to notice. She was a blank. Stories weren't told about her. In 2019, an ancient uncle of mine asked me to find what I could about Maud. He knew so little. I dug out some books. It wasn't long before I was looking at a photograph of her father in the uniform of the Native Police.

I was appalled and curious. I have been writing about the politics of race all my career. I know what side I'm on. Yet that afternoon I found in the lower branches of my family tree Sub-Inspector Reginald Uhr, a professional killer of Aborigines. Then I discovered his brother D'arcy was also in the massacre business. Writing is my trade. I knew at once I had to tell the story of my family's bloody business with the Aboriginal people. That led me, step by step, into the history of the Native Police.

Language keeps shifting. In the times I am writing about, Aboriginal Australians were called blacks, natives and Aborigines. The language of today and the values it represents were not in the minds of colonists then. To be true to the history, the politics and their thinking, I have used the language of that time.

The AustLang database has been my guide to the names of Aboriginal peoples. For their territories I have relied on the map of Indigenous Australia produced by AIATSIS, the Australian Institute of Aboriginal and Torres Strait Islander Studies.

I wrote on Gadigal land.

D.E.M.

I

MR JONES

No man, who comes to this Colony and has ground and cattle and Corn, can dispassionately view the subject of the Blacks, their interest says annihilate the race.

Lancelot Threlkeld, 1826

LIVERPOOL PLAINS

1

CROSS-BREEDING

The young man drove his flock over the Liverpool Range. The sky was immense. Magnificent plains lay before him. Grass ran for miles as level as the sea. This was country where squatters would make fortunes and found dynasties. But fortune was a fickle thing in the Colony. So far, she had favoured Edmund Blucher Uhr extravagantly, plucking him from a poor street by the Thames when his sister married the Sydney merchant whose sheep he was driving down to a crossing on the Mooki. It was spring. The air was full of birds.

Is it not a good place, Uhr asked. His guide agreed. "But I should not like to put my sheep on it and drive away the cattle of those who have sat down here." Two huts stood on the far side of the river. Uhr didn't care. "They are a set of cattle-stealing rascals, and I should have no compunction." His guide agreed they were rascals. "But I should not trouble myself about that. I should go farther, and look out for myself. They are here." Uhr was unpersuaded. He had crossed the range with orders to seize a great swathe of the finest land in New South Wales. "My sheep will soon scatter the cattle."

The two men rode down the river for 12 miles, claiming 150,000 acres of the Liverpool Plains for the merchant Richard Jones. The soil was black and deep. This is Kamilaroi* country, but neither Jones nor Uhr doubted for a moment the land was theirs for the taking. Jones

---

* Also Gamilaraay or Gamilaroi.

paid nothing for these acres. His only obligation was to stock them. Uhr would soon be running 30,000 sheep along the Mooki. New South Wales was perfecting a unique form of colonial conquest: invasion by sheep.

The Kamilaroi call this corner of their country the great plains, Corbon Comleroy. "Big fellow water all over the plains," one of the old people told a stockman. "They used to have canoes and go fishing from one island to the other." The Kamilaroi were a warrior nation about 12,000 strong and their country covered 30,000 square miles running from the plains west and north into the valleys of the Peel, the Barwon, the Gwydir and the Macintyre. These were the Welsh, Scottish and English names the invaders pinned to the map. But ancient Kamilaroi names survived, perhaps too beautiful to be lost: Quirindi, Wee Waa, Collarenebri, the Mooki. Even before Edmund Uhr brought his sheep to the plains in 1835, maps had begun to mark the places Kamilaroi would be slaughtered. The names are still there: Waterloo Creek, Gravesend, Slaughterhouse Creek, Vinegar Hill and, most haunting of all, Myall Creek.

*

Richard Jones never raised his voice. Not for him the caterwauling and brawls dubbed *Botany Bay tactics*. He was quiet, fearless and a mighty Christian who would seize from the Aboriginal people by influence, chance and cunning 600,000 acres of their country. His lieutenant in the enterprise was the young man he rescued from the London slums. Though Jones became one of the richest figures in New South Wales and shaped its politics under four governors, this silky man with a plain name makes only fleeting appearances in the big histories. Many dismissed him in his own day as pious and penny-pinching. But Richard Jones was a great white carp in the colonial pond, half hidden in the weeds, always feeding and always dangerous.

He came to Sydney in 1809 as a clerk in a merchant house. The Joneses had land and a little brewery on the Welsh borders. "Small country gentlefolks," his daughter Elizabeth called them. "Papa was sent to London for educational advantages & when fitted for it, he obtained a clerkship in a leading London Mercantile Firm." This was Alexander Birnie & Co., traders in wool and whale oil. As an elder of the Scottish church, Birnie worked hand in glove with the Missionary Society in the Pacific, where God and trade were advancing together on the fringes of the Empire. His house shipped evangelists to Tahiti, New Zealand and the Marquesas, whence their boats returned to London laden with timber, flax and oil. Neither trade nor evangelism extended to the Aborigines of New South Wales. How different this story might have been had they anything to sell the invaders.

Birnie sent his restless brother James to set up a branch of the house in Sydney. He in turn brought out twenty-three-year-old Jones. Birnie was a drunk who left his young clerk in charge of the business for months and years at a time. Responsibility came easily to Jones. Over the next few years, he sold rum from Bengal and household goods from London. He set up a whaling fleet in the Tasman and began to ship wool to England. He handled other people's money with faultless tact. He collected debts for merchants in India, China and London; he administered the estates of the mad and the dead. Trust was his capital. His prospects grew as he became known as a Christian merchant of impeccable honesty.

Sydney was a makeshift town built on a few bays of the finest harbour in the world. Its imperial trappings were modest. Windmills lined the hills. Pubs were dotted everywhere. Stock wandered the streets. A gallows stood close to the graveyard. Though there was money to be made in the town, punishment remained the purpose of the place. Chain gangs clanked through the streets every morning. Hundreds of convict servants worked for masters who had only to feed, clothe and house them in return for their labour. Jones employed and despised them. "Very bad indeed," was his verdict of the labour they gave. And convict discipline? "The punishments are much slighter than they were; which, no doubt, is the cause of all the insubordination." All his life Richard Jones was a committed foe of insubordination. He would not have convicts in his house. "My own private servants were always free."

The Colony had yet to recover – if it ever did – from the upheaval of the Rum Rebellion that overthrew Governor William Bligh. Though a petty tyrant, Bligh was often in the right. He thought army officers and wool growers like John Macarthur should obey the law like everyone else. So they deposed him. Jones was there to watch the fireworks that marked the arrival of his successor, Colonel Lachlan Macquarie, who already knew a thing or two about insurrection. Macquarie had fought the American rebels in Charleston and New York. After the American War of Independence, rebellion was never entirely out of the question in the Empire. Men who overthrew a governor might once have been dragged back to London and hanged. These rebels were barely punished. The enduring lesson of the Rum Rebellion was the power of the big men of New South Wales. Governors took them on at their peril.

The day after Macquarie stepped ashore, on New Year's Eve 1809, he delivered a short speech on the Grand Parade. The new Governor hoped that "the dissentions and Jealousies of the Colony might now give way to a spirit of conciliation, that all classes go to church on Sunday and the native peoples be treated with kindness". Macquarie had been given the same Royal Instructions issued to the governors who came before him:

> You are to endeavour by every possible means to open an intercourse with the natives, and to conciliate their affections, enjoining all our subjects to live in amity and kindness with them. And if any of our subjects shall wantonly destroy them, or give them any unnecessary interruption in the exercise of their several occupations, it is our will and pleasure that you do cause such offenders to be brought to punishment according to the degree of the offence.

That had not happened. Twenty years of European settlement had seen many massacres of Eora and Dharug* people. After one or two attempts

---

* Also Darug.

to punish settler vigilantes, the authorities in Sydney turned a blind eye to killings in the bush. In town, Aboriginal people wandered the streets free and naked. They laughed and made friends. They fished the harbour and showed settlers where to fish. Bennelong and his wife Barangaroo dined at the Governor's table. But out along the Hawkesbury River (Dyarubbin), the Dharug were murdered by farmers planting the Colony's first corn. The blacks killed in return, which settlers declared was evidence of black savagery. Few colonists could admit the underlying provocation that set black against white. David Collins, the Colony's first judge, saw the situation with clear eyes: "While they entertained the idea of our having dispossessed them of their residences, they must always consider us as enemies; and upon this principle they made a point of attacking the white people whenever opportunity and safety concurred."

Sin was everywhere. Sydney was indifferent to the Christian faith. Men outnumbered women more than two to one. Crimes of the flesh too terrible to mention were commonplace in the streets. Marriages were few. Hardly anyone went to church. The Colony's first newspaper, *The Sydney Gazette*, which Jones would one day own, begged all ranks to "unite in the highly meritorious Service of Suppressing Vice in all its Forms, and in pointing out to their tender Offspring and Servants the Paths of Virtue, by themselves uniformly regarding the Sabbath Day, and regularly attending the Church." Nothing changed.

The loudest voice beseeching citizens to return to the ways of the Lord was that of the Reverend Samuel Marsden. He was many things in the Colony – a hellfire preacher, a magistrate of notorious cruelty, a wool grower at Parramatta, a trader in the Pacific Islands and valued client of the house of Alexander Birnie & Co. Jones was quickly absorbed into Marsden's family and became, for the rest of the preacher's life, his friend and defender. Both men were of the Evangelical wing of the Church of England. Their loyalty to the Established Church came with a strong dash of Methodism. They had no time for the eighteenth-century romance of the Noble Savage. The native peoples of Australia were seen, instead, to be unredeemed, fallen and in desperate need of salvation.

But could they be redeemed? Marsden once believed so, but by the time Jones came into his circle he had become, through bitter experience, convinced that everlasting life was beyond the grasp of the Aborigines.

Two black boys had jilted him. Taking an Aboriginal child into the household was an early fashion in the Colony. It rarely turned out well. Marsden's first disappointment was young Harry, a boy left an orphan after a reprisal raid:

> I entertained very great hopes that from conversing with him upon the comforts of Civil Life, the nature of our Religion, and such subjects as I thought were best calculated to enlarge his mind, he might become civilized. But at length he joined the Natives in the Woods.

That Harry might grow up to want more from life than virgin service in the Marsden household seemed not to cross the chaplain's mind. Undeterred by Harry's betrayal, Marsden took in four-year-old Tristan Mambe. Over the next dozen years Tristan learned to read the Bible, sing hymns and wait at table. He was a little wonder in the Colony. But when the chaplain tried to take his protégé to London to show off to his Evangelical friends, the young man got drunk in Rio de Janeiro, stole money and went on a spree. The ship sailed on without him. The sin of ingratitude bit deep with his master. Marsden never forgave Tristan or his race. He considered blacks incapable of instruction. Two faults put civilisation beyond them, he told Macquarie:

> The first was, they had no wants, they lived free and independent, and thought little more of to-morrow than the fowls of the air or the beasts of the field, and put no value upon the comforts of civil life. The second was, it had been found hitherto impossible to attach them, either to places or to individuals in the Colony who wished to benefit them.

Marsden backed missions to the Māori and Pacific Islanders, but never saw the point of trying to lead Aborigines into the Light of Christ. Jones was of the same mind. He never thought they might be *civilised*. He was to be a founding father of many charities in the Colony, but the charity of Richard Jones never extended to Aboriginal people.

Exasperated by the failure of the Established Church to engage with Aborigines, Governor Macquarie established the Native Institution in Parramatta in 1814 as an experiment in "Educating, and bringing up to Habits of Industry and Decency, the Youth of both Sexes". Enrolments were pitifully thin. That Aboriginal parents were so reluctant to part with their offspring was taken as yet another mark of their savagery. As a concession to their affection, an open slat fence was built to allow parents – on application – to watch their children in the school yard dressed in linen pretending to be white children. To encourage enrolments, Macquarie held a feast every year in Parramatta where Aboriginal families assembled to pay obeisance – or so it seemed – to the Governor and the leading citizens of the town. Tables were set up in the marketplace and loaded with beef and drink. Children from the institution were put through their paces. "Several of the little ones read, and it was grateful to the bosom of sensibility to trace the degrees of pleasure which the chiefs manifested on this occasion," reported the *Gazette*. "Some clapped the children on the head, and one in particular turning round towards the Governor, with extraordinary emotion, exclaimed 'GOVERNOR,—that will make good Settler—that's my Pickaninny!'"

Marsden would have nothing to do with the Native Institution. But his boycott of the 1816 feast was notably ostentatious. That year the Governor had a grave purpose: to seek peace after sending his soldiers to massacre "Black Natives of this Country" he held responsible for the deaths of men and women on farms south of Sydney. Macquarie wanted the perpetrators taught a lesson:

> You must fire upon them; saving the Women and Children
> if possible. All such grown up Men as may happen to be
> killed you will direct to be Hanged on the highest Trees and
> in the clearest parts of the Forest where they fall.

The soldiers were asked, while they were at it, to scoop up a dozen boys and half a dozen girls for the Native Institution. Near Appin in April 1816, soldiers drove at least seven men, women and children over a 200-foot drop into the Cataract gorge. Many others were shot. In the wake of the operation, Macquarie invited the leading citizens of the town to assemble at the feast in the hope of reaching some sort of understanding with the Aboriginal peoples of Sydney. But the Reverend Samuel Marsden, who had been seen in Parramatta that morning, didn't bother to attend. This insult provoked the Governor's secretary, John Campbell, to deliver in the *Gazette* a magnificent broadside under the pseudonym "Philo Free", accusing Marsden and his missionaries of making extravagant profits from spirits, timber and flax in the Pacific while doing nothing to introduce "the pure doctrines of the Christian religion among the sable sons of Australia".

Marsden sued. Claims that he neglected Aborigines didn't upset him. He wanted Philo Free punished for accusing him of profiteering in the Pacific. In the tight little world of Sydney, this was seen as a proxy battle between Marsden and the Governor. Would-be witnesses fled. But Richard Jones did not flinch from the task of dissembling for his client and mentor. He admitted in the witness box that Marsden owned the *Active*, a brig that traded with New Zealand and Tahiti. He had filled the ship's hold with goods for seven years but he insisted the *Active* sailed at a loss. "I believe that the London Missionary Society make an allowance to Mr. Marsden of £250, and the Church Missionary Society make up any other deficiency." That was not true. Jones denied Philo Free's charge that the missionaries had taught the peoples of the South Seas how to brew spirits. That was also a lie. He denied the missionaries had ever distributed guns and cutlasses. Another lie. Every accusation Philo Free made against Marsden and his missionaries was indisputably true. But Jones' testimony secured the chaplain's victory. Campbell was ordered to pay Marsden damages of £200.

At the age of thirty, Jones left his old house to join Alexander Riley, a clever and moody businessman who came to the Colony early and

RICHARD JONES

prospered first as a merchant and later as a wool grower. Riley's claims
on history include his part in building Macquarie's notorious Rum
Hospital. The deal yielded him little and nearly ruined his partners, Gar-
nham Blaxcell and D'Arcy Wentworth. But from 1815, Riley and Jones
grew rich together. Merchants all around them were failing, but Riley
and Jones were sound. To Macquarie's government they sold everything
from iron to twine. They shipped cedar from Port Stephens to Sydney.
They owned ships carrying goods and people to London. Whaling was
their most profitable business, so profitable that Jones saw it as the commercial future of Australia. They introduced marine insurance to the
Colony and made a fortune as agents for Lloyds.

    Through Riley, Jones came to know Walter Davidson, the most
important commercial connection of his life. Davidson was a landowner

who fled Australia after the Rum Rebellion and set up on the China coast, where he grew rich selling opium to the Middle Kingdom and tea to the Empire. Davidson's tea was hugely profitable for Riley & Jones. Everyone drank tea. Every hut in the bush had its chest of tea. Convict rations included a pound a month. When tea was short, authorities feared for public order. Davidson shipped tea from Canton by the ton, adding rum and cigars to the cargo on the way. Though Jones had a puritan distaste for opium and applauded China's later attempts to suppress the trade, he made his early fortune in the tangled commerce of opium and tea. All the way to the crash, tea was the business closest to his heart. Merchant Jones became China Jones.

Macquarie loathed the firm. In May 1818 news reached Sydney that the Secretary of State for the Colonies, Lord Bathurst, had prohibited convict ships from carrying, as they always had, commercial cargoes. The Governor blamed this on the London manoeuvres of Alexander Riley and Richard Jones. He protested to Bathurst:

> It renders the Colony (at present but Scantily furnished with Merchants of Capital or Character) altogether dependent on the ill Selected and precarious Supplies which one solitary Mercantile Firm (namely, that of Jones & Riley) may Chuse to Import. By these Means, all Competition in Trade and Price is at an End, and the place reduced to the Necessity of dispensing altogether with its accustomed Imported Comforts, or obliged to purchase them at the grasping Extravagant prices which a Selfish, Sordid Firm Chuses to demand.

Prices soared. Macquarie suspended the ban and asked Bathurst for fresh instructions to put trade with the Colony "at once on a permanent and a Free, Fair Footing". Bathurst agreed to withdraw his edict. Jones said of Macquarie: "The more I view the man's conduct the more I am confirmed in the vile malignity of his disposition."

*

When news of his father's death reached Jones in July 1818, he prepared to leave for home. He planned to be away from Sydney only long enough to administer his father's modest estate in Shropshire. But it would be over six years before he returned. He put his commercial affairs in order. Alexander Riley had left for London already, having ceded his place in the partnership to his son Edward. The firm was now Jones & Riley. Jones also farewelled the many charities where he was, almost always, treasurer. The Auxiliary Bible Society of New South Wales held a special meeting at the Court House in September to thank him for "his cheerful and ready, honourable and faithful discharge of the Duties of that Office". A week later he sailed for China on the *Magnet*. In Canton he met Walter Davidson for the first time and they became firm friends. His health broken but his fortune made, Davidson was about to join his family's bank in London and hand the Canton business to his partner. The house of Dent & Co. became one of the great British *hongs* on the China coast. Tea and money would flow from Canton to Richard Jones for another twenty years.

WALTER DAVIDSON

In London, Jones took a desk in the Broad Street office of his agent, Stuart Alexander Donaldson, a canny shipowner whose alliance with Jones in Australia was enriching them both. From this perch in the City, Jones kept an eye on his Sydney house and its whaling fleet. Nothing earned him so much at this time as whale oil from the Tasman fisheries, shipped to England in his own boats to light lamps, make soap and lubricate the machinery of the new industrial age. Jones found himself comfortably settled in Broad Street. He took on a new partner in Sydney – thirty-three-year-old William Walker, late of Calcutta, who brought £7000 and a good deal of talent to the house – and he ordered the sale of his household furniture, plate, china, earthenware and library in Sydney. But as he was deciding to stay in London, the price of Australian wool rose sharply. "German wools, except the very best, were falling back, while Spain, racked by political disorder, no longer counted," wrote the historian Stephen Roberts. "Australia was forging to the front." The famous inquiry into Macquarie's regime conducted by John Bigge seized on wool as "the principal, if not the only source of productive industry within the colony". This aristocratic lawyer saw many difficulties ahead – labour shortages, a long voyage to market, British import duties – but he could see no problem finding land for the immense flocks he had in mind. Small grants ended with Bigge. After him, land went to the gentry in huge slabs. And the native peoples? Bigge saw them dying off as settlement advanced. "As an unfettered range over a large tract of country seems to be indispensable to their existence, the black population will undergo a gradual diminution in proportion to the advances of the white population into the interior."

As wool prices continued to climb, Jones and Walter Davidson decided to invest heavily in Saxon sheep. Spanish merinos were flourishing in Australia but the finest clip in the world came from the pampered merino flocks of Saxony. These were housed at great expense in barns through the German winter, but perhaps in Australia they would flourish all year in the open air, tended by a few convict shepherds. It was a gamble on which they were willing to bet large sums of money. When

Davidson married in 1824, Jones joined him and his bride on an extended honeymoon in Germany, inspecting and buying expensive sheep. Jones spent over £5000 in Saxony and another £3000 on fine stock in England. They planned to run their flocks together. Davidson would remain in London and Jones return to Australia. Both expected to be granted thousands of acres in New South Wales. England was still giving away land to respectable suitors – theft by gentlemen for gentlemen.

Jones approached Lord Bathurst, bragging to the Secretary of State for the Colonies of all he had achieved in New South Wales and all he might yet achieve with his pure Saxons. His tone was superb:

> I trust your Lordship will view my exertions for the benefit of that rising Country with your usual liberality, and give me an order on the Local Government for a Grant of Land proportionate in your Lordships opinion, to those exertions and the amount of Capital embarked in the agriculture and Commerce of the New World.

Davidson called on his wife's grandfather, Viscount Strathallan, to remind the Secretary of State that Walter Stevenson Davidson was family, a partner in the bank Herries, Farquhar & Co., and nephew of the late physician to the King. "And therefore, in every point of view, I know no one in the Kingdom better entitled to obtain such a grant as my friend Davidson, or one more likely to do it justice and follow up the plans and wishes of government." Without waiting for Bathurst's verdict, the partners fitted the *Hugh Crawford* out at great expense to carry in comfort to Australia 122 rams and ewes plus Jones and his wife, Mary. The arrival of the *Hugh Crawford* in Sydney in April 1825 is a moment marked in the history of wool in Australia. It was a tight race, many more Saxons would follow, but Jones could boast for the rest of his life: "I am the first person who imported from Saxony, Sheep of pure blood and first character, into this Colony."

So much about his alliance with Mary Peterson was unlikely. Her family sold slops – sailors' work clothes – and her father died when she was six. Her mother, a tailor, next married Johan Uhr. They had five boys. Nothing certain is known of Uhr's birth, death or background. He was called a mariner and my family believed he was German. They all lived in the same house in Cannon Street by the Thames, but he seems to have disappeared soon after the birth of his youngest son. There's scant evidence of him being about when his stepdaughter Mary married a colonial merchant on Christmas Eve 1822. Jones was thirty-six and Mary was nineteen. She left to live with him in Pall Mall.

The family had illusions of intimacy with the Scottish aristocracy. Mary's grandfather John was a Ker, who saw himself one of the family of the Dukes of Roxburghe. The stories were vague, something about a military Ker who lost his fortune and an unmarried duke who *may* have sired a child. A piece of cloth embroidered with a ducal crest was considered evidence of the link between the families. There was a close link once, in the seventeenth century. But John was a fancy fan painter and broke. He showered the fifth duke, James Innes-Ker, with letters and turned up uninvited one day at Fleurs, the family's pile in Scotland, where he claimed to be "most nobly entertained, and politely treated by all". But then he took a step too far and the duke snapped. "I am informed, *I hope groundlessly*, that *you* gave out, that your son is *next after me* to the succession of the Roxburghe estates," he wrote in February 1812. "This I know to be contrary to fact; it may injure you and him, but cannot serve." John's begging letters didn't stop. None were answered. When John threatened to publish their correspondence, the duke's office advised him to go right ahead. He did. In 1814 an infinitely sad pamphlet appeared: *The Breach of Promise or Mis-Led Nobleman, by Artful Teachers; or Honor Sold for the Sake of a Trifle*. Price: one shilling. He was still begging: "Any nobleman, lady, or gentleman, who should think proper to subscribe to relieve my loss, it will be thankfully received, and gratefully acknowledged."

The fan painter was encouraged in these Roxburghe claims by his wife, the author of several Gothic novels that sold poorly and earned critical ridicule, not least for their immoral tone. Though not much of a writer, there was a good deal to admire about Anne Ker. She was determined and outspoken. She stood up for herself, condemning the "devouring watchmen" who sneered at her novels in literary periodicals. Her last great effort was a three-volume saga, *Edric, the Forester,* the adventures of a lost heir in the time of William the Conqueror. Her husband used the title page to attack the fifth duke in doggerel:

> There is a man on Scottish ground,
> Caus'd me to lose two hundred pounds
> Surely how could such things be?
> Why, in promising to provide for me!

Edric's failure left Anne begging the Royal Literary Fund for help, "having lately sold all her furniture and the money expended, and at this time nearly in want of bread to exist". She received five pounds.

This curious London pair, novelist and fan painter, lived to see their family rescued by their granddaughter's marriage to Richard Jones. The future of the Peterson and Uhr boys was now assured for Jones took responsibility for them all, shipping them out one by one in their teens. This was not entirely selfless. At his age Jones ought to have had sons of his own in his businesses. These London boys would serve until his own came along, and they could take with them to New South Wales the comforting notion that however rough life might be herding sheep on the Liverpool Plains, or boiling down carcasses in the bush, or slaughtering Aborigines in the Gulf country, they had this splendid – and forever unproved – connection to the Roxburghes.

The first to arrive in Sydney, Daniel Peterson, was apprenticed on one of Jones' whaling boats. The next, John Uhr, was sent at the age of thirteen to learn the ways of sheep. The next boy was Edmund. The family had a taste for grand names that survived generations. Born five weeks after Field Marshal Gebhard von Blücher drove Napoleon into exile, the boy was christened Edmund Blücher Uhr. The umlaut was lost at sea. When he stepped ashore in Sydney in 1827 at the age of twelve, he was sent to Richard Jones' new estate south of Sydney, Fleurs.

2

LORDS OF THE SOIL

J ones had hoped for better country. The Hunter Valley had been opened for settlement while he was in London. By the time he returned to the Colony, every square inch of land along the river had been taken. He was given 2000 acres of "Badly Watered Fine Open Country" near Patrick's Plains – later Singleton – with permission to buy, if he wished, another 4000 acres. He pestered Governor Ralph Darling for more promising country up the coast. Darling refused. Jones kept nagging: "I have invested a large Sum of Money in the importation and improvement of fine Woolled Sheep, and also being in possession of a large Herd of Cattle I am now much in want of pasture for them." Finally, Darling gave him 10,000 more acres, officially in recognition of his services to wool, whaling and banking. Lord Bathurst confirmed the second gift while observing it was rather extensive. But this was the colonial way: to those given much, yet more would be given. Jones purchased a few extra blocks to give his stock access to the river and named his accumulated run Black Creek, after a stream that flows down from the Broken Back Range. A long time later, under the name Pokolbin, this became famous wine country. But it was taken from the Wonnarua in the 1820s for cattle and sheep. Jones did not move his stock north from Fleurs until the killing was done.

The Wonnarua called the river Coquun. Years later, when this world had vanished, a boy who once stood on the riverbank watching the Wonnarua at play wrote about this time so that it might be remembered how kind and funny and handsome the Wonnarua were, "swimming hither and thither, diving great distances, and unexpectedly seizing a companion by the legs, who would disappear under the water with a cry, a strange admixture of shout and laugh, to again appear with the aggressor choking with laughter and water". He delighted in their banter. "You ugly fellow, your face is like a pumpkin," they told him. "Your hair is like a brush, plenty wallaby sit down there." The men took him hunting and in the evenings let him listen to their singing, "the voices of the females harmonising well with those of the men". In old age the boy also wanted to celebrate how beautiful the valley was before the axemen came:

> The aromatic cedar, redolent when cut with exquisite perfume, alike remarkable for its beautiful foliage and enormous size; the gigantic fig tree; and the monarch gum ... The contrast between the brush as felled but recently, and the adjacent wall of living timber, may be more readily imagined than described. The one a picture of extreme loveliness, and the other of desolation.

The Wonnarua resisted the invasion of their land by stripping farms of crops and robbing travellers on the road. From hilltops, they rolled boulders down on their pursuers. Deaths were sporadic. When a stockman known for beating blacks was killed near Putty in 1825 and two more deaths followed in the nearby mountains, soldiers from Windsor killed at least six blacks in a dawn raid in Garland Valley. It turned out they had nothing to do with the deaths of the stockmen. In early 1826, Darling posted half his newly formed Mounted Police to Wallis Plains – later Maitland – under the command of Lieutenant Nathaniel Lowe, a young man itching for action. After two fencers were attacked on Ravensworth, Lowe's men tied a rope round the neck of a captive Wonnarua man and forced him up a tree.

> He was directed to crawl to the extremity of a bough of the Tree, when he had done this, he was commanded to tie the rope tight to the branch; the other end being fast round his

neck, this he did, and sat crouched and trembling on the tree:— One then fired at him, wounded him; another fired and wounded him again; a volley was then discharged at him which knocked him off and left him suspended by the neck on the tree!

Lowe shot prisoners in the bush. One morning, he ordered Jackey Jackey, a prisoner being held in a cell at Wallis Plains, to be taken out one morning, tied to a sapling and executed.

So war broke out in the valley. Payback drove both sides but the rules were different for whites and blacks. "In the Aboriginal justice system," wrote the historian Grace Karskens, "guilt was shared communally, so the family and friends of the guilty person could suffer punishment for their wrongdoing." Settlers complained long and hard of blacks attacking families known to be "good" to them. Did years of kindness count for nothing? But payback by the blacks was focused and was thought to leave both sides square. "Plenty shake hands." But the whites played by different rules. Their retribution was massive. They shot anyone they could find. Years of friendliness earned the Wonnarua nothing then. When whites were out to kill, any black would do. Henry Reynolds, the great historian of dispossession, called this a shift of decisive importance. "For the groups in question the constraints of custom had been circumvented, they had moved from feud to warfare."

As the Hunter was invaded, several newspapers began publishing in Sydney. The *Monitor*, edited by that "testy, talented, and versatile genius" Edward Smith Hall, spoke up for blacks, Catholics and convicts. Hall was the first to report the execution of Jackey Jackey at Wallis Plains, and as he learned more about Lieutenant Lowe's campaign in the valley, he laid out arguments he would pursue for years:

> If the blacks commit larceny, burglary, or arson, deal with them *according to law*. That is, apprehend them, try them, and punish them … The blacks deserve better treatment at our hands. Have they not inherited the lands, we have

wrested from them, *for ages?* Is it not reasonable we should, when they wrong us, *forbear* as much as possible? Are we not infinitely the most powerful? Should we not, therefore, be magnanimous?

William Charles Wentworth's *Australian*, on the other hand, ceaselessly urged Darling to take violent action against these *savages* and *predators*, these *wild beasts* and *sable subjects of the Crown*. He and his editor William Wardell called for a reign of terror: "Treat them as an open enemy, and let them have enough of red-coat-and-bullet fare." With relish *The Australian* reported the last great slaughter in the Hunter, a reprisal raid in 1826 carried out by police and armed settlers led by the bloodthirsty young magistrate Robert Scott of Glendon. They cornered their prey in Garland Valley. "A hot conflict followed, the natives maintaining their ground, and making the most dexterous use of their spears. At last they were obliged to yield, betake themselves to flight, leaving behind them about eighteen of their comrades who were numbered with the dead. A man and his gin were taken prisoners. The attacking party sustained no loss of lives." Once again, it turned out the slaughtered Wonnarua played no part in the attacks being avenged.

Governor Darling was impatient with the wool men of the Hunter, first for provoking trouble with the Wonnarua and then for doing so little to protect themselves. He, too, had been sent out with Royal Instructions to "prevent and restrain all violence and injustice" against the Aborigines. Yet Darling was happy to tell the settlers: "Vigorous measures amongst yourselves would more effectually establish Your ascendancy than the utmost power of the Military." Nevertheless, Darling was perturbed by the slaughter in the Hunter and especially by the execution of Jackey Jackey. He ordered the settler magistrates of the valley – including Robert Scott – to inquire into the killings. They prevaricated. Thus began a stand-off between the Governor and the settlers of the Hunter, which dragged on for six months until the splendid missionary Lancelot Threlkeld persuaded two witnesses to testify against Lowe. The officer was arrested and charged with Jackey Jackey's murder.

Lowe was not the first European to be tried for killing an Aboriginal person. But he was an officer, not a renegade convict. For his defence, Lowe engaged Wentworth and Wardell, who tore Threlkeld's convict witnesses to shreds. All juries in the Colony were made up of military officers. Lowe's jury took five minutes to acquit him. Another result might have changed the history of this country, for his acquittal in May 1827 signalled that the murder of Aborigines by officials would almost certainly go unpunished, even when damning evidence was available and the government had the courage to prosecute. "The numerous friends of Lieutenant Lowe crowded round to congratulate him on the happy termination of the trial," *The Australian* reported. "A second burst of applause was given as he triumphantly left the Court."

*

Jones was busy in Sydney. Apart from The Rocks, where convicts lived in squalor by the wharves, he thought the town presentable. "It is the general wonder of strangers to find so respectable a place." He was one of Sydney's most respectable citizens. Wealth gave him high standing but not always regard. There was something slippery about Jones. No faction could depend entirely on his support. Some things were bedrock: his horror of convicts, Catholics and government extravagance. But he was showing signs already of becoming a master of the volte-face, which left him loathed by many for his "inconsistencies" and admired by some for his independence. "Mr. Jones," wrote *The Sydney Monitor*, "is one of those singular Tories, who do not hesitate to adopt a good measure, even if it be scouted by his own party and upheld by the Radicals." He defended the privileges of the Established Church though his own faith was coloured with radical Methodism. He imported rum and campaigned for abstinence. He was a Christian warrior with, it seemed, a magical way with money. Now in his early forties, having

SYDNEY, 1824

made one fortune in trade and oil, Jones was chasing another in wool.

The Macarthurs, haughty woolgrowers of Camden Park, mocked Jones behind his back for years, sneering at the high price paid for his Saxon merinos: "The purchasers all admit their folly." They admired Merchant Jones – and borrowed money from him – but they ridiculed the ambitions of a city businessman too busy to learn the ways of sheep and supervise his flocks. They also mocked the entertainments given by the Joneses in their elegant house in Hunter Street as "A strange mixture of finery, ostentation and vulgarity." The press gushed:

> On the evening of Thursday last, the Lady of Richard Jones, Esq., gave a most splendid Ball and Supper to a very large party of Friends; amidst the gay throng were to be seen the first rank and fashion, and as for beauty the constellation was so imposing as to acquire the appellation of the Australian galaxy. The dancing was nearly confined to quadrilles – the Band of the Buffs played the most bewitching airs – and the Supper exhibited a rich display of elegance, neatness, profusion, and variety; the wines were the oldest in the Colony, and of the best kind. Some of the old bon

vivants expressed their pleasure so heartily as to give every token that they felt "quite at home."

A butler ran the household. Once a week, the family was on display riding to St James' Church in a yellow carriage. Their son Richard was born in London. More children followed in Sydney. They christened their second daughter Mary Australia.

Jones' warehouse was out the back. The firm – now Jones & Walker – had six ships in the Tasman fishery, a store and wharf on Sydney Harbour and a gross return on sperm oil in the three years after Jones' return of nearly £100,000. Jones' brother Edward worked in the warehouse. "He is a very steady young Man and an excellent Bookkeeper," Jones reported to his London agent. "I intend he shall eventually have a share with me." Rather less promising was Mary Jones' brother Daniel Peterson, whom Jones made master of the whaler *Juno*. He was twenty-two with a wild temper. Off the coast of New Zealand, one of the sailors, fearing the ship might run aground, queried Peterson's order to raise the anchor. *The Sydney Monitor* reported the grim scene that followed. Peterson called the sailor over:

> Johnstone went close up to him to shew himself, when the Captain pushed him with his left hand; Johnstone said to him, "Don't shove me Captain Peterson!" Captain Peterson replied, "Yes, you mutinous rascal I will shove you," and again shoved him with his left hand, and presenting a pistol which he had ready in his right hand, shot him dead. The ball entered at the left jaw, came out through the top part of the head, and lodged in the right head of the brig. The chief mate immediately took the pistol out of the Captain's hand and threw it overboard, saying "You shall do no more mischief with that; you have done a pretty thing for yourself!" When the Captain drew the trigger of the pistol, he said, "He struck me first," when the crew answered, "He did not."

Peterson fled and sheltered for a time with the Māori, before disappearing for ten years to America.

By contrast, all was prospering at Fleurs under Edmund and John Uhr with their sixteen convict servants. This is Dharug country, where low hills fall to river flats that run for miles towards the Nepean River, the Yandhai. In the distance are the scrubby foothills of the Blue Mountains. Around Fleurs were some of the finest farms in the Colony, but Jones' 4000 acres on South Creek were thought to be the best of them all. The Uhr boys sent milk and butter from his 200 cows up to Sydney. His vines produced 2000 gallons of wine a year. But his Saxons were the glory of the place. They became a craze in the Colony. Rams from Fleurs fetched £70 to £80 each. Jones and Davidson's gamble was paying off magnificently. The Saxons did not need to be pampered in Australia. "The climate has a most extraordinary effect upon the fleece," a London wool merchant told an 1828 House of Lords inquiry. "Latterly they have been of varied qualities, but all possessing an extraordinary degree of softness, which the manufacturers here so much admire, that they are sought for more than any other description of wools."

Jones began to stock his Hunter Valley lands in 1827. Though he never lived at Black Creek, he was regarded as one of the big men of Patrick's Plains, a troublesome cohort of Tories mocked as the *junta*. Jones' loyalties were engaged entirely by his neighbours. Beside Black Creek lay Castle Forbes, an unhappy estate owned by "Major" James Mudie and his son-in-law John Larnach, renowned for their brutality to convict servants. Over the river was Glendon, the mighty run of Robert Scott, a man whose loathing of blacks and whose efforts to mask the crimes of Lieutenant Lowe made him notorious in the Colony. Scott and Mudie were magistrates, country gentlemen appointed as in England to uphold the law in their districts. With barely any police on hand, they were the law. Terrible consequences flowed from this. Landowners were left to punish each other's convict workers and did so with notable brutality. Even worse, it was not in their interests to protect blacks.

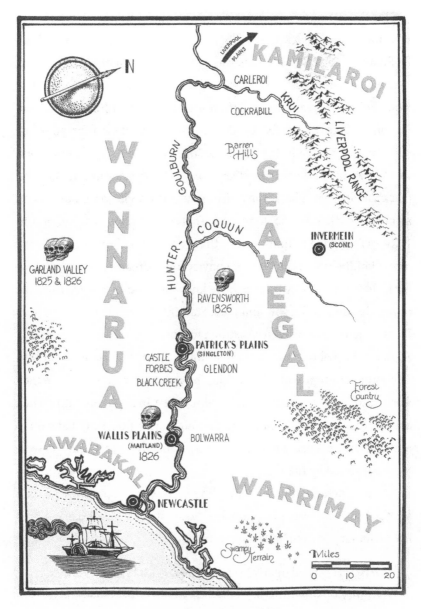

HUNTER - COQUUN

These bush magistrates were supposed to investigate the killing of Aboriginal people in their districts. They almost never did. The killers were, after all, their neighbours. But none of this touched Jones' admiration for the big men around Black Creek. Half in jest, perhaps, he called them by a name used to mock blacks: "Lords of the Soil".

Jones bought his most valuable run on the Hunter in 1833. Bolwarra lay miles below Black Creek on a huge bend in the river near Wallis Plains. The soil on the flats was inexhaustibly rich. Fields of hops, maize, wheat and tobacco flourished where impenetrable forests had stood only a few years earlier. "There are several beautiful and extensive lagoons or lakes on the Estate, and several extensive swamps, affording sufficient pasturage in the driest season," reported *The Sydney Monitor*. Work was underway to clear more red gums, swamp mahogany, blackbutt and paperbark. On a rise above the floods, Jones built sheds, a house and a handsome stone barn. That still survives. A squad of convicts was assigned to him to work the land. One had a place in history. John Standfield was the kind of convict Jones dreamed of working for him. He was not a city criminal. He knew one end of a horse from the other. He could milk, sow and reap. Standfield was one of half a dozen Dorset men transported to Australia for forming a Friendly Society of Agricultural Labourers – a trade union – in the village of Tolpuddle. The indignation provoked in Britain by the punishment of these men was already being reported in the Sydney press in September 1834 when Standfield arrived at Bolwarra. Jones fought with Bourke to hang on to a useful worker even when it was known the Tolpuddle Martyrs were to be pardoned by the King.

After much aristocratic wrangling in Westminster, Jones' partner Walter Davidson was given a magnificent stretch of 5000 acres on a high tributary of the Hunter. Jones reported:

> It is not excelled by any Estate in New South Wales, for either beauty of situation or fertility of soil. A great deal of it is naturally clear of Timber; and the remainder of it so Park like, that the Timber is not thicker upon it than you would wish for ornament and shade: added to this, it is exceedingly well watered, having the Krui River for one boundary.

Not naturally cleared: the grasslands in that broad, shallow valley had been fire-farmed by the Kamilaroi and Geawegal forever. Davidson called his run Carleroi. Higher up the Krui, Jones leased several blocks of land that climbed like stepping stones towards the Liverpool Range. He called these 20,000 acres Cockrabill. This is noble country. In cold winters, snow covers the range. The two runs between them commanded most of the Krui, which left the hinterland without water, useless to anyone else, and theirs to graze as their own. It's a tactic called peacocking. Cockrabill and Carleroi were run as one operation with fourteen *government men* – convict servants – and eight free shepherds working the sheep. "Mr D's and my Saxon and Merino flocks are increasing fast," Jones told his London agent in 1829. "Next year we shall have about 1200 Breeding Ewes and as you know the value of their Wool you will be able to form some estimate of their worth, and with good luck in a very few years we shall arrive at the number of 10,000 beyond which I have no ambition to go, but afterwards to cull and keep the finest." Sometime in the early 1830s, Edmund Uhr left Fleurs for the Krui, the first step in the long journey north he would take in Jones' service. He was still a teenager.

*

Ralph Darling was a governor after Jones' heart: a conservative Christian devoted to public order, financial probity and the rigid separation of colonial society from the convict underclass, whether emancipated or in chains. When the Bank of New South Wales, brought to its knees by reckless lending, came begging for a bailout in May 1826, Darling made the first condition of any rescue that Richard Jones be appointed to the bank's board. Jones was a founding director of the rival Bank of Australia, but he was happy to execute this little volte-face. *The Sydney Gazette* applauded his defection. "Mr. Jones, as one of our first Merchants, is known to be a man of extreme caution and immense wealth." Months later when the bank needed a second bailout, Jones became its president, a post confirmed by the board every year for the next sixteen years.

Darling's autocratic gloom, his generosity to the colonial rich, his attacks on the press and the closing of theatres made him deeply unpopular. When William Charles Wentworth sent an angry impeachment of the Governor to London, Jones' name was among the Landed Proprietors and Merchants of the Colony who signed a grovelling address to Darling, accusing his critics of encouraging a second Rum Rebellion:

> It has been with deep regret that we have long observed every measure of your Excellency grossly vituperated by licentious public writers in a manner calculated to inflame the minds of the lower orders of the community against your Excellency's Administration, and to produce discontent and insubordination among the prisoners of the Crown.

Richard Jones Esq. was named a week later among the seven citizens who would sit on the Governor's new Legislative Council. The other independents – as the citizen members were known – included John Macarthur of Camden Park; Sydney's other big merchant, Robert Campbell; landowners Alexander Berry and John Blaxland; Captain Phillip Parker King, son of the former Governor and manager of the Australian Agricultural Company; and a Hunter River magistrate, Edward Close, forgiven, it seemed, for his part in trying to shield Jackey Jackey's murderer from prosecution. *The Sydney Monitor* saw the independents as an unhappy lot, split between the ultras led by Macarthur and the rest into "the old poisonous two-edged faction, which hate each other so cordially".

The Council met in private. Only the Governor could introduce bills. The seven officials who sat with the independents were supposed to back him.* In the unlikely event that a measure was defeated, the Governor could put it into operation anyway while his masters in London decided the final outcome. The power of the independents

---

* The Lieutenant Governor, the Chief Justice, the Colonial Secretary, the Attorney-General, the Treasurer, the Senior Chaplain and the Collector of Customs.

lay over there. Brawls that began in the Colony were fought to the finish on the far side of the world, where the wool men and merchants of the Council had bankers and agents to lobby Westminster on their behalf. As they all grew rich from wool, their London connections were listened to more and more attentively. In all his time on the Council, Richard Jones ceaselessly urged economy on the government in everything except immigration. No sum was too great to spend shipping decent free labour to New South Wales. Through it all he remained low-key, indeed often inaudible. He whispered at the table. Manning Clark declared him: "Not a stooper to the ways of the mocker, the slanderer, or the overstater."

In Jones' fourteen years as an independent, from 1829 to 1843, the Council initiated no laws to protect the native peoples of the Colony. These were the years when Britain freed its slaves, emancipated Catholics and passed the Great Reform Bill. Yet all this time, the Legislative Council of New South Wales stayed sunk in the politics of the past, impervious to change and unwilling to hinder the conquest by settlers and sheep of Aboriginal lands. This was not surprising. When Darling appointed Jones, the independent members of the Council held between them 140,000 acres. A decade later, under Governor Bourke, they were running sheep and cattle on nearly 600,000 acres. Under Governor Gipps in the early 1840s, they held a million acres of their own, and Captain King managed another million for the Australian Agricultural Company. This was a Council of citizen dispossessors and, almost from the first, the councillor with the greatest individual stake in the land was Richard Jones.

A fever to invest in sheep gripped London. Jones wrote to his old partner Alexander Riley in 1834: "All the Sheep pastures not very distant from Sydney will be valuable and people must look forward to secure in time, whilst the opportunity offers, as our Sheep Farmers will become so rich that once the Lands become into their possession there is little chance of their becoming in the way of sale again." Jones was seen as a man of infinite caution, but in truth he had a taste for risk.

Every gamble he had taken in business paid off. He told Riley about the huge land purchases he was making in the valley. "I am somewhat plagueing my Pocket to do this, and to make the matter secure, I am abridging my commercial affairs for this purpose."

3

RACE AND FAITH

illiam Grant Broughton was the Duke of Wellington's gift to New South Wales. Broughton had impressed the Prime Minister as a scholarly curate on his country estate. So he appointed him the first Archdeacon of the Colony. Though not thrilled by the prospect of service on the far side of the world, this prickly divine arrived in September 1829 and was immediately one of the most influential figures in the Colony. He sat on the Council. Though he and Jones were from opposite ends of the church – Jones an Evangelical and Broughton a man of High Church ritual – they became allies. Both were Tories. Both recognised that order and punishment were necessary to achieve God's ends. Both were committed enemies of Rome. Neither believed anything material was owed the native peoples for their land. Broughton thought Christ alone was sufficient compensation for their acres:

> Natural and much more Christian equity points out that as in the occupation of their soil we are partakers of their worldly things, so in justice should they be of our spiritual. As through the tender mercy of our God the day spring from on high has visited us, we are solemnly engaged to impart to them the glorious beams of Gospel truth to guide their feet into the way of peace.

Broughton was not a man to throw himself in the path of colonisation. How could he? Westminster was endowing the Church of England in

Australia with great swathes of black land. The Home government knew it could trust Broughton not to upset things in New South Wales. Had anyone at Home had any doubts, he would not have been allowed near the Colony. Every preacher and priest in New South Wales was on the public payroll. The servants of God were under strict political supervision. They could be ejected at any time. When Father Jeremiah O'Flynn turned up in Sydney without approval in 1817, Macquarie deported him. Jones approved. "I think he acted very properly for the peace and good order of the country."

Soon after Broughton arrived, he chaired an enquiry in Hobart into the violence that racked Van Diemen's Land, the war between black and white which over forty years had claimed a thousand lives. That most lucid historian of frontier conflict, James Boyce, calls the Broughton inquiry of 1830 "one of the great whitewashes of Australian history". Though the committee conceded the settlers had done much to provoke violence in the early days, they believed those days were long past. They blamed continuing violence on the island on the "wanton and savage spirit inherent" in the natives. They urged settlers to remain charitable in the face of threats. "As Men, as Englishmen, and as Christians, the Committee are sensibly persuaded that every degree of moderation and forbearance is due to an ignorant, debased and unreflecting race." But if forbearance failed, brutal retaliation was justified. The committee recommended that guns be supplied to settlers and vigilante reprisals officially sanctioned. It was imperative, they said, that the natives learn once again a "dread of the effect of firearms". The Broughton rule of dealing with native peoples – restraint where possible but brutal punishment if necessary – was to become the default Christian position in the century ahead. The Archdeacon and members of his committee were pleased with their work. "They venture to express a hope that the experience of present transactions may be even rendered useful in the history of the World."

Broughton was a builder. Jones soon held the purse strings on his committees, raising funds for parish churches and schools. They sat

together on the Legislative Council, where Jones defended the Archdeacon's £1000 salary against critics who wondered why he was paid
many times the stipend of the Archbishop of Paris. Jones backed the
Archdeacon's ruthless efforts to keep public funding out of the hands
of faiths other than their own. And while working in tandem to block
the plans of two governors to educate every child in the Colony, Jones
and Broughton collaborated on the mighty task of founding the King's
School in Parramatta to educate the sons of the gentry.

Broughton preached to his clergy with fervour about their mission
to the blacks. God had triumphed over "the obstinate superstition of the
Jew" and He would triumph yet over "the erratic habits and inconsider-
ate disposition of the native tribes". But missionary efforts in Australia
were, if anything, petering out. Macquarie's Native Institution, having moved from Parramatta to the Blacks Town, shut its doors in 1829.
Lancelot Threlkeld's mission at Ebenezer on the Hawkesbury failed,
not least because so many Awabakal – for whom he was translating the
Gospel of St Luke – had died. The Methodists, now establishing themselves as a separate denomination, were delighted when Richard Jones
agreed to chair the tenth anniversary celebrations of the Wesleyan Auxiliary Missionary Society of New South Wales. "Mr Jones' assistance was
gratifying, not merely as shewing a personal good feeling towards the
Society, but more particularly as denoting the good-will of the Established Church, of which he was so highly respectable a member." But the
Methodists were doing nothing in New South Wales. The congratulatory
speeches concentrated on Methodist endeavours in Calcutta, Mauritius,
Honduras, Ceylon and the South Seas. But there was more to celebrate.
The Reverend Ralph Mansfield reminded the assembled believers of "the
advantages which would accrue to the mercantile interests of New South
Wales by the christianization" of those "unnumbered islands, whose
inhabitants are covered with the thickest darkness of pagan superstition".

Home to be enthroned in Canterbury as the Lord Bishop of Australia in 1836, Broughton displayed his shaky grasp of the calamity that
had befallen the Aborigines. "They seem to me to wear out, from some

cause; wherever Europeans meet with them," he told a committee of the House of Commons. "They appear to wear out, and gradually to decay." He couldn't put his finger on the reason. He admitted having abandoned all efforts to bring these people to Christ. "Any attempt to allure them permanently into a civilized life would be utterly ineffectual." Was the committee to understand these unfortunate persons were entirely abandoned to ignorance and degradation? "With a very trifling exception indeed, they are." It was not a question of intelligence. "They are not of a dull disposition," he explained. "They are a quick, intelligent people; but they have, I may say, no wants; you find it impossible to excite any want in them which you can gratify, and therefore they have no inducement to remain under a state of restraint, nor are they ever willing to leave their children." He could see that they had lost their hunting grounds. "They have a conception of our having excluded them from what was their original property." Did that produce feelings of indignation? "I think not. I have found them always exceedingly obliging, good tempered, and quite satisfied with any little benefit you might confer on them."

*

Fate handed Jones a remarkable gift. After a rackety youth, Robert Howe had converted to Methodism and on inheriting the *Gazette* from his father he turned it into a voice of Wesleyan virtue. He stood up for Aboriginal peoples. Of course, troublesome blacks had to be punished but squatters were condemned for "starving, insulting, and forcibly destroying those myriads of ill-fated natives, amongst whom our lot has been providentially cast". Howe was a family man. He and his wife, Anne, had three children. He was also cautious. He wrote a will appointing Richard Jones, a man of his faith with an impeccable reputation, as his executor. Howe was only thirty-four when, fishing on the harbour with his son and a servant one summer afternoon, a gust of wind overturned his boat. He struggled in the water. "Oh! William," he called to his groom.

"I can swim no more—I am drowning—look to my poor wife—she will soon be a widow!" A few sailors appeared as Howe sank out of sight. "One of the party touched him with the oar; and had it been a boat-hook, the unfortunate gentleman would have been saved," reported *The Sydney Monitor*. "None on board the boat had courage to jump over and dive for Mr. Howe, which we consider a little singular among sailors." Howe's corpse was found next morning. "The fishing lines had got so completely entwined around his limbs and body, as actually to resemble a net; the wrists were tightly laced together, and had he been purposely bound, it could not have been done more effectually."

Soon after Howe's death, the *Gazette* announced that the affairs of his estate were now in the hands of Richard Jones. At first, the grieving widow left Jones to handle the money and Jones' protégé, the Reverend Ralph Mansfield, to edit the paper. This did not last. One day she burst into Wentworth's office at *The Australian* in a great state of perturbation. Mansfield was ruining the *Gazette*! "After listening to her complaint, Wentworth gave this advice: 'You go back, Mrs Howe, and kick him downstairs.'" She did so in early 1832. Jones sacked the next editor she hired after he wrote a glorious editorial condemning the privileges enjoyed by Jones' friend the Colonial Secretary Alexander MacLeay, blasting the Emigrant's Friend Society – whose president was Richard Jones – and reproaching Bishop Broughton for political meddling: "An effective, unpolitical Clergyman, is one of the greatest blessings which a neighbourhood can enjoy." The contest between Jones and Mrs Howe was brutal even by the standards of the Sydney press, as silent Mr Jones schemed to make himself heard.

Jones was the head of a crowded house. His wife was about to have their fifth child, a second son after three daughters. Living under the same roof in Hunter Street was his sister Elizabeth – fast in danger of becoming a spinster – and his brother Edward, working for him in the merchant house and running sheep on Cockrabill and Carleroi. The Jon-eses continued to entertain. This penny pincher with an uneasy attitude to alcohol loved to open his doors to visitors to Sydney. In September

1831, he entertained the officers of the twenty-four-gun French discovery ship *La Favorite*, which had caused high excitement when it sailed through the Heads. Governor Darling took a party to visit the ship where he was greeted with the greatest attention by Captain Cyrille Pierre Théodore Laplace, who later eulogised Sydney:

> The scholar who travels through the Roman countryside or in the sandy wastes of Egypt is going to have philosophical thoughts on the grandeur and decay of nations about whom we barely recall anything. Oh! How he would find sweeter thoughts and ones more practical for humanity at least, if he wandered through the capital of Australia, a populous city which rises majestically on the very site where not so long ago thick bush stood as a sinister mass.

Edmond de Boissieu was among the officers entertained by the Joneses a few nights later. He kept a diary:

> The only businessman at whose house we were often received and who gave dances in our honour is Mr Jones. He is one of the richest men in the colony and he has joined the aristocracy. They say he is a very decent man with great business ability. It is mainly through whale-catching that he has made his fortune which is entirely self-made, having come to the country as a simple clerk — he belongs to a lower class in society as does his wife, daughter of a fruit seller in London, whom he had educated before marrying her. She is still pretty, but with excessively affected manners, a trait which she shares with her sister-in-law Miss Jones who is also a beautiful woman.

Boissieu had picked up a little gossip concerning Mrs Jones and the Governor's much-disliked brother-in-law, Henry Dumaresq:

MARY JONES

The story that nobody contradicts goes that Mr Jones was warned by his sister that every time he went to the bank, of which he is one of the directors and where he was forced to stay several hours, Colonel Dumaresq, then a single man, went to his wife's house … he came back and caught them … there is no doubt about it. And furthermore had a great wish to be and to appear amiable. These ladies do not speak French at all.*

* Le seul négociant chez lequel nous ayons été reçu souvent et qui nous ait donné des bals est Mr Jones. C'est un des plus riches de la colonie et il s'est attaché à l'aristocratie – on le dit très honnête homme et d'une grand capacité pour les affaires – c'est surtout par la pêche de la baleine qu'il a fait sa fortune qu'il ne doit qu'à lui seul, étant venu dans la colonie comme simple écrivain – il appartient à une classe inférieure de la société ainsi que sa femme, fille d'une fruitière de Londres qu'il a fait élever avant de l'épouser. Celle-ci est encore jolie mais excessivement minaudière, manière qu'elle partage avec sa belle-sœur Miss Jones qui est aussi une belle femme. La chronique que personne ne contredit raconte que Mr Jones, prévenu par sa sœur que toutes les fois qu'il s'absentait pour aller à la banque dont il est un des directeurs & où il était obligé de rester plusieurs heures Le colonel Dumaresq alors garçon entrait chez sa femme, revint et les surprit … pas moyen d'en douter – du reste grand désir d'être et de paraître aimable. Ces dames ne parlent pas du tout français …

Jones had suffered a commercial blow. He had five whaling ships and 44,000 acres of good land in New South Wales. He was hungry for more. The tea trade never failed. But in the winter of 1829, his partner William Walker withdrew to set up his own house. Walker had proved immensely capable, particularly on the whaling side. He had brought significant capital to Jones and took £30,000 with him when he left. That was essentially all the ready capital Jones had at his command. "Thus prematurely closed one of the safest concerns in the New World," he told his London agent, Stuart Alexander Donaldson. But Jones was putting on a brave face. "I am no enthusiast. I have lived long enough in the World to be cured of this, but I have also lived long enough here to know I have been instrumental in raising an honourable structure of Commercial importance that I will not resign into other hands it being as I consider purely my own fee simple." He assured Donaldson he would not be deflected from his plan to spend, perhaps recklessly, on sheep and land. "It is true I have invested a large sum in Colonial property, and my Sheep promise in another year to become a source of great wealth to me, indeed sufficient for all my wants."

More than ever, he presented himself as a model of colonial respectability. His presence on charitable committees declared their high moral purpose and careful management of funds. The cause closest to his heart was the distribution of Bibles, they being the true path to Salvation and a mighty weapon against the deceptions of Rome. Though once a great importer of rum, he had come to blame ardent spirits for the crimes that caused convicts to be transported, for most crimes committed in the Colony, and for so many business failures. He became a stalwart of the Australian Temperance Society and would have no rum on his whaling ships. The society allowed drinkers a little beer and wine. The more radical Total Abstinence Society regarded that position as fraudulent. Their iron rule: Teetotallers Only. Yet Jones was in the chair to celebrate their first anniversary. He was a catch for any cause. He didn't promise to foreswear alcohol entirely. Rather than sign the pledge, he declared, "As he had always been temperate, he was willing to do what he could to put down intemperance." He made wine at Fleurs and wine kept flowing in Hunter Street.

In a town of wild sectarian warfare, the Benevolent Society's care of the poor crossed all religious lines. It does to this day. As its treasurer, Jones worked alongside Catholics, Quakers, Presbyterians and Methodists to combat what he identified as a curse of the time: promiscuous charity. The Benevolent Society assisted only the deserving poor. Jones wrote:

> Think of the annoyance of having your houses besieged from morning to night by beggars of every description—the deserving and the undeserving—the aged and the young—the blind and the wounded, and the diseased—without the possibility of inquiry into the circumstances of each; the incessant knocking at the door, or ringing of the bell, with the servants announcement, "It's only a beggar." Who would not willingly pay an annual sum in order to procure exemption from such an annoyance?

The proper answer to a mendicant at the door was not a shilling but "Go to the Benevolent Asylum" where shelter was offered to about 500 poor, invalid and blind. But there were no beds for the original peoples of the land. No Bibles were distributed to the blacks. Nor did the Temperance Society offer destitute Aborigines a chance to acquire useful habits. For Jones and the forces of charity in Sydney, care might leap faith lines but not straddle the race divide.

Jones signed the Bishop of Australia's letter to the Governor in 1830 claiming the school they planned at Parramatta would be "as little exclusive" as possible and open to all classes of the community. They lied as they begged for money. Elsewhere, His Grace was more candid about the purpose of the King's School:

> The inheritors of even large properties who are thereafter to take the lead in Society and to occupy a station of

importance in the Country are too often destitute of the
requirements which should qualify them for such a situation. In too many instances I have heard of their sacrificing
all their respectability and influence by associating habitu-
ally with their own Convict servants. Such a forgetfulness
of what is due to themselves and to Society, I need scarcely
remark, could not occur if their minds were duly cultivated.

Colonial fantasies of high connection were allowed free play at King's.
Godfathers to the project were said to be William IV and Broughton's
patron the Duke of Wellington. The name was taken from a school which
had stood in the shadow of Canterbury Cathedral for centuries. But
Parramatta offered a ragged version of the original. None of the head-
masters lasted long. They broke down, died, went bankrupt or fled. The
first pupils were a scrum of missionaries', farmers' and merchants' boys.
Jones' son was pupil number seventy-six. His reverend headmaster was a
man of dignified bearing and violent temper, a flogger who beat the boys
with a quince stick and an ebony ruler. His single aim was to make each
and every one of them learn by heart the Eton Latin Grammar.

*

Jones and the Governor were friends. So were their wives. But towards
the end of Darling's time, he and Jones had one or two differences. For
forty years colonists had been calling for civilian juries in criminal trials. Men as far apart in their politics as Chief Justice Sir Francis Forbes
and the people's tribune, William Charles Wentworth, were demanding
an end to the old rule that only military officers could sit on criminal
juries. But when Darling attempted to make the change, he met a wall
of Tory opposition on the Council. The problem was that his proposal –
to have the same juries in the Colony as in England – might mean that
decent citizens would find themselves on a jury with prosperous former
convicts. Jones told Darling:

> The less we have for some years to come of the free insti-
> tutions of the Mother Country amongst us, the better it
> will be for the peace and good Government of the Colony.
> Property here forms no criterion of a Man's fitness; Charac-
> ter is infinitely of more consequence ...

Darling's plan was defeated. The task was left to the next Governor, and Jones would again oppose the reform. Postponing the future was one of his enduring causes.

Darling ended his time in the Colony a hated figure. He had med-dled in the courts, jailed newspaper editors, shut theatres, enriched his favourites and revenged himself in so many petty ways on his oppo-nents. The farewell ceremonies were muted. But Jones had so much to thank him for: tens of thousands of acres, membership of the Legis-lative Council and the presidency of the Bank of New South Wales. Darling had made him a great citizen of the Colony. As the Governor prepared to depart in October 1831, Jones gathered signatures for an address of farewell, which the *Monitor* denounced in its pages as an "AUDACIOUS FORGERY" got up by order of Darling:

> He has set that famous grantee and reservee Mr Richard
> Jones to go about the Town, spending a dollar at every shop,
> and begging the unwary shopkeeper's signature in return for
> his custom! By these ingenious means it is said, Councilman
> Jones has *bought* a dozen or two of signatures for his Patron;
> and thus concocted, the Address was yesterday presented to
> the General by a number of the Governor's favourites.

Having been imprisoned by Darling half a dozen times, the paper's editor – Edward Smith Hall – was venting his bitterness. But he was right to point out that in the fawning rhetoric of the address, only one paragraph mattered – the one condemning London's plan to make the occupiers of vast grants in the Colony pay a little for their land. The signatories urged Darling to attend to the matter the moment he reached London. A few days after he sailed, landholders decided to alert the King to "the most ruinous consequences to the Agricultural Interests, and to the Community at large". The wool barons put aside their enmities to campaign for the right to graze their stolen lands free of charge.

The future was rushing towards them. A hard drought had broken. Prices were climbing in London. "The character of the Australian fleece continues to rise yet higher and higher in the British market." British banks were mustering capital to invest in Australia. Cloth makers in Bradford were mechanising. Bushmen had learned to read the land, allowing shepherds "to graze stock over wide areas of the interior with an ease which would have amazed and perplexed hesitant shepherds of the eighteen hundreds". The year Darling arrived, New South Wales sent 275,000 pounds of wool to London. When he left seven years later, it was 1,401,000 pounds. Money and sheep were pouring into the Colony. But the grass in the Nineteen Counties was eaten out. What the wool men needed in the early 1830s was more land. Much more land.

4

BREAKOUT

When he took Jones' sheep over the Liverpool Range, Edmund Uhr crossed a boundary men and stock were not supposed to cross. London had drawn a line on the map running along the range, out in an arc beyond Bathurst and back to the sea 140 miles south of Sydney. All settlement was supposed to be contained in Nineteen Counties, behind what was called the Limits of Location. This was both a way of saving money and an arcadian delusion that the bush in the counties could be tamed and something like an English landscape would appear, a countryside of villages, farms and churches. The British had drawn such lines before. One ran down the Appalachians, reserving all the territory on the Mississippi side of the mountains for Native Americans. Barring those lands to settlers and speculators like George Washington was a root cause of the American Revolution. Britain had learned its lesson. The line around Sydney would never be allowed to provoke rebellion. Its proclamation in 1829 came with no guarantees for the Aboriginal people beyond. Policing the line was half-hearted. Settlers soon began moving their sheep out into what they called – with a certain hunger – the wastelands of the blacks. In a famous despatch to London, the new Governor, General Richard Bourke, argued that trying to prevent this breakout "would seem a perverse rejection of the Bounty of Providence".

The appointment of a liberal, Irish patrician to govern New South Wales was a sign of great change in Britain. The Whigs were back in power. Old wrongs were being tackled after decades of Tory rule. As the new government dealt with slavery, rotten boroughs, child labour and the poor, it was also bent on advancing the prosperity of the Empire. Whigs believed prosperity was virtuous, an idea that set policy towards the Australian colonies on a profoundly conflicted path. While London officials began to query the great lie that Australia was an empty country that anyone might claim, others in Lord Grey's government were keen to see the wool industry boom. God's mandate was to replenish the Earth. The God of the Europeans was a colonising God. As men and stock burst through the Limits of Location, London did nothing to bar their way and nothing to protect the people whose country they were invading.

Uhr did not go far. The rocky crossing at Wallalla where he made his headquarters was less than 50 miles from Cockrabill. First, he had to build a slab hut with a bark roof that could double as a fort. Then huts had to be scattered across the country for his shepherds. In a world without wire, sheep had to be watched day and night. "A flock of sheep," said Jones, "should never exceed from 300 to 350 placed under the care of one man, constantly with them." A man did chores around the hut all day and watched over the sheep at night when they were brought back to the yards. This was lonely work for a strange army of often eccentric, difficult men. They knew that in hostile country, they would be the first to die at the hands of the blacks. Uhr soon had sixty people on his three runs down the Mooki: Wallalla, Doona and Breeza. Half were convicts or ex-convicts. Fifteen were women. The men wore the familiar uniform of the bush described by William Telfer of Wallahbadah, a local bushman with a sharp eye and wretched punctuation: "Scotch twill shirts moleskin trowsers blucher boots Cabbage tree hats with two long streamers of black ribbon hanging over the leaf of the hat also a blue smock shirt instead of a Coat for all weathers wet or dry." In early summer the flocks were washed in the river and shorn once their wool was dry. Bullock wagons took the clip over the range and down to a steamer at Wallis Plains. Rain might drag this operation out for months, for when it rained the black soils of the Liverpool Plains turned to deep, adhesive mud. Thirty bullocks were then needed to move each wagon.

MURRI.

A KAMILAROI HUNTER

"Those days when they got bogged the Crackin of the bullock whips was like the report of a lot of firearms reverberating through the forrest," wrote Telfer. "The swearring was something to be remembered by those sun tanned rough men of the roads."

Uhr's neighbours thought him unscrupulous, but travellers found a hospitable host at Wallalla. In the way of the bush in those days, the homestead was an inn along the way. Shepherds slept in a hut out the back. Magistrates and schoolteachers shared Uhr's table and stayed overnight under his roof. Most were gone in the morning.

The ornithologist John Gould stayed for weeks. "This part of the Mokai was one of the most beautiful, and to me, one of the most interesting localities, I had visited in New South Wales," he wrote in his masterpiece *The Birds of Australia*. "I therefore encamped on its banks for some time, during which I experienced much hospitality from Mr. Uhr." Gould's mighty find on the Mooki was the Warbling Grass-Parakeet:

> This lovely little bird is pre-eminent both for beauty of plumage and elegance of form, which, together with its extreme cheerfulness of disposition and sprightliness of manner, render it an especial favourite with all who have had an opportunity of seeing it alive ... Their flight is remarkably straight and rapid, and is generally accompanied by a screeching noise.

He shot and ate them. His wife, Elizabeth Coxen, drew them. Gould's black guides called them by the one Kamilaroi word known to the whole world: Betcherrygah.

The Kamilaroi lived along the Mooki in big huts, fishing and hunting all summer. They assigned to Baiame, the greatest of their gods, responsibility for the seasons and weather. "His stature is immense," recorded the poet Eliza Dunlop. "Whenever he dies the world will be destroyed by huge rocks which fall from Heaven." She jotted down Kamilaroi expressions in her notebook:

> What are you laughing at
> Mina thina gindamilla
>
> Hold your tongue you have said plenty
> Thirima thirima wana Gwaldendi geerma
>
> You are stingy & won't give it
> Gouranda goor caumil oora
>
> Did you eat plenty
> ya geer booruldee

I'll put a spear through your bowels
Quia thuree thooloo thooree

Half a dozen years before Uhr's arrival, a slaughter near Wallalla had – at least for a time – broken Kamilaroi resistance on that part of the plains. The massacre was unprovoked. A peaceful body of men, women and children who had gathered near a hut at Yarramanbah were driven off with whips. They fought back. After interrogating witnesses, Richard Sadleir, a lay teacher of religion, reported to the church:

> One man, who was struck over the legs, resented the insult with a blow of his waddy, which led to a more general scuffle, and the whites, as usual, resorting to the use of fire-arms, poured in several destructive vollies, firing on the blacks as they climbed the trees for security; and in one instance, as related, ripping open with a knife the bowels of an unfortunate being who had fallen wounded from a tree.

It took stockmen days to burn the bodies. Horrified settlers reported the massacre to the Colonial Secretary. Nothing was done.

These were early days out in the wastelands of the blacks. For a while the original inhabitants of the land expected the whites and their sheep would go just as they came. It took time for them to learn that their land was lost to them. Only then did resistance intensify. Henry Reynolds wrote:

> While conflict was ubiquitous in traditional societies territorial conquest was virtually unknown. Alienation of land was not only unthinkable, it was literally impossible. If blacks often did not react to the initial invasion of their country it was because they were not aware that it had taken place. They certainly did not believe that their land had suddenly ceased to belong to them and they to their land. The mere presence of Europeans, no matter how threatening,

could not uproot certainties so deeply implanted in Aboriginal custom and consciousness.

Squatters crossed the plains, occupying the country as they went. By 1833 they had reached the Namoi. Sir John Jamison lost five stockmen to the Kamilaroi at Barber's Lagoon that year and another two on his Baan Baa run. Sir John, knighted by King Charles XIII of Sweden for curbing an outbreak of scurvy in his navy, was a big figure in the Colony, a man of wealth and liberal principles. He sat on the Council and entertained distinguished visitors at Regentville, his elegant house that still stands by the Nepean. The deaths of his shepherds struck alarm in the Colony. The *Gazette* appealed for squatters to treat the Aboriginal natives of the Colony kindly, but also demanded government protection for settlers who came under attack in the wastelands. "We care not whether this is done by means of a military, or of a police force—but protection the settlers expect, and to protection they have a right." The *Gazette* was calling not for the arrest and trial of blacks, "raised a little above the brute species", but for their summary punishment. "We desire that they should be shot or hanged—not for the sake of vengeance, or of retributive justice, but for the sake of example, and its effect in deterring others from the commission of similar atrocities."

When Governor Bourke refused to send soldiers to help Jamison hunt down the killers, the distinguished squatter sent one of his convict shepherds, William Bean, to capture the supposed ringleader, Six Toed Jackey. Bean shot him one night on the road back to Baan Baa apparently trying to escape. Bourke had the convict shepherd charged with murder. The trial of Jamison's man in late 1835 was designed by Bourke to send a message to the bush that such killings had to stop. Bean's prosecutor was the Solicitor-General, John Plunkett – an Irishman, a Catholic, a fine lawyer and a Whig. He told the jury that Six Toed Jackey was not in lawful custody and had a *right* to escape.

There was an erroneous impression entertained by overseers and stockmen, in general, that the Native Blacks were

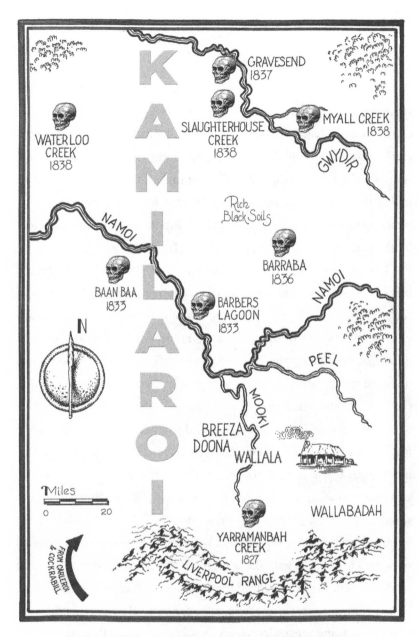

LIVERPOOL PLAINS – CORBON COMLEROY

not protected by Law, and that therefore, they might be shot
at pleasure; but His Honor will tell you ... that, however
low they may rank in the scale of intellect or intelligence,
the British Law watched over and protected their lives with

the same solicitude, it would show to the most eminent or
exalted white men.

Plunkett argued in vain. A jury of military officers took only a few
moments to acquit the convict shepherd. Bourke was at a loss. What
the missionary Lancelot Threlkeld called "the melancholy state of warfare" on the Liverpool Plains rolled on, claiming perhaps ten times the
number of black lives that had been lost in the Hunter. Bourke continued to refuse to deploy the army against the Kamilaroi. From his time
as acting Governor at the Cape of Good Hope, he knew that set-piece
battles were no way to bring peace to the frontier.

The apparently civilised argument that British law protected
blacks and whites alike was a lie that stripped Aboriginal peoples of
the sovereign standing they needed to come to terms with the invaders. The inhabitants of the continent were left with no more authority
in British eyes than, say, itinerant farm workers in Kent. The Crown
does not make treaties with its own people. None were made in Australia, a situation unique in the Empire. The treaties Britain struck
with Native Americans, the Māori and the people of the Cape were
not always honoured. But in Australia, there were not even prom-
ises to break. Bourke set nothing aside for the blacks. No provision
was made to arbitrate between the invaders and the invaded. Many
squatters reached private accommodations with the peoples whose
land they were taking, but conflict between the invaders and invaded
remained inevitable, with the most likely resolution: violence. Bourke
made matters worse by telling the squatters to look after themselves.
"If Gentlemen Farmers chose to go so far away, they must endeavour
to find out some means by which they could protect themselves." He
expected decent restraint from men of that class, but the result was
vigilante slaughter.

*

Richard Bourke gave the squatters all the land they wanted, yet they came to loathe him. They grew rich under Bourke. Money was pouring in from London. The wool market was booming. But Jones and his kind set out to humiliate and thwart the man. Every great reform Bourke proposed, Jones opposed. Hand in hand with the Lord Bishop of Australia, he worked to block any change that might advantage Catholics, convicts and the Irish. That Bourke was a Whig made him suspect. That he wished to break down barriers that protected respectable settlers from the rabble beneath made Bourke, in the eyes of the colonial Tories, a great danger to the Colony. They attacked him as an ignorant humanitarian who misunderstood New South Wales. *The Sydney Herald* found the phrase Bourke's critics would use to belittle his policies all the way to the end: the *soothing system*.

> Sir Richard's career in this Colony bears a strong resemblance to the course he adopted at the Cape. The soothing system was the order of the day in both instances; and admirable as that system is, when applied to a community of honest, intelligent, and well educated people, we must contend that it is quite erroneous and mischievous when applied to the ferocious Kafir or the demoralized Convict.

Bourke was a patrician Protestant who had grown up in County Limerick with Catholic relatives and friends. He respected their religion and scorned sectarian hatred. This attitude alarmed men like Jones all the more when London sent a Catholic to the Colony to be Solicitor-General. John Plunkett was the first Catholic to hold high office in Australia, a narrow-faced man devoted to his faith and the common law. He was Irish and knew about occupation. He sat on the Council for twenty-four years and never owned sheep. Manning Clark wrote: "His great passion was to introduce equality before the law and liberty of religion for all men in New South Wales." Plunkett was soon Bourke's most trusted adviser. His care for the original inhabitants of the land put posturing men like Bishop Broughton to shame. Plunkett did more than pray. He fought in the Council and the courts. He was of the family of the last Catholic martyr in England – Oliver Plunkett, who was hung, drawn and quartered in 1681 after a trial before an all-Protestant jury at which he was denied both counsel and witnesses. John Plunkett believed in due process.

Bourke had barely settled in Government House when he discovered that gentlemen magistrates in the bush were inflicting punishments on convict servants that would be considered too brutal for slaves in the West Indies. Without much fuss, he and Plunkett persuaded the Council in 1832 to forbid magistrates sitting on their own from ordering more than fifty lashes. Harsher punishments could still be inflicted when two or more magistrates sat on the bench. But it was no longer possible for settlers to go next door and persuade a neighbouring magistrate to have their convicts whipped almost to death. The cat-o'-nine-tails was banned at the same time. All whippings were henceforth to be carried out with a government whip, not one "varied according to accident or caprice". Magistrates were also instructed to report on each whipping they ordered. At Wallis Plains in September 1833:

1. Dennis McDonald, per ship *Asia*, insolence and neglect, 50 lashes. This man's back appeared much lacerated, and the blood appeared at the 20th lash, and continued to bleed much ...

4. Henry Brown, Rosslyn Castle, drunkenness, 25 lashes. Back did not appear lacerated, but the offender screamed out greatly ...

17. Joseph Gibson, Captain Cook, neglect of work, 50 lashes. Bled greatly, and appeared much exhausted ...

18. John Orr, *Hercules*, neglect of duty, 12 lashes. (A boy); cried out very much.

The wool men were furious. Much fine rhetoric was thrown about accusing the Governor of failing to respect gentlemen magistrates, men clothed in the ancient garb of judicial independence. Within weeks they claimed insubordination was now rife on their runs. Much more was at stake here than hurt feelings. Bourke was seen as mounting a Whig attack on the power of the gentry to set their own rules in the bush, to decide for themselves what laws applied and did not apply beyond the city. They demanded to be free to deal as they wished with sheep, convicts and blacks. The political contest in Australia between city and country which began at this time has never died.

The junta of Patrick's Plains led the charge against Bourke. Jones backed his neighbours entirely. He was not a flogger but saw Bourke's changes – which he had, in fact, voted for on the Council – put order itself at risk. Jones apologised for the uncharacteristically sharp language about Bourke in letters to his London agent. "But when I see such a studied indifference as regards the moral welfare of the Colony, I cannot help feeling warmly on the occasion." In August 1833, 130 land-holders and free inhabitants of the district of Hunter's River signed a petition to Bourke, protesting the loss of their powers. The first to sign was Robert Scott of Glendon, over the river from Black Creek. Scott was the magistrate who led the slaughter of Wonnarua in 1826. Next to sign was James Glennie, who had also taken part in killings in the valley. The third of Jones' neighbours to put his name to the petition was mad Major James Mudie of Castle Forbes. He was a huckster with a ruddy face and spectacles, whose connections in Britain gained him this magnificent grant. His castle was a bark cottage that looked across hundreds of acres of the richest river flats, worked by sixty-four convicts hauled regularly before Mudie's friends on the bench to be flogged for idleness, sleeping in the fields, neglect, disobedience, breaking axes and, the great catch-all, insubordination.

On the night of 4 November 1833, three of Mudie's convicts took to the bush, stole a pistol and returned next morning to Castle Forbes. They threatened to blow out the brains of Mudie's daughter, Mrs Larnach;

looted the kitchen; stole horses and set off to deal with John Larnach. They found him at the creek with a dozen convicts washing sheep. "You villain, you tyrant," one of the mutineers shouted. "I'll make you remember flogging, I will, you tyrant." Larnach plunged into the water and took cover behind the convicts around him. "You will never take another man to Court," someone shouted. Shots were fired but no one was hit. Larnach staggered up the far bank, tripped and fell on his face. The men rode off. Soon captured, they all faced hanging.

Convicts did not have lawyers. But when the Castle Forbes rebels came to trial, they were represented by Roger Therry, another Irish Catholic lawyer Bourke had brought to Sydney. Therry was head of the small debts court, but this minor post left him time to have a practice of his own. He was good at this work and favoured by Bourke with government briefs. Who paid him to represent the mutineers was never clear. Therry knew before he walked into court that he would enrage the junta by leading evidence from outcasts like Anthony Hitchcock:

> I had the misfortune to go to Mr Larnach, who took every opportunity of keeping me from getting my ticket of leave; his men are flogged nearly to death, starved and badly clothed. Dying bullocks are served out to the men in a stinking state, and their wheat is the refuse of the grain. When taken to Court, a man is sure to receive what punishment is promised him by Mr Larnach or Mr Mudie, and if a man attempt to make a defence, the Magistrates immediately exclaim—"Hold your tongue you d—d rascal, or I'll give you fifty for contempt of Court." The bread made from the wheat served out to the men, is as black as your Honour's hat, and so rank, that it is not eatable, except by a starving man; if a man go to the master to complain, he gets his eyes d**d, and is threatened to be taken to Court and flogged, which he is sure to be if taken there. Nothing but flogging and starvation made me take the bush.

Roger Therry

Hitchcock and his fellow prisoners asked if they might "exhibit their lacerated backs to the public gaze in Court, to show what torture they had endured". Permission was denied. All were convicted. A boy among the mutineers was sent to the penal settlement on Norfolk Island for life. The rest were hanged at Castle Forbes. Thus the rule was established: kill a black man and be acquitted; threaten a gentleman and you hang.

The junta was unhappy with Therry for making martyrs of the mutineers. Bourke reported to London that the evidence of the men and their conduct at the trial "obtained in a very remarkable degree the sympathy of the Public". This popular feeling determined the junta to back Mudie. Bourke ordered a feeble inquiry that absolved Mudie of every charge except serving his convicts rotten food. By this time, the junta had his measure: Sir Richard Bourke found grappling with the Tories beneath him. Mudie proved one of those madmen deranged by victory. He took his exoneration badly. He declared it degrading – an unprecedented indignity to a gentleman's honour, etc. – even to face questions about life at Castle Forbes. When he found the Governor had struck his name from the list of gentlemen magistrates, his protests became hysterical. Jones backed him. Though he conceded his neighbour's rhetoric was at times a little exaggerated, Jones endorsed Mudie in the diatribe he published in London, *The Felonry of New South Wales*:

> I have been acquainted with you upwards of ten years, and during that period, I have never known anything in your conduct discreditable to you either as a magistrate or as a private gentleman. On the contrary, I believe you to have been an active, useful, and independent justice of the peace; and I consider your recent dismissal by his excellency the governor, from the commission of the peace, an arbitrary act, and an unjust abuse of the power vested in him as supreme ruler in this colony.

Jones had not signed the 1833 petition but when the Scotts of Glendon called a meeting at Leeds Tavern on Black Creek in February 1834, he put his name to a second petition denouncing Bourke's "hasty, unnecessary and premature" reforms, which had left landowners and their friends "suffering in their property and peace of mind from the insubordinate state of the Convict Population". In a colony like New South Wales, petitions were the only democratic way citizens could make their opinions felt. Etiquette mattered. They were supposed to be open to all. After being drafted at public meetings, copies were left about in banks and stores for signature. Newspapers advertised where copies might be found to sign. But what became known as the Hole & Corner petition was a private affair. No public meetings were held. No public appeals were made for signatures. It circulated quietly. Its existence was unknown to the public for three months. Signing the Hole & Corner petition was a bold move on Jones' part. He was the only member of the Council to sign either. Its purpose – and the reason for all the secrecy – was to persuade the Home government to sack Bourke. After reciting their woes, the petitioners told the King: "All hope of redress in this Colony is at an end."

5

BOTANY BAY TACTICS

William Watt, transported for embezzling a London haberdashery, was the best journalist in Sydney. Five blameless years in the Colony had earned him his ticket-of-leave – not a pardon, but the freedom to get on with his life. That the newspapers of Sydney were densely populated by criminals made many, from the Governor down, uneasy. But there was nothing they could do about it. Talented journalists are always in such short supply. The *Gazette* housed two felons: the editor Edward O'Shaughnessy, an Irish poet and drinker transported for fraud, and Watt, who did the editor's work and dashed off columns under the name "Bow Wow". Jones had a formula to explain the incongruous situation at the paper: "I do not consider it disgraceful to associate with an emancipist of good character in the literary business."

Jones and the widow Howe often found themselves at odds, but for two or three years – by flexing his muscles as executor of her drowned husband's estate – Jones was able to control the *Gazette*. He fiercely policed the paper's political line. When the Reverend Henry Carmichael, an editor, attacked Jones' friends on the Council he was shown the door. Watt gave the executor-proprietor satisfaction by raging against Bourke and flattering the gentlemen of the Hunter. "What possible interest can they, as magistrates, have in an extension of powers?" Bow Wow asked. "Is it to be assumed that they desire to flog and banish their fellow-creatures, merely to satiate an appetite for inhumanity? No!" His scorn of Bourke was electric. "Fifty lashes! Why, this is a mockery of punishment." He pictured sad magistrates sitting alone in the bush, laughed at by ruffians in the dock. He saw disorder everywhere threatening the Colony. He told a fellow journalist at the time that when he called at Mr Jones' office in Pitt Street, he "had a hand for him to shake, a seat for him to sit on, and it was how do you do Mr. Watt?"

But when he and Anne Howe became lovers in the winter of 1833, Watt had a sudden change of heart. After months of mocking Bourke, he began to offer full-throated support for the Governor. He wanted readers to make no mistake. In October he declared: "The *Gazette*, yielding at length to sober conviction, evidently retracts its former opinion." Jones tried to bring the paper to heel in the usual way by sacking the editor, but Howe found the strength to block the move. Watt was triumphant: "Mr. E.W. O'Shaughnessy ... *scorned* to yield to the dictation of a base faction, and write right and left against the Governor and Chief Justice without any just occasion. The attempt, however, proved abortive! A woman's hand arrested the blow!!!" The next months were tangled with Watt moving backwards and forwards to the *Monitor*, but as the Hole & Corner petitioners began plotting against Bourke in early 1834, Watt was back at the *Gazette* and running the show. Charles Gibson wrote: "Mr. O'Shaughnessy depended too much on the bottle for his editorial inspiration, and as Mr. Watt was a moderate man, in this line, the latter soon gained the entire control of the paper." For the next two years Jones schemed to be rid of Watt, Howe and Sir Richard Bourke. As far as possible he kept himself hidden. But he drove the disruption and was never more dangerous.

The secret petition, still unseen, was reported for the first time by the *Monitor* in April 1834. It was still circulating and struggling to find signatories. Fewer than a hundred citizens had put their name to the document. Watt declared the Colony was facing a choice between "a government based upon principles of liberality and even-handed justice" and the selfish intrigues of "hole-and-corner malecontents". The name stuck. Watt weighed into Jones' friends with a will in the *Gazette*.

Mudie was frequently ridiculed in its pages. The old warmth between Watt and Jones evaporated. "In consequence of the change in my politics, he became inimical to me." In June, Watt took delight in reporting the petition was in trouble. The Hunter gentlemen had split. Mudie was refusing to sign. Sir Edward Parry – Arctic explorer and promoter of the Australian Agricultural Company, with its immense landholdings – had refused to carry the document to London. Copies were still impossible for the public to find. Watt wrote, "We are bound to express ... our utter contempt for the hole-and-corner cabal who would endeavour to effect that in private, which they will know, if it were openly avowed, would expose them to the just indignation of the colony." But Bourke had at last found a copy and saw the petition for what it was: a conspiracy aimed at his overthrow.

Watt had been working for months on one of the great pamphlets of the age under the pen name "Humanitas". It was published in July and caused a mighty din.

"HUMANITAS"
ON THE
PRESENT SYSTEM
OF
CONVICT DISCIPLINE
AND
PARTY POLITICS
IN
NEW SOUTH WALES:
WITH
Comments on the Recent Enquiry
AT
CASTLE FORBES.
——ooo——
SOLD AT THE SYDNEY GAZETTE OFFICE.
Price, Three Shillings.

The identity of Humanitas was soon known. That this homily was the work of a felon outraged Jones' allies. Berating the cruelty of the Hunter River magistrates, the evils of brutal punishment and the dignity of emancipists was a man on a ticket-of-leave. The Tories began eyeing his ticket.

Watt's voice was calm. His analysis of the Hole & Corner plot was a piece of fine reporting. He did what Bourke had flinched from doing after the uprising on Castle Forbes: laying out the heart-rending facts of convict life under Major Mudie. He wrote sharp sketches of notables in the Colony. Broughton: "A mere cypher in the State machinery." Hannibal Macarthur: "The whole of this family are determined foes to every measure that has even the show of liberality." And Jones:

> Mr. Richard Jones is a fiery Darlingist. He is said to be a moral man—one who treats his servants with leniency, and they acknowledge his tenderness with a corresponding anxiety to promote his interests. This ought, at least, to convince him that insubordination, so loudly proclaimed to exist, must proceed in a great measure from ill-treatment. He is known to have been formerly a "high Tory," and he is now a "Radical," and one of the Governor's sturdiest opponents: nevertheless I do not think he could assign a reasonable motive for his conduct. He is supposed to be a tool for others. These paltry few it is, who have gathered around them a host of hornets, to buzz about and annoy the Government.

Roger Therry then entered the fray with a pamphlet of his own under the title "Observations on the Hole and Corner Petition" by an "Unpaid Magistrate", in which he defended Bourke and attacked the gentlemen magistrates for their disloyalty and incompetence. He accused them of sending convicts illegally to the hulks on mere suspicion. Therry claimed only a few of them were up in arms against Bourke, a faction that would "arrogate to themselves all the wisdom, and all the virtue,—as they would engross all the wealth—of the community". The identity of the Unpaid Magistrate was never a mystery, but it took a little time to emerge that Therry was commissioned by the Governor to write the pamphlet. When Bourke sent a copy of the petition to the Secretary of State for the Colonies in late 1834, he included Therry's pamphlet, "containing a refutation of the charges alleged in that Petition, drawn up with perfect truth and great clearness". It was not, he confessed, an official document but "may safely be consulted for information, if at any time the matter of the Petition should be brought into discussion".

*

Disputes with London played out so slowly. A year could pass between a complaint leaving Sydney and a decision from the far side of the world landing on the Governor's desk. While waiting for London's verdict, Jones and the petitioners had work to do. First, Watt had to be destroyed. Tickets-of-leave were easy to lose. Immorality was enough to send a ticket-of-leave man back to the chain gangs. Bourke was told Watt had – before his present liaison with Mrs Howe – a child out of wedlock with a prisoner. He refused to cancel Watt's ticket. His tormentors then had Watt charged with receiving stolen goods: to wit, two sheets of paper taken from a rubbish bin at *The Sydney Herald*. At a mischievous moment in the never-ending warfare between Sydney's mastheads, Watt had persuaded a compositor at the *Herald* to dig up and deliver to him proof sheets of an abandoned story. For those bits of paper Watt was charged and put in prison. He continued to edit the *Gazette* from behind bars.

Jones sat among the Hole & Corner petitioners who crowded the gallery of the court to watch the trial. Roger Therry, the prisoner's barrister, mocked the very idea of bringing a prosecution over "a piece of useless dirty paper". The jury agreed. Undaunted, Mudie charged Watt with being "a notorious liar". The falsehood that might put him in chains was a claim that Jones used to shake his hand and offer him a chair when he visited the merchant's counting house. The bench at the Police Court was packed with five of Mudie's magistrate friends. The trial lasted ten days. Jones played his part to perfection:

> I know the prisoner at the Bar; I never shook hands with him,
> nor handed him a seat in my life; he never was in my house,

he has been two or three times in my office on business from
The Gazette Office to which estate I am an executor; if he has
made these assertions he has been guilty of telling the grossest falsehoods; I should never think of allowing such as he to
behave in such a way; I never had any connection with him
in politics, if he has said so it is also false.

He turned to face Watt:

I have a very bad opinion of you, and have had it for a long
time; I have had abundant reason for it, which I will state
if you wish it; I know that Major Mudie had a bad feeling
towards you, and for very good reasons ... I am sure the
repeated attacks upon Major M. in *The Gazette* were sufficient to cause him to have an ill-feeling towards you; I know
sufficiently well, that you were the author of those attacks.

Jones reassured the court he was untouched by Watt's lies:

I hope my character stands too high to be injured by any thing
such a man as Watt could say of me; I do not think it will
injure my character, either as a Member of Council, a magistrate, or a gentleman, but I should feel much ashamed to have
it supposed that I could have any intimacy with such a man.

The *Gazette*'s reporting of the trial was Watt's work. Even *in
extremis*, vivid prose poured from him. Mudie only abandoned the
chase when Watt threatened to call eighty witnesses to his good character. Even before a tribunal stacked with Mudie's friends, the charge
of lying failed. Bourke nevertheless ordered Watt into exile at Port
Macquarie, the gulag for educated convicts north of Newcastle. This
was not brave. "Watt had assumed a position in society inconsist-
ent with his condition," the Governor explained to Therry. "To avoid
general scandal, it was necessary to remove him, though without sub-
jecting him to the severity of forced labour, which would have been

the consequence of cancelling his ticket." In mid-September 1835, his ticket-of-leave intact, Watt left for Port Macquarie. Anne Howe followed soon after and with Bourke's permission, they married in the new year. Watt continued to edit the *Gazette*.

As Watt's trial was sputtering out, the Chief Magistrate and Chairman of Quarter Sessions let it be known he wished to retire. The magistrates were to choose his successor. Roger Therry was the only candidate. He had the backing of the Governor. Jones set to work. "Having called a Cabinet Council in Hunter-street, he and his partizans cast about to consider how best to defeat the election of Mr. Therry, and they selected Mr. Riddell as a fit opponent." The Colonial Treasurer, Campbell Riddell, was a man of grievances. He moaned about the burden of his work, his pitiful salary, the land grants that failed to come his way, and London's failure to make him Colonial Secretary. He had asked Bourke if he might stand in the election for Chairman of Quarter Sessions, but Bourke refused and wrote to his son in London: "I told him I could not allow him to hold that office in conjunction with that of Treasurer and a seat in the Ex. Council. He appeared to acquiesce in the propriety of my decision and left me stating that he would give up all thoughts of standing." But Riddell made himself available to Jones' faction – emboldened, perhaps, by Lord Glenelg, Secretary of State for the Colonies, being an old friend of his family.

The canvass for Riddell was quiet. Almost to the end, Therry was unaware of the campaign against him. "Letters of pressing solicitude traversed the country in all directions," *The Australian* reported when the plot later came to light. "Family connexions were hunted up to procure suffrages in every quarter." Jones wrote asking the magistrate son of his old partner Alexander Riley to switch his vote. "I shall feel obliged by you not attending to vote for him. I am not on speaking terms with him, and as he has behaved most discreditably towards me I trust you will assent to my wishes." Riley obeyed. That a contest was afoot only became clear when Jones, late in the day, had to break cover to nominate Riddell. Bourke was furious that Riddell had broken his word.

The vote took a week to count, a week that saw the factions brawling extravagantly in public. Once more the horrors of Castle Forbes were raked over while the convict Watt and the lawyer Therry were abused as dangers to society – Watt for climbing above his station and Therry as an Irishman "found continually at his Excellency's elbow 'breathing soft whispers' into his willing ear".

Riddell won by a single vote. Once Therry's humiliation was complete, Riddell assured Bourke that he had no intention whatever of taking up the post. In a letter filled with awkward lies, the Colonial Treasurer claimed to have been surprised to hear rumours that his name was even in contention. Jones offered his own lies. "He only disgraces himself," the Governor told his son. "Jones attributed his conduct to excitement. It has however become the subject of general animadversion and is considered a very gross act of political fraud, for which many assert he ought to be removed from Council." But once again, this civilised Irish gentleman showed himself unwilling to grapple with his enemies. He left Jones alone and merely banished Riddell from the Council. "I cannot with due regard for H M.'s service and my own Honor any longer sit in Council with Mr Riddell," he told Glenelg, adding that if London did not back his decision he would resign. When Bourke heard the Secretary of State had dismissed the Hole & Corner petition, he had every reason to be confident Glenelg would approve Riddell's exile. Yet Bourke wrote to his son to be ready to lobby for him in Westminster: "As extraordinary things do sometimes happen in this best of all possible worlds it is right to be prepared."

*

Jones seized absolute control of the *Gazette* in February 1836. The Watts were in exile in Port Macquarie when he went to the Supreme Court for an injunction to prevent Mrs Watt from "meddling or at all interfering with the management or conducting" of the paper. He listed her sins: she had married a convict; appointed "persons of the lowest description" to write for the paper; and under her management sales had greatly decreased, much to the loss of her late husband's heirs. Mrs Watt's rejoinder was blunt: "Jones only wants to retain the said Newspaper in his hands to further his political views and ends, and not for the good of the said Estate." Jones won in the Supreme Court. Mrs Watt fought on for a time but the litigation petered out, leaving the *Gazette* in Jones' hands. To be his editor, he promoted one of her enemies, a talented bachelor called George Cavenagh, whom *The Australian* dismissed as Jones' "pliant and obsequious minion".

For the next five years, the *Gazette* spoke with Jones' voice, calling for order, punishment, temperance, charity (whites only) and the rights of squatters, while condemning the Governor, convicts, the Irish and – with absurd passion – Rome. Editorial after editorial in the *Gazette* dwelt on Bourke's secret machinations to promote papists and popery. As clashes with Aboriginal people grew more frequent and more bloody, the *Gazette* counselled restraint: "For the life of every savage unnecessarily sacrificed, a score of white men, will still have to atone." Beyond such warnings the paper offered only pessimism, parsimony and greed. This was pure Jones. His *Gazette* saw no hope that the blacks might be civilised; no reason to waste money on their welfare; no limit to what might be spent crushing black resistance; and no question that their lands were there to be taken by the squatters.

6

DEATHS AND ARRANGEMENTS

After marvelling at the giant tortoises of the Galápagos, Charles Darwin set sail for Sydney, curious to observe the society evolving there. He found the "Aboriginal Blacks" skilled, good-humoured and acute, "far from the utterly degraded beings as usually represented". But the whites appalled him:

> The whole community is rancorously divided into parties on almost every subject. Amongst those who from their station of life, ought to rank with the best, many live in such open profligacy, that respectable people cannot associate with them. There is much jealousy between the children of the rich emancipist & the free settlers; the former being pleased to consider honest men as interlopers. The whole population poor & rich are bent on acquiring wealth; the subject of wool & sheep grazing amongst the higher orders is of preponderant interest. The very low ebb of literature is strongly marked by the emptiness of the booksellers shops.

He did note: "The capital of a person will without trouble produce him treble interest as compared to England: & with care he is sure to grow rich." The rich were moving into houses along the ridge of Woolloomooloo Hill, where a few windmills still stood about, relics of another time. As Darwin was casting his eye on the Colony, Richard Jones moved his family to a large, plain house on the hill. As an insult to Bourke, he renamed the place Darlinghurst. Today's suburb grew from its three-acre garden.

At the age of fifty, Richard Jones was known as the "inevitable president of all Sydney commercial institutions in King William's time". He was president of the Bank of New South Wales, president or treasurer of a slew of charities, his flocks were grazing 200,000 acres and he employed nearly 300 men on seven whaling stations in New Zealand. Edmund B. Uhr was managing an enormous extent of country on the Liverpool Plains and his troubled older brother John was working here and there for Jones in the Hunter. Uhr boys were still arriving from London. Cornelius William, a sweet child everyone loved, arrived at the age of seventeen and was already working sheep. One more Uhr boy was waiting his turn by the Thames. The oldest Jones boy was at King's, praised for his exemplary conduct, fine translations from the Greek gospels and mastery of the flute. The year the family moved to Darlinghurst, the thirteen-year-old opened the King's School concert with a rendition of "The Last Rose of Summer". He did not seem destined for the land.

For years Jones had been urging his London agent, Stuart Alexander Donaldson, to send his son to Sydney: "I will receive him into my House of business and give him a share of it, and I trust therewith as respectable an introduction to the World as falls to the lot of many young men." Jones made no secret of the commercial advantages for both of them. "You will on your son's arrival in this Country doubtless feel a deeper interest in the welfare of my establishment ... and will be naturally anxious that the amount of business done will be greater than heretofore." The young man arrived in May 1835. His furniture followed. "I have had your crest put upon your silver," wrote his mother. "I wish my dear son to be thought somebody." Stuart Alexander Donaldson junior would be the first premier of New South Wales, but first Jones made a merchant of him. He proved able and, after a brief apprenticeship, Jones took him into the house.

Sailing to Sydney with Donaldson was young Patrick Leslie, sent out to learn the ways of sheep at Cockrabill and Carleroi by his uncle and Jones' partner, Walter Davidson. Patrick Leslie is honoured today

PATRICK LESLIE

as a great pioneer of Queensland. But that doubtful achievement lay on the far side of a brutal public falling-out between this conceited boy, his uncle and Jones. All went well at first. The Joneses opened their arms to him. "They are excessively kind & such a thing as stiffness or reserve is not known in their house," he told his uncle. The lad was relieved to find snobbery rife on the far side of the world: "It is quite delightful to see the line that is drawn between the different classes of society here – I mean between Classes No. 1 & 2." He trusted their choice of friends. "Those with [whom] they associate may be companions for anyone." For all the welcome and good cheer, he did come to realise how opaque Jones was: "If you do ask his advice he gives it willingly but in such a way that you are not sure whether he would advise one thing or the other."

Jones' sister Elizabeth married as the family was settling down in Darlinghurst. She had met John Stephen Ferriter, purser on Her Majesty's war sloop *Alligator*, a couple of years earlier when the ship called at Sydney after carrying out Britain's first armed conflict with the Māori. The *Alligator* and the *Isabella* with sixty soldiers of the 50th Regiment were sent to rescue the survivors of a whaler wrecked and looted by the Māori on the coast of the North Island. The rescue complete, they set about a slaughter. "There being about 103 natives assembled on the beach, we fired upon them," sailors told the *Sydney Times*. "Numbers of their dead strewed the beach." A heavy gun was wheeled up to destroy their fort, or pā. "We found the natives ready to receive us—they fired upon us, but as soon as we discharged our carronade at them, they fled to the bush, where the military being ready to receive them, a great many were killed." After meeting Miss Jones in Sydney, Ferriter sailed home, left the navy and returned to the Colony. He began working for Jones even before he and Elizabeth were married by Samuel Marsden at St James' Church, King Street. They were both thirty-four. "Aunt Ferriter was a very particular woman in every way," wrote her great-niece. "She had a soft voice and held herself upright to the end of her days. She never lolled."

The move to Woolloomooloo Hill was also a time of family tragedy. On a voyage home, Edward Jones died in Manila. As well as working in his brother's Sydney office, Edward had been running 5000 sheep on the Liverpool Plains. Jones sold these to his brothers-in-law, Ferriter and Uhr, for the colossal sum of £10,406. This was far out of reach of either man. At the same time – at least on paper – Ferriter and Uhr became partners in Jones' operations on the Liverpool Plains and beyond, apparently holding some of the land and the vast flocks grazing on them. Whether these arrangements were designed to hide Jones' assets isn't clear. But that was how they operated when hard times hit. Meanwhile, after a brief time in Sydney, the newlyweds moved to Black Creek where Ferriter joined the Patrick's Plains junta, first as a magistrate and later as a local councillor. The Ferriters remained part of the formal life of Sydney, on the list for levées at Government House.

*

With Australian wool fetching wild prices, flocks of young men from every corner of Britain were arriving in the Colony to make their fortunes. All they needed was capital to buy sheep. Some had old family money to draw on; others borrowed from banks and merchants; many scraped together whatever savings their families could spare. Poet and former convict William Wilkes wrote:

Many a fond mama brought forth her hoard,
To lavish on the child her soul adored;
Old orange-coloured guineas saw the light,
Jingling on burly crowns, and sovereigns bright;
The savings-up of many a careful year
Were parted with, yet not without a tear.
One last fond look upon the coin was bent—
Oh could the dear old dames have seen it spent!

That so many came to the bush burdened by debt mattered for Aboriginal people. When deciding what lives to take or spare, what country to take or share, squatters had to keep in mind obligations on the far side of the world. Often at stake – particularly as the great boom of the early 1830s faded – was the survival of families back Home. This encouraged desperate measures. George Augustus Robinson, that equivocal figure in the history of Van Diemen's Land, noted in his diary: "It is a fact and deeply to be regretted that men, settlers, go into the wilds of Australia, natural Humans; at Length become cruel."

Governor Bourke hoped the Aboriginal people of the grasslands of Port Phillip might be encouraged to abandon hunting as sheep poured in from Van Diemen's Land. He tried to settle them in villages. Ending the wandering of blacks was touted as the first necessary step to their civilisation. But there was this advantage too: peoples who once required rivers and plains for their survival might be contained – in the most Christian way – in a few huts in the corner of a settler's run. Bourke failed. John Batman struck a deal with the leaders of the Kulin peoples to purchase 600,000 acres of their land. Bourke repudiated the deal. The meaning of this is fiercely debated still: was Bourke saving these people from a rotten deal – all that land for blankets, tomahawks and flour – or denying their sovereign right to make a treaty with the invaders? James Boyce argues that a deal of some sort was made but the written record was a lie: "There was no possibility that the Aborigines had consented to the incomprehensible concept of selling their land by signing a written treaty." Lord Glenelg congratulated Bourke for protecting a helpless people from "private adventurers" while guarding "the foundation on which all Proprietary rights in New South Wales at present rest". Bourke and Glenelg were not interested in deep issues of native title. They would be attended to by the High Court 150 years later. What mattered to colonial officials was making sure that any and all revenue earned from the black lands of Australia flowed to the Crown.

Bourke's position on the natives of his little realm was a mess. One afternoon when entertaining two Quaker missionaries at Government House, Parramatta, he mentioned "the desirableness of doing something for the Aborigines of New South Wales, and the difficulty of knowing what to do in order to promote their improvement". James Backhouse and George Washington Walker had spent five years in the Colony and found the Aboriginal peoples skilful, cheerful, intelligent and dignified. On Flinders Island they were appalled to find exiles from Van Diemen's Land dying. They spent time at Lancelot Threlkeld's mission and with squatters on their runs. They served on Richard Jones' temperance and education committees. A few weeks after their meeting with Bourke, Backhouse offered him a critique of the grim history of the Colony so far:

> It is scarcely to be supposed that in the present day any persons of reflection will be found who will attempt to justify the measures adopted by the British, in taking possession of the territory of this people, who had committed no offence against our nation; but who, being without strength to repel invaders, had their lands usurped, without an attempt at purchase by treaty, or any offer of reasonable compensation, and a class of people introduced into their country, amongst which were many, both free and bond, who, regardless of law, and in great measure exempt from its operation by the remoteness of their situation, practised appalling cruelties

upon this almost helpless race. And when any of the latter have retaliated, they have brought upon themselves the
vengeance of British strength, by which beyond a doubt,
many of the unoffending have been destroyed, along with
those who had ventured to return a small measure of these
wrongs upon their white oppressors.

Backhouse did not plead for dispossession to cease. The point of a colony was, after all, to occupy the territory of conquered peoples. The
missionary argued instead that the Aboriginal peoples ought to have
first call on the revenue raised on their lands "to whatever extent may be
required for their benefit" to supply them with food, clothing, shelter,
cash wages – "in order to teach them its use and value" – and education,
plus land of their own if they wish to cultivate it. But that Quaker good
sense collided with the iron law of New South Wales that anything done
for Aborigines had to be cheap. Divide the land? Too expensive. Feed
the dispossessed? Too expensive. Fund teachers? Too expensive. Send
enough police into the bush to protect the original lords of the soil?
Much too expensive. The refusal to spend cramped every response to
the horrors of the frontier.

So did Bourke's refusal to punish the murders among his officials.
Returning from the country he named Australia Felix, the Surveyor-
General Thomas Mitchell reported, in rather a jaunty way, a massacre
he conducted on the Murray by trapping about 180 "lynx-eyed" savages
in a pincer movement:

Attacked simultaneously by both parties, the whole betook
themselves to the river; my men pursuing them and shooting as many as they could. Numbers were shot in swimming
across the Murray, and some even after they had reached
the opposite shore, as they ascended the bank. Amongst
those shot in the water, was the chief (recognised by a particular kind of cloak he wore, which floated after he went
down). Thus, in a very short time, the usual silence of the

desert prevailed on the banks of the Murray, and we pursued our journey unmolested.

As many as forty died. To commemorate the rout, Mitchell named a nearby hill Mount Dispersion. It still bears that name. Bourke was appalled by the killing and the tone of Mitchell's report. But Mitchell wasn't charged. He wasn't even dismissed. All Bourke and his Executive Council delivered was a withering rebuke.

The story of Mitchell's slaughter in the south was broken by *The Australian* – no longer owned by Wentworth and no longer barracking for brutality. But *The Sydney Herald* greeted the news with one of the most bloodthirsty tirades in the history of colonial journalism. It began with an attack on the "humbugging maniacs and hypocrites who write and prate of matters of which they know nothing whatever" and went on to urge squatters to follow the lead set by the settlers of North America:

> If nothing but extermination will do, they *will* exterminate
> the savages as they would wild beasts. And thus it will ever
> be: it is the law of nature that civilized man shall drive the
> savage before him; for it was never yet known that a savage
> people were subdued by persuasion.

The *Gazette* spoke with the voice of Richard Jones. It deplored unprovoked violence towards the blacks. It feared for the revenge attacks that would inevitably come – and they did. The road south would become one of the most dangerous in the Colony. The *Gazette* mocked the man – "The fact is, that Major Mitchell is, and always was, dreadfully frightened of the blacks" – and deplored the slaughter. "Is there any thing that could justify a *second* volley, and a *third* being discharged with the same awful effect?" And why shoot like dogs men swimming away from the scene? But in almost the same breath the *Gazette* was demanding Bourke put down the blacks on the Liverpool Plains.

This was personal. Blacks and drought were threatening Jones' flocks. The rain had stopped. Competition with the Kamilaroi for water

and grass was growing fierce across the plains. Five stockmen and timber cutters were killed in 1836 and 1837. Two of the dead were shepherds
on John Cobb's run on the Gwydir and a party of stockmen set off in
pursuit of the killers. Through his network of black informers, the missionary Lancelot Threlkeld heard that the vigilantes "came upon the
tribe, found some with the clothes of the murdered shepherds on their
backs" and set about killing them. As many as 200 died in reprisal raids,
their bodies buried on a mountain still called Gravesend. Threlkeld
reported to the Colonial Secretary:

> If Government were to institute an enquiry into the con-
> duct of some Europeans in the interior towards the blacks,
> A War of extirpation would be found to have long existed in
> which the ripping open of the bellies of the Blacks alive;—
> the roasting them in that state in triangularly made log
> fires, made for the very purpose;—the dashing of infants
> upon the stones; the confining of a party in a hut and let-
> ting them out singly through the door-way, to be butchered
> as they endeavoured to escape, together with many other
> atrocious acts of cruelty, which are but the sports of mon-
> sters boasting of superior intellect to that possessed by the
> wretched Blacks!

The squatters were circulating a list of fourteen – but always said to
be fifteen – names of martyrs to black violence since explorers first
came to Corbon Comleroy. But as far as Bourke was concerned, the
old deal with settlers beyond the Limits of Location was unchanged:
those who took their sheep deep into the wastelands had to look after
themselves. He stuck to this though the outcome was appalling. By
Threlkeld's count, the killing of those fourteen or fifteen whites on the
Liverpool Plains provoked the deaths of at least 500 Kamilaroi. Bourke
also refused to send troops to put down the blacks of Port Phillip Bay.
But he did authorise the settlers there to set up a corps of native police.
It was an old Empire strategy he knew from his time at the Cape of

Good Hope, where white officers led local black troopers in a force known as the Cape Mounted Rifles that proved cheap and effective in frontier wars with the Xhosa.

*

But Bourke was done. As the furore over Mitchell's killings was raging in the local press, Glenelg's verdict arrived from London: Campbell Riddell was to be readmitted to the Council. Bourke wrote at once resigning his commission. Glenelg's ridiculous decision had many fathers, chief among them his ties to the Riddells of Argyllshire and the endless whinging of squatters and their London agents about the liberal Irishman who was their Governor. But the plotter who brought Bourke undone was Richard Jones. Bourke's fall shaped the Colony. His fate demonstrated all over again the danger of trying to rein in the squatters of New South Wales, particularly the squatter magistrates. For decades to come they would be left with their summary powers intact to rule the bush in their own interests. It would have terrible consequences for the Aboriginal peoples of the Colony.

Bourke's permission to return arrived in October 1837 by the same ship that brought the news to New South Wales that a new monarch, Victoria, was on the throne. The *Gazette* struggled with its emotions: gloom at the passing of William IV, and profound satisfaction at the confirmation of Bourke's departure: "The inhabitants of this portion of Her Majesty's dominions are at last about to be set free from the thraldom of a convict-ridden Government—we trust for ever." The people of Sydney did not share the verdict of the Tory press. A huge crowd the *Gazette* called "a felon mob" gathered along the shore to farewell the Governor. Small boats escorted his ship down the harbour and Bourke stood bareheaded on the deck as it slipped out to sea. He was not sorry to go.

7

THE CREEKS

The soldiers Bourke would not dispatch left Invermein for the Liverpool Plains a month after he sailed. Reports had reached Sydney of fresh depredations by the Kamilaroi. The *Herald* was baying for blood.

THE POOR BLACKS—Letters have been received from the Northern parts of the Colony, which state, that the Blacks are murdering the shepherds and stockmen with impunity. These letters also inform us, that the same tribe of Blacks are destroying the cattle by hundreds.

While waiting for the new Governor to arrive, the Colony had been left in the hands of Colonel Kenneth Snodgrass, a capricious veteran of the Napoleonic Wars who gave Major James Nunn of the 80th Regiment a free hand to deal with trouble on the plains. "You are to act according to your own judgement," said Snodgrass, "and use your utmost exertion to suppress these outrages." At Waterloo Creek on 26 January 1838, Nunn's troops and Mounted Police drove a large number of Kamilaroi into a swamp and slaughtered at least fifty. Afterwards, Nunn found a few bits and pieces in their camp which convinced him he had punished blacks involved in the murder of Cobb's shepherds on the Gwydir, a crime for which hundreds had already been killed. Back at Cobb's head station, Nunn boasted to the appalled squatter of "[p] opping off with his holster pistols the Blacks whenever one appeared from behind a tree".

WATERLOO CREEK

The new Governor, Sir George Gipps, was a dour military man of Whig sympathies and some administrative skill. He brought with him the usual Royal Instructions to safeguard the native peoples of New South Wales. He was keen to comply. When squatters in the south petitioned him in June to send troops to protect them on the track to Port Phillip, he refused.

> Sir George Gipps desires it to be intimated to the gentlemen who have signed the memorial, that as he has the most positive directions from Her Majesty's Government to treat the aboriginal natives as subjects of Her Majesty, it is entirely out of his power to authorise the levying of war against them, or to give sanction to any measures of indiscriminate retaliation.

To make himself absolutely clear, Gipps declared a new start. Rhetoric of this kind had never been used by an arriving Governor before.

In order that no misapprehension may exist on this subject, he feels bound to declare that nothing which has been
done In this Colony in former times, or in any other place
or Colony whatsoever, would, in his opinion, be a justification for departing from the strict obedience which is due
to the order of Her Majesty's Government.

Only days after this mighty rebuke was issued, a squatter from the
north of the Liverpool Plains arrived in Sydney with news that twenty-
two Aborigines – Wiriyaraay people of the Kamilaroi nation – had been
slaughtered at Myall Creek. Frederick Foot told the Colonial Secretary,
"As I reside in the neighbourhood where this flagrant violation of the
Law took place, I consider it a duty incumbent on me, to submit this
statement for the information of the Governor." When he left, corpses
were still burning on a pyre: "The head and part of the body of one,
the head of another, besides several sculls and bones still remained
unconsumed." On his way down to Sydney he had alerted Denny Day,
the Police Magistrate in Muswellbrook, who had set out for the scene
of the massacre. A fortnight after Foot's arrival in town, news broke in
the papers of a slaughter "of the most shocking enormity". Details were
sparse but it was known that nine men were already on their way to
Sydney under arrest.

In the shadow of this news, the new Governor gave his Legislative
Council two documents: James Nunn's account of Waterloo Creek –
which he knew to be a whitewash – and the final report of Fowell
Buxton's Select Committee on Aborigines (British Settlements), which
he had brought with him to Sydney. The humanitarians of the Whig
government, having ended slavery in the Empire and paid slave owners £20 million compensation – cash that built elegant country houses,
drove the industrial revolution and sent sheep deep into Australia – next
turned their attention to the fate of the native peoples of the Empire.
Here was a more complex challenge, one that could not be solved with
a mountain of money. The natives of the Cape were the main concern

of Buxton's committee, but they spent some time looking into the fate of the Aborigines of North America and New Holland. Their approach was peculiar: this was an inquiry into morals, not money. In the city of London were bankers and merchants who might tell the committee what was driving dispossession and violence in the Antipodes. None gave evidence. Apart from colonial and military officials, almost the only witnesses before the committee were clergy. Broughton was quoted lavishly.

The final report of June 1837 is a wretched mix of fine rhetoric and muddled argument that recommended no brake on colonisation. How eloquently the committee sided with the dispossessed native peoples of half the world.

> Too often, their territory has been usurped; their property seized; their numbers diminished; their character debased; the spread of civilization impeded. European vices and diseases have been introduced amongst them, and they have been familiarized with the use of our most potent instruments for the subtle or the violent destruction of human life, viz. brandy and gunpowder ...
>
> It might be presumed that the native inhabitants of any land have an incontrovertible right to their own soil; a plain and sacred right, however, which seems not to have been understood. Europeans have entered their borders uninvited, and, when there, have not only acted as if they were undoubted lords of the soil, but have punished the natives as aggressors if they have evinced a disposition to live in their own country.

And what were the natives owed after fifty years of this? Not restoration of their lands. The committee thought it too late for that. "Whatever may have been the injustice of this encroachment, there is no reason to suppose that either justice or humanity would now be consulted by receding from it." Once again, the true answer to the woes of colonisation was God. Indeed, the committee saw the Empire's true purpose in the world was not conquest and exploitation but "to carry civilization and humanity, peace and good government, and, above all, the knowledge of the true God, to the uttermost ends of the earth".

The Council considered the report on 10 August 1838. They met, as always, in a bare room in the Rum Hospital on George Street. The councillors sat at a long table with Gipps at their head displaying his usual "choking rigidity". The doors were open to the public. Under Gipps, debates could be watched and reported for the first time. Though the journalists sat only a few feet from the table, they complained for a dozen years that Mr Jones "spoke too low to be audible in the gallery". The councillors were not much concerned with Buxton's flights of rhetoric that afternoon. They focused instead on the few measures which had, to their surprise, already been put into effect by London. Part of the revenue from the lands of New South Wales – held in London – was henceforth to be spent protecting the Aboriginal people and educating their youth. A band of Protectors was already on its way to Australia, men who would live among the natives, learn their languages, win their confidence and be their advocates in disputes with settlers. The Protectors were also to try to persuade these people to give up their wandering ways while ensuring, in the meantime, that they were free to hunt and gather on their lands. "So long as agriculture shall be distasteful to them, they should be provided with the means of pursuing the chase without molestation."

The squatter councillors were restless. Sir John Jamison (140,000 acres) deplored the Colony's revenue being spent on Protectors simply to satisfy the members of religious societies at Home. "The subscribers were very rich, and they subscribed munificently, and if they sent people out, they ought to pay them." Hannibal Macarthur (113,000 acres) called for a local inquiry into the Aboriginal question. Gipps agreed. Richard Jones (183,000 acres) took up a theme he would pursue for the rest of his life: the impractical, expensive, ultra-humane and ignorant thinking of London:

Mr Jones said it was clear that her Majesty's government had very little idea of the condition of the natives of this Colony; and the Committee of the House of Commons appear to have no knowledge of the subject whatever. This was clearly to be seen from the appointment of the Aboriginal protectors, whose duty it would be to follow the tribes about the bush—to live with them and build them huts, which everyone who had the least knowledge of the natives of this Colony knew to be impracticable.

Buxton wanted to see an old promise fulfilled: the release on the mainland of the imprisoned survivors of the native peoples of Van Diemen's Land. John Blaxland (72,000 acres) had already condemned the idea as "extremely hazardous and expensive". Jones met the proposal with his bedrock belief that the blacks could never be civilised, a belief he saw confirmed by the infamous Black Line of 1830.

As to saddling the Colony with the expense of maintaining the miserable remnant of the tribes of Van Diemen's Land, at present on Flinder's Island, it was quite preposterous. In Van Diemen's Land they were never civilized, and if they were all brought here, and Mr Robinson with them as chief protector, and turned into the woods, what would be the result? They would commit the same outrages here that they did in Van Diemen's Land, where the inhabitants formed a military cordon, to drive the wretched natives into one corner of the island, where they were seized and conveyed to Flinders island for the purpose of being civilised; and that experiment having failed, they were by way of another experiment, to be turned loose on the Colony. It would only be saddling this Colony with a heavy expense, and to send them here would be of no use.

JOHN PLUNKETT

Jones' rage against the Protectors ran long and deep. The *Gazette* ridiculed these "humbug" appointments as "the rankest pieces of jobbery" ever conceived by a corrupt and venal Whig ministry. They were no more use than "the protectors of the Esquimaux, for all the good they do". Why, asked Jones' paper, should blacks be given officials to advocate their cause? "Let them send agents of their own, and at their own cost." Jones and the *Gazette* saw the Protectors as the best evidence of all that London was ignorant of the needs of the squatters and the true nature of the blacks. When Lord Melbourne proposed setting aside 15 per cent of land revenue to pay for civilising the Aborigines, the *Gazette* responded with brutal ridicule: "We think it is about as feasible as the project of the laundresses in the fable, who set about washing a black fellow white, but unfortunately, just as they were about completing the bleaching process, the obstinate fool took it in his head to die."

*

John Plunkett charged eleven shepherds and stockmen with the murders at Myall Creek. Now Attorney-General under the new Governor,
Plunkett was more determined than ever to show that the law protected black and white alike in the Colony. An ancient obstacle to
the prosecution was the principle that heathens could not give evidence. The best witness to the killings was an Aboriginal boy who
stood behind a tree, watching the slaughter. He spoke English. But
Davy could not go into the box because, having no fear of the after-
life, his oath had no weight. While useful for silencing the slaves and
savages of the Empire, the rule made things awkward when there
was business to do with Jews, Hindus, Muslims and Chinese. Loop-
holes had been found for them over the centuries but the evidence of
other native peoples of the Empire remained inadmissible. As Plunkett said: "A person can fearlessly commit any crime if none but the
blacks are present."

Sydney responded with horror to the news of Myall Creek. As the
trial approached, the Presbyterian John Dunmore Lang set up a local
branch of the Aborigines' Protection Society, formed in London in the
wake of the Buxton report "to protect the aborigines against the hard-
hearted aggressions of the white man". As its meetings were held in
Exeter Hall in the Strand, *Exeter Hall* became for decades squatters'
slang for everything they despised about sentimental British humanitarians. The Sydney meeting was held over two weeks in the Mechanics'
School of Arts. Nothing like this had been attempted in the Colony
before. Gipps was very much in favour. The Lord Bishop of Australia
was nowhere to be seen and no followers of Rome were among the
organisers, who included Richard Jones, the only man of business and
by far the largest landowner on the committee. His presence was not
incongruous. Myall Creek was everything he deplored: an unprovoked
massacre that would lead to yet more killings in the bush. He was sitting
with his friends: half the committee worked with him on the Religious

Tract Society, circulating Bibles to the ignorant and the poor of the Colony. Now they were turning their attention to the plight of the native blacks. *The Colonist* reported its brave beginnings:

> The two public meetings which have been held in this town for the purpose of taking the sense of the inhabitants on this great national question, have been such as the warmest friends of the Aborigines could have desired. Crowded to excess by respectable persons of both sexes; addressed by eloquent advocates for the rights of the injured race; marked throughout their lengthened sittings by the profoundest attention, and by unequivocal expressions of sympathy for the wrongs inflicted, and of zeal for the immediate application of all possible means for the redress of those wrongs; these meetings have done much to rescue New South Wales from the odium which had been not unjustly cast upon its name.

It proved a total failure. Many were uncomfortable with the London society's credo: "By fraud and violence Europeans have usurped immense tracts of native territory, paying no regard to the rights of inhabitants." What were those rights, asked lawyers among them? Richard Windeyer, just arrived in the Colony, cited the ancient Greek principle that wilderness belongs to no one. He took issue with the Exeter Hall view that the blacks could own land. The *Herald* reported:

> He could not look upon the natives as the exclusive proprietors of the soil. He viewed colonization on the basis of the broad principle laid down by the first and great legislator, in the command he issued to man "to multiply and replenish the earth." He considered in fact that the land belonged to him who should first cultivate it.

Windeyer saw this as fundamental to the moral position of the colonists. "If we have no right to be here, we have nothing to do but to take ship and go home." The brief life of the Aborigines' Protection Society in New South Wales ended that night.

The squatter who led the murdering stockmen at Myall Creek was not facing trial. Exasperated by the loss of a few cattle and the narrow escape of a couple of shepherds on his Gwydir run, John Fleming of Mungie Bundie had recruited twenty convict and ex-convict stockmen to ride along the river, armed with swords, guns and pistols, looking for blacks to kill. The Wiriyaraay of the Kamilaroi nation sheltering on Henry Dangar's station on Myall Creek had nothing to do with any of the outrages in the district. Fleming directed his men in their slaughter. His role and identity were known. But not even the offer of a free pardon, a passage to England and £50 saw him betrayed. He lived out his days untroubled on the Hawkesbury. His men bore the brunt of the punishment alone when the trial of eleven stockmen began in November. Each was charged with murder. Plunkett and Therry were their prosecutors. Three of the best lawyers in the Colony defended them, their fees paid by the Black Association of squatters recruited by the odious Robert Scott of the Patrick's Plains junta. He urged the prisoners to stay united to the end and sat at the bar table with the defence team throughout the trial. Though Plunkett could not call on Davy's testimony, the evidence he could lead was so powerful that the newspapers of the town condemned the killings as atrocious, wanton, horrific, diabolical, revolting and unpardonable. But the jury acquitted. In the uproar of the court, Plunkett ordered the prisoners not be set free. He had fresh murder charges to lay.

The Sydney Herald did not join "the wailers over the aborigines". The arguments the paper advanced against the prosecution have barely changed in two centuries. The *Herald* abused virtue-signallers: "Theorists, and others desirous of acquiring a reputation for humanity." And city elites: "Philanthropists, who sit at ease at home to talk and write of the 'poor aborigines." And groupthink: "It is quite evident that the sentimentality and ravings of a parcel of European 'canters' have had their effect on the minds of many mistaken men in this Colony." And those

who have so lost perspective that they "weep over the perhaps necessary shooting of a black" and fail to bear in mind the tragic fate of so
many innocent whites. According to the *Herald*, the "most glaring and
oppressive" outrage was the money wasted on missions to the Aborigines "when our revenue will barely pay the salaries of our Government
Officers!" During the Myall Creek uproar, the paper ran a long letter
from a squatter on the Murrumbidgee who claimed to be intimately
acquainted with the blacks:

> Hordes of Aboriginal cannibals, to whom the veriest rep-
> tile that crawls the earth holds out matter for emulation, and
> who are far, very far, below the meanest brute in rationality ...
> every man of common experience in the Colony, and of com-
> mon sense, has long known, viz:—that the aboriginals of my
> native country, are the most degenerate, despicable, and bru-
> tal race of beings in existence, and stand as it were in scorn "to
> shame creation"—a scoff and a jest upon humanity ... they
> will, and must become extinct—civilization destroys them—
> where labor and industry flourish, *they* die!

The second trial took one long day. Plunkett charged seven of the
stockmen with killing four children by kicking, beating and decapitat-
ing them before throwing their bodies onto the fire. The prosecution's
best witness was George Anderson, a young convict from London
who had had the moral resolution not to join the killers that day. The
Black Association was still paying the defence lawyers and steadying
the accused. Plunkett denounced the association as a criminal body
and vowed to prosecute its members if only he could identify them.
To this day they remain unknown. The *Gazette*, the *Monitor* and *The
Australian* joined the attack on the Black Association. Without naming
Fleming, they regretted with one voice that the ringleader of the massacre was not with his men on trial.

The judge finished summing up after midnight and the jury returned
at two in the morning with a verdict: they found the seven guilty of the

murder of one unnamed child. All were sentenced to hang. The *Gazette* applauded the decision. Jones believed in punishment, even capital punishment. His paper had no doubt the executions would prove useful. "We sincerely hope that it may strike a terrible warning among those who like these men consider themselves out of the reach of the law." For fear of an angry mob, the public was kept away on the morning of the execution. A priest and two clergy attended the condemned in the empty yard. After the warrant was read, the prisoners kissed and shook hands. The hangman placed ropes around their necks. They prayed as the drop fell.

Gipps and Plunkett had made their point. "One thing of lasting benefit only came from Myall Creek," wrote Plunkett's biographer John Molony. "Henceforth all were aware that there was equality before the law for the white and the black inhabitants, in so far as the sacredness of human life was concerned." But the squatters easily countered the danger. After the executions, the silence of the bush that protected so many killers would be imposed with a severity that lasted a century. And the men of the bush discovered more discreet ways to kill. The *Monitor* vouched for "the very *words*" of an exchange overheard after the executions:

> Country Gentleman—So, I find they have hanged
> these men?
>
> Town Gentleman—They have.
>
> Country Gentleman—Ah—hem—we are going on a safer
> game now.
>
> Town Gentleman—Safer game? how do you mean?
>
> Country Gentleman—Why, we are poisoning the Blacks;
> which is much safer; and serve them right too!

Gipps at last established a police force for the bush. The Mounted Police operated only inside the Nineteen Counties. The new Border Police would follow where the squatters went. Gipps imagined

the force as a band of even-handed men, ready to prevent "the outrages which have been committed on the Aborigines, as well as by
them". Jones welcomed the new force. For years he had condemned
the Mounted Police, which he thought particularly useless against
the bushrangers robbing travellers, drays and stations up and down
the Hunter. The pub at Black Creek had been robbed "in open day"
of cash and rum. One of Jones' men had been severely wounded by
these banditti. John Uhr had found himself staring at the musket of a
bushranger while dining one evening with his friend James Canning
Pearce on a run near Invermein. Opossum Jack and his men stripped
the place of "cash and orders £15, dresses, blue cloth suits, tobacco,
waistcoats, boots, shooting jackets, clothes, powder, pistols, cutlass,
carbine, shawls, muslin, nett, knives, razors, saddle, bridle, &c, &c".
The loot was loaded onto a couple of horses held by Pearce's own convicts. "They then politely bid us good night and left us."

Gipps made the squatters pay for his new Border Police with a levy
of a penny a sheep and sixpence a horse on top of the pitiful licence
fees already charged for their land – a flat £10 a year no matter how
enormous the run. Jones suggested the levy be raised a little to pay for
"religious instruction to these people who might be said to be out of
the pale of the law". His proposal failed. The Border Police would last
seven years. There were never enough – only sixty-eight to patrol many
hundreds of thousands of acres. They spent much of their time collecting the licence fees that paid for their existence. For that, the squatters
came to despise them. "Little time was left for patrolling the large area
of the district to keep the peace between settlers and Aborigines," wrote
Leslie Skinner in *Police of the Pastoral Frontier*. "Even then, in practice,
protection of the settler was the main objective."

Jones' early enthusiasm soon died. He and his paper condemned
the force as ineffective, leaving squatters with little choice but to use vigilantes to combat the blacks. The *Gazette* argued that vigilantes led to
unnecessary violence. What was wanted was effective professional protection in the bush. This was a Christian point of view – not to spar the

blacks but spare the settlers from having to kill. Discipline and speed remained everything. Mercy taught the blacks no lessons, for savages saw leniency as cowardice or impotence. Blood would have to be shed, but on the other side of swift retribution lay the hope of lasting peace:

> Nothing but summary measures of coercion will check the sanguinary disposition of the Blacks, or put an end to the fearful waste of human blood ... we cannot, from whatever cause we may conceive it to have arisen, consent to see our fellow-colonists butchered and their property destroyed by ruthless savages without calling upon the Government to lose no time in reducing the hostile tribes to subjection.

8

HIS GIMLET EYE

"**1837** 1838 1839 three years nothing but dust,"
wrote William Telfer, the bard of Wallabadah. The drought would not let up.
Much quoted in pulpits at this time, a passage from Jeremiah seemed to
be describing the plight of New South Wales:

> Because the ground is chapt, for there was no rain in the
> earth, the plowmen were ashamed, they covered their heads.
> Yea, the hind also calved in the field, and forsook it, because
> there was no grass.
>
> And the wild asses did stand in the high places, they
> snuffed up the wind like dragons; their eyes did fail, because
> there was no grass.
>
> O LORD, though our iniquities testify against us, do
> thou it for thy name's sake: for our backslidings are many;
> we have sinned against thee.

John Dunmore Lang named those sins: foul deeds committed against
the blacks.

> They are still bone of our bone and flesh of our flesh—for-
> med originally after the image of God, like ourselves, and
> guilty only, as far as we are concerned, of an Ethiopian skin,
> and an untutored soul.

He did not persuade the Colony to change its ways. A day of fasting, humiliation and prayer mandated by Gipps was given the credit for a brief opening of the heavens in the autumn of 1839. "Rain has descended in copious showers; occasionally in torrents; and now all is life, and greenness, and beauty," sang *The Colonist*. "Our ponds overflowing— our fields smiling in their ancient verdant gladness—our gardens springing up into prodigal luxuriance—our arable lands richly prepared for the plough and for the seed." Up on the Liverpool Plains, the Mooki flooded. Sheep were washed away. Edmund B. Uhr and his neighbours sustained great losses. Then the rains stopped again. Dust returned.

Uhr spread his sheep far and wide. Driving off the blacks was only one way squatters won country. Another was to invade their neighbours. Boundaries were vague. What began with sheep so often ended with lawyers. Unwisely, Uhr ignored the complaints of Edward Nowland, the overseer next door:

> I spoke to Mr Uhr & told him the injury is sheepe was doing the cattle & he said he would tel the men not to go their any more. but they still continue their old beat & since that I have got the sheep on the grant. wich satisfys me that they are wilfully attemting to destroy the cattle.

In the depths of the drought Uhr was sued for moving mobs of sheep onto Doona, the central block of Jones' claim along the Mooki. Behind their backs a wild highlander working for Jones at Black Creek had sold the grazing rights to the run. Telfer called the man: "A terror to the aboriginals and lawless white men in those days of Early Settlement." But even after his sheep were pulled back from Doona, Jones had 130,000 acres on Wallalla and Breeza – superb when it rained.

The drought broke days after Edmund Uhr married Amy Kemp in February 1840 at St James' Church in Sydney. The couple may have reached Wallalla in time to see their sheep being washed down the Mooki. *The Australian* reported Uhr suffered "great losses" in his flocks. Their first child, Edmund Ker "Ned" Uhr, was born in their fortress hut the following year. Seven more children followed over the next fifteen years. They would all carry the bloodlines of German sailors, Aldgate traders, would-be aristocrats and one of the bad men of early Australia, Amy's father, Anthony Fenn Kemp.

He ran through a small fortune as a youth; hung about the edges of the French Revolution; was entertained in America – or so he claimed – by his hero George Washington at Mount Vernon; and turned up in New South Wales as the paymaster of the Rum Corps. Kemp swindled the troops, embezzled military funds and took a leading role in the Rum Rebellion. After a few years in exile in London, he persuaded a hapless merchant – never repaid – to trust him with a shipment of goods to sell in Hobart. He was soon a prosperous rum merchant in the town and bought a sheep run he called Mount Vernon. He used dogs to drive off the original inhabitants of his acres. He backed the Black Line, the largest force ever assembled in Australia to kill Aborigines. The shame of that colossal fiasco has never died. The plan was to clear the island of blacks by beating them out of the bush like grouse at a shoot. These lumbering Europeans were easy to avoid and, mercifully, only two palawa were killed and two captured. But Kemp rose at a public meeting to urge citizens on: "Let us unite with one accord to strengthen the hands of Government by every means in our power, till we succeed in obtaining security for our settlers in the Interior against the atrocities of the Aborigines, who are like all other Savages, expert in ambush, and ferocious in vengeance."

Kemp and Jones had known each other for years. Kemp was married to the sister of Jones' first business partner in the Colony, Alexander Riley. Kemp had bought a second run he called Mount Vernon near Fleurs, where he and Jones exhibited their Saxon rams. Perhaps they brought the couple together. Amy had married a well-connected military man posted in Hobart. Alas he drowned in the winter of 1837, trying to run an overloaded boat through the surf at Little Swan Port north-east of Hobart. His "most amiable and accomplished" widow was in need of a husband and found one 800 miles away on the Liverpool Plains.

*

Jones was busy in the city, promoting one company to buy steamers for the Hunter River run and another to light the streets of Sydney. The Australian Gas Light Company survives today. He founded and chaired the Australian Auction Company, an ill-managed cabal intent on putting the town's auctioneers out of business. His whaling fleet was at its most profitable. The tea trade flourished. He was shipping sandalwood to China. Yet in 1837 he decided to sell the great bulk of his merchant business to his partner Stuart Donaldson, keeping for himself only whaling and tea. "The business most to my taste is the China trade," Jones told Donaldson's father. "I have been a large participator through the kindness of my friends Dent & Co for many years ... if the trade is profitable to any one it will be to me." His daughter Elizabeth remembered him trading after that "in a very small private way—himself & one clerk—in two hired rooms in Town; chiefly I think if not only as Agent for Dent & Co in China."

Jones was under pressure. As the wool market began to fail and the Australian Auction Company became mired in debt, money from Canton had become crucial to Jones' survival. This flow of cash was put at risk when a feud erupted in the late 1830s between Walter Davidson and his nephew Patrick Leslie. When that arrogant young pup arrived in Sydney to learn the ways of sheep at Cockrabill and Carleroi, the Joneses had opened their arms to him. So had the Macarthurs. At princely Camden Park, the Macarthurs showed showed off their Spanish merinos and poisoned his mind against Richard Jones. The Macarthurs' scorn for the merchant grazier seeped into Leslie's letters home. Without visiting either run, the young man condemned Fleurs as "a losing concern" and dismissed Black Creek as "horribly ill watered and a bad pasturing country". He relayed rumours that things at Carleroi and Cockrabill were in terrible confusion, "and how can it almost be otherwise?" After only a few weeks in the splendour of Camden Park, Leslie was confidently advising his uncle that it would be best to divide the joint flocks on the Krui and that he, Patrick, would earn the family the returns they deserved from their sheep, relying on his "first rate advisers", the Macarthurs.

The country was in poor shape when Leslie finally reached the Krui. It hadn't rained in months. A twenty-year-old who knew no one in the Colony except a few elegant families found himself rubbing shoulders with "the greatest scoundrels I ever saw in my life". He was supposed to be taught the ways of sheep by an ex-convict overseer, whom he believed was robbing the place blind by indulging the men. "I have seen eight or ten of them out in a day shooting and fishing for their own amusement, and the rascally Overseer never take any notice of it, but pass it over for a duck or two, or a few fish." In a brutal account of things on Cockrabill and Carleroi written to Walter Davidson only weeks after his arrival, Leslie identified the fundamental problem: Jones' generosity was ruining the business.

> Mr Jones gives his assigned servants much larger rations than any other person I have met with in the Colony, and, instead of doing any good, does a great deal of harm; as, indeed, the conduct of the rascals sufficiently shows, and his overseers have more indulgences than any other person: they have only to ask for what they want. What does more harm than any other thing among the men here, is giving the assigned prisoner servants wages; a great many of these fellows have ten, twelve and fourteen pounds per annum: that runs away with money.

Accounts Jones sent Davidson showed Leslie was lying. Yet in what Davidson came to regard as "an evil hour", he granted his nephew's wish. After a dozen years of partnership with Jones, the flocks were separated. Leslie had to find shepherds and build huts and yards on Carleroi. The bills went to his uncle.

Uncle and nephew soon fell out. Every boast Leslie made proved hollow. Though their sheep were "precisely the same character and race", the wool from Carleroi arrived in London filthy and fetched far less than Jones' wool from Cockrabill. Without Davidson's permission, the young man began to pay himself under a traditional system known as thirds: for managing Davidson's flocks he kept for himself a third of the lambs and a third of the wool. On discovering this, Davidson furiously demanded proper accounts. They never came. Davidson wrote to the boy's father at Warthill House, the toy castle in Aberdeenshire where the family still lives: "I think you will agree with me that figures of arithmetic are far better, because more intelligible, than figures of speech, in matters of dry business." He blamed Leslie's engagement to Hannibal Macarthur's daughter Kate:

> From this moment, he entirely lost sight of his true position, and quickly evinced such inconsiderate and unreasonable haste to become independent, as gave rise to his assuming an importance as inconsistent with his true position, as it was unwarranted by any views or prospects ever held out to him by me.

The spirit of Jane Austen hovered over the ruckus. When Mrs Hannibal Macarthur saw in one of Davidson's letters a slighting reference to her daughter having turned the boy's head with "flattering approbation and partial smiles", she fired off a defence to Warthill:

> Be assured, my dear Mrs. Leslie, of the unshaken integrity of your Son; he is respected by all. Mr. Davidson's opinion of [Kate] is, indeed, quite erroneous; and I could have hoped he would have given me credit for instilling something more solid, which would protect her from the fluttering nonsense of romantic love; and to have cherished an affection whose superstructure is religion and prudence.

Leslie walked off Carleroi and joined his more capable brothers Walter and George on a pioneering exploration of the Darling Downs that earned him his fame. On his return to Sydney, he presented his uncle with a last bill for £4000 and, flush with money, married Kate Macarthur. Davidson refused to pay "this vast pretended debt". Carleroi was sold on his orders and fetched a bad price. Uncle and nephew pursued each other with lawsuits and pamphlets.

This family melodrama might not have hurt Jones, but Davidson, keen to secure the future of his nephews, had also sent Patrick's brother William to Canton to learn the ways of opium and tea at Dent & Co. As Jones was relying more and more on the revenue of the China house to keep him afloat, the brothers sided against him. Dent & Co. was growing exasperated, and for good reason. When the *Lord Amherst* limped into Sydney Harbour in late December 1839, rather battered after a long voyage from Canton, Jones auctioned the cargo – 763 chests of hyson skin tea, 364 chests of twankey green tea and 2300 bags of Java rice – and kept the proceeds. The ship also brought news of a battle between war junks and British cutters at Kowloon, the opening round of the First Opium War. Jones applauded the moral energy of the Chinese government without quite thinking things through: Dent & Co. was a principal target of Peking's wrath, and if the opium trade were quashed the flow of money south to him would inevitably dwindle. Jones would not be indulged much longer.

When young Donaldson took full control of Jones' old business in Sydney, he was surprised to find the books in some confusion. The various strands of the business were tangled together. Available cash was being used to meet any payments as they fell due. Jones delayed again and again paying £4000 due to Donaldson, who wrote to his father: "Jones grows more and more Intimate with me a trait which is gratifying as it increases with acquaintance – I believe he has a very good opinion of me – but he is withal his good qualities a singularly mean man in some things." He had asked the young man to sell a wharf on the harbour. "Jones handed over all the papers and powers to me – they entailed upon me an infinity of trouble and annoyance – at last I sell the property for £5400 – He then comes in and takes a little concern with the matter and with the concern one half of the commission."

Most troubling was the discovery that the capital Jones had promised to leave in the business didn't exist. "Between you and me, Jones never had much actual Capital engaged in business," Donaldson told his father. "His credit has always been immense and so will mine be if I require it – but Jones' actual property has been nearly all excepting a few thousands engaged Solely in Estate and landed property stock." Jones was using about £30,000 of other people's money as it flowed through his hands. The young man began to wonder if he had sold the business to him to free himself from financial difficulties.

*

Few squatters celebrated the end of transportation to New South Wales in 1840. Most were distraught at the prospect of losing their free labour. But Richard Jones was delighted, for it brought closer the day when New South Wales would be rid of criminal contamination and its government relieved of the cost of feeding and housing these felons. With renewed determination he campaigned for London to ship out decent, hardworking Protestant families in the place of criminals to work the land. "So important is it that immigration should be continued, that he would pledge the general revenue, the land, houses, wives, children, any thing, rather than it should be discontinued." On this issue Jones was never quiet. It was a cause that perfectly united money and morals: populating the bush with free men and women would mean more work done and less trouble with the blacks. Jones' fearless attacks on London over immigration earned him high praise from the *Herald*:

> It is this fact which causes the sturdy, English-like independence of Mr. Jones to stand forth so prominently, and which causes him (deny it who may), to be looked upon as the representative in the Council of the independence of the Colony. There is nothing *mincing* about *him*—there is no deprecating any intentional disrespect, forsooth, to

the Secretary of State—there is no cringing to, or fawning upon, any man;—no, Mr. Jones speaks out, and for so doing he is deserving of the thanks of the Colonists.

Shepherds were blamed for a great deal. Squatters who could not see that invading the land inevitably provoked violence blamed evil shepherds for all the troubles of the frontier – evil shepherds and runaway convicts living with the blacks. Shepherds certainly had to take a share of blame. Their kidnapping and rape of Aboriginal women and children incited violence on the frontier for over a century. But contrary to Jones' high hopes, there was nothing to suggest free men were any better behaved than convict shepherds in the bush. Some saw their deaths at the hands of the blacks as yet more proof of native savagery. Others observed that most white men speared in the bush "were killed under provocation which would fully justify one white man in killing another". Threlkeld wondered why more of these abductors did not die. From his new mission at Lake Macquarie, he wrote to the Attorney-General in 1825:

> I have … heard at night shrieks of Girls, about 8 or 9 years of age, taken by force by the vile men of Newcastle. One man came to me with his head broken by the butt-end of a musket because he would not give up his wife. There are now two government stockmen, that are every night annoying the Blacks by taking their little Girls … My wonder is, that more Whites are not speared than there are considering the gross provocation given.

More sodomy might have meant a quieter frontier. Instead, clerics like Father William Ullathorne, Catholic Vicar-General of New South Wales, threw himself into excoriating crimes in huts and on chain gangs so frightful that even to name them would "make your blood to freeze, and your hair to rise erect in horror upon the pale flesh". This delicate Benedictine said he became aware that the Colony was a pit of Sodom in the confessional. The *Gazette* insinuated he may have had some personal interest in the issue, calling him "a dapper little gentleman of exceedingly mild and fascinating manners, more resembling in appearance what is generally called 'a ladies' man' than a strict adherent to the stern doctrine of clerical celibacy". Sir William Molesworth, chair of the House of Commons Select Committee on Transportation, took Ullathorne seriously:

> Are unnatural crimes common in country districts amongst the convicts?
> —I believe that where they do exist on farms, it is where a number of them are brought together on the large farms.
>
> That they are not common amongst the shepherds, who are separated?
> —I do not think they are so common amongst the shepherds as they are amongst a much more dissolute set, the stock-men.
>
> Are they common amongst these stock-men?
> —I believe that there is a great deal of that kind of crime amongst the stock-men.
>
> Is it supposed that they have introduced those crimes amongst the natives?
> —Yes.

Here was fresh proof, if any was required, that the best hope for missionaries was to reach Aborigines before they saw with their own eyes how God's word had failed so conspicuously to make the invaders models of Christian virtue.

With labour short and no convict ships on the way, the government turned its mind to a radical alternative: employing the native blacks. Jones joined a committee of Council chaired by Broughton to examine the issue. Some squatters and country magistrates brutally dismissed the notion. Others gave the committee encouraging accounts of blacks willing – for the odd shilling, a tomahawk, clothes and food – to wash sheep, cut wheat, gather potatoes, grind corn, strip bark, track stock, milk cows, wait at table, drive bullocks, build fences and shepherd flocks. Hugh Murray, Esq., of Lake Colac said:

> I consider them apt to learn, and clever at work, trustworthy when property is put into their charge, submissive, and easily taught obedience and respect, but on the whole, naturally inclined to indolence.

Kindness might cure that. "Kindness and justness in all dealings with them will attach them to the service of a settler," wrote James Walker of Wallerawang. Many understood from the first their workers expected fair exchange from them, an expectation known these days by the Pitjantjatjara term Ngapartji Ngapartji: I give you something and you give me something. What was promised to black workers had to be provided. Breaking your word to the men who looked after your sheep and cattle was the end of all trust. It could lead to violence.

From all corners of the Colony, the committee heard of trouble between blacks and convicts. Henry Bingham, Commissioner of Crown Lands on the Tumut River, told the committee: "The assigned servants have generally a great dislike to them, and are jealous of seeing them employed, and threaten them, and the natives, finding themselves uncomfortable, will not of course remain at the stations." They could be wise to flee. Shepherds were known to murder black workers, "from the idea that the rate of wages is lowered by their unpaid services".

The sudden disappearance of their most hardworking blacks baffled squatters. J.W.D. Passmore of Molong Nyrang told the committee: "They invariably resume the roving life they have been accustomed to, returning only at uncertain intervals, when hunger, or the caprice of the moment, may direct them." That their workers had other lives in the bush, including important obligations to Country, passed the squatters by. Their thinking had barely changed in the thirty years since Marsden

was jilted by his boys. Squatters could not imagine ways of incorpo-
rating the family and ritual obligations of their workers into the life of
their runs. They wanted an obedient, menial and celibate workforce.
Thomas Wilson JP of Braidwood brought a measure of wry understanding to the issue: for two years a young man had worked for him,
apparently becoming civilised, waiting on the Lord Bishop of Australia
when he came to lunch. "But after having obtained possession of a new
suit of clothes, &c., he left the place about midnight, and the next time
I saw Mundilly, he was, (perhaps more becomingly) dressed as a savage
chief; he evidently preferred a precarious existence—perfectly uncontrolled—to every comfort in a state of thraldom."

How to make blacks reliable was the key question Broughton's committee set out to answer. The evidence was clear: kindness, fair dealing,
blankets and food. "They frequent those stations most where they are
best fed," observed Benjamin Barber of Hume River. But the committee sketched out a complicated scheme of punishment that would see
all the squatters in a district band together to refuse employment to
any black who should quit the service of his master "without leave or
sufficient warning". It goes to Gipps' credit that the idea of blacklisting
blacks never got off the ground. What the committee made absolutely
clear was that, despite all the difficulties involved, squatters were going
to need black workers more in difficult times ahead. At last the Aboriginal people had something to sell: their labour.

*

Jones' passion for small economies risked making him ridiculous. Peppered through newspaper reports of Council debates are his objections
to spending. He would not have money wasted on Protectors of Aborigines. He objected to anything spent on Catholics. He deplored the size
of teachers' salaries. Why should Mr and Mrs Hume of Berwick-upon-
Tweed leave that uncongenial climate to "come to this beautiful country,
and expect £200". He disapproved of pensions being paid in England

from the revenue of New South Wales. Ditto the cost of colonial officials
working in New Zealand. He queried the expenses of the superintendent
of Port Phillip, Charles La Trobe. *The Port Phillip Patriot* offered La Trobe
its condolences: "We much fear that the gross parsimony of the Sydney
Council, led by that old woman, Jones, who appears at all times eager to
thwart the good measures of the covenant. We say, we much fear, that the
folly of this 'OLD LADY,' prevents your Honour from performing those
useful public acts which require money to bring them into operation."

Jones wanted every spare penny spent on immigration. But in the
depths of the drought, when calls were being made for the salaries of
high officials to be cut for a time, Jones staunchly defended the pay
of his friends. The *Monitor* painted a sad picture of the Jones family
besieged by their neighbours on Woolloomooloo Hill:

> First would come the venerable Bishop, with a face preg-
> nant with grief and dismay; next the Colonial Secretary ...
> next the Colonial Treasurer. After listening to the groans
> of these, the continual guests of his hospitable table, then
> the lady of the worthy Councilman would have her Bou-
> doir besieged by the ladies of the same officers, and be bent
> to the ground with sympathising grief, in listening to their
> sighs and tears. Flesh and blood could not bear it.

When Jones condemned the "foolish appropriation" of £200 for
lectures on poetry at the Mechanics' School of Arts, Gipps sprang to
the defence of Art. Only a few nights earlier, he and Lady Gipps had
been to a lecture there on the Romantic poets which their Excellencies
found "was every way calculated to improve the mind". At the lectern
was William à Beckett, a barrister newly arrived in Sydney, who had
confessed that night to be no fan of the "the namby-pamby, nimini-
pimini style of modern versification" of Wordsworth. To much laughter
and applause, he recited an ode in the manner of the poet, "describing
the palpitations and sorrows of a young lady from Wollongong, anticipating a visit from a young gentleman with whom she had danced on

board the steamer during the passage down". Alas à Beckett's work has not survived. He waited until he was lecturing on his hero Byron before replying to Richard Jones. He paused after declaiming a speech from *Marino Faliero, Doge of Venice* to wonder:

> Where is the cold-blooded wretch—the low and sordid groveller—the dull and miserable clod of earth—who, after reading such a passage as this, would ask with imbecile and avaricious sneer, "what is to be gained from poetry?" What is to be *gained* indeed? *Not perhaps gold nor wool!* But do we not feel, in listening to the glorious and majestic picture—to these classic and sublime reflections—our imaginations enchanted, our fancy captivated, our passions warmed, yet chastened, our tastes refined, and our capacities for all that is grand and graceful, lofty and lovely, both in art and nature, exalted, purified, and encouraged?

Jones' capacity for the lofty also failed him when considering the education of the children of the Colony. The great Whig cause of free education was opposed by the Church of England throughout the Empire. Bourke had come in 1831 with orders to set up schools along Irish lines with trained teachers in decent classrooms. The Bible would be read every day and clergy would have generous access to the children of their faiths. Men like Jones and Broughton thought it better children be left in darkest ignorance than be exposed to priests in the corridor and Catholic children in the playground. Jones brought a petition to Bourke's Council, damning his plans as "unworthy of this enlightened age, and subversive of the Constitutional rights of a Protestant people". Bourke pulled back. To the Governor's chagrin he was directed by London at the same time to give £2000 to the King's School, which he reminded his masters in London was "for the Sons of the wealthy Colonists and Civil Servants of the Government, whilst the Children of the poor are educating in mere Hovels under Convict School Masters". It did no good. King's had to be paid.

Gipps arrived with the same orders to set up the same schools and found himself facing the same opponents. At a public meeting in October 1839, Jones made a remarkable suggestion that his political opponents would use against him when the time came. He proposed that the religious education of every child in the Colony regardless of their faith should be supervised by the Church of England. He moved and it was so resolved:

> That it is an object of the highest national importance to provide that instruction in the truths and precepts of Christianity should form an essential part of every system of education intended for the people at large; and that such instruction should be under the supervision of the Clergy, and in conformity with the doctrines of the Church of this realm, as the recognised teacher of religion.

The Council debated Gipps' plan for six hours. Broughton spoke for three. Jones stared down the Governor. "His Excellency had said, that those who voted against it should bear the blame, which would descend to their children's children to the remotest posterity. For his part, he was quite willing to bear the blame, and that his children should suffer the consequences of his voting against a system which had no religion in it." With the church and the Tories against him, Gipps abandoned the plan. It was another decade before the Church of England withdrew its veto. By then it could barely afford to educate its own.

*

The collapse came suddenly. The price of wool in London had been slipping for years but Sydney was living as though the boom would never end. From the winter of 1839 to the winter of 1840, the Colony had imported goods worth £2 million. But there was no way to pay for them. In August 1840, the banks sharply tightened credit. In these dark weeks, Alexander Brodie Spark, director of the squatters' Bank of Australia, kept a diary:

November 3: Town in a nervous state. Did what we could at
the Bank to relieve the pressure.

November 7: Afraid on entering town to hear of fresh failures—groups about the street earnestly talking. Run on the
Commercial Bank.

The financial press switched between despair and nervous optimism.
Surely wool prices were about to rebound? Surely flushing out the insol-
vents would restore confidence? All would be well, newspaper sages
declared, when the next clip sold.

Jones discovered his latest initiative, the Australian Auction Company, was a cratered ruin. The idea had been to sideline local auctioneers.
Instead of having them sell their cargoes as they arrived from London,
Calcutta and Canton, "eighteen of the leading and most opulent of the
mercantile body" banded together to run the auctions themselves. The
deep pockets of the merchants would also allow them to offer cheap
credit to buyers and sellers. The company appeared to flourish. One of
the first cargoes it handled was the tea and rice on the *Lord Amherst*. As
businesses all around them were failing in August 1840, the company
promised a dividend that year of 25 per cent. But the press began asking questions. Vast debts were discovered. Jones, who had attended few
board meetings, found the business had been abominably managed.
"He never saw such a mass of confusion." Credit had been recklessly
extended to buyers and sellers. After operating for only ten months,
the Australian Auction Company closed down once it was decided it
could not carry on "with such an immense mass of arrears on hand, and
under the existing depression of trade". The banks compelled Jones and
two other directors to back the company's debts. If the worse came to
the worst, they faced liabilities between them of £60,000.

Jones raised what cash he could. Black Creek and Cockrabill went
under the hammer for about £20,000. He mortgaged Bolwarra for
another £5000. He sold the *Gazette*, which soon folded. The Bank of New
South Wales, notoriously generous to its directors, allowed President

Jones to run up an overdraft of more than £10,000. He continued dip-
ping into other people's money as it passed through his hands. Having
kept all the funds from the *Lord Amherst*'s voyage, he remitted nothing
to Dent & Co. after the next shipment of tea was sold in Sydney. Nothing
was said in public but the Canton house was demanding payment. All he
had to keep his creditors at bay by the winter of 1841 was his impeccable
reputation for caution and probity. When Alexander Young, the sacked
manager of the Auction Company, attacked him in the press, Jones made
a rare public rejoinder:

> I have nothing to fear from Mr Young's personal abuse
> of me, but I may be permitted to remind him that I have
> now resided nearly thirty-two years in this colony, and if it
> should please God that he should reside here a like period,
> and then retire from the active concerns of business with
> the reputation I possess, I feel assured he will be thankful,
> as I am, for the state in which he shall be then placed.

In truth, Jones was at the end of his tether. But he had a plan. He
would save himself by seizing a fresh empire of land. Thirty years in
the Colony had left him with no doubt that the hunting grounds of the
blacks were there to be taken by men like him. The government asked
only that he stock the acres he stole. The price of sheep had collapsed.
He was buying them by the thousand. He would drive them north in
the footsteps of the Leslie brothers, first taking land on the Darling
Downs and then at Moreton Bay. He would dispatch Edmund Uhr to
mind the new runs. In good times, the Aboriginal people of Australia
were dispossessed of millions of acres by squatters eager to make their
fortunes. In the dark years of the early 1840s, yet more were lost to men
like Richard Jones desperate to stave off ruin.

9

MOVING NORTH

Morris Townsend Somerville was a run-hunter, an adventurer who found land for squatters. Tall tales would be told in the colonial way about Somerville's aristocratic connections in Ireland. In truth, he was the offspring of a respectable family with more sons than capital. One day his older brother would be High Sheriff of Cork. Young Morris arrived in New South Wales at the age of sixteen with influence enough to be granted a couple of thousand acres at Wallis Plains and a few convict servants. He may have worked in the 1830s as an overseer for Jones. Though he never served in the army, he came to be known as Captain Somerville. A superb horseman, he rode with a cornet slung over his shoulder which he blew as he galloped across the country. He recruited blacks as guides. He also shot blacks who stood in his way. Somerville was a genial and unscrupulous gentleman of the warrior class.

For three months he lumbered north with a dray, bullocks, stockmen, many dogs and thousands of sheep. On the Condamine he staked out for Jones 80,000 acres of Barunggam and Giabal country and called the run St Ruth. He then drove on to the lip of the Great Dividing Range, where the land falls sheer nearly 2000 feet to the grasslands below. The view swept Ludwig Leichhardt away:

> I entered on my journey over the Coast Range opposite
> a spectacle of nature, as is only rarely granted to a capti-
> vated poet in visions; when the sunny green of the forested

foothills, the dark blue of the rows of the rugged mountains, the purple grey haze around the grotesque mountain shapes in the distance; the lonely roaring of the waterfall; when all these powerful impressions crowd into my mind feeling all the more sensitive in this solitude, I believed in the urge to spread out into the magnificent natural world, and from the trembling as one senses the presence of a higher being, my mind would return, in keeping with the feelings of most heartfelt, purest pleasure, cleansed and purified to the old equilibrium.

Bullock drivers called the track down the precipice "Hell Hole". Perhaps it was true as claimed that the sight of campfires in the valley at night made settlers think of the fires of hell. More likely, it was the name bullock drivers gave to a fearful descent. "Deep ravines lay on all sides of us, and the stones loosened by the horses' feet went thundering down their precipitous sides to the bottom," wrote the adventurer James Demarr. "But difficult as was the road, it was the customary one for drays to and from the Downs and Brisbane Town."

Leaving his men to begin to make their way down, Somerville rode off to fetch an American living nearby who knew the country in the valley below. John "Tinker" Campbell was astonished to see Somerville sounding his horn as he galloped towards his hut. "I had known this gentleman before, and did not feel at all inclined to accompany him over the Range." But over dinner and with a promise of tea, "of which I was short", Campbell agreed to go with him. It was midnight and pouring rain, "the roads mountainous and as slippery as glass", when they caught up with the stockmen camped well down Hell Hole. Some blacks faded into the night as the two men rode up. Next morning they reappeared, naked and armed. Campbell said to Somerville, "Don't leave until I get my horse." Somerville said: "No, I will not leave you." When Campbell returned he found the whole party had set off without him. "I must own my reflections were not pleasant." A black appeared brandishing a club. "As he approached me I caught his eye, and looking him steadily in the face began talking to him in his own lingo, taking care never to take my eyes off his. After a minute his eyes quailed and his looks fell to the ground. I knew I had him then." Campbell wrote that he jumped onto his horse, put his pistol to the warrior's head and held him hostage until they overtook the dray. Campbell dismissed the young man with "some flour and sugar, and we parted very good friends". His friendship with the handsome Multuggerah survived the war between black and white about to fill the valley.

Somerville claimed 50,000 acres of sandy ridges and loamy flats along Lockyer Creek at the foot of the range. This was Yuggera and Giabal country. One half he called Tent Hill and the other Helidon. The boundaries of the two were vague. Wallaby and kangaroo roamed the flats, the creeks were full of eel and mullet and when large flocks of ducks, geese and pelicans rose on the wing, they darkened the sun. But this paradise of abundance came with a drawback: the grassland was interspersed with large tracts of scrub where blacks might hide. A squatter wrote, "I consider that part of the Country to be most dangerous in consequence of large impenetrable Scrubs being so very numerous, & the forest ground generally to be so thickly timbered."

Whites spoke of the scrubs as the *fastness* of Aborigines. So many chases would end with Aboriginal men slapping their bums in derision and disappearing into tangled masses of vegetation where whites could not follow. Frontier wits called the worst of the spiky plants *Wait-a-While* and *Lawyer Vine*. A squatter tried to describe these little jungles to his father in Scotland: "Such country is of course utterly impracticable for a horseman and not to be rashly ventured upon even on foot. I have myself entered, a very decently dressed bushman and returned in almost a state of nudity."

The first squatters arriving from the Downs were made to take their sheep many miles up the Brisbane River. An old rule decreed all country within 50 miles of the Brisbane penal settlement had to be left unoccupied. Brisbane was on Turrbal country at a place they called Meanjin. The convicts had gone but the rule remained. Commandant Owen Gorman dutifully rejected any claims within a 50-mile radius of outlying Ipswich, where convicts once quarried limestone. That ruled out most of the good pasture of Moreton Bay and forbade Jones taking land at the foot of the range. But once his sheep were on Tent Hill, he asked Gipps in Council when he would "throw open the Moreton Bay country, which is anxiously looked for by the people settled beyond the mountains". The Governor confessed he was seeking but did not yet have permission, but he made it clear in

A Squatter's dray of Darling Downs

their exchange that he drew the circle of exclusion not from Ipswich but from Brisbane. That opened half the district of Moreton Bay to squatters. Newspaper reports of Jones' exchange with Gipps were on Gorman's desk within a fortnight. Jones' runs along the foot of the range were secure.

But Tent Hill and Helidon were only staging posts. Somerville waited a few months before driving a fresh mob of sheep a little beyond Ipswich, where he staked out another 115,000 acres on the Brisbane River. This was audacious. The land was empty because every acre lay too close to Gipps' reading of the rules. Yet Jones was strangely confident the Governor was about to scrap the exclusion zone entirely. He was right. Gorman made Somerville pull back from the boundary of the Government Stock Station – that was too cheeky to be allowed – but Jones' claim to the fine stretch of country he called River Station would never be challenged. He did not put his name to the run. As far as his creditors would ever be able to tell, these acres and the tens of thousands of sheep grazing them belonged to his brothers-in-law, Ferriter and Uhr.

*

Tent Hill lay in the country of Old Moppè or Moppy, father of Multuggerah and head man of the Yuggera nation. "A more formidable looking fellow than Moppè I never saw," a settler wrote after watching him fight in a tournament. "He was about forty years old, upwards of seven feet high, beautifully proportioned, and the muscles of his upper arms reminded me of the gnarled trunk of an oak." Moppè was straightforward, determined and not a man to cross. The clans he led extended from the Darling Downs into Moreton Bay and up to the headwaters of the Brisbane River. Moppè formed an early bond with Commandant Gorman. His diplomatic dealings with the Europeans had made him a notable figure in the penal colony. In the way of the time, he was given a brass plate to wear round his neck that read:

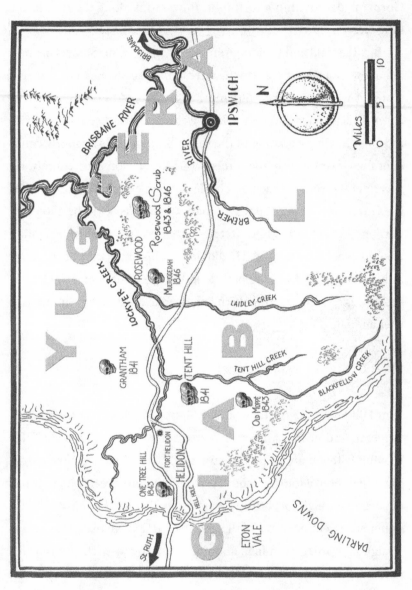

TENT HILL

Moppy, King of the Upper Brisbane Tribe. When he and the Yuggera
elders came to understand what those words meant, the plate was
angrily returned.

It might have seemed to Moppè when he and his people left for a
gathering on the coast in June 1841 that the whites were leaving Moreton Bay. The prison had shut down. The convicts and their jailors were
departing. But while Moppè was away, Somerville and his fellow run-
hunters were doing their work in the once-forbidden valleys. Soon after
Somerville set down at Tent Hill, James "Cocky" Rogers seized 30,000
acres over Lockyer Creek on behalf of his employer, George Mocatta.
He called the run Grantham. Rogers was an evil little man with a long
black beard who carried a double-barrelled musket as tall as himself.
He found an empty blacks' camp on Grantham and stripped the place
of 400 sheets of bark, the universal building material of the bush. Old
Moppè returned from the coast to find thousands of sheep in his country and his camp destroyed. He confronted Rogers, who shot Moppè's
dogs and threw his people off Grantham at the point of a gun. So the
war at Moreton Bay began.

Moppè first attacked the Scottish grandees who had seized half
a million acres in the upper reaches of the Brisbane River. Awkward
David McConnel put his sheep on Cressbrook, where the family still
lives; the Mackenzie brothers named their infamous run Kilcoy after
the family's castle in Scotland; the Archer brothers seized Durundur on
the Stanley; and middle-aged John Balfour took Colinton on the Brisbane. Gaelic was the language of their highland shepherds. As Balfour's
men were splitting timber in September, a mob of three or four hundred blacks appeared, threatening their lives and scattering a flock of a
thousand ewes. The sheep were recovered. When the blacks appeared
on Kilcoy the next day, Mackenzie's men found themselves "under the
necessity of firing repeatedly upon them". When they returned in great
numbers "fearless of fire arms", all the Scots retreated to Cressbrook
where their host sent to Sydney for guns, pistols and cartridges. All
went about heavily armed. McConnel wrote to his brother that the

men of Cressbrook, Kilcoy and Colinton were prepared for the worst, "together, able & ready to resist 1500 blacks".

The Scots learned a thing or two from the Highland Clearances about shifting people to make way for sheep. Unwanted tenants and unwanted blacks were much of a muchness – though the blacks weren't free to emigrate to America. We are indebted to the lairds at least for this: they wrote fine letters home. David McConnel could sketch colonial society on one page – "There has been little or no restraint to their pride, which shows itself to an amazing extent in Sydney and astonishes all newcomers" – and confess without a qualm on the next to killing blacks. "Many of us think it no harm to shoot any of them that we meet & any number, anywhere beyond settled districts, until they are thoroughly pacified." These men were clear-eyed about their role as dispossessors.

> In every district that is occupied by settlers, the blacks have been fought & driven away with loss; these battles have principally been with the settlers; it is very seldom that soldiers or police are brought or have been brought into action; and from the blacks method of warfare, it is difficult for them to do so; & in all new districts there seldom is protection from government until the third year, when the blacks are beginning to be more afraid to do wrong. Government seldom hears of these skirmishes with the blacks as they are concealed and obliged to be so to prevent bad consequences.

Soon after the retreat to Cressbrook, Cocky Rogers rode out to a distant hut on Grantham to investigate reports of Moppè's people stealing sheep. He found the hut-keeper missing. When night fell he crept close to Moppè's camp, which lay on the far side of a dry creek. Fires were burning in the dark. Rogers decided on a dawn raid. All hands on Grantham were ordered to muster for the attack. A messenger went to Tent Hill, asking Somerville for reinforcements. Rogers also sent for his friend Arthur Hodgson of Eton Vale on the Downs where he once worked. They called Hodgson: "That prince of squatters—'King

Arthur'—who, under all circumstances, never forgot to play the *rôle* of an English gentleman." He was also a magistrate. Rogers would need him when the killing was done.

The Grantham shepherds arrived after dawn. Half a dozen men on horseback and half a dozen on foot advanced on the sleeping camp. All had muskets. Six had pistols. Rogers carried his long musket, a brace of pistols and a sword. At Rogers' signal, they charged into the camp all guns blazing. George "Black" Brown woke suddenly. He was the rarest of beings at such a slaughter: an eyewitness who was not Aboriginal. Brown was from Ceylon, a convict who became a bush constable at Moreton Bay and spoke Yuggera. He was there to recruit guides to help build a new road up the range. On Brown's arrival in the camp, he had found the blacks still "in a state of uproar" over Rogers' dealings with them, "which caused them to kill his sheep in return". The raid had begun without warning. Brown spoke of men firing on people as they slept. Those who could, fled.

> The Natives were making their escape to the scrub as Horsemen were riding after them, the Natives were ja[bbing] their Spears at them. the parties had gathered together where I was standing the firing was continued about 1/2 an hour I cannot say the number that were Killed.

Somerville arrived with men from Tent Hill to join a chase that continued all day. How many died has never been known. Moppè's warrior son Wooinambi made his escape. The only captive the vigilantes bothered bringing away with them was Brown, handcuffed and in chains. He was a problem.

Next day, Hodgson arrived from the Downs and opened an inquest. As he began taking depositions, news came from Tent Hill that a shepherd had been killed by the blacks. The squatter magistrate rode over with a large escort to find the old man "brutally murdered, with 3 spear wounds in his belly, & his Brains & Eyes knocked out". The man had worked for Jones for a dozen years and died for the sins of Cocky Rogers.

This grisly sight reminded the magisterial party that the hut-keeper on Grantham had not shown himself. They rode over to find his hut looted, with "money scattered about the Ground" and his body lying there, his throat cut, his belly slashed and his brains dashed out. Hodgson took a pair of wool shears covered in blood to be the murder weapon. That night, as the cycle of retribution continued, a carpenter on Tent Hill was robbed of all his tools and rations. Tinker Campbell was one of the horsemen who rode over the next day to investigate:

> Some half-dozen of us jumped into our saddles and gal-
> loped for Tent Hill—only about three miles from Grantham.
> We were quickly upon the spot, but too late to prevent the
> blacks from robbing the place, which they did of all the iron
> tools lying about a new hut in course of erection, and what-
> ever else they could conveniently lay hands on.

Somerville was already in pursuit. Campbell's men joined the chase. A black with a spear was seen gliding out of the trees.

> Never men spurred or rode harder than we did to cut off the
> blackfellow before he reached the scrub, but we had lost too
> much time, and, slapping himself in a very significant and
> expressive manner, he darted into the scrub.

The horsemen returned empty-handed to Grantham that night, where a grave had been dug for the slain men.

> Two sheets of bark had ... been procured, one to lay under,
> and the other over them. After reading the Church of Eng-
> land service over them, they were both laid in one grave, the
> bark their only coffins. "Peace to their manes."

At Tent Hill a fortnight later, Somerville shot Wooinambi. The circum-stances of the killing remain a mystery. Hodgson held a quick inquest and ruled the young warrior had been shot in self-defence. Richard Jones appears to have been untroubled by Somerville's part in the Grantham

raid or the killing of Wooinambi. Somerville was to remain working for
Jones for some time, even after Edmund Uhr and his family came north
to take charge of his new runs.

The Darling Downs J.P. set about saving his friend Rogers' life.
To the Colonial Secretary he sent a bundle tied in a pink ribbon of
carefully crafted statements. In his, Rogers spoke of the raid in chivalrous terms: as the shepherds and blacks faced each other across the
dry creek, their champions engaged in lone combat until Wooinambi
speared two of his horsemen. Only then, and reluctantly, had Rogers ordered his men to charge. None of the statements in the bundle
detailed what followed. Rogers thought men had been wounded. Some
of the shepherds reported hearing shots; one or two admitted firing
over the heads of the blacks; but nobody saw a black body the whole
day. Hodgson did not include in the bundle George Brown's eyewitness
account of the slaughter. The magistrate blamed Brown for what had
happened that morning: "The Natives had committed no depredations
until 'George Browne' had appeared amongst them." So certain was he
of Brown's guilt, he said, that he had no alternative but to commit him
to prison. Brown was sent in custody to Sydney.

Gipps was not impressed. He told Owen Gorman, "I cannot in these
instances look upon the natives as the aggressors and that I am bound
to protect them as much as any other portion of the Inhabitants of the
Territory." Roger Therry, acting Attorney-General while Plunkett was
on leave in Ireland, was far from convinced by Hodgson's bundle. He
told Gorman:

> It is manifest these depositions do not disclose the whole of
> what took place on that occasion.
>
> The expression in Mr. Rogers' deposition that "He regrets
> to add that he has reason to believe that several men were
> severely wounded" falls very short indeed of what might
> be disclosed as the Effect of the firing that took place. The
> wounds inflicted on the members of his party are detailed

with great minuteness, but a general and vague expression
is deemed sufficient to describe and comprehend the extent
of the injury done to the party which Mr. Rogers and his
armed assistants endeavoured (I know not on what authority) to capture.

An anonymous letter had reached Therry which gave an account of the
slaughter that did not square with the evidence presented by Hodgson.
Therry directed Gorman to convene a full bench of magistrates – including Hodgson – to hold a second inquest, "with the fullest confidence
that you will sift to the bottom a transaction that has justly excited much
painful interest, and which it is equally your duty and mine to fully
investigate". Therry ordered witnesses to be asked a few plain questions:

How many shots were fired? How many (if any) of the Native
Tribe were killed? Of how many did Mr. Rogers' party con-
sist and of them how many were armed?

Rogers and the shepherds held their ground at the second inquest.
Somerville was not called. Brown was left in prison in Sydney. The
anonymous letter did not move the magistrates and enraged the squatters. Someone had broken the silence of the bush! A Latin quotation
suggested an educated man, perhaps Dr Goodwin newly arrived at
Moreton Bay. Tinker Campbell wrote: "The poor Doctor suffered great
obloquy and abuse, being for a long time supposed to be the author of
the letter which was believed to be false, or if not false at least treacher-
ous." The squatters on the bench laid no charges against Cocky Rogers.
"So the whole thing was voted a bottle of smoke. The night after was
spent in jollity, and what two days before threatened to be a *tragedy*,
turned out to be a *farce*."

Cocky Rogers was not satisfied. Drunk and enraged one day, he
fought the man he blamed for all his troubles. Gorman described the
scene to the Governor: "He came close up to me with his hand stretched
out saying 'you are a Liar – you are a Liar – you are a Damned Liar' – his

hand touched against my face and considering myself most shamefully abused and assaulted, I regret to say that I struck him." The two men were rolling in a Brisbane street, with Gorman's hand round Cocky's throat, before they were separated. Gorman had to go. In his place Gipps installed Dr Stephen Simpson as Commissioner of Crown Lands. A homoeopathic practitioner with atheist and liberal views, Simpson had practised medicine for some years on the Continent. He had come to the Colony looking for a fresh start, armed with a single asset: a letter of recommendation from His Grace the Duke of Sutherland, whose son he had treated in Rome. That was enough.

*

William Fanning disembarked in Sydney in March 1842. The young emissary from Dent & Co. had warned no one he was coming. "Land at nine, put my traps into a dray & bend my steps to Petty's hotel. Hire a room, dress and taking my letters in my pocket start for Mr. Jones' office – find he is not in town." Dent & Co. had lost patience at last. Fanning had come to take over the business of the house and make Jones pay.

> Wander about, disgusted with dirt and filth, of the streets, return to Mr. J's office & find him. Hand him the Letters, & as was to be expected they produced no very pleasing effect. The poor old man was totally upset, – his Eyes filling with Tears more than once, & alternately swayed by feelings of regret & indignation he indulged in the metaphor of a town dependent on one pipe for a supply of water, suddenly deprived of its support.

Jones was affronted. How, he wondered, could a relationship of so many years be so suddenly and so rudely broken? He "burst out in no measured strain against the altered tone of the China house, the unprincipled men now in it – Messrs. Braine and Leslie". That was

William, brother of Patrick. Fanning only interrupted Jones when he complained of being sacked without warning.

> I hinted that ever since I had been in China the letters of the house had endeavoured to impress on him the necessity of a change in the way of doing business – that he had at one time agreed to what they said, at another hesitated and finally done nothing in the way of Remittances more regular than before or putting them in funds for investment on his own account, and that they had thus reluctantly been driven to a change, which he ought to have expected unless he thought they were playing with him.

Fanning took his leave, returning every few days to Jones' office, perplexed and even disgusted by the reception he was given. "Can get scarcely anything out of him but surprise regret at what has happened." Fanning handled the situation with great tact. No humiliating announcements were made in the press. As far as the Colony knew, Jones was still a commercial force and a mighty voice for financial probity. Patrick Leslie wrote to his brother in Canton: "I think you are extremely lucky in your agent Fanning he is a fine gentlemanlike fellow and sticks to his business like a leech & I can assure you it requires a sharp fellow to get out of old Jones what he has done."

The Colony was on the edge of insolvency. The Bank of Australia was sliding under, taking with it half the old families of New South Wales. Private money still poured into Sydney to be lent at rates of interest that had *The Sydney Monitor* railing against the town's "insane craving after money, in order to rush headlong into fresh speculations … the extortionate demand of the Usurer and the reckless folly of the borrower". Creditors and debtors were brawling in the courts. Jones won case after case against the men who owed the Australian Auction Company thousands but he saw little of the money. Bills were everywhere brutally discounted. The price of wool had halved in four years. And another year had passed on the Liverpool Plains without useful rain. The ground was bare and the river putrid. "No less than five hundred head of cattle have died from want in the immediate vicinity of the Mooki," one of Edmund Uhr's neighbours reported. "The banks of the water holes are literally covered with dead carcasses, which have been taken out of bog by the stock-keepers, being unable to again rise." He added: "The destruction among the sheep of Messrs. Uhr, Richards, &c., is very great."

The Uhrs' murdering sibling Daniel Peterson reappeared in Sydney with a wife and three children, having lived for years untroubled in Boston. He was learning the ways of wool. He told his half-brother John on the Isle of Jersey that he'd promised to buy a few thousand sheep from Jones at ten pence per head. It was not proving a good deal:

> The sheep are much cheaper now some of Capt. Piper's best breed of sheep have been sold at auction, a few days since, for sixpence per head. Money I have not any having spent all, mainly for shoes, etc., and God knows what I shall do. No person has money here. Sydney present a scene of poverty & distress & thousands leaving daily altho everything is so low. Good cattle £1 per head. Horses will scarcely be received as presents. Butter 6d. per lb. We have not sent anything to Sydney for some time it will not pay.

Squatters had begun boiling down their sheep for tallow. A fleece might be worthless but the fat on a carcass could fetch six shillings to be made into soap and candles. Boiling down would prove the salvation of the bush. "It seems like a flattering dream," wrote *The Sydney Morning Herald*. "Like one of those gorgeous visions of the imagination in which the waving of a wand, the rubbing of a lamp, or the utterance of a cabalistic word, can transform pebbles into gold, and hovels into palaces." So savage was the culling that wool merchants in London began pleading with squatters to spare their finest stock. "Let only those be sacrificed whose ovary is mixed with alloy." Their pleas were ignored. Up and down the Colony, fires burned under iron pots of slaughtered sheep. Roger Therry recalled: "Sydney became for a time surrounded with boiling-down establishments at short distances from the city, and, in whatever direction one travelled, his sense of smell was revoltingly assailed by the tainted breeze wafted from these establishments along the road."

When Gipps first proposed reforming the insolvency laws of the Colony along British lines, no one opposed the idea more staunchly than Jones. Debtors must be punished, he told the Council. They must be made to pay all they could to their creditors. "He had every objection to allowing a parcel of fellows ... to walk into an Insolvent Court and come clear out, to recommence plundering again." So strong was his opposition and so urgent his predictions of doom that Gipps' bill was withdrawn. But a year later, when Gipps reintroduced his reforms, Jones had changed his mind. His own creditors were gathering. The price of wool had not recovered. The rains had not come. Jones asked only that the bill be delayed a little, for the reforms were provoking such feverish agitation in the town that it was feared the whole Colony was about to be declared insolvent. No delay was granted. Hundreds of people were immediately bankrupted. Jones dismissed them contemptuously. "They had been well known as persons possessed of nothing." But the *Monitor* had a word of warning for the big men of the Colony: "Those who have as yet succeeded in resisting the pressure, whose names are highest and most trusted amongst us, stand on slippery sands which may be swept away by the next opposing wave."

II

EDMUND B. UHR

The Colonial Treasurer: What do you mean by dispersing?

Lieutenant Frederick Wheeler: Firing at them …

10

VALLEY OF THE SHADOW

Edmund Blucher Uhr took the *Shamrock* to Brisbane in January 1842 to take charge of Tent Hill. On the steamer were several squatters who were, like him, visiting their Moreton Bay runs for the first time. They knew they were sailing to bloody country. The Yuggera were not quiet. Shepherds had died on Tent Hill and the warrior Wooinambi had been shot there. In the coming weeks, the *Gazette* would report more shepherds would die at Moreton Bay, "murdered, by these miscreants who first stripped their victims, and then broke their skulls with waddies". But these would prove mere scuffles in the months ahead.

Uhr was twenty-seven, lanky and self-important. The faux mantle of the House of Roxburghe hung on his shoulders and a decade under the wing of Richard Jones had given him an exaggerated sense of his standing. He saw himself as a leader, a man who cut a swathe. But in truth he was a dogged follower, a tetchy colonial saved by his connections. He enjoyed his standing at Tent Hill as a squatter among squatters. Helidon had passed into other hands, but Tent Hill carried more than 14,000 sheep on what seemed, for a time, superb pasture. Uhr had twenty shepherds, a mix of convicts and free men, working the grasslands along the creeks flowing down from the escarpment. His wife, Amy, arrived in May. She had stayed behind at Bolwarra for the birth of their second child, Louisa Amy. They settled down in a homestead on a little conical hill overlooking Lockyer Creek, the last of the Uhrs still in service to Richard Jones. After fifteen years, Edmund proved the only one of the Thames-side brood to show much return on the old man's investment in their lives.

John Uhr, the oldest, was broken. In his mid-twenties, while "labouring under an aberration of mind", he was admitted to the Liverpool lunatic asylum. Jones had the place inspected to see if it was "fit for the reception of a person of respectability". Though the opposite was the case, that's where he remained for some months. On his release, Jones sent him to the bush to test the restorative powers of running sheep on Bungebar, a 16,000-acre run on the western edge of the Liverpool Plains, owned by James Canning Pearce, a colourful figure the family kept bumping into. John also owned a little run of his own and had half a dozen convict servants, but not long after he and Pearce faced the muskets of Opossum Jack and his highwaymen, John shipped out to London, where he lived, at first, with one of his Peterson sisters in Lambeth before settling down on Jersey with a Jones cousin. The family called him in their letters *Poor John*.

After King's, Jones found the youngest of the boys, George, a perch in the office of the Sheriff. He would end his days Sheriff of New South Wales. The third son, Cornelius William – always known as William – was a sweet boy everyone loved. He arrived, too old for school, at the age of seventeen. He had musical ambitions. Jones found him a job at the *Gazette*. But by the time his brother Edmund sailed for Moreton Bay, William was some way down the road to ruin. He vanished and a sad advertisement appeared in *The Sydney Herald*.

> Unless Mr. WILLIAM UHR, now, or late of the *Gazette* Office, calls at Mrs. Butler's, No. 1, Macquarie-place, and pays his bill for board and lodging, his clothes, trunks, or anything else in her possession, will be sold by auction, to discharge the debt, fourteen days after this notice.

He was bankrupted at the age of twenty-three, owing £41 to two tailors, a draper and his bootmaker. Jones did not ride to his rescue. William disappeared for a time to New Guinea.

On board the *Shamrock* with Uhr was Colin Mackenzie of Kilcoy, one of the lairds of the upper Brisbane Valley. A week after he disembarked, at least fifty Aboriginal people were poisoned on his run. The deaths of two shepherds and the spearing of a bullock had provoked the Mackenzies' supervisor to ask: "Don't you think it would be a good thing to give these fellows a dose?" When blacks next gathered asking for flour, tobacco and sugar, a meal of maize porridge – or perhaps stewed mutton – mixed with arsenic was given to them. Back at their camp on the lagoon, the poison soon took effect. "The first pangs experienced: the ferocious wrath upon the discovery of the trap into which they had fallen: the increasing agonies: the crawling to water: the insatiable burning thirst: then—death." In the grim history of frontier slaughter in Australia, the Kilcoy poisoning of February 1842 carries a unique stench. Blacks thereabouts came to call poison *Mackenzie*. Bloody as the fighting had been at Moreton Bay, it grew even bloodier. The Kilcoy killings set off a war that lasted many years. Yet no one was ever punished for this crime. It was barely investigated.

Governor Gipps was in Brisbane soon afterwards to declare the place open for business: "The ... District of Moreton Bay shall be no longer continued as a Penal Settlement, but that the same shall be open for Settlers, and all Free Persons desirous of proceeding thither." His proclamation secured River Station. Jones' timing had been perfect. The new Commissioner of Crown Lands, Dr Stephen Simpson, had by this time heard extraordinary rumours about killings at Kilcoy "first brought here by the Limestone Blacks & since repeated on all hands". He was a doctor. "From the remarkable minutiæ with which the symptoms were described by the Aborigines", Simpson recognised arsenic as the poison. He raised the rumours with the Governor. Nothing happened.

Every three years, tribes from as far afield as the Darling Downs and the Mary River gathered in the forests at the headwaters of the Brisbane River to feast on the nuts of the bunya pine. Runners and signal fires along the mountain tops summoned thousands to feast, play and dance. Quarrels were settled, boys initiated, marriages arranged

STEPHEN SIMPSON

and news shared. These gatherings held particular terrors for squatters nearby. They lost stock and feared plots were hatched against them. That was true in the aftermath of Kilcoy. Moppè was present at one meeting – or *toor* – after the feast that sent word of the poisoning north and south. Settlers were attacked. A second toor was held in the middle of 1842 near Brisbane. "With the incidence of the arsenic in the flour, the elders of every tribe in the South-East Queensland met for the very first time in conference in the Jimna Forest," wrote the Butchulla historian Olga Miller. "Upwards of fifty elders representing many Tribes, were at this meeting." One of those elders was her great-grandfather. Ray Kerkhove and Frank Uhr wrote: "Some seven to 14 tribes declared their intention to drive the whites off their lands, and issued declarations of war, circulated by the missionaries and escaped convicts."

Two renegade convicts brought evidence of the poisoning to Dr Simpson. James Davis, who had lived in the bush for a dozen years under the name Duramboi, told him of losing two adoptive brothers in the slaughter. David Bracewell, who had been present at the great toor, left Simpson more certain than ever that arsenic was the cause. He warned Gipps of a general feeling in Brisbane that a mass poisoning had taken place up at Kilcoy. "These Tribes vowed vengeance & said they had had some already but would have more." Gipps did nothing. The Aboriginal people were as good as their word. In July Simpson reported to Sydney:

> The Stations to the North of the Brisbane are suffering considerably from the hostile proceedings of the Aborigines, who appear to be carrying out their vengeance in a very insidious manner ... Plunder does not appear to be so much their object as the destruction of life.

Investigating the Mackenzie brothers of Kilcoy was a daunting prospect for the Governor. They outranked him. The Mackenzies were friends of Lord Glenelg, the old Secretary of State for the Colonies. After the poisoning, Gipps even appointed Evan Mackenzie a magistrate. On his father's death he would return as a baronet to his family's castle on the Black Isle in the Highlands.

In June, two German missionaries were exploring the Bunya Mountains when their native guides suddenly refused to take them further. Pastor Karl Wilhelm Schmidt made a note in his diary: "A large number of natives, (about 50 or 60,) having been poisoned at one of the squatter's stations. The neighbouring tribes are going, we are told, to attack and to kill the whites, wherever they meet with any." Schmidt, fearful, did nothing. But it was his duty every year to submit his diaries to John Dunmore Lang. Appalled by what he read, Lang sent the diary to Government House. It was returned, he said, with those few lines about the poisoning underlined in red. Gipps still did nothing.

Lang's views on the blacks were tangled. He saw the colonisation of Australia as a great work of God but from the pulpit and in the pages of his newspaper, *The Colonist*, he condemned the ruthless way it was being carried out. Lang attacked the failure to compensate those people

who lost their land and the refusal to share with them the inexhausti-
ble bounty of the country. Above all he condemned the bloodshed on
the frontier.

> Not only have we despoiled them of their land, and given
> them in exchange European vice and European disease in
> every foul and fatal form, but the blood of hundreds, nay
> of thousands of their number, who have fallen from time
> to time in their native forests, when waging unequal war-
> fare with their civilized aggressors, still stains the hands of
> many of the inhabitants of this land!

Lang had seen Kilcoy coming. After Myall Creek, *The Colonist* reported
squatters recommending poison as a safe and swift way of ridding their
runs of blacks. One of these men the paper called a "vampire of hell".
With *The Colonist* now defunct and the Governor unresponsive, Lang
gave Schmidt's diary to *The Colonial Observer* to "stir up His Excellency's pure mind by way of remembrance".

The story of Kilcoy finally broke in the press ten months after the
massacre. Schmidt was attacked viciously for making such wicked
accusations, but there was horror, too, as the Colony learned of this
scarcely imaginable crime. The *Australasian Chronicle* took aim at
everyone who had known of the poisoning but said nothing for so
long. "We have no words to express our sense of their conduct in allowing this deed of darkness to sleep for so long a period. They have all to
a man chosen to be either actively or passively partners in the crime."
The new *Sydney Morning Herald* demanded an investigation. "If so foul
a murder has been committed, we trust the guilty parties will be found
out, prosecuted, and meet with the punishment due to the perpetrators of so diabolical an act." Every squatter in the vicinity of the killing
should, the paper said, come forward for questioning. "It will not be
difficult for all who feel confident in their own innocence to unite in
denying any knowledge of the transaction." Gipps' only response was
to ask Dr Simpson to speak to the missionaries. Schmidt tried to claim

he had no duty to do anything about the poisoning because he was not a Protector of Aborigines. But Simpson discerned the real reason: "It is very evident that the disinclination to follow up the investigation, has been caused by the fear of offending the squatters generally."

Kilcoy reignited Plunkett's determination to have Aborigines give evidence. There were so many eyewitnesses to the poisoning that day, but none could appear in court. The Conservative government of Sir Robert Peel recognised such reform was "indispensable to the protection of the Natives", but declined to pass one law in London that would open the courts to every subject of the Empire. Instead, the Conservatives left the task to each individual Colony. It was a profound betrayal. When Plunkett brought a bill to the Council in Sydney, all the squatters were opposed. That great windbag of liberty William Charles Wentworth said, "It would be quite as defensible to receive as evidence in a Court of Justice the chatterings of the ourang-outang as of this savage race." The bill was defeated by fourteen votes to ten. Not until 1876 would the sworn testimony of Aboriginal people be heard in New South Wales and Queensland. British justice was ceaselessly applauded for protecting black and white alike, but through the bloodiest years in those colonies no Aboriginal person could bear witness in court to the truth about life and death on the frontier.

*

An alliance of tribes from the Darling Downs north to the Mary River was at war with the settlers. Yet few of these sheep men had the courage to see themselves for what they were: conquerors of country. To the raw squatter mind, the land belonged to no one. It was waiting to be taken. Settlers saw themselves as defending *their* land against bands of vengeful savages. Outgunned but not outnumbered, Aboriginal people hoped either to expel the intruders or reach some accommodation that would allow them to hunt and fish on their lands. Negotiation with individual squatters continued all the time. But while the lie of *terra nullius* – the unoccupied country – survived, overarching negotiation between black and white, between the colonial government and the peoples of the Colony, was impossible. Australia was fought for in an endless war of little, cruel battles.

Jones' run on the Darling Downs, St Ruth, came under attack six months after Kilcoy. A shepherd was killed at St Ruth and stockmen retrieving his body were menaced by the Barunggam. Armed men rode out every day with the shepherds, who grazed their flocks within sight of each other. Yet they still came under attack. The *Gazette* reported in August: "On the blacks attempting to surmount them, a skirmish ensued, when one of the white men, in attempting to take one of the blacks alive, was so severely speared by him, that not the slightest hopes of his recovery are entertained." Working on Jones' run at this time was another convict runaway, James Baker or "Boralcho", who had lived with Multuggerah's people for fourteen years before returning to the European side of the frontier. Multuggerah used Baker to warn Brisbane town of his peoples' intentions: "They are determined upon murdering a white man whenever they can obtain an opportunity, and for this purpose, the tribes on the Downs have joined those on this side of the range."

On the upper Brisbane River, the lairds found themselves fighting an elusive enemy. "They never show a bold front," complained David McConnel. "A person might ride in the centre of 200 of them & still not see one." The preferred squatter strategy was to attack their sleeping camps at dawn. It didn't matter that in the barely lit confusion of horses, bodies and guns it was impossible to identify the men the vigilantes were pursuing. Nor did it give them pause that only after the sun came up could they hunt for some shred of evidence – a shirt, a tomahawk, a book or a side of beef – to justify the attack. Prisoners were never safe. To his brother in Europe, McConnel described the fate of four men he locked in a hut one night during the fighting in 1842.

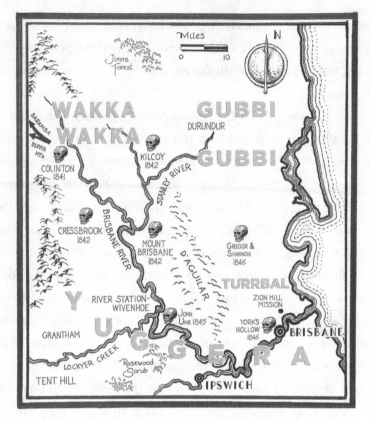

MORETON BAY

They became desperate & being very strong men, they all broke loose; so we fired on them; killed one, Commandant, a fellow 6 ft 3 high & strong in proportion, on the spot, stabbed one twice with a bayonet, put 4 balls into him besides, & 2 balls into the third; the 2 latter got off, but I am sure, could not go far; the boy got out by the chimney at the commencement, no one touching him ... they were stripped before the fight, & we could not get any firm hold of them; their hair being very greasy. We were not at all sorry that they were killed; for they attempted murder long before, killed two men of Mackenzie's, rushed Oliver's sheep, & rushed our own 2 days before this battle. We were all determined on getting rid of the bloodthirsty scoundrels; & there are yet several more as bad.

The McConnels kept Commandant's skull on display at Cressbrook.

The Archers of Durundur did not join the fighting. They had reached an accommodation with the Wakka Wakka that kept the peace on their 38,000-acre run. As Charles Archer explained to his father, accommodation took some effort:

> Davie ... considers the Black as the hereditary owner of the soil and that it is an act of injustice to drive him from his hunting grounds – at the same time punishing any case of sheep stealing or petty theft when the culprit can be got hold of. The result has been that the Blacks here appear to have acquired some idea of the rights of property, and this tribe, so far from doing any injury, are of the greatest assistance in procuring bark, breaking up ground with the hoe, carrying rations to the sheep stations &c. &c. ... They see us approach the camp without alarm, and I have been present at several of their Coroberees, or dances, and the other day at a Bullan-bullan, or fight, without interrupting their proceedings.

The Archers were great letter writers. Thomas Archer supplied ruthless pen portraits of fellow squatters to his family on the far side of the world. McConnel of Cressbrook he found: "too rich, and not obliged to do anything for himself". John Balfour of Colinton had imbibed notions prevalent in France not consistent with morality and propriety.* "He is therefore no desirable companion." The Mackenzies of Kilcoy he found of good stock and amusing company. "But their misfortunes I am afraid have caused a good deal of recklessness, and sharpness in business which is not at all pleasant."

Tent Hill became a killing ground once again when Cocky Rogers, for no known reason, shot Moppè on the run in early 1843. Some accounts have the warrior chased and cornered by Rogers on a creek still called Blackfellow Creek. Others say he was fishing there with his

---

* Homosexuality.

daughter Kitty. When mourning his death, the Ipswich *North Austra-lian* declared Moppè: "A very influential blackfellow, chief of the tribes on the Lockyer. He always exerted himself to restrain his followers from collision with the whites. He was shot at Tent-hill, under circumstances which, at the time, were not held to justify the act." After his death, his son Multuggerah took command of an alliance of tribes above and below the range. He was thought to have 2000 warriors at his call. The fighting intensified. Simpson had only a handful of troops and a few Border Police to keep the peace. In September 1843, attacks on stock around Tent Hill reached a new pitch. Simpson gave Sydney a report of the losses:

> On the 1st of September they attacked Mr Jones' Station on Laidley Creek & took away about 150 Sheep & injured many more.
>
> On the 5th they again attacked Mr Jones' Station on Sandy Creek but were driven off with the loss of one sheep only.
>
> On the 6th they came in a large body to the Shepherd at the same Station & would have murdered him but for the timely aid of a party of horsemen.
>
> On the 7th they attacked a Shepherd of Mr C. Browne & took part of his flock; the man however escaped from his dog barking at one of the Blacks who was in the act of spearing him.
>
> On the 8th they killed a horse, a cow and two bullocks belonging to Mr Jones.

The Tent Hill shepherd was attacked again, this time by about twenty warriors in red and yellow war paint. They ignored his gun. "A tall black man threw a boomerang at me, which went over my head; they all shouted and leaped, and threw a shower of spears, seven of which struck me; one through my hand, one on the right side, one on the left, one under my left shoulder, and one on the back." The shepherd retreated towards the road, firing as he went. "They threw waddies at me, several of which struck me." He was saved by the chance appearance on the road of another armed shepherd from Tent Hill. The blacks vanished. "I was weak at the time, and he pulled me under the shade of a tree." He was taken by dray to a surgeon in Ipswich who treated his wounds.

Tent Hill was a busy house. Another daughter had been born to Amy, and Edmund's younger brother, William, had turned up from New Guinea. Reports were good. "He does not keep so much company, he was also steady and sober," wrote their murdering Peterson brother, Daniel. "He possesses very superior talents and I am rejoicing at his determination to make good use of them." But Tent Hill was not safe. Edmund does not emerge a hero from the skirmishes of these times, but a hair-raising story was told of Amy beating back the blacks. Perhaps the story is true, though it's strange it did not reach the press until years after Amy's death. As told in 1908, the Uhrs were greatly harassed by the natives.

> Mr. and Mrs. Uhr were sitting on the verandah of their thatched bungalow when suddenly a spear hurtled through the air and struck the wall close beside them.
>
> To rush inside and bar the doors was the work of a moment, but it was executed none too soon, for, before the guns and muskets—there were no rifles in those days—could be taken down from the walls, the house was surrounded by yelling warriors.
>
> A few well-directed shots from cleverly-concealed loopholes beat the enemy off for a while, but presently spears began to find their way through the windows and the thinly-thatched roof—for, of course, bush houses were devoid of ceilings.

The couple continued to hold off the attackers with firearms until they saw spears tied with blazing bark aimed at the grass roof. Fortunately, the thatch was damp from recent rain. Only patches caught fire. Nevertheless, the danger was great.

Then it was that the pluck of the little British lady came in.
Telling her husband to keep up a brisk fusillade from the
side of the house on which the thatch was smouldering,
she unbarred a door, and rushing out seized a long handled garden rake that was on the verandah and, regardless
of the spears and nullah-nullahs which flew around her, she
was just able to reach the burning thatch and tear it down.

She got back inside without a scratch. But the attack was not over.

Just as another fiery missile lodged in the thatch, and Mrs.
Uhr was preparing for another sortie, the sound of galloping hoofs, a couple of shots and a ringing cheer, fell upon
the ears of the besieged, and a mounted detachment of
military police, which had been patrolling in the neighborhood, made its appearance, and the savages melted from
sight—except the few who lay dead around, to bear testimony to the strenuousness of the fray.

Multuggerah sent a message to his old friend Tinker Campbell in
Brisbane, warning him not to return to the Downs. "It was to be war
now in earnest," wrote Campbell. "Their intention was first to spear
all the commandants, then to fence up the roads and stop the drays
from travelling, and to starve the 'jackaroos' (strangers). Altogether,
they, in fact, intended to let no more rations go to the Darling Downs."
Campbell laughed at the idea. The messenger grew angry. "By God,
Mr. Campbell, baal* you go."

Hell Hole had been abandoned. A better way down had been found
which ran along a ridge past Meewah or One Tree Hill, before burrow-
ing through the scrubs for miles to emerge near Tent Hill. Campbell
helped cut the track and knew its shortcomings: "When the scrub was
reached all parties were about sick of the job. It was, therefore, resolved
to make the narrowest possible cutting through, so that a dray could

---

* Don't.

just pass and that was all. I do not think the road here averaged more than eight feet wide." Multuggerah and his men were already ambushing drays as they lumbered through the scrubs, but his new plan was to lay siege to the settlers on the Downs by blocking the road entirely. A band of squatters decided to assert their right of way by sending up to the Downs a convoy of three drays drawn by about fifty bullocks guarded by fourteen armed men. They set off on the morning of 12 September 1843 after a long night at a shanty pub on Tent Hill. A few miles into the scrub, they found their way blocked and both sides of the track fenced high with tightly woven vines and saplings. As Multuggerah's hidden warriors let out a mighty yell, the whites abandoned the convoy and fled back the way they had come. Spears rained down on them. Campbell reported: "The blacks robbed the drays of everything they could carry away—flour, sugar, sheep-shears (the latter they broke, and armed the point of their spears with them)."

The terrified men steadied themselves back at the pub, where much of the crowd from the night before was still drinking. They all saddled up. Thirty or forty armed men rode back up the track. What followed is celebrated in Indigenous lore, bush yarns, songs and histories as the Battle of Meewah or One Tree Hill. In their forensic account of the clash, Ray Kerkhove and Frank Uhr describe the vigilantes trying, in blind confusion, to find Multuggerah's men in the scrubs. Then suddenly, the warriors broke into the open and headed for the summit of One Tree Hill. The pursuers scrambled after them. "This was a fatal mistake, as the incline is so steep and gravelly that even skilled walkers today lose their footing." Out of range and out of sight on the heights, the warriors rained boulders and stones down on the squatters and stockmen, who fled into the forest and sheltered for the night under their looted drays. The rout on One Tree Hill was a signal Aboriginal victory in colonial Australia. Moppè's son proved himself a general.

But it had to be avenged. About 150 settlers gathered for what Kerkhove and Uhr call "undoubtedly the biggest combined drive in the history of the frontier wars in Queensland". Every reliable man in the

THE RAID

district was there with a gun. The McConnels of Cressbrook rode down
with Balfour of Colinton and Hodgson of Eton Vale. Dr Simpson arrived
with a few police and rushed back to Brisbane for reinforcements – ten
soldiers of the 99th Regiment. Edmund and William Uhr were at the
muster. A young convict shepherd on Helidon was given a gun and
ordered to attend. His name was William Wilkes, later editor of *The
Moreton Bay Courier* and a figure in literary Sydney who turned the
chase for Multuggerah into "The Raid of the Aborigines", a comic ballad recited in pubs for the rest of the century.

> The dunghill cock his clarion blew,
> And swift the sportive echo flew,
>   Down Lockyer's pleasant vale.
> When every squire and gallant knight,
> With bosoms burning for the fight,
>   Assembled in the dale.

After two days' chase, Multuggerah took refuge in Rosewood Scrub
near Tent Hill. As usual, the whites charged at first light. Details are
scant. *The Sydney Morning Herald* reported most of the goods looted
from the drays were recovered. "An immense number of tomahawks,

waddies, spears, and other offensive weapons were also taken." Blacks were killed but the paper's correspondent was coy about numbers: "Some of the ringleaders … have, I believe, fallen victims to the vengeance of the white man." William Coote's 1882 history of Queensland admitted "no small number of the savages" were shot in the operation. Multuggerah escaped.

No one dies in Wilkes' ballad. Few wounds suffered are worse than black eyes. The black warriors are heroes, handsome and oiled. Their women are beautiful. The whites who pursue them are fat, broke, drunk, love-struck, filthy, proud and timid. Wilkes sorted Edmund Blucher Uhr among the cowards. True or not, this conceited man had to live with Wilkes' ridicule for the rest of his life:

> Then on a sorry jaded hack,
> With feet extended—bridle slack,
> Long Blucher came—but he turned back,
>   Before the fight began.
> His heart was base—the Craven Knight,
> And home he fled in shameful fright,
>   The battle's brunt to shun.
> Goaded by fear within an hour,
> He housed him in his lady's bower,
>   From danger far remote,
> Nor thought himself secure from death,
> Till he had thrust his head beneath
>   Her flannel petticoat.
> Oh, why should such a haven be
> Reserved for coward loon like he?
> Then there was half a dozen more,
> Perchance there might be half a score,—
> The first was pretty Billy Ure,
>   His mammy's pride and joy.

The squatters are driven on by Justice Ferret of Tent Hill. The portrait of Uhr's brother-in-law is not the least flattering. Lord Ferret is pompous, long-winded and gutless:

> For proudly bringing up the rear,
>   The mighty Ferret comes.
> Shouting "on, on—your laurels reap,
> "Fight for your cattle and your sheep,
>   "Your altars and your homes."

Rather than dispersing on Lord Ferret's command, the blacks make a stand. Ferret is chased from the field by a dog. Pretty Billy gets it in the rump:

> While one of the gins, with a kangaroo spear,
> Had sadly annoyed Billy Ure in the rear;
> You may see to this day the part is affected,
> He waddles along with it greatly projected.

The whites find the blacks' camp deserted. They carry away what booty they can find – bits of pipe clay, an old tomahawk, a dead dog – and retire to the pub to humiliate each other with drunken accusations of cowardice and defeat.

> My story is told, and my harp is unstrung,
> Farewell to the heroes whose deeds I have sung:
> Their praises must live in the songs of the just,
> When the bones of the minstrel are crumbled to dust.

Only fiction provides neat endings. The Rosewood raid did not end the violence along the foot of the range. Edmund Uhr's sheep were still stolen and his shepherds threatened. Simpson sent troops to Tent Hill once more in December 1843 "to assist in keeping off aborigines". Soon he permanently stationed a dozen men from the 28th Regiment where the road up to the range enters the scrub. Fort Helidon on Darkey Flat was a watchtower with barracks built of slabs with gun slots.

Troops rode up and down with the drays. Order of a kind was brought to the surrounding country but at a high price. "This period of military supervision was one of terrible slaughter, scores upon scores of the aborigines falling victims to the white man's gun," wrote the journalist John James Knight in the 1890s. "One of the men who assisted in putting many of the unfortunate blacks out of existence told the writer several incidents which if repeated here would scarcely be regarded as pleasant reading, nor yet redound to the credit of persons even now living."

*

Jones filed for bankruptcy in August 1843. His new acres had not saved him. The price of wool, rock bottom when Somerville set out for the north, had not recovered. The price of whale oil had fallen by nearly half and would never recover. Only his reputation for absolute propriety had kept his creditors at bay for so long. He owed young Donaldson thousands, and thousands more to several other Sydney merchants. He wasn't paying his overseers or licence fees on his runs. He hadn't paid his lawyer, Mr Norton, for years. He had unpaid bills with his butcher and with David Jones. Thousands of pounds invested for his sister had vanished. He owed most to those who had trusted him most: £9000 to Dent & Co. and £11,000 to the Bank of New South Wales. The bank moved against its president in July 1843, when Jones was made to pledge most of his properties to secure his mighty overdraft. The bank's auditors insisted no director ever be allowed to amass such an overdraft again. Jones ceased appearing at board meetings, and on 1 August the directors sent a messenger to tell him to resign. He prevaricated a little before facing the inevitable. The bank began proceedings against him at once, not for the overdraft but for the immense debts of the Australian Auction Company.

As Jones slid towards bankruptcy, he sold Wallalla and Breeza to John Eales, a land-grabber with deep pockets. Eales was willing to ignore the warnings of Jones' neighbours on the Mooki that any sale of Wallalla and Breeza would be challenged. The result was one of the great lawsuits of the Liverpool Plains. Victory and defeat turned on the testimony of old stockmen willing to swear to the history of disputed runs. "Each squatters in those days had a few good swearing men," wrote William Telfer. "One of those got the Title of King of the liars as he would swear anything for his master ... those law cases was their harvest ... a fifty pounds cheque would be paid them in Sydney for wich they were ready to swear what suited best." Squabbles over Wallalla and Breeza lasted twenty years. Jones was happy to take a few hundred pounds and leave the brawl to Eales.

He resigned from the Legislative Council in early November 1843 and was declared insolvent two days later, owing £48,000. William Fanning, the young man from Canton, led the trustees in bankruptcy. They took Fleurs with its vineyard and dairy; Darlinghurst and its furniture, china, silver and a "very beautiful and valuable" carriage; Drayton, the last of Jones' holdings at Patrick's Plains and lately the headquarters of the Ferriters; Cockrabill, under the Liverpool Range, with its Saxon flock; his licences to graze both St Ruth on the Downs and Tent Hill at Moreton Bay plus their 24,0000 sheep; and Jones' most valuable property, Bolwarra, touted in the press as "being probably, without exception, the most fertile, well watered, and advantageously situated agricultural property in the colony". One day, Jones bumped into the ruined merchant Alexander Spark in George Street. Spark wrote in his diary: "He held out his hand, and on my asking how he was, and observing that I had not seen him for a long time, a small sad shake of the head followed, and patting him gently on the back, we parted without words, but there was a glistening in his eye. God help us, how awful a thing it is, at our time of life, to be struck down from eminence and affluence to utter poverty."

Jones had other plans. At this distance it is impossible to track all he did to evade his creditors, but a few of his strategies are clear. At some point he gave his wife a dower – a 10 per cent share of the value of everything he owned. As his houses, acres, sheep and the bright yellow carriage at Darlinghurst went under the hammer, Mary

Jones took 10 per cent of the proceeds. That was really small change. Jones saved a larger slice of his fortune by driving thousands of sheep from St Ruth and Tent Hill over to River Station. Those 115,000 acres and all the stock grazing there were never listed among his assets. On paper they belonged not to Jones but to the partnership of Ferriter & Uhr. Once the wool price rose, that land and those sheep would be the key to his commercial resurrection. Jones was bankrupt for less than a year. Under laws he once opposed, he was free to return to business once his debts were known and the trustees had gathered all the assets they could find. Not much. Only £14,400 was raised to meet his debts of £48,000. Young Donaldson, badly burnt by Jones' collapse, wrote: "There is neither any special lustre nor are there any particularly pleasing recollections attached to the name of R. Jones Esq." But the future Premier of New South Wales had the consolation of buying Darlinghurst for a song.

"All passed for ever from his possession!" wrote Jones' daughter Elizabeth in her little memoir that portrayed her father as a good – even saintly – man brought undone by the times:

> In the terribly sudden & disastrous storm that overtook all financial interests throughout Australia at that time; he suffered a deep reverse of fortune ... But we were not entirely reduced to penury ... we were still in comfortable circumstances. And also we were allowed to live at Bolwarra, as "tenants at will," for nearly two years during the winding up of the "Insolvent Estate". And when in the latter part of 1845, we had to leave Bolwarra; and made our course to Brisbane; we were still placed in easy & pleasant circumstances even then: & by degrees also things continued to improve. But the affluence of years gone by, was never to be recovered.

Jones still had clout despite his ruin. Before leaving Bolwarra, he asked Gipps to make his wife's brother a magistrate. Jones listed his qualifications: "Mr. Edmund Blucher Uhr of Brisbane River Moreton Bay ...

is a young man of excellent character, is married to a Daughter of Mr. Kemp of Van Diemens Land and in partnership with Mr Ferriter in a large sheep establishment ... and should your Excellency be pleased to confer the honor upon him, I feel assured he will prove himself worthy of it." In July 1845 His Excellency announced Uhr's appointment as a Magistrate of the Territory and its Dependencies. To mark the occasion, Uhr ordered a signet ring engraved with the crest and motto of the dukes of Roxburghe: *Pro Christo et Patria Dulce Periculum* – For Christ and Country Danger is Sweet.

11

KILLERS OF MR UHR

As Jones' runs were sold under them, the family gathered on River Station. The Uhrs came across from Tent Hill in July 1844 with a newborn son, Reginald Charles Heber Uhr, named for no known reason after the Bishop of Calcutta, writer of the mighty hymn "Holy Holy Holy! Lord God Almighty". The Ferriters arrived at much the same time and built a large cottage a few miles upstream where the Jones family – Richard, Mary and half a dozen children – joined them nine months later. Over lunch there one day, Charles Archer of Durundur inspected the Jones women: "The younger pert and pretty, the elder pleasing in appearance with a quite sensible manner, that is as far as I could judge from being three hours in their society; Mrs Jones looks very young to have a grown up family – the old gentleman himself was not at home." Thomas Archer had earlier reported on Edmund and Amy Uhr at Tent Hill: "I stayed at the station of a Mr Uhr who is married and one of the largest proprietors in the district – Tho' he is a great humbug in some points he was very kind to me and Mrs Uhr a handsome and rather ladylike person showed me every attention." At some point, River Station was renamed Wivenhoe.

John Uhr turned up in 1845 after spending five years in Europe. He was not well. Friends called him "Cranky Uhr", which in those days meant crazy rather than angry. His brother gave him menial work as a hut-keeper on a remote corner of the run between the Brisbane River and the foothills of the D'Aguilar Range. The Yuggera seemed quiet, but Dr Simpson feared this only signalled a shift in strategy.

"They no longer adopt a system of open war, but visiting the Stations in small mobs in the guise of friends they allow no opportunity to escape them of pilfering the huts or destroying any stray Cattle they may meet with."

In December John and a shepherd were minding 800 sheep. His hut was full of stores. On about 16 December, the shepherd brought the flock home in the evening to find the hut plundered and no sign of the hut-keeper. He slept that night among his sheep and began searching for Uhr in the morning. Some blacks appeared who told him Uhr was dead in the river. The shepherd snatched a gun and ran. The river was in flood and he could not cross. He hid in the reeds for hours until his cries alerted men working on the far bank. They rescued him and found Uhr. According to reports, his body had been treated "with the greatest indignity".

John Uhr was the first *gentleman* to die in the fighting at Moreton Bay and the news of his death was reported across the Colony in tones of high indignation. Though nothing whatever was known of the circumstances of his killing, graphic reports were soon in print: Aborigines arrived at the hut, clamouring for tobacco; Uhr refused their demands; a mob attacked all at once; Uhr died fighting gallantly and his body, "presenting innumerable wounds of the most frightful nature", was thrown into the river. Papers reported the death had thrown the district "into the greatest alarm and consternation". The Commissioner of Crown Lands hurried to the scene. Tracks were followed to a deserted camp in the scrub where articles stolen from the hut were lying about. Simpson concluded whoever was responsible for the killing was, by that time, far away. Jones demanded protection and a corporal and eight men from the 99th were sent to guard the families at Wivenhoe. Other squatters could only dream of the authorities taking such care of them. Simpson explained to the Colonial Secretary: "I certainly do not myself see any necessity for their presence beyond calming the fear of the inmates, including a large proportion of women & children; as I know that the aggressive party has crossed the D'Aguilar Range." An inquest held by the Uhrs' neighbour over the river, Major North, blamed "blacks unknown", but the squatters were convinced the guilty party was a warrior of the Garumngar clan of the Wakka Wakka named Waakoon or Horse Jemmy. The evidence against him was always feeble. The day before Uhr's death, Waakoon had come to the hut offering to cut brush in return for food. That was all. Simpson refused to offer a reward for his capture.

SPEAR GRASS

Jones was preparing to take his sheep out of Moreton Bay. This was not provoked by Uhr's death. All the wool men of Moreton Bay were facing the same problem: their country was proving unsuitable for sheep. Pastures that were so wonderful only years earlier had been eaten away, allowing spear grass to run rampant. The pointed seeds of *Heteropogon contortus* wounded men, lacerated sheep and contaminated the clip. Jones might have turned Wivenhoe over to cattle instead, but wool prices were rising sharply again in London. He and his neighbours wanted vast new inland acres for their sheep, country they would once again take from the blacks without a qualm. In April 1846 Jones and Edmund Uhr joined David McConnel of Cressbrook on a journey to see what lay over the Cooyar Range. McConnel assembled a dray, ten bullocks, seven horses and eight or nine men including black guides to take them over the mountains. The expedition left McConnel with a low opinion of Uhr: "He is no bushman, & he had not the slightest idea of the 'lay' of the country." But he was impressed by old Merchant Jones joining this pioneering journey into the bush.

> We ascended the ranges & kept on the top of them, trav-elling North till we saw a perspect of good country, which we soon did; descended to a creek running due North, through a fine open country, very well adapted for sheep, & the grass abounding in herbage; & after riding over this country & ascertaining that there was abundance of water, & the country was well adapted for stock, being situated on a land 2000 feet above the sea, & very open, & free from scrub, & sufficient to hold 50000 sheep at least ... Our adventures were not numerous; we saw no blacks to disturb us, & we had fine weather, except one heavy thun-derstorm; so that altogether I enjoyed the expedition very much. It is exceedingly delightful & causes great excitement to the mind to travel over new country in which white man has never trod.

Jones staked out the first and biggest run on what turned out to be the upper reaches of the Burnett. In twenty years of land-taking, these 164,000 acres of Wakka Wakka country were the most he had ever seized at one time. He called the run Baramba. Once again, he kept his name off all the official papers. Though clearly in command, he insisted this immense new run belonged to his brothers-in-law, Ferriter and Uhr. Jones had had enough of the bush. With Baramba secure and his fortunes rising once more, he took his family to Brisbane where he bought ninety acres on the river which he called New Farm.

Brisbane was struggling. A gulag at Meanjin made sense, but not a city so far up that difficult river. One or two large buildings were left from the town's convict past. The old barracks in its walled yard had become the centre of government. A few houses stood about. On the skyline was the mill where convicts once ground corn. Still busy were the gallows nearby. Stores and wharves had appeared along the river. One was the store of Daniel Peterson, Mrs Jones' murdering brother, who was at last making a fortune, this time by selling to squatters, among other things, arms and ammunition to shoot blacks. Turrbal, Yuggera and Wakka Wakka people wandered the streets. They were essential to the town, supplying firewood and fish, oysters and clothes props*, bark and flowers. Whites called their main camp in the town York's Hollow as a complicated tribute to the Turrbal leader, Daki Yakka or Duke of York. In time, York's Hollow would disappear under Victoria Park and the Exhibition Ground. But for the moment, the camps there and at Breakfast Creek made Aboriginal people endlessly familiar to the whites of Brisbane. Yet the townsfolk remained nervous. From time to time, shepherds were killed on runs within a day's ride of Brisbane. Rumours of violence swept the town. Blacks were kept off the streets at night.

At the age of sixty, Jones built a bungalow for his family at New Farm. The children were disappearing. After excelling in Greek, scripture and the flute at King's, Richard left for Cambridge where he was reading for the ministry. He never returned. In the depths of the Jones' financial catastrophe, their daughter Mary Australia had married William Bligh John O'Connell. The families had known each other for years. Richard Jones had campaigned for the groom's brother Maurice Charles O'Connell when he stood – unsuccessfully – for a seat in the House of Assembly. Sir Maurice later entered the Queensland Parliament, a decent figure in the squalid politics of the new Colony. That left four children at New Farm: Frances, a daughter of four; Thomas, a boy of fourteen who loved sailing; and two daughters in their late teens, Louisa and Elizabeth. They were taken into society.

Sitting in Brisbane one day, drowsing over a book, Thomas Archer of Durundur found a gentleman and three ladies at his door.

---

* A long pole used to raise a line of washing.

The former I soon recognised to be Mr Jones, at one time
a leading merchant and MC in Sydney, but much reduced
by the late hard times. I of course introduced myself to
him and was in my turn introduced to Mrs and two Misses
Jones, the latter very pretty and highly accomplished
young ladies.

In a very short time I found myself on very easy terms
with them all, and to my own astonishment found myself
buttering toast & doing the amiable, to perfection, a style
of business to which I have been rather unaccustomed for
the last ten years; next day I had the honor of escorting
them to their cottage about ¼ mile from town where I have
been every day since, boating, shopping and visiting with
the ladies, and in fact acting as their "Chaperon" on every
occasion. During this time I have led a very agreeable life,
and was within an ace of falling in love with one of them
when to my horor I was told that she is engaged to be married next month!

Louisa's husband, Robert Ramsay Mackenzie, having clawed his way
out of an extravagant bankruptcy, was on his way to being rich again.
Though he was not a Kilcoy Mackenzie, there was a baronetcy on its
way. As he waited for his inheritance, this handsome, stupid and genial
man would be Treasurer and Premier of Queensland. In both posts he
would serve squatters and the Uhrs generously.

Jones planted indigo, sugar cane and cotton along the river. Cotton
especially seized his imagination. The master of Baramba was ready for
another volte-face. He sent samples of his cotton to Manchester, assur-
ing the Chamber of Commerce this was the future of Australia. "Before
another quarter of a century passes away, if our difficulties are removed,
this branch of commerce will become more important than our present
large export of wool." Pickers would be needed by the thousand. The
great cause of Jones' political life, bringing workers to Australia, was

once more pressing on his mind. He could not understand why Britain wasted money on starving Irish.

> How much better employed would have been the £8,000,000 that was spent in the Irish famine, had it been spent in sending your excess of numbers here and elsewhere—where, in time, they would acquire happy homes, and be surrounded with comfort; but the English government, by its absurd economy, will give no assistance to emigration—thus retaining the starving people at home, waiting for another visitation of the kind.

Jones was among the first at Moreton Bay to hire indentured Chinese men shipped down from the Fujian province. He took sixteen as shepherds for Baramba, promising them six pounds plus two suits of clothing per year for five years. In business Jones did what he had to do, but he still yearned to see Australia peopled by cheap British labourers.

*

Any Aboriginal man slain at Moreton Bay at this time was declared a killer of John Uhr. No proof was required. The warrior Multuggerah was killed on the Rosewood run of John Coutts in August and with him died two "supposed murderers of the unfortunate Mr. Uhr". In June *The Moreton Bay Courier* appeared and was almost at once the most influential paper in the town. The capture of Waakoon, aka Horse Jemmy, "the principal in the murder of the late Mr. Uhr on the Brisbane River", was the paper's first crusade. A reward of £40 was offered. The paper's attitude to the blacks would shift dramatically over time as owners and editors came and went. But under its founder and first editor, Arthur Lyon, *The Moreton Bay Courier* backed the squatters and dismissed the blacks:

> Shall a handful of miserable savages, secure in the supinity of our rulers, go on adding victim to victim, robbery

to robbery, until their thirst for blood and plunder, growing by what it feeds on, becomes so enormous that we must either flee like cowards from the land, or sweep them from existence.

The reward worked. In November, three convict workers were given permission by the government overseer in Ipswich to capture Waakoon in return for the £40 and their tickets-of-leave. Their leader, Daniel Doyle, a street thug, had a warrant for Waakoon's arrest – not for murder but spearing a cow. The three were issued arms and ammunition. They soon found Waakoon or Horse Jemmy in a camp of about 200 blacks in Rosewood Scrub. Doyle promised him flour. He and another black called Mayhall walked with Doyle for about 50 yards before becoming suspicious. They refused to go further. Doyle said at the inquest:

> I then told him that I had a warrant against him for the murder of Mr. Uhr, and that he was my prisoner. I then laid hold of him and the other black. We struggled together, and I got thrown down. Mayhall got loose, and threw a waddie, which knocked the hat off my head. I had pistols in my belt at the time, which were hidden by my blue shirt. Immediately afterwards Horse Jemmy released himself from my grasp, and rose up. As he was going away, he turned round and looked at me. I then pulled out a pistol, while rising on my side, and discharged it at him. I fired because I heard the blacks yelling, and thought if I did not do so, they would attack me.

Waakoon died as he was being carried to Major North's run nearby. Though his son had been in the shooting party, North held an inquest into the death immediately. Plunkett was not satisfied. He ordered a full bench of local magistrates to reinvestigate Waakoon's shooting. Major North sat with them. They found "that no undue violence was in this case exercised towards the blacks, in endeavouring to apprehend a known murderer, for whom a warrant was out for this apprehension". A few months later Doyle and his convict companion, Joseph Reynolds, were given their tickets-of-leave.

To add to Brisbane's nightmare at this time, Andrew Gregor and his pregnant housekeeper, Mrs Shannon, were killed 25 miles from town on their Pine River run. "A very bad specimen," Thomas Archer called Gregor. "Very ignorant very narrowminded and very stingy." Suspicion for the deaths fell on Jackey Jackey, a man already accused of being among the killers of John Uhr. One night in October, Constable Peter Murphy led a party into York's Hollow, found Jackey Jackey and put a noose around his neck. He broke free. Shots were fired. In a melée of conflicting testimony in the police magistrate's court, Constable Murphy insisted Jackey Jackey was alive and happy in the Bunya Mountains. The camp blacks thought differently but the police refused to hear evidence that Murphy had killed two men in the raid that night from their leader, Daki Yakka, that Murphy killed two men that night. The Turrbal chief, known in the town as the Duke of York, cut firewood for the Inspector of Customs, William Duncan. The two men had grown close. Duncan insisted on reading the man's evidence into the record:

> White fellows had fired at them in the camp, and that they had shot two black fellows; one Bobby belonging to him, and another named Jackey Jackey. I asked him if it was Bobby, who was a little palsied; he said it was. He said that they had destroyed the camp, and taken away all their utensils and weapons; that all the blacks ran away; that a Mary, whom I understood him to say was his daughter, was taken in childbirth—pickaniny tumbled down—and that she herself was very sick.

The baby died immediately and the mother a few days later. Daki Yakka's evidence was ignored. Murphy was untouched.

Newspapers in the south challenged *The Moreton Bay Courier* to produce evidence that these dead blacks were all involved in the murder of John Uhr. The paper published in reply a slather of lies about the victims and sage advice for those city folk in the south whose "enthusiasm has warped their benevolence". The paper set out the squatters' position with timeless concision: "We have seized their country by the right of might, and by the right of might the whites will continue to possess it. When all other remedies, and amicable means, have failed, they ought to be civilized by compulsion."

12

TROUBLESOME BUSH LAWYER

Within a year of sighting the grasslands, Richard Jones had 25,000 sheep grazing on Baramba. Fifty shepherds worked to bring his flocks over the mountains from Wivenhoe. Eventually, John Ferriter took charge of more than 60,000 sheep grazing 164,000 acres of Wakka Wakka country cut up into mighty blocks named Charleston, Cherbourg, Murgon, Johnstown and Brisbane Range. Jones was still cautious. Everything here was in the names of Ferriter & Uhr.

His flocks were infected with catarrh. It strikes suddenly. "The head and mouth become much swollen, and an offensive matter runs from the nostrils, accompanied generally with severe purging, which in a few hours terminates in death." Catarrh was so infectious that squatters expected their neighbours to cull sick sheep promptly. Jones' inaction was so notorious that years after his death he was still being denounced: "Those sheep had been diseased … first at Tent Hill, then removed to the Brisbane River, near Wivanhoe, they were diseased there; then removed to Barambah, and were there diseased." Finally, at Baramba, Jones began the cull. It was a big operation. "There were 25,000 head of diseased sheep slaughtered for boiling," wrote a Baramba stockman, George Dart. "Some mornings you would see 20 or 30 fine large fat sheep dead in the yard. During the boiling of those diseased sheep all hands on the head station were working between two and three months amongst the slaughtering and boiling." Carting tallow to a boat at Ipswich might take two or three months, so Jones decided instead to walk his sick sheep over the Wide Bay Range and down to the Mary River to be boiled down and their tallow shipped to market.

After Kilcoy, the Butchulla and Gubbi Gubbi had cleared the Mary River. It was a significant black victory. Half a dozen shepherds were killed; the rest fled and their masters followed. For five years, squatters hesitated to return, though the district of Wide Bay was such promising country, well-watered and fire-farmed for centuries. But as *The Sydney Morning Herald* remarked, the quality of the soil was more than counterbalanced by "the untameable qualities of the aboriginals". In September 1847, the daring and unscrupulous George Furber braved the danger to build a store at the head of navigation of the Mary to ship out wool for the squatters of the hinterland. A few Butchulla worked on the store with half a dozen ticket-of-leave men. One day in October one of the blacks flung an axe that scalped Furber. Widely reported as an act of unprovoked savagery, the assault was industrial action of a kind familiar in the bush. Furber had promised provisions and not kept his word. A local squatter wrote:

> From my own experience nothing seems to annoy them more than for white men to promise and then to shirk performance. This is not the way to deal with the natives; and I would advise no one to attempt evasion after promising them anything for work that has been cheerfully done.

Dreadfully injured, Furber was helped to Ipswich while his convicts remained terrified on the river. But they gathered themselves and began to deal out punishment to the assailants. So began a process that went on for years. Many Butchulla would be slaughtered en masse or shot one by one in Wide Bay, accused of having assaulted this litigious and violent man.

Neither Furber's bloody fate nor talk of abandoning Wide Bay to the savages deterred Jones. He poached one of Furber's men, William Clements, to find land on the riverbank where he might build a boiling-down for the slaughtered sheep of Baramba. Clements arrived in early

1848 on the ketch *Aurora*, which almost came to grief at the mouth of the Mary. Angry blacks looked on:

> I shall never forget the hideous yell of those incarnate fiends—on the rocks, when they saw us escape their clutches, and believe me, a good lookout was kept on board the Aurora that night, for their canoes.
>
> Next morning we weighed, and took the Bar without further mishap, and proceeded up the Bay, the channel being so intricate that we grounded several times during the day; however, having made the mouth of the river, after mistaking half-a-dozen openings, for it, we got alongside a landing place ... and made fast.

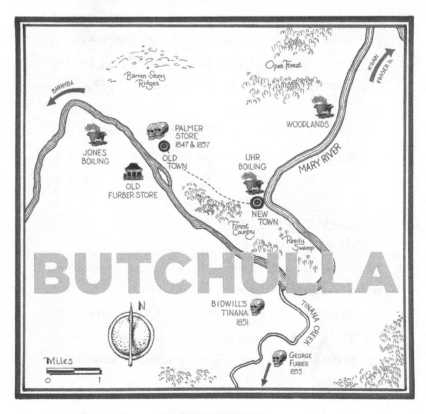

MARYBOROUGH

Here on the south bank of the river – Gooroomandoom or place of kangaroos – the settlement of Maryborough began with a wool store and a boiling-down. The only whites around when Clements arrived were Furber – back from Ipswich – and his convict workers. The first wool was shipped down the Mary at this time, the Baramba fleece. Jones had high hopes for the new settlement. He and Furber joined forces to tout the "easy and safe navigation" of the Mary in the Brisbane press. They claimed Wide Bay was a fine harbour and the bar at the mouth of the river posed no problems for navigation. They were lying. Clements returned safely on the *Aurora* in April 1848, with a team of men armed to the teeth and ready to start building on the land he had taken for Jones:

> We laid in twelve-months' supply of rations, three or four large pots for boiling purposes, a number of casks in "stacks", and all the paraphernalia necessary for the carrying on the sheep, and boiling establishment. We had a cooper, butcher, blacksmith, and nine shepherds for Mr. Jones ... I need not say that we were well supplied with cutlasses and fire-arms, "Old Brown Bess" and her bayonet included, and any amount of ammunition; indeed, I have a faint recollection of clearing out Peterson's store, South Brisbane, of arms and ammunition on this occasion. The most formidable weapon in those days, before the age of breech-loaders and revolvers, was the muzzle-loading double-barrel, and cutlass. The blacks had a most holy—if anything connected with the wretches could be holy—horror of a cutlass ...
>
> We erected four huts, each having a front to the cardinal points, so as to enable us, in the event of being attacked by the blacks, of showing a front to whatever quarter that attack might come from.

The settlers who followed made up their own minds where to build their huts, choosing an open ridge on the north bank of the river.

The government surveyor explained: "For safety sake, and mutual protection from the Aborigines, they sat down on a clear bit of ground
immediately opposite to Mr Furber." Safety may not have been their
only consideration, for in the middle of 1848 Jones' pots began their
filthy work. When his first batch of tallow was ready to ship south,
Jones came up to inspect the operation. Liking the look of the country,
he directed Clements to seize 80,000 acres of river flats at Owanyilla, a
dozen miles upriver. As the run was being stocked, the Butchulla carried off seventy sheep. Clements led the pursuit. The awkward sarcasm
of *The Moreton Bay Courier* points to a bloody conclusion:

> We cannot offer, any apology for Mr. Clements, for his
> behaviour was really very unkind. He assembled a small
> party of about ten persons, including himself, and set out
> with the avowed object of rescuing Mr. Jones's sheep—if he
> could find them. After some tramping, they succeeded, with
> the assistance of a black guide, in reaching the camp of the
> enemy; and, finding that the latter were enjoying themselves
> in the real old English style,—roasting the sheep whole upon
> their fires,—Mr. Clements entered against their proceedings
> a protest, which he found it necessary to enforce by a volley.
> The last named argument had the effect of dispersing the
> "Young New Hollanders," who chiefly shine in private assas-
> sination, but it is probable that Mr. Clement's party were
> rather bad shots, or else that they purposely fired wide. At
> all events it is certain that the killed and wounded conveyed
> themselves from the field of battle on their own legs.

Through all this, Edmund B. Uhr of Wivenhoe sat on the Ipswich
bench, dealing with assaults, drunks, absconding servants, forged orders
and squabbles over stock. Without any formal knowledge of the law, he
issued summonses, arrested suspects and presided over trials. He loved
the work. The Uhrs had had another son in 1845, whom they christened
Wentworth D'arcy. His mother Amy's links to the Wentworths were old

and sordid. Her father had plotted the Rum Rebellion with handsome, quarrelsome D'arcy Wentworth, whose son William Charles was now the democratic tribune of the Legislative Council, execrating the blacks and mocking those who called for their protection. Perhaps something of the grubby panache of the Wentworths passed to the boy as water was dribbled on his head at St John's in Brisbane. He was known all his life as D'arcy.

*

Jones no longer needed to hide his land and flocks in the names of his brothers-in-law and in March 1849 they began to disentangle themselves. Perhaps Uhr and Ferriter also thought it time they went their own way. After years of service to Jones, they emerged barely prosperous. Ferriter was forty-seven and borrowed heavily to stock Toomcul, a 30,000-acre run near Baramba, which became a place of killing and fierce reprisals. He didn't last there long. Edmund B. Uhr at thirty-five was done with the bush. Mary McConnel of Cressbrook visited Wivenhoe at this time and found the family packing. "Mr Uhr's brother had been murdered by the natives," she wrote. "As they continued troublesome, the family decided to move to town." In the division of assets, Uhr took the Maryborough boiling-down. He and Ferriter made an early sortie to Maryborough in June and sat for a few days as the first bench of magistrates in the settlement. *The Sydney Morning Herald* approved. "By administering a few wholesome lessons in the shape of fines and imprisonments", the two men "made this a comparatively quiet and orderly city!" The Uhrs arrived with servants and labourers in August. Once more, the Sydney paper applauded: "I am glad to inform you that E. B. Uhr Esq., J. P. has come to reside here, and intends opening stores, and also to boil down on a large scale."

The place was primitive: two pubs, a store and about 100 settlers living in shanties on the bank, waiting for the government to survey the place and offer them plots to buy. Edmund B. Uhr didn't wait. In the

spirit of Richard Jones, he simply took what he wanted. Uhr could see
the rough village was at the far end of a great loop in the river. He took
some acres a couple of miles across country but eight miles closer to the
sea. There he built – without permission on land he didn't own – a store,
a wharf and a boiling-down. "In a very short time houses were erected
by Mr. Uhr for himself and family, as also for the butchers, coopers,
stockmen, and laborers attached to the boiling down," wrote Clements.
Cattle and sheep were soon cooking in the vats. Consignments of Uhr's
tallow were fetching excellent prices in Sydney within twelve months.

From the first, Maryborough was known as a place of quarrels.
Uhr took an energetic part in them. He nevertheless saw himself as
a custodian of order. Time on the bench was making him even more
self-important and endlessly demanding. One of his passions was getting up petitions urging the Governor to do this or that for the benefit
of the settlement. His first petition, sent within weeks of his family's
arrival in Maryborough, asked His Excellency to save the settlement
from drunks:

> Violent assaults, Robberies, Forgeries, and other crimes are
> daily committed with impunity, and in many instances the
> culprits are well known, and escaped punishment from the
> want of a Police force ... shearers and laborers who are a
> most lawless, and abandoned class of men of the "Wide Bay",
> "Burnett," and adjacent districts; resort there in great num-
> bers, among whom it is well known that the settlement is
> without Police ... from an assembly of such Characters, with
> the means of intoxication at command frightful scenes may
> be anticipated.

Most of Uhr's petitions in these years begged Sydney for protection
from the blacks. Maryborough was under siege. Whether it would survive was an open question. Huts were stripped and drays plundered.
Every man carried firearms. Flocks along the river were double-
banked – each mob guarded by two armed shepherds. Having once

cleared the land of whites, the Butchulla of the coast, the Gubbi Gubbi of the upper Mary and the Wakka Wakka of the Burnett stubbornly resisted their return. "It became obligatory to decide whether the blacks or whites were to hold the land," wrote one of the squatters. "Numerous were the parties formed to hunt up the murderers and rescue the stolen sheep." Hungry blacks raided the boiling-downs. Workers at the pots kept horses and rifles always at the ready. In mid-1849, *The Sydney Morning Herald* detailed the latest attacks:

> I am sorry to inform you that the blacks are becoming very troublesome here. They rushed Mr. R. Jones's boiling-down establishment; next day bailed-up Mr. Walker's people (another boiling establishment); the day following took the whole of Mr. Furber's fat sheep, which he had got down for slaughter; the same day endeavoured to steal Mr. Jones's fat wethers, but were driven off by the shepherds. Two days since they tried again to rob Mr. Jones's establishment, but were driven off; to-day, in the very heart of the settlement, a blackfellow threw spears at one of the inhabitants.

The Border Police never operated in Wide Bay. The settlers had only their own men to ride against the blacks. Stockmen from Baramba took part in the bloodiest reprisal raid of the time after two young shepherds, the Pegg brothers, were killed on Gregory Blaxland's 75,000-acre run, Gin Gin, on the lower reaches of the Burnett. Weeks later, Blaxland led fifty or more squatters and station hands on a dawn raid of a Gooreng Gooreng camp at The Cedars on the river. Eyewitness reports are supposed to exist but cannot now be found. Historian Arthur Laurie wrote in 1952 that "the blacks were shown no mercy" but "put up a mighty fight against the firearms of the whites, they of course having no better weapons than spears". He added: "Over sixty years later ploughmen unearthed skulls, bones and weapons." It is thought that sixty died in the raid, blacks who seem to have taken no part in the killing of the shepherds. A year later, Blaxland was killed in reply. Another round of

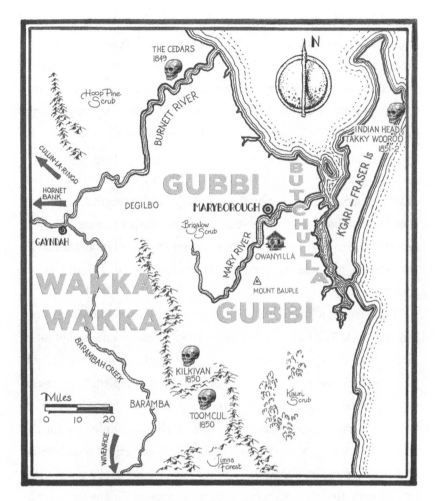

WIDE BAY & BURNETT

violent reprisals followed. A local stockman turned journalist, George Loyau, wrote: "I believe I am not wrong in stating that every acre of land in these districts was won from aborigines by bloodshed and warfare."

The government's man in Maryborough was the famous botanist John Bidwill. After losing a promised appointment as director of the Sydney Botanic Gardens, Bidwill asked for a post in the north and was made Commissioner of Crown Lands for Wide Bay. He and Uhr sat together on the bench. For a time their court was the bar of the FitzRoy Inn. There was no lock-up in the settlement. Bidwill's achievements as a botanist are honoured still – the mighty bunya pine is *Araucaria bidwillii* – but his efforts to govern Maryborough, a place he called "as regard Law and Morals ... California on a small scale", were unimpressive. He was standing outside Palmer's store one day when Furber walked up to some Aboriginal men unloading stores, drew a pistol from his breast pocket and shot one dead. With his weapon smoking, Furber declared: "That is the man who tried to murder me, and very nearly succeeded." Bidwill reported the killing to Sydney. He was not much troubled when no action followed. "We are here, a mere handful of white men, surrounded by thousands of black savages who understand no law but the law of self defence and the lex talionis," Bidwill remarked. "Furber has removed a murderer in the only way the blacks understand, and our lives will be all the safer for it. I shall leave it at that."

Bidwill built a house and planted gardens on the good black soil of Tinana Creek. The Butchulla ignored his botanical specimens but often raided his vegetable patch for sweet potatoes. One morning Bidwill found a black carrying off his flowerpots. They grappled. "I managed to fling myself clear of him and fire the pistol." He missed. The man fled and minutes later Bidwill found himself surrounded by Butchulla. Two of his workmen appeared. "A fight commenced which lasted for two hours and half," the botanist reported. The Butchulla were driven off and from that time Bidwill stationed six men at Tinana for his protection and surrounded the vegetable garden with a tall fence. He went further. "Mr. Bidwell was determined to try and frighten them," wrote one of his men. "He got a large man-trap from Sydney, and it was so strong that it took two strong men to set it. It was bolted to a large stump with a strong chain, and was set every night. One night there was a great yelling and noise by a black who was caught in it. In fact, his leg was nearly cut through, and early in the morning, one of the men put an end to his pain and misery."

*

To his chagrin, Uhr discovered the government wanted his wharf and land. When Hugh Labatt arrived to survey the town in mid-1850, he saw what Uhr had seen: the settlement was too far upstream. "It could not be in a worse position," he reported, for the last long loop of the Mary added "always two and sometimes three and four days to a voyage in working up and down the River". He proposed Maryborough start all over again – around the site of the boiling-down. Uhr told the surveyor "he would exert himself to the utmost to prevent his boiling Establishment being disturbed". His opposition exasperated Sydney officials, who began to brand Uhr a pompous troublemaker. When Labatt's plans for the new town were published, Uhr persuaded sawyers, labourers, storeowners and publicans – including George Furber – to petition the Governor to leave Maryborough alone and build a new port near the mouth of the river. Labatt warned the Surveyor-General not to be too impressed: "Mr Furber ... a small Publican, appears to be much influenced by Mr Uhr, who is a particularly interested party, and has the character of being a troublesome bush lawyer." The petition failed. So did Uhr's sad plea to be compensated for spending "upwards of three hundred pounds (£300) in building with the full intention of purchasing the land as soon as your Excellency had authorised the land to be exposed for sale". All he won in the end was the right to stay for a few years until the land was required. "Rent" scribbled an official on the file. Another replied: "Yes!"

"Uhr, of boiling-down fame", turned sheep and cattle into tallow. His men fattened, slaughtered, skinned, gutted and packed the carcasses into iron vats to be stewed until the last ounce of fat was drained away. The stench was terrible. The hides were tanned; the bones were burnt for fertiliser; and the sodden mass of flesh was given to the blacks who worked for Uhr and gathered for the spoils. "Mr. Uhr's boiling place is more like a blacks' camp than anything else; hundreds of camps being round it, numbers being employed by the proprietor to carry on his operations," complained *The Moreton Bay Courier*. But Maryborough needed the blacks. After a mass exodus to the Victorian goldfields in the early 1850s, labour was short and for a few pennies, a little tobacco or a billy of overcooked mutton the Butchulla chopped wood, fetched water, lumped cargo, dug holes and butchered beasts for the boiling-down. They were pilots on that difficult river. Steamer captains gave the Butchulla rations and fishing lines to guide their boats up the Mary and back to Wide Bay. Travellers arriving for the first time by sea were astonished by the sight. Bidwill's gardener, George Dart, remembered:

> After we crossed the bar and coming into the river, scores of naked blacks swam to the schooner and boarded. They explained to the captain where the deep water was, pointing the way the schooner would have to go. When we arrived at the wharf at the "Old Township" there were more naked blacks, male and female, about the wharf, more so than whites. As soon as they commenced to discharge the cargo of the boat, which was principally flour, a train of blacks began carrying the 200lb. bags of flour to Mr. H. Palmer's store and other places on their heads, and all in rotation. In fact, nearly all the discharging of vessels in those days was done by the naked blacks.

A *pullen pullen* was staged every season outside Uhr's plant. The champions were paraded, oiled, powdered with crushed charcoal and decorated with feathers. These contests were choreographed but violent. They might last for weeks. At night, men and women sang and danced by their fires. These gatherings at Uhr's place in Maryborough became a staple of colonial memoirs. A squatter on the Mary remembered, years later, a mighty *pullen pullen* when the Gubbi Gubbi of Mount Bauple faced the Butchulla of K'gari, which the whites called Fraser or the Big Sandy Island:

> The Boppleites had close on five hundred men, and what they lacked in numbers they certainly made up in manly physique and martial bearing. Hostilities commenced about

3 p.m., and did not cease till near sundown, when the King of Fraser Island was laid low by a spear right through the abdomen. About a dozen other warriors were killed on both sides, but the allies were completely routed. They appeared to be quite crestfallen, and did not offer the least resistence when a Bopple chief, attended by a crowd of fighting men, rushed on to claim the young princess, daughter of the fallen monarch, or whilst, as afterwards happened they carried her away in triumph.

That Maryborough lived so intimately with Aborigines did little to temper the fears of the town and nothing whatever to reassure squatters on the Mary and Burdekin. More loudly than ever, town and country alike demanded police protection. Up and down the Colony, the same was true. The Border Police were long gone, unloved almost from the day Gipps established this force in the aftermath of Myall Creek. They were so loathed for collecting licence fees on stock and runs that the squatters in Council abolished the force in 1846. Much as they wanted protection from the blacks, they craved protection from tax collectors more. The Governor sailed home, leaving them to it. For the next bloody years all the squatters had to keep them safe were a handful of constables – Maryborough had one – very few soldiers and their own station hands, armed and willing to kill.

13

MY ROGUES

S ir Charles Augustus FitzRoy, the tenth Governor of New South Wales, was an aristocratic soldier and Whig politician, the grandson of one duke and son-in-law of another. He fought at Waterloo. FitzRoy had already served the Empire at the Cape of Good Hope and as Governor of the Leeward Islands in the West Indies. He came to Sydney with the usual instructions to safeguard Her Majesty's black subjects. But he was particularly instructed to make peace with the squatters, who had broken the last two men sent out to govern the Colony.

Their most urgent demand was to own their acres. All Bourke and Gipps had ever given them was a licence to run sheep on Crown land. The squatters wanted title. Stephen Roberts wrote that this "led to a degree of political organisation hitherto unknown in Australia and caused a campaign which extended from Calcutta to Canada, from Sydney to the remotest coffee-house in the Scottish Highlands". The wool men peppered their fantastical claims to rights and liberties with elegant threats of rebellion. "The word *resistance* is not, with us, the effect of American feelings or principles," wrote Wentworth's *Australian*. "It is simply *English*." The black lands of New South Wales were an immensely valuable asset of the Crown. Half a dozen British governments had refused to give it away to settlers. But after a decade's pressure from wool-growers, their London agents, merchants, bankers and mill owners, Westminster's resolution collapsed. The shift began under Gipps, and FitzRoy arrived in 1846 with instructions to give squatters leases and eventually the right to buy their runs at ridiculously low prices. Few gifts in the history of the Empire would prove so lavish.

Life for Aborigines was supposed to go on unchanged. Lord Grey, the Secretary of State for the Colonies, wrote to FitzRoy: "These Leases are not intended to deprive the natives of their former right to hunt over these Districts, or to wander over them in search of subsistence, in the manner to which they have been heretofore accustomed, from the spontaneous produce of the soil." But no one had the courage to tell the squatters. Grey's fine rhetoric lies buried in the correspondence between him and the Governor of New South Wales. When a draft of the Sale of Waste Land Bill reached Sydney in late 1845, nothing was said about Aborigines and squatters sharing the land and rivers. Nor was it mentioned when the bill was debated in Westminster. Grey might have endorsed in the House of Lords the rights of the original inhabitants of the land for whom he expressed, in private, such tender care. Instead, he talked about the value of wool to Britain and the number of Australian acres it took to feed a sheep. Even before reports of his speech reached the Colony, the Chief Protector of Aborigines, George Augustus Robinson, had warned London:

> Unless suitable reserves are immediately formed for their benefit, every acre of their Native Soil will shortly be so leased out and occupied, as to leave them, in a legal view, no place for the sole of their feet ... I have great reason to fear the legal rights acquired under a lease would be fully acted upon and the unfortunate Natives might be hunted from Station to Station, without a Spot they could call their own.

London had set aside reserves for the native peoples of Canada, the Cape and New Zealand. But Grey refused to consider the same course in Australia. Reservations, he told FitzRoy in early 1848, did not suit Australia because both sheep and blacks needed so much land.

I think it has been generally agreed that this system is inapplicable to the circumstances of Australia. The necessity under which proprietors of flocks are placed of extending their occupation of Land, such as it is, over wide tracts of Country ... the barren and inhospitable character of large tracts of the Australian soil, the migratory habits of the scanty Tribes in search of sustenance which the earth very sparingly affords them, all seem to render the establishment of native reserves of Land on a large scale of very doubtful utility, even if practicable.

FitzRoy

Grey saw sharing the land as a pathway to peace: "A distinct understanding of the extent of their mutual rights is one step at least towards the maintenance of order and mutual forbearance between the parties." But the new law was silent on this. It gave the squatters no power to expel the original inhabitants of their lands. Grey as good as ordered FitzRoy to issue a proclamation making this clear to the squatters, but the Governor's courage failed.

A law passed in London guarding the rights of Aborigines to live, hunt and fish on their lands would, if enforced, would have transformed the history of Australia. A law proving impossible, Plunkett proposed embedding that right in squatters' leases. FitzRoy agreed. This required a fresh order from London. The Governor asked that the rights of the Aborigines be set out "in the clearest and most explicit manner" but the Colonial Office advised against: "Such a broad limitation of the rights originally held out for the acquisition of leases … would be complained of with great force." So the order of 1849 hid its purpose behind talk of the peaceful and effectual occupation of the land. One day, the great humanitarian principle that black and white might share the land would be resurrected by the High Court in the *Wik* judgement, but until then it survived only as a ghost in the fine print of pastoral leases:

> We do further Reserve to the Aboriginal Inhabitants of Our said Colony, such free access to the said Run … and to the trees and waters thereon as will enable them to procure the Animals, Birds, Fish, and other food on which they subsist.

The squatters paid no heed. Nor did colonial governments. Squatters went on clearing the land of blacks for over sixty years. The result was slaughter. The Whigs of Great Britain are rightly honoured for taking on the sugar planters of the West Indies and freeing the slaves of the Empire, but they would not face down the squatters of New South Wales.

*

Pitting native against native is a strategy as old as empire. The Romans, the Spanish, the French and the English all enlisted the conquered to fight on their side. How they came to fight against their own people is a matter of sharp contention, even centuries later. But once under the command of their conquerors they proved ruthless, loyal and cheap in advancing the cause of Empire. In the nineteenth century, the British used sepoys in India and Malays in Ceylon. Governor Bourke, knowing the Cape Mounted Rifles of southern Africa – a force of Hottentots (as they were then called) led by white officers – had given permission to Christian De Villiers, a merchant from the Cape, to set up a corps of mounted Aborigines along those lines to keep down the blacks of Port Phillip. The fortunes of this little private army were mixed. De Villiers was mocked by some as a killer of blacks and praised by others for his efforts to check indiscriminate slaughter in the bush. Either way, the idea of using blacks to fight blacks took hold in New South Wales. *The Sydney Herald* ventured that blacks drilled in military tactics were "from their superior animal sagacity … the most proper to employ in protecting the whites and blacks mutually from each other".

For almost a decade, squatters had been asking that the Port Phillip experiment be extended to the whole Colony. Gipps had refused. But FitzRoy, also familiar with the Cape Mounted Rifles from his time in Africa, asked his Council in mid-1848 for a modest £1000 to fund "the formation of a small corps of Native Police". His request was accepted without fuss. The new force would operate only in the north and have no role collecting revenue. To command the Native Police, FitzRoy chose Frederick Walker. A more complicated figure could hardly be imagined. "A tall, handsome, yellow-haired, blue-eyed Saxon—the beau ideal of a pure Anglo-Saxon", Walker was also a drinker and a big talker who touted himself as a man of peace, a man who loved the blacks and was loved by them in return. Yet he already had blood on his hands. A horseman on a vigilante party in the Riverina remembered:

> At that period the blacks were giving great trouble. They had extensive swamps filled with reeds in which to retreat when pursued by the settlers. A large party was at last organised,

and Mr. Walker showed such aptitude for command upon
one occasion that he was by common consent made leader-
in-chief. By his exertions the blacks were rendered quiet,
and the stations in those parts were no more molested.

Walker effortlessly talked away his past. He was good at spinning his
own story, particularly in the press. He was deft with people of power
and managed for a long time to charm and argue his way out of trouble.
He was called Filibuster Walker. Before it acquired its particular American meaning, the word meant freebooter or adventurer.

William Charles Wentworth had employed Walker as superintendent
of Tala, his 200,000-acre run on the Murrumbidgee. He recommended
the man to FitzRoy as commandant of the new corps. An even warmer
advocate was Augustus Morris, who had also worked at Tala before moving north to the Macintyre River to set himself up as a squatter. In this
new country, resistance by the Kamilaroi and Bigambul was intense.
Morris had been one of those lobbying FitzRoy to set up a force like
De Villiers' troop at Port Phillip and suggested it should be led by "his
old friend in the south country", Frederick Walker. In August 1848, the
young man was sworn in as a Justice of the Peace and Commandant of
the force. He was twenty-eight. The Governor fell in with the suggestion
that the headquarters of his experimental force would be on Callandoon,
Augustus Morris' run near what would become Goondiwindi.

Walker recruited his men in the country around Tala. In time, a
certain mystique attached to the sable warriors of the Murrumbidgee
and Murray, "in form and gait as fine fellows as would be picked up
by a recruiting sergeant in an English county". But Walker recruited
there for two reasons. He had worked with many of the men and spoke
a smattering of their languages. And their country was a long way
from the territory they would patrol in the north. Walker's ground
rule was: "No blacks ought to be made use of as Police in their own
country." They were also, in the jargon of the day, *tame* blacks, not
hunters in the bush. Working for squatters meant they knew the ways

of the whites. Squatters were annoyed to lose them. Luring their workers away caused tension between squatters and the Native Police from
the start. There was talk of banning the practice. Walker claimed he
had the needs of squatters in mind when he took only some of the
many stockmen eager to join the force. To be forbidden to enlist them
altogether, he said, "would have amounted to an Order not to raise a
Native Police Force".

The great blank in the history of the Native Police is the absence
of any account from any recruit over the next fifty years of what was
in his mind when he joined the force. There was never any doubt their
duties would involve killing other Aborigines. At that time, this could
not be seen as collaboration against their own. Many years would pass
before the Aboriginal peoples of Australia came to see themselves as
a nation. Colonial governments in the nineteenth century knew there
were divisions among them they could exploit, just as the British had
done in North America, were doing in South Africa and would soon
do in New Zealand. Walker could count on his Murrumbidgee men
regarding the Aborigines of the north not as brothers and sisters but as
strangers in strange country. What made them strange and dangerous
to each other was being away from their own country, the country that
made them who they were. Here was a deadly conundrum. While officially denying their attachment to land, colonial authorities would rely
on that profound attachment – and the divisions it provoked – to raise
a black force that would strip them of their country.

Men were forced into service with the Native Police in the following decades. They were trapped, kidnapped and threatened at gunpoint.
Black prisoners of the Crown would serve their terms in the force. But
there is no evidence Walker coerced or tricked his men into leaving the
Murrumbidgee behind and saddling up as killers. "Victims don't make
good choices," said Wiradjuri scholar Mina Murray. "They don't have
options. I'm sure there were some who joined of their own free will
sensing a change in the balance of power on the frontier, recognising an
opportunity, circumventing traditional power structures. Others I am

very sure were coerced into it through any number of ways and probably hated themselves their whole lives."

They were young men in a broken world. Walker was promising
them adventure, horses, guns, uniforms, women, a few pence a day and
food. He regretted they were not issued with swords: "It would greatly
add to their good opinion of themselves and also impress the Natives
in the distant districts with greater fear of the force." They got their
sabres. That Aboriginal men could live off the land for weeks at a time
was a great argument for employing them as troopers. But with their
rivers ruined and their hunting grounds overrun with sheep, Walker
was offering to feed them well – to match the rations they were given
by squatters. Troopers would eat a lot: two pounds of meat, one pound
of flour plus a little tea, sugar, salt and tobacco every day. When the
force was out on patrol, local squatters were obliged – and paid – to
feed them. Richard Jones, with his usual generosity, would grumble that
feeding the Native Police "creates a famine on some stations".

In December 1848, Walker led his new troopers up the Darling (the
Barka) on a journey that would take four hard months. He called them
"my rogues" and spoke of belonging to them as much as they belonged
to him. "They have left their own country to follow me, on the faith
of my word alone," he told the Colonial Secretary. "The men are very
anxious to please me." He encouraged the troopers to call him Morubil-
lah, which appears to mean "big legs". It was all rather cloying. But *The
Queensland Times* reported Walker was not all sweet affection:

> Mr. Walker had the rare gift of managing in a complete
> manner the aboriginal population. His slightest nod was a
> command which none ever dreamt of disregarding. There
> is no doubt, however, that he ruled his black boys more
> through love than fear ... but if his confidence was betrayed,
> the constant state of armed peace, which was his normal
> condition in the bush, enabled him to teach his assailants a
> lesson which was learnt at one sitting.

A TROOPER OF THE NATIVE POLICE

He assured his men that service with the Native Police put them a cut above their fellow blacks: "I want you to shew everybody that I *command* a body of *clean, sharp* and *good* policemen not a lot of *dirty, lazy* charcoles." Out of sight they were free to hunt for women: "Keep away from Gins* when you are at a *gunya*.** Do what you like when you are *in the bush*. I will not be angry with you then." They were to cease seeing fighting as mere fun. Now it was duty. They could fight as they wished and kill if attacked: "I must not have any charcoles beat my police ... If the charcoles begin to throw spears or nulla nullas *then* don't you wait but close up knock them down." He urged the troopers to be grateful

---

*   Not at this time an insulting term.

** A hut.

to him, to the Queen – who gave them their rifles and horses – and to FitzRoy: "The Governor has been *very good* to you and *he* will expect *you* to do your duty."

As they rode and walked up the Barka, Walker made sure their progress was attended with applause all the way. To the Colonial Secretary he sent crisp reports of hardships endured and natives – both friendly and hostile – encountered. The troopers began killing about a hundred miles below the town of Bourke. Out looking for their horses one morning, Larry and Geegwaw were confronted by seven Nhaawuparlku men. Spears flew. When a man tried to seize Geegwaw's carbine, Larry picked up a spear and killed him. More blacks appeared. So did Walker. "Luckily myself and several troopers reached the spot in time," he told the Colonial Secretary. "My men firing as they came up killed four more natives." After the encounter, Walker led his men east and when they reached Warialda in late April, he gave to *The Maitland Mercury* the first of many newspaper interviews in his career, boasting of the dangers faced, the privations endured and the blacks dispatched by his men.

> During the last three hundred miles of their journey the horses of the policemen were much distressed and exhausted for want of grass and water, owing to the continued drought, and some of the horses died; and the last two hundred miles the whole party travelled on foot. During seventeen days, also, the party were without rations of any kind, and had to subsist on emus, kangaroos, *native dogs*, and sometimes some fish and ducks.

The paper's correspondent had also clearly fallen under the Commandant's spell:

> The whole party of police seem to be a very orderly and well-behaved set of men, and their commandant, Mr. Walker, appears well qualified for discharging the very intricate and

important trust committed to him. I have no doubt they will soon restore confidence and tranquillity in this part of the country, and ensure the safety of life and property on the McIntyre, where latterly there has been so much loss and danger.

This heroic account of the new force and its splendid Commandant was published in the leading papers of Melbourne, Brisbane and Sydney. *The Sydney Morning Herald* seemed to fall in love with Walker, an amour that lasted years. The Governor was deeply impressed. Walker claimed he was civilising the blacks where missionaries and the Protectors of Aborigines had failed. *The Sydney Morning Herald* lapped it up:

These despised denizens of our woods and forests are not only veritable human beings, but are capable of rendering substantial service to the community, in one of the most important of its public departments. With all their rudeness and barbarity, they are found to possess qualities which eminently fit them for employment as guardians of the lives and properties of their white brethren. Bold, courageous, active, strong, hardy and enduring, obedient, orderly, zealous, and incorruptibly faithful, they have turned out to be capable of discharging the duties of a Mounted Police force in the most efficient and praiseworthy manner.

By June, Walker and his men were at their headquarters on Augustus Morris' run, Callandoon. They began patrolling the Darling Downs. "I found the Condamine country in a very disturbed state," he told the Colonial Secretary. "Several of the stations had been abandoned, twelve white men had been murdered, and the loss in cattle and sheep was immense." FitzRoy scribbled: "This Report of the Commandant of the Native Police is very satisfactory & the Comm't should be informed of the approbation of the Government of the zeal & activity he has displayed in effecting so much with so small a force." Others were less sanguine. William Telfer, the Bard of Wallabadah, heard of a raid carried out at this time by twenty squatters, their shepherds and Walker's men on a camp of three hundred warriors:

> Just at daybreak they made an attack on the sleeping camp
> some of them fled hearing the horses coming. making for
> the scrub but were met by the native police who drew their
> swords cutting and slashing the fugitives a great number
> were slain also a lot shot dead … the old cheif fought on his
> knees using his spear bayonet fashion trying to stab their
> horses until he was shot dead … thus was broken up this
> large tribe nearly one hundred perished under the sword
> and bullet of the white man.

Walker could see that most of the violence in the district was caused by squatters clearing blacks from their runs. He knew there was no empty territory for Aborigines to retreat to. Everywhere was black country. For one people to move onto the lands of another was an unpardonable violation of law. Stay or go, the people who once hunted and fished the squatters' runs faced reprisals. Fighting to stay was the more honourable course. Walker offered FitzRoy a practical plan to address the problem: he would refuse the assistance of the Native Police to squatters who cleared their land:

> As every black has his own hunting ground from which he
> is thus expelled, and he is not allowed to trespass for any
> length of time on that of others he is compelled for his own
> subsistence to kill cattle.
>
> It is my wish that the marauding parties which now
> infest the brigalow should be broken up, which can only be
> done by allowing each native to return to his own ground.

While FitzRoy agreed clearing the runs was much to be regretted and did the squatters who did so no credit, he would not use the Native Police to discourage them doing so – despite London's expectations and the terms of the squatters' leases. FitzRoy noted on Walker's letter: "I cannot authorise assistance being withheld."

The impact of the Native Police was swift along the Macintyre. Walker was delivering what Morris and his fellow squatters had demanded for so long: speedy and brutal punishment. Shepherds became cheaper to recruit on the Darling Downs. Runs fetched higher prices. Newspapers gushed over the "indefatigable exertions" of the Commandant and his men:

> Where but a year since the shepherds dare scarcely leave their huts, and every person went about armed for fear of the blacks, all is now as quiet and settled as in the districts that have been occupied these twenty years, and it is now very uncommon to meet a person armed even when he is travelling from station to station.
>
> Much of the success that has attended the experiment in this district is doubtless to be attributed to the personal character of the commandant, FREDERICK WALKER, Esq.

FitzRoy admired Walker's zeal but ordered him not to display too much enthusiasm in his reports, a problem that came to a head after a Native Police operation against sheep-stealers in the scrubs of 80,000-acre Carbucky, next door to Callandoon. The run was in the hands of one of the brutal men of this narrative: John Larnach, the convict-flogger of Castle Forbes. It was already late in the day when Walker went after the thieves in the Carbucky scrubs.

> My party accordingly rushed in on foot and delivering their fire at twelve paces, at first staggered the insurgent blacks and at last drove them from their cover, my orderly Edgar was speared through the leg, but he immediately drew the spear out and drove it several inches into the body of his adversary. Mr Rens was also wounded by a bomerang in the face.

I now joined the main body of my men but the blacks escaped in the dark.

On visiting the scene of action the next morning we found one black dead and saw that several had been badly wounded, having crawled off on their hands and knees leaving a trail of blood ...

I much regretted not having one hour more of daylight as I would have annihilated that lot.

FitzRoy gently reminded Walker that the force was entrusted to him "for the maintenance of order & Peace & not for the purpose carrying war into an enemy's country". He did not ask about casualties. A hundred are thought to have died at Carbucky, which proved a pivotal engagement: it convinced the squatters of the Macintyre that the Native Police could transform their lives; it brought a bloody kind of peace to that country; and Walker's report was one of the last vivid accounts by an officer of the Native Police at work. There would be no more talk of *annihilation*. Such things in future would be taken for granted.

Walker's difference with the Governor left him wondering once more what his operating instructions were as Commandant of the force. FitzRoy forbade him to conduct war, but how far could he and his troopers go? Riding into camps at dawn with all guns blazing was not police work as it was generally understood. He defended himself to the Governor. "In no case whatever have I acted beyond what I deemed was my duty." He begged His Excellency to set out exactly what course the Native Police should follow when they next found themselves pursuing sheep-stealers in the scrubs. FitzRoy would not be cornered:

> It is impossible at this distance to give particular instructions
> as to the course Mr. Walker is to pursue in the performance
> of his duties ... He must be guided by his own discretion
> and I have no doubt that the zeal and ability which he has
> undoubtedly displayed in the management of the Native

Police will be so tempered by that most essential quality as
to merit no further cautioning on my part.

Walker was flattered but dissatisfied. He continued to ask for written
instruction to protect him and his men as they carried out their bloody
work. He knew that in law he had not even the authority to discipline
his men for disobeying orders. Yet he did. "The fact is," he told the
Colonial Secretary, "the Troopers would not submit to it from anybody
except myself."

So pleased was the Colony with the force that FitzRoy decided to
triple its size. In January 1850, Walker went down to the Murrumbidgee
to recruit another thirty men. Before he left Callandoon, he swore in a
second-in-command. Richard Purvis Marshall was just the sort of man
he wanted leading the troopers: a promising gentleman from a naval
family whose time as a squatter near Callandoon had left him with an
intimate knowledge of the district and an animus against the blacks: "It
was almost impossible to reside there," Marshall said. "They were killing people and driving stock away in all directions." The Commandant
left Marshall unsupervised, to kill for nine months on the Condamine
and Macintyre. FitzRoy's officials were disturbed by what they heard.
Augustus Morris warned his protégé of troubles looming: "'Entre nous'
The sooner you get here the better. Marshall does his best but you and
Marshall are very different persons amongst the men. They have not the
same reliance and affection for him as for you. Still nothing is wrong."

Walker was back at Callandoon in September. "The new recruits
are all in great spirits," he assured the Colonial Secretary. "I have left
hundreds of Ab Natives much vexed that they were not enlisted." He
was distressed to find troopers had died of influenza while he was away.
"Take care of yourselves," he instructed his faithful companions. "Don't
get sick any more for it breaks my heart." He handed the new men over
to be drilled in the use of carbines and sabres, on foot and on horseback. The camp was alive with the din of the Sergeant-Major's orders:
parry, thrust, cut, guard, advance. But the squatters were impatient.

They wanted the new troopers out on patrol, not hanging about at Callandoon. FitzRoy abruptly ordered Walker to move a detachment of
Native Police north but the Commandant did not budge as he tried,
once again, to persuade FitzRoy to give him written terms of engagement. The lack of clarity here he called "one of the greatest difficulties
I have to contend with".

He asked what law allowed him to punish the blacks when he could
not precisely identify those who committed the crimes? He set out a
typical case:

> Sheep are stolen in large numbers and men are constantly
> murdered, no man is identified as one of the murderers or
> thieves. the only evidence which can be obtained is that with
> my men I can generally (almost always) track the aggressive
> party, but this if it implicates anybody would implicate any
> blacks who have joined the party since the offence.

John Plunkett, the hero of Myall Creek, might have forbidden such
reprisal raids altogether. He might have directed the Native Police to
take no action except against individual, identified suspects. He might
have ordered Walker to bring suspects in for trial rather than punishing
them in the bush. But the Attorney-General did none of these things.
He gave Walker only two instructions. First, after every clash in which
Aboriginal natives were killed there was to be an inquiry – essentially
an inquest – and the sober details of the deaths sent to him. He would
not be happy with "a mere statement of resistance by the Blacks". He
wanted to know the details of the acts done by both the blacks and the
troopers. He told the Colonial Secretary: "The duty thus imposed will
probably operate as a sufficient check upon the Corps." It would prove
no check at all. His second instruction was as feeble: "It cannot be too
strongly impressed on Mr Walker and his officers, that they should
only fire in extreme cases, when the necessity of it is clear and obvious."

In the history of the force, no written instructions were ever issued
limiting, with any clarity, the actions the Native Police could take against

Aboriginal Australians. The pioneer historian of the force, Leslie Skinner, wrote: "No measure of law was enacted nor any official policy declared to determine the functions of the force or its duties and obligations." Without anyone saying so, Walker and his successors had been handed the power of life and death.

*

Richard Jones was telling the Governor to hurry the Native Police to Wide Bay and the Burnett. News that they were on their way had seen the blacks settle down, he told FitzRoy in October. "But in consequence of the delay, they now think it is all gammon, and are become more daring in consequence." The town's constable was utterly useless, Jones said. "Nothing but a strong body of Native Police will restore and keep order in the frontier districts."

His attitude to the blacks had hardened. He never believed they could be civilised; never approved revenue being spent on their protection; never saw them as worthy of charity; and never doubted their lands were there for the taking. But he had always deplored vigilante violence. He and the *Gazette* had called for order in the bush to prevent further enraging the blacks. Forbearance where possible, punishment when required was the old formula he and Bishop Broughton espoused. But that was before John Uhr was murdered at Wivenhoe and Jones, as a ruined merchant, came to live in the bush. He wasn't on his Moreton Bay acres for long, but long enough to acquire what had not been there before: a personal grudge against the blacks. "Whenever opportunity presents itself, they are sure to plunder," he told FitzRoy. "And if in their power they will commit murder at the same time. I had a shepherd in charge of a flock murdered about fourteen months ago, and since then I have been plundered several times by the savages; in fact the rapine is general." With the Native Police still stuck fast at Callandoon, he sent the Governor a dossier of complaints from local squatters listing fearful losses of life and property. One ended: "Our curses rest upon the

Government for so neglecting us, and at their door does the guilt of these murders lie."

The first detachment of Native Police under Richard Marshall left for Gayndah and Wide Bay in November. Walker was thrilled by the sight of them riding out: "They average 5 feet 10 inches in height and 11 st 5 lbs in weight. I have not hitherto been able to turn any party out in such a good state of discipline." Marshall's men were soon on John Stephen Ferriter's Toomcul, where a shepherd had been killed and sheep taken. Tracks led the troopers and station hands to a camp which they rushed in the evening. "The blacks dispersed with an awful howling into the scrub, pursued by police," reported Ferriter's Superintendent. He saw two dead. Next day, Marshall's men returned to destroy their nets, hooks and fish traps – a brutal punishment. Eight hundred sheep were recovered. Days later, the troopers on the nearby Kilkivan run were shooting blacks accused of nothing more than gathering in large numbers. Riding with Marshall's men that day was John Murray, a local squatter who was soon to lose his run and join the Native Police. Murray gave *The Sydney Morning Herald* a heroic account of the battle on Kilkivan:

> The blacks immediately attacked the police, and stood for a considerable time, when a running fight for upwards of an hour took place, the blacks disputing every inch of the ground obstinately, the police behaving with the most determined gallantry. Trooper Boney was wounded in the shoulder with a spear, and cut on the hand in two places with a nulla nulla; however, his enemy did not escape him. This man's bravery and coolness would have done credit to a soldier of any nation. The blacks suffered severely.

By this time, a second division of twelve troopers was moving north under the freshly recruited George Fulford of Rayleigh. Walker had not looked far to find him: Fulford was yet another Macintyre squatter who came to the force with a furious thirst and a grudge against the blacks

for spearing nearly a thousand of his cattle. His drinking grew worse
in the service: "He was addicted to habits of intemperance, and in the
habit of remaining on the spree, as it is commonly called, at squatters'
stations." Fulford joined Marshall in the hinterland of Wide Bay.

Walker was the last to move north in December. He had invented
his own rules of engagement, or so he later boasted. "This Force never
acted unless I knew that a felony had been committed, and I had reasonable grounds of suspecting the offenders, warrants had been issued,
or affidavits, clearly pointing out the offenders, sworn to." This was non-
sense. From the first, mere suspicion was enough for Frederick Walker
to send his troopers into the bush. Warrants were useful cover when
blacks died at the hands of the force – escaped while resisting arrest,
etc. – but a squatter's complaint was enough reason to kill. Being an
Aborigine in the vicinity of a crime was a death sentence. But there was
one demand of the squatters Walker baulked at – dispersing gatherings
of perfectly peaceful blacks. This infuriated Jones and became, almost
at once, a point of intense dispute between the Native Police, the squatters and the government.

Early in the new year of 1851, Walker's detachments were proving
their worth fighting in the scrubs of Moreton Bay. Calls were made many
times in the history of the Native Police for black troopers to be replaced
by whites, men supposedly more disciplined, more restrained, less savage and hardly more expensive. Governments ignored these pleas for
three reasons: black troopers could not give evidence of what happened
in the bush; their supposed savagery gave cover to government for the
fundamental savagery of the force; and only black troopers, it was said,
could pursue their prey into the scrubs. That they went naked about
that work proved endlessly fascinating to newspaper readers in Australia and abroad. The *Manchester Evening News* reported in the 1870s:

> It was very curious to see how eagerly on some occasions,
> when the poor hunted savages had taken refuge in a thick
> scrub, the black troopers would strip off their uniforms,

and, carrying only their carbines and ammunition, enter with gleaming eyes upon the work of extermination. Meantime, the white officer waits outside, and listens approvingly to the dropping shots which tell of the work being done within the close-clinging tangle of tropical vegetation.

That paper edged up to the truth. Aborigines who could hunt in dense forest certainly made effective troopers, but the real reason for leaving them to enter the bush alone was to license slaughter. Sitting on his horse outside, an officer saw nothing and heard only the patter of gunfire.

One Sunday in February, Maryborough was thrown into a state of excitement by the sight of the whole Native Police force arriving in town. Forty-seven troopers and their three officers had joined up in the bush to make this entrance. The troopers looked "very natty", thought Edmund B. Uhr. He was most impressed. "The men were well disciplined, and there was every energy used to suppress the aggressions of the blacks." With the arrival of the Native Police, the town's magistrates could at last execute their plan to clear K'gari (Fraser Island) of its criminal blacks. The island was a place of dread for settlers – a stronghold, they thought, for vicious blacks who hid in its immense scrubs, re-emerging at will to commit fresh crimes. Uhr and his fellow magistrate the Commissioner of Crown Lands, John Bidwill, were convinced that until these blacks were dealt with, "the lives and property of the inhabitants of Wide Bay District will not be safe". Frederick Walker took little persuading. A few days after riding into town, he, Murray and Fulford – all justices of the peace – joined Bidwill and Uhr on the Maryborough bench to issue warrants against thirty-five men believed to be hiding on the island who were wanted for felonies and murder:

"Neddy" "Jacky Jacky" "Iowrning", "Nosy", "Boomer", "Mr Bunce", "Ineway", "Grassoom", "Bobby", "Iangera", "Ben Bullen", "Jimmy", "Pepo", "Coola" "Coola", "Wananinga", "Perika"

"Charlie", "Bungalee", "Tom", "Old Athlone", "Old Diamond", "Peter", "Puckemall", "Toby", "Tiear", "Boney", "Paddy", "Tommy", "Doughboy", "Lawley", Big Diamond, "Peter with one eye", "Athlone", "Woolge" and Diamond.

Walker sent the warrants to Sydney with two questions: would a raid on this scale be legal and where could he find a boat? His troopers could not row: "The Native Police have never yet seen the sea." He asked for a swift answer for he saw the future of Wide Bay in the balance. "A large number of naturally well disposed blacks have abandoned the murderers and are shewing a wish to live peaceably with the whites. I am therefore very anxious that the Natives on Frazers Island should learn that they cannot place the law at defiance by retreating to that place." Months passed with no answer from Sydney.

14

TO THE ISLAND

Jones was swept back into politics in 1849 when London began once again shipping convicts to New South Wales. He was sixty-three. The appearance of the first prison ships galvanised the Colony. Anti-transportation meetings from Brisbane to Hobart talked rebellion. Fearing the worst, Jones wrote to *The Sydney Morning Herald*:

> It is fresh in the recollection of most now living, that by the misrule of the English government, the present United States of America withdrew their allegiance from the parent state; and it does not require the spirit of prophecy to foretell that, from the course she is pursuing towards this country, similar results will follow; but I hope unattended with the direful consequences of the American revolution.

A few days after the first convicts landed in Brisbane after nearly ten years, Jones led a protest meeting on the verandah of the Immigration Office:

> He was totally opposed to their being received on any terms. (Applause.) He had been forty years in this colony, and his experience led him to the conclusion that convict labour had been the bane of the country. (Applause) ... They were told, at last, that transportation to this colony should cease, and on the faith of that promise hundreds of respectable families had come to the colony. (Hear, hear.) On a sudden

the system was resumed, at a time when the colony ... had arrived at an eminence, morally, physically, and politically, which rendered convict labour unnecessary and injurious—(Applause.) Yet people were longing for it again, but we would not have it here.

That Richard Jones had returned from the political dead to fight transportation was regarded as a curious and significant event. Once again, he was chairing meetings and writing letters to newspapers, arguing – with figures to back his case – that the prosperity of New South Wales had never depended on convicts. After a year of this, he announced in late 1850 that he would stand at a by-election for the seat of Northern Counties in the Legislative Council.

For the first time in his life, Jones found himself on the hustings. "Old Dickey Jones" was attacked as a squatter turncoat, a bigot, a former bankrupt, a notorious employer of Chinese shepherds and a man of "numerous inconsistencies which have marked his public career". He returned fire, attacking the "squatting lords" as liars for telling London that all they needed to extend their flocks and herds beyond the power of counting was the return of prison labour. He thought otherwise. "My impression is, the present race of squatters have as much land and stock as they can well manage." He called them purse-proud and accused them of wanting convicts simply so they could pay as little as possible for labour. "He was a squatter himself, and he felt justified in making that statement."

His old antagonism to the Irish boiled over. After wasting a fortune on the famine, Lord Grey was now spending £60,000 to ship Irish pauper girls to Australia. "Glaring and improper as has been this vast expenditure for such useless wares." At times on the hustings, Jones rambled on about the fine prospects for cotton and once or twice he veered off track to condemn the neglect of Christians in the bush:

The sound of the Gospel is seldom heard in their tents, and the performance of a religious rite almost a stranger in their land. Contrast this spiritual destitution with imperial Sydney, her viceregal palace, her many towering and costly churches, her courts of justice, and other paraphernalia of greatness, one stands in amazement to contemplate that the people contributing largely, as they do, to the General Revenue, should be so much neglected.

Though he had little to say during the campaign about the depredations of the blacks, it was in these weeks that he began forwarding complaints from the northern settlers to FitzRoy. That he did not canvass the issue was curious but not unusual. The native question seems rarely to have been mentioned during election campaigns in these years. Perhaps neither ferocity nor charity swayed voters. Only once his election was confirmed in November did Jones take the extraordinary step of publishing his private correspondence with FitzRoy in newspapers. The letters included His Excellency's sharp rebuke for sending him the "coarse and underserved reflections" of the settlers. The Governor was particularly irked by thoughts of curses raining down on his head. Jones didn't care. He had faced down tougher governors than FitzRoy. *The Sydney Morning Herald* backed him and the settlers who, it declared, had endured long and unmerited suffering at the hands of the native blacks: "They would not be men if they did not feel; they would not be Englishmen if they did not complain, and complain pretty roughly too."

Though transportation brought Jones back into politics, his chief cause once elected was seeing the Native Police freed from all restraint. "Being under the impression that they were fettered by particular restrictions, they had shrunk from acting." Now Jones was on the side of ferocity. He saw immigration and protection as intimately connected. Both were required to deliver labour to the bush. You might land a shipload of yeoman labourers on the wharf at Brisbane, but they were not going to go to the Burnett – or not for a reasonable wage – unless the Native Police could keep them safe.

In April 1851, Jones took the steamer to Sydney to be sworn in. He was back in the Council, where he felt he belonged, but his old influence was gone. When bankruptcy forced him out, he was one of fourteen members. Now he was one of thirty-six. He could still not be heard when he spoke. "Mostly inaudible," declared *The Empire*. "Totally inaudible," complained *The Maitland Mercury*. There was little business for the Council to deal with but the separation of the Port Phillip district into the new Colony of Victoria. That triggered new elections in New South Wales, with new electorates under a new franchise that gave every adult male the vote. FitzRoy would become Governor-General. After sitting for only a dozen days, Jones returned to Brisbane to begin campaigning all over again, this time for the seat of Stanley Boroughs, which covered the towns of Ipswich and Brisbane. Transportation was again at the centre of contention, with squatters demonised everywhere for polluting a pure young nation – not by slaughtering the original inhabitants of the land, but by importing British prisoners to mind their sheep.

Jones was never more a master of the volte-face. Though his hold on Baramba's 164,000 acres had just been officially confirmed, he backed the growing political movement to have the huge runs of the squatters broken up. He was not backing small settlers trying to find a patch of land. He had an eye for lost revenue:

> The lands thus unholily alienated belong to the Colonial Crown; or, in other words, are held in trust for the people. I hope to live to see the day when an essential change will take place in the government of this country: then will this oligarchy be broken up, and what remains unsold of these vast tracts of country be surrendered to the rightful proprietors, and administered solely for the public benefit.

He did not mean the blacks. He ridiculed the magistrates who had petitioned London to send out more convicts:

Why, magistrates here were as thick as bees. Any boy in
the bush might be a magistrate. In England none but men
of the highest standing and experience were invested with
the commission of the peace; but here J.P.s were as thick
as sheepfolds. It was only necessary to ask the Governor
to make brother Tom or cousin Jack a magistrate, and the
thing was done.

He would know. His backers dubbed him "the poor man's friend" and
urged the electors of Stanley Boroughs to unite under the banner: "NO
CONVICTS, AND RICHARD JONES FOR EVER."

The second campaign was tougher than the first. Placards denouncing Jones as an anti-Catholic bigot appeared in the streets of Ipswich
and Brisbane. When William Duncan – Catholic, Inspector of Customs and friend of the York's Hollow blacks – rose to challenge Jones
at a meeting in Ipswich, the candidate replied rather sharply that he
should go back to his office. So, under the pen name "Cato", Duncan
wrote to the press about Jones' long history of bigotry and contempt
for Irish immigrants:

> It can scarcely be wondered at, therefore, if our fellow Elec-
> tors from the sister isle should, on such an occasion as this,
> remind him of his connection with a movement so outrag-
> eous to their feelings and the feelings of their wives and sisters.

Cato's letter was nearly Jones' political obituary. It appeared the day
before the poll at which he scraped back home by three votes.

Jones' first task was to destroy Duncan. He demanded the Collector
of Customs in Sydney sack the man for publishing this "mass of scandalous charges". But the time was past when Jones could demand such
things. He kept nagging the Collector of Customs. None of it worked.
Duncan became the Collector of Customs for New South Wales, a post
he held for many decades, and retired with honours as a Commander
of the Order of St Michael and St George.

Jones became in the Assembly the conduit for squatter fury at the failings of the Native Police. The bunya season had come around again and the Commandant was refusing to disperse gatherings of peaceful blacks feasting in the mountains. Squatters petitioned the government to end absurd restrictions which they saw making the Native Police a laughing-stock of cunning savages. "Great services were anticipated from the doings of this Corps upon its arrival in the frontier districts, and the result has proved thus far to have been severe disappointment," Jones told the Governor. He acknowledged the high character and discipline of the force, "[b]ut it is said to be trammelled with such restrictive orders from the Executive, as to render its services useless for the purposes intended, and the sooner we are rid of them and left to manage the Savages ourselves the better". FitzRoy again sharply reproached him: "He is entirely in error in supposing that the movements of the Comm'r of the Native Police are tramelled by the restrictive orders from the Executive." Frederick Walker defended his record in the press. FitzRoy promised: "As long as he continues to perform the arduous and responsible duties entrusted to him with the same zeal & efficiency, as have hitherto been displayed by him, he will continue to receive the support of the government."

Jones demanded again and again that the Native Police raid K'gari, which he knew as the Great Sandy Island. He warned the Council in November 1851 of the peculiar dangers that needed to be addressed there:

> The aborigines of the north were a most numerous and powerful body, who required to be vigorously guarded against. They came in canoes and in large bodies from a place called the Big Sandy Island, whence they came in canoes across a sheet of water as smooth as Port Jackson. This island ought to be visited and examined.

Days later he was complaining of a fearful increase in murders by the blacks of Wide Bay, a claim dismissed curtly by the Colonial Secretary, who accused new settlers in the northern districts of thinking the duty of the force was "to keep up a constant aggressive warfare against the blacks;—a state of things which no Christian Government could sanction".

FitzRoy's government was not to blame for delaying the invasion of K'gari. Plunkett had approved the raid. His argument was plain: if lawless whites were hiding on the island, police could be sent to round them up. Why not lawless blacks? That blood would be shed did not deter him. "It must, unhappily, be expected that the proposed attempt at arrest may lead to a warlike conflict and perhaps to loss of life, but the aim of the law must not be paralysed by the expectation of such results." All the Attorney-General did when giving Walker's plan his imprimatur in April was make a feeble plea for restraint:

> Notions of humanity ought to suggest that in executing these laws against these unfortunate beings, a more than ordinary anxiety should be manifested to act with the utmost amount of forbearance consistent with the supply of the Police and the effectiveness of their operations.

One condition he made perfectly clear: the black troopers were at all times on the island "to be entirely under the well regulated control of their officers".

Finally in December 1851, after months dispersing blacks on the Burnett, Walker reappeared in Maryborough with two dozen men ready to launch the most ambitious operation in the brief history of the Native Police. One of the most relentless critics of the force, William Henry Walsh – Superintendent of the mighty Degilbo run on the lower Burnett – watched the chaos Walker brought to Maryborough:

> The town was full of blacks; a vessel lay at the boiling place, and which had been piloted up from the bay as usual by the natives. Three was the number, and these three Mr. Walker resolved to catch. The vessel was accordingly surrounded by the police, and two out of the three poor creatures caught;

and, Sir, if ever under the disguise of law, an atrocious act was done, this is it. Without rhyme or reason, these men were dragged to the lock-up, and there, upon an order of Mr. Walker's, confined "to the 27th of the month"—rather more than a week.

Walsh rated utterly futile Walker's attempt to keep news of the coming raid from reaching the island. "The troopers were night and day mixing with all the other blacks." But that was only the start of the chaos. "Their freaks did not stop here."

Plunkett had given the raid his blessing as an operation to execute warrants against thirty-five blacks accused of murder and felony. But it became clear in the days before the expedition set out that Walker had no intention of bringing a mob of prisoners back from the island. The little schooner he chartered for the expedition, the *Margaret & Mary*, could scarcely carry a dozen troopers let alone return from the expedition with thirty-five felons in chains. Whatever the original impulse, massacre had become the purpose of the expedition. As a cover to take his men out there, Walker needed to be seen to be executing a few warrants. The list of thirty-five known felons no longer mattered. All Walker was after on the island were Durrugguree and Perriha, the men accused of flinging that axe at George Furber four years earlier. Like the death of John Uhr, the scalping of Furber continued for years to be a useful excuse for killing blacks.

Furber was obviously the man best able to identify the suspects, but he refused to abandon his mail run to Gayndah for a fortnight. Walker then approached the Superintendent of Uhr's boiling-down, Duncan Cameron, who was said to know more blacks than anyone in Maryborough. Uhr forbade him to leave his post. Early in the evening the expedition was set to sail, there was an ugly confrontation between the two justices of the peace in Cameron's hut. Walker tried to compel Cameron to join the expedition, "but Mr Uhr by his violent conduct prevented us from taking his deposition". Uhr could not stand to have his authority questioned even in the smallest way. "I informed Mr Walker that Mr Cameron was my superintendent, that I could not let him go with him as the station he was at was in a very unprotected state & that he had property under his care to the amount of some Three thousand pounds."* Walker wrote: "Mr Duncan Cameron was ready to go with us; but E. B. Uhr Esqre JP ... not only refused to allow him to go, but made use of threatening language to him if he did."

The boats were at Uhr's wharf waiting to catch the tide. "Great preparations were made for the jaunt," wrote "Vox" in *The Sydney Morning Herald.* "Squatters and storekeepers swelled the party—moist and dry provisions were abundantly laid in." The plan hatched on the Maryborough bench a year earlier had been abandoned; but Walker told the Governor: "Having engaged the Margaret and Mary schooner I considered it would be wrong if I did not go to the Island and see if I could not do something to put a stop to the felonies of the Fraser's Island Blacks."

*

K'gari is the largest sand island in the world, a great dune sitting in the mouth of the Mary River. According to Butchulla legend, K'gari was a spirit who thought the earth too beautiful to leave so she was changed into this island. Along the ocean flank is a beach 70 miles long. The landward shore is lined with swamps and forests. Oyster middens here are thousands of years old. Lakes of freshwater perch in the high dunes and clear streams flow over beaches into the sea. Forests grow in pure sand. The scrubs of K'gari were endless. The Butchulla gathered in large numbers on the island in winter, feasting on crabs, turtles, mullet and dugong. In summer, most Butchulla moved back to the mainland. Even so, some thousand stayed on through the hot, wet summer months, hunting kangaroo, snake and possum. Men and women carried initiation scars across their chests and painted their bodies with ochre.

---

* Three hundred pounds was the value he put on the plant months earlier when begging FitzRoy for compensation.

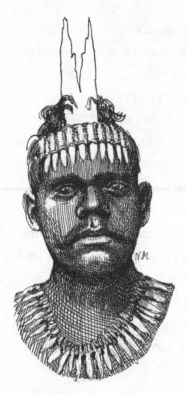

A BUTCHULLA MAN

The men plucked their beards and stuck feathers in their hair. They were renowned fighters and musicians.

Walker had taken aboard the *Margaret & Mary*: Sergeant Major Dolan, twenty troopers and a horse. Captain Charles Currie and his crew had been sworn in as Special Constables for the expedition. In convoy with the schooner as it slipped away from the wharf late on Christmas Eve were two boats provided by the Leith Hay brothers, also sworn in as Special Constables. The Leith Hays were military Scots. Their father was a general and their uncle an admiral. Home was Leith Hall in Aberdeenshire. Their passion was the track. One brother, James, was a magistrate. They were busy accumulating a quarter of a million acres in the hinterland of Wide Bay. The troopers in their boats were commanded by Lieutenant Richard Marshall. Somehow the brothers' faith in the Native Police as a force "essential to the protection of life and property" survived the next ten days. "The Native Police are of the greatest service," James and Norman Leith Hay told *The Sydney Morning Herald*. "The officers of the corps never shrink from doing their duty."

After crossing the Great Sandy Strait, the main party disembarked at their rendezvous point on the swampy inner shore of the island. The flotilla sailed south under Marshall's command, with orders to scour the coast there and return in three days' time. Walker's men began by ransacking a nearby camp. Butchulla attempting to escape were stopped by Marshall's boats. Their dinghy was one of the few prizes to end up back in Maryborough. When a second, larger boat broke from the shore, "The Police fired into it and several balls struck," reported Walker. "Two troopers jumped into the sea to try and capture it but it had got too far. They of course lost all their cartridges." That boat was never seen again. It rained heavily that night. "The Blacks made frequent attempts to surprise the Native Police Camp but without effect." At least two were killed in the process. Walker now regretted splitting the party and sent James Leith Hay and six troopers to call the flotilla back. "But it was too late." Little went right after that.

> I started with the remaining troopers in pursuit of the blacks who had annoyed us during the night; when we came up with them, they being on the top of the range, escaped. We found a large fresh water Lagoon on the table land. The rain was heavy all this day as well as the night previous. The scrubs were so dense that with difficulty the Police forced their way – worn out with fatigue we returned to the rendezvous having walked and waded at least 25 miles.

The flotilla reappeared. What Marshall's party had done down the coast remains a mystery. Walker carefully reported nothing to the Governor: "It is needless for me to say more than that he acted with his usual energy and discretion." Marshall had brought several prisoners back with him. Two were thought to be Furber's assailants, Durrugguree and Perriha, but no one could put a name to the others, so they were set free.

K'GARI – FRASER ISLAND

At this point, they might all have sailed for Maryborough. Their discomfort was acute. Walker told the Governor: "It is difficult to explain to you the hardships from rain at one time excessive heat at another and from miriads of mosquitoes and sand flies which the whole of the party have suffered." Despite this, they stayed on. From this point, Walker's already scrappy report became risible. He told FitzRoy: "The Native Serjeants Edgar and Willy asked me to allow them to pursue the hostile blacks. I considered it necessary." He sent twenty-four troopers into the scrubs for three days all on their own. "I was too footsore to accompany the men." This was a direct breach of Plunkett's order that the troopers were never to operate unsupervised on the island. Walker's excuse was far from convincing. The historian of the early force, Leslie Skinner, wrote: "He was a good bushman to whom danger, fatigue, discomfort, privation, and even monotony were inseparable from the callings he pursued." The truth is simple and grim: the Commandant was allowing on a vast scale what officers of the force were used to doing by this time: sitting outside scrubs as their troopers killed out of sight. He wrote of his men: "They followed them from the 31st Dec to 2nd January inclusive never getting up to them until they reached the East side of the Island, where the blacks took to the Sea." He reported nothing more.

According to rumour then and traditional owners now, there was a massacre on the beach at this time, probably at Takky Wooroo (Indian Head). "A lot of our people were killed there," a traditional owner told a 2017 investigation into the heritage significance of the site. Another said:

"All's I know is about the massacre and I know that it was true; it's true! It is! It's true; it was handed down." Walker and his men were so tight-lipped after the raid that suspicions were immediately aroused that something terrible had happened out there. "So much secrecy really makes the whole matter look bad," Vox told *The Sydney Morning Herald*. The people of K'gari were known to be kind to shipwrecked mariners, but a few months after the raid they treated the survivors of the wreck of the *Thomas King* with unusual barbarity. William Henry Walsh put it down to a fresh spirit of revenge among the Butchulla.

> Frequent allusions have been made to the extraordinary secrecy of the result of that jaunt, and much surprise expressed at the profound silence maintained concerning their exploits, by this most heterogeneous body of black hunters. True, now and then we receive little bits of information from Sydney, (of all places in the world), that rumours are afloat that the natives were driven into the sea, and there kept as long as daylight or life lasted.

While the troopers were still at their work on the far side of the island, Walker and James Leith Hay sat at the rendezvous point writing letters. One denounced Edmund B. Uhr. They let FitzRoy know they wanted nothing more to do with the man: "In future we cannot act in concert with Mr Uhr as a magistrate." Uhr had, of course, already written his own complaint to the Governor. "I have had the honor of being a Magistrate for many years & owing to the unfortunate illness of our Commissioner of Crown Lands Mr. Bidwill, whose duty I am now doing in his absence, the whole of the arduous Police duties of this place have devolved upon me." FitzRoy backed neither side. Could they not calm down and think of their clash as the product of excessive zeal? They could not. For the next four years Walker mocked Uhr's repeated pleas for police protection in Maryborough. God knows how many lives that saved.

When the troopers stumbled out of the scrubs, they were in wretched shape. "One half of the Police are lame," reported Walker. They brought nothing and no one with them. Next day, the *Margaret & Mary* sailed for Maryborough with a parcel of books found in one of the camps, the dinghy and two prisoners. Given the public justification for the raid, this haul was evidence of ludicrous failure. Walker and his men could not boast of what had happened at Indian Head. Despite the obvious gaps in Walker's report and his open breach of Plunkett's orders, the Governor and the Attorney-General accepted that everything on the raid was above board. FitzRoy scrawled on Walker's report: "The Commandants movements appear to have been conducted with much judgement & Lt Marshall & the Gentlemen who accompanied the Police are entitled to the thanks of the Government." At Walker's suggestion, Captain Currie of the *Margaret & Mary* was given a reward of ten pounds.

Durrugguree and Perriha were swiftly acquitted. As disobliging as ever, George Furber refused to go to Sydney for their trial. He sent, in his place, a deposition the judge found "very insufficient" and "extremely vague". When he directed the acquittal of the prisoners, voices were raised in alarm. Squatters seized on the outcome in Sydney as fresh proof that judges were on the side of the blacks. The squatters *knew* who assaulted George Furber. They *knew* who killed John Uhr. They *knew* who was guilty of murdering their shepherds and stealing their sheep. But the courts asked for proof. What was the point of tracking down malefactors, taking them to a lock-up, turning up at a trial to give evidence against them only to have a judge acquit them for want of witnesses to their crimes? Justice was surely more efficiently delivered in the bush with a gun.

15

RETRIBUTION ALONE

A speech of three hours was no long haul for William Charles Wentworth. On 25 August 1852 he spent those hours in the Council proposing serious mischief: an ultimatum to London that if self-government was not granted within a year, the Council would block FitzRoy's next budget. The Governor would be left without funds to govern. Despite their many differences, Richard Jones agreed with the point he was making. For decades he had argued, as Wentworth was arguing that day, that New South Wales alone should decide how the Colony's revenue was spent. A dramatic debate followed Wentworth's vast oration. Jones was silent but his vote that evening gave the radicals their victory of one.

After the Council adjourned at 8.30 p.m., Jones was walking back to his room at Petty's Hotel when he was felled in the street by a stroke. A passing colonel helped him home. A doctor was called. So was William Uhr, who sat with Jones for weeks until he was strong enough to take the steamer home. William, still unmarried, was leading two lives: working for his brother George as a clerk in the sheriff's office and composing songs for the musical theatre. "Bandbox" Uhr was only months away from his one great success: "You Love Me Not", an unhappy ballad sung to rapturous applause at the Royal Victoria Theatre in Sydney and recommended by *The Sydney Morning Herald* for "every lady's drawing-room". In late September, the two men took the *Eagle*. Off New Farm, the steamer hove to so Jones could be rowed ashore. He recovered a little but was seized by a fainting fit on 6 November, and "becoming aware that his end was approaching, took an affectionate farewell of the members of his family present, and expired, apparently without pain, between ten and eleven o'clock A.M". The funeral followed next day.

> The remains of the deceased were brought up by water to the ferry wharf at North Brisbane, where nearly the whole of the inhabitants of Brisbane, of any note, were waiting to pay the last tribute of respect to their departed fellow colonist. Here the procession was formed, Messrs. Thomas Jones and J.S. Ferriter, and Messrs. Daniel Peterson and William Uhr, following immediately after the coffin, as chief mourners. The other gentlemen who were in mourning, consisting of persons of all classes of Religious and Political opinions, followed. Others joined the procession from time to time, and many ladies and children, belonging to the families of the townspeople, accompanied the body to the burial ground. Between three hundred and four hundred persons were present at the interment ... and the body was consigned to the grave in the presence of a sorrowful and attentive assemblage.

Jones' obituaries left unsaid nearly everything that mattered. They noted the distinguished marriages of his daughters and celebrated his role in the anti-transportation movement. But men like him were already being farewelled as "Old Colonials", code for having lived through dark days that need not be remembered in any detail. Not noted were his great appetite for land, his humiliating bankruptcy, his growing enthusiasm for punishing the Aboriginal people and his failure, in all his years on the Council, to advance a single provision for their benefit. In fairness to his memory, it must be noted that while supplying goods to the Germans at Zion Hill in 1838, he donated one pound to their missionary efforts. His daughter Elizabeth thought it best not to dwell on "the things that are behind" as she recalled how he "sought to serve God in his generation, & was an influence for good throughout the land". His reward would come, she believed, in the "Day when God shall judge the world in righteousness".

Edmund was not among the mourners. Nor was he remembered in the will. He could have done with a hand. His store and boiling-down were struggling. The store sold "every description of merchandise suitable for the interior": flour, sugar and tea, strong boots, rum and castrating knives. But he had no instinct for trade. By charging a little too much he lost a useful contract to supply the needs of all the officials in the district. He quarrelled with a local publican over selling brandy and rum, a squabble that fuelled another rancorous correspondence with Sydney until the government gave up and took no action against either man. Uhr sold the store to his managers, who made a fortune. His grandson summed up Uhr's life in business: "Various schemes tried, always money lost."

He wanted a government post. Four months after Jones' death, John Bidwill died of privations endured while lost for days in the scrub. Australia's great botanist could not, it turned out, live off the land. Uhr wasted no time. Next day he wrote to the Colonial Secretary asking to be appointed Commissioner of Crown Lands in Bidwill's place.

> He has left me as one of his Executors and also desired that I would take charge of his Government duty, which I intend doing till I hear from you ... as I have a large family depend-ant on my exertions I should be very grateful if you will recommend me to His Excellency the Governor General for the situation now vacant ... I beg leave to mention that I was a Squatter for many years on the Darling Downs & Brisbane River districts, in partnership with my Brother-in-law the late Mr. R. Jones.

FitzRoy turned him down flat. Haggling over his land in town, quarrelling with townsfolk, constantly demanding protection from the blacks and his bizarre behaviour at the time of the Fraser Island raid did not recommend Uhr of the boiling-down for such a post. On hearing the news, Uhr asked instead to be appointed the town's salaried Police Magistrate.

> I have accomplished all the duty of this office here for the last three years, & mostly unassisted by any other magistrate, at times it has been arduous & not unattended with inconvenience to myself, but I felt it a duty imperative on me being the only resident magistrate in this locality.

He dropped other names. He found eighteen citizens to sign a petition on his behalf. But FitzRoy once again rebuffed him. Next he asked to be paid Bidwill's salary for the months he held the fort until the arrival of the new Commissioner, a dull public servant called Arthur Halloran. Uhr wanted £350. His begging letters followed one after another to Sydney for nearly sixteen months. He was becoming pathetic. Drawn into this tedious correspondence were the Governor, the Colonial Secretary, the Auditor-General and the Chief Commissioner of Crown Lands. But as no one could identify the work Uhr had actually performed as self-appointed acting Commissioner, he was offered only his expenses. By this time, Uhr was abasing himself for a pittance. He requested £50 and was given £20.

Edmund B. Uhr was most himself on the magistrates' bench. Nothing kept him from his duties. Little had been done since Bourke's time to curb the power of magistrates like him. In Sydney and Brisbane lawyers kept an eye on these amateur JPs, but out in the bush they exercised their jurisdiction unsupervised. "In no part of His Majesty's Dominions are the duties that belong to the Magistracy, more arduous and complicated, than they are in this Colony," Plunkett wrote in *The Australian Magistrate; or, A Guide to the Duties of a Justice of the Peace for the Colony of New South Wales*. "Upon their proper discharge, depends very much the well being of its anomalous community." Plunkett's lucid manual defined murder as a crime blind to the race of its perpetrators and its victims.

Murder is the killing [of] any person under the King's peace, with *malice* prepense* or afterthought ... *Express malice* is when one person kills another with a sedate, deliberate mind, and formed design ... Malice is *implied* by law in several cases ... Poisoning implies malice.

In Plunkett's book, vigilantes were murderers:

Whenever a person in cool blood, by way of revenge, beats another in such a manner that he afterwards dies thereof, he is guilty of Murder ... [W]here the defence rests upon some violent provocation, it will not avail, however grievous such provocation may have been, if it appears that there was *an interval of reflection*, or a reasonable time *for the blood to have cooled*, before the deadly purpose was effected.

Plunkett made this clear:

As to the word "the King's peace," in the definition of murder, they mean merely that it is not murder to kill an alien enemy in time of war ... The Aboriginal Natives of the Colony are within "the King's peace," and the unlawful killing of them is as much murder, as the killing of any other of the King's subjects.

So how was murder to be punished? If gentlemen of the bench heard of vigilante slaughters, they might bring any witnesses before them for interrogation. That was almost unknown. Plunkett imagined a world where witnesses to slaughter would volunteer their evidence to magistrates bound by law "to probe well" those allegations. But that required white men and women brave enough to face down the squatters and break the silence of the bush. Across the colonies, decade after decade, witnesses to massacres almost never came forward. Why would they risk everything going to a magistrate more than likely too gutless

* Premeditated.

to take action? The Myall Creek prosecution was remarkable from the first, for the white man who saw those bodies burning on the pyre rode down to a good magistrate in the Hunter Valley, who set the machinery of the law in action before anyone in Sydney heard of the slaughter. But after Myall Creek a curious but brutally effective omertà was imposed in the bush, a code that let so much be written in the papers about massacres but saw nothing done about them in the courts.

Uhr is not known to have taken any initiative to investigate the killing of blacks. On the other hand, he showed a good deal of ingenuity enforcing an unwritten rule of the bush that no black ever accused of a serious crime should escape punishment. One day Uhr noticed a gold ring on the finger of the notorious Make-i'-light or Mickaloe as they passed in the street. "Having heard of the loss of a ring when the shipwrecked seamen of the *Thomas King* were murdered, Uhr suspected this might be the same." He bought the ring for a fig of tobacco and then arrested the man. Nothing whatever linked the ring to the shipwreck.

That was not the point. By this time, Make-i'-light was known for escaping two murder charges. Five years after the killing of the squatter Andrew Gregor and his pregnant housekeeper, he was charged with participating in their murder. The committal proceedings in Brisbane were held before John Stephen Ferriter and William Duncan, the Customs man and friend to the blacks of York's Hollow. The case was collapsing when, from nowhere, an ex-convict appeared claiming to have witnessed Make-i'-light murder a sawyer on the Pine River. For that crime only, the prisoner was committed for trial and eventually convicted by a jury.

The judge was Roger Therry who, troubled by the verdict, persuaded the Governor to quash the conviction. Make-i'-light's release provoked fury from squatters and jubilation among the Aborigines of Brisbane. *The Moreton Bay Courier* reported: "Drunken orgies were held in the evening, at which threats and defiance towards the whites were very freely circulated."

When Edmund B. Uhr pounced on the man, a Mrs Cash of Pine River came forward to say the ring was hers, stolen from her house by a party of blacks. But she couldn't swear that Make-i'-light was among the thieves. After a year in prison and a failed attempt to implicate him in the death of a shepherd, Make-i'-light was once again set free and, again, the papers despaired of the pernickety rules of British justice. According to *The Moreton Bay Courier*, a notorious thief and murderer had now been "once more turned loose upon society, to continue his career of crime and blood".

The blacks had not forgotten Furber. Early one morning he left Uhr's wharf with a team of men to gather timber. They worked out of sight of one another. When Furber and his son-in-law failed to appear for lunch, a search party found them dead. "Mr. Furber seems first to have got a fearful tomahawk cut on the head, but seems to have fought most desperately, even after he received the murdering blow, for his hands were severely cut, and his shirt torn to ribbons," reported *The Moreton Bay Courier*. "The finishing blow was another tomahawk cut on the back of the neck, re-opening a wound made by the blacks some seven years ago." The bodies were brought down to Maryborough. Only eight or nine days later did the Native Police arrive on the scene. "Truly this is shameful. All the white population of Maryborough ... without any exaggeration, might be cut, drawn, quartered, roasted, and eaten, before the tardy assistance we might hope for could be got on the devils' tracks."

*

By 1854, Frederick Walker's little band had grown to a hundred. The Native Police were at work from the cedar forests of Kempsey north to Rockhampton. From a distance the force still inspired praise. *The Sydney Morning Herald*'s effusions could be set to music:

Ill or well, hungry or thirsty, whether half blind with sandy blight, or suffering from fever and ague, from rheumatic pains, and all the diseases to which this worst of Australian climates is subject, with the thermometer ranging between 100 and 125 degrees of Fahrenheit in the shade—early and late, night and day, week after week, with knocked up horses or on foot, deterred by nothing, never daunted, never discouraged, never delaying, never halting, till the men and horses gave in under them,—sometimes without water, for days together without food, save an occasional snake, an iguana, or an opossum, snatched up hastily, in passing, by a native trooper, which was shared by the division,—onward these courageous and indefatigable officers marched their men, subduing tribe after tribe, recovering thousands of sheep, carried away by the wild savage. Protecting one station from incendiarism, another from murder, taking and shooting hosts of murderers, never stopping, never tiring, until every station in the Burnet district was as secure as those within 100 miles of Sydney. The Burnett country is now as quiet as any district in the colony that has been inhabited for fifty years.

Not according to squatters there. William Henry Walsh of Degilbo continued his attacks on Walker's "inert, inexplicable, and inferior force" in the pages of *The Moreton Bay Courier*.

If a commission were appointed to enquire into the merits and demerits of this sadly managed corps, strange things might transpire; reasons would be ascertained ... from whence those melon stealing, garden robbing troopers, obtain their authority or orders to attack, and violently beat, our servants for approaching too near their encampment? If the same regulations require them to take possession of all the "gins" on the establishment, where they may happen to be for the night? Whether such acts are likely to promote morality, health, or quietness in our tribes, and particularly what promise, or return, do they make the husbands, in this unrestrained intercourse with their wives?

Squatters accused Walker of favouritism. "Are we poor devils to have no benefit from the Native Police," asked William Forster, "merely because we cannot make friends with the Commandant, or write such sweet little letters as the Messrs. Leith Hay?"

As angry squatters took pot shots at Walker in the press, the Governor allowed him to publish in reply a majestic account of the history, the aims and the methods of the Native Police. The Commandant lavished praise on his own efforts to civilise the troopers. "I lost no opportunity of improving the men morally, of practising the memories, teaching them to reflect, and argue among themselves; also in inculcating habits of regularity, obedience, and cleanliness." He spoke of putting into the past the "harshness and abominable cruelty" once exercised against the Aborigines. He showed, by contrast, supreme confidence in his own dealings with them. "I have always thought that I was right, morally and legally." But the principal purpose of his manifesto was to blast the squatters for continuing to clear blacks from their runs. This contradictory man understood as clearly as anyone how this provoked constant violence in the bush. He recalled arriving on the Darling Downs for the first time to find the blacks outlawed in their own country.

> Driven to desperation, they carried on a constant war of retaliation with the whites, and lived solely on cattle. So accustomed were they become to this life, that force had to be resorted to, to make the ringleaders submit.

Once subdued – he gave no details of the violence involved – the blacks were allowed back onto their old lands. So ended, he said, nine years of war on the Macintyre. A better class of shepherd was working there now. "A run which would not have fetched £100 in May, 1849, was disposed of in January, 1850, for £500." Unless squatters let the blacks in, Walker could see only endless violence ahead.

> So long as settlers carry on the system of preventing the blacks from obtaining their lawful means of livelihood, and persist in not showing to them that all old grudges and vindictiveness are thrown on one side by the whites, which the blacks will believe when they are allowed at the stations, and not till then, so long will a system of depredations be carried on which the Native Police may check, but cannot permanently put an end to.

Walker's argument, laid out in *The Sydney Morning Herald* and *The Moreton Bay Courier*, infuriated those squatters determined – in the jargon of the time – to keep the blacks *at a distance*. That was almost all of them. Few were willing to *let the blacks in*, which became known – and reviled – as the Walker policy.

The squatters struck back. Walsh of Degilbo rounded up fourteen neighbours to write to the Governor, condemning "the calumnious misrepresentations of an individual against a large and respectable community". They dismissed the Walker policy: "It is too well known that most of the murders and outrages perpetrated by these savages have taken place on stations to which they were admitted, and where they were supposed to be on friendly terms with the residents." With some daring, they sheeted home to FitzRoy the troubles of the frontier: "We have little hope that the force will ever be useful without a complete reform of its present defective management, which seems to us to be in a great degree owing to that unlimited confidence reposed in the Commandant by his Excellency the Governor-General." At this point, FitzRoy might have reminded Walsh and his neighbours on the Burnett that they had each signed leases promising the Aboriginal inhabitants of the Colony "such free access to the said Run ... and to the trees and waters thereon as will enable them to procure the Animals, Birds, Fish, and other food on which they subsist". But he did not. Despite his private endorsement of Walker's views and his agreement with Lord Grey from half a dozen years before, FitzRoy ventured nothing in public and left the squatters free to decide for themselves what they did with the blacks on their land.

Walker's force began to fall into disarray. Discipline was fraying. Rations were short and officers were not being paid. Efforts to make sense of his accounts revealed that Walker had blown his budget. FitzRoy advanced him the money he needed but was beginning to doubt his Commandant. Walker's supporters spoke of his brain being too lofty to grapple with details. "His intellect was keen, his brain capacious, but, like many others similarly gifted, he was incapable of descending into minute details of schemes which, in the gross, he sketched with great power of mind." The truth was that by early 1853 Walker was drinking heavily. Brandy was his poison. Many officers in the force drank, but the most notorious drunk in the Native Police was its Commandant. Five years of killing blacks was taking its toll. His patron Augustus Morris wrote:

"That terrible failing, as I have warned you so often will I fear be the ruin of you." FitzRoy ignored for some time complaints by squatters and magistrates of Walker's drinking, but in the winter of 1854 the officers of the Native Police began complaining too. They accused their Commandant of "irregularities, drunkenness, and abuse to them, as well as his general irregularity in the management of the Force". They threatened to resign en masse. Walker was stood down pending an inquiry. Marshall took his place. In late September, Walker was ordered to present himself for questioning to a board of inquiry in Brisbane.

He prevaricated. He was seized with the notion that he would take his rogues with him if he were sacked. He sent messages to them, promising to take them back to their own country. After years of service, the men he had brought from the south remained virtual prisoners in the force. They could not walk a thousand miles home. They needed horses. Marshall told the Colonial Secretary: "Should Mr. Walker be in a position to take the Murray men back to their own country mounted as he brought them from there, there is no doubt but that they would be glad to return but most of those I have seen express a most positive determination not to walk back." Walker wrote to a favourite in the fourth division:

> DEAR NED,
> Mr. Marshall, Mr. Irving, Mr. Fulford, Mr. Nicoll have made the Governor COOLA* with me and I think I shall go away altogether – Write to me what you are going to do suppose I go – and Larry and Tahiti too. Ask all the No. 4 and the new Policemen. Some Policeman say they stop with Mr. Marshall some say go back Murray and others say when Morubillah go they no more Policemen. I been write Governor all No. 4 go with me. Yes.
> FREDERICK WALKER

---

* Angry.

October and November passed, and Walker still did not present himself. Finally, on 19 December, he appeared at the Brisbane Court House with eight or nine troopers in full uniform. They were refused entry. He was drunk. "Mr. Walker took his seat, evidently in a state of intoxication, bordering on stupidity, so as not even to recognize his first Lieutenant, Mr. Marshall, who was sitting at his side." He was asked to leave. "This, however, he declined to do, and conducted himself in such a haughty and insulting manner to the Board, that, without removing him by force, they had only one resource—to adjourn the Court." Walker led his little troop back to the river. Their billet was on the far side. Marshall appeared on the wharf and persuaded all but two of the men to abandon their commander. Hours later, those two reappeared, also anxious to leave Walker but afraid to collect their arms and belongings. When Lieutenant Irving and the Chief Constable of Brisbane crossed the river to see to this, the drunken Commandant drew his sword and threatened Irving. That was the last straw.

*

Edmund B. Uhr was happy to see Walker go. Since their quarrel, Maryborough had been left to fend for itself. His men had been killed and his house robbed. The blacks were worse than ever. Uhr blamed their knowing the ways of the white man. "Civilization always seems to make these fellows more troublesome than when in their wild state; they come to know their power." Sawyers were so afraid to work in the scrub that building was at a standstill for want of timber. Palmer's store was broken into again and again. But what was the point of capturing the culprits, Palmer asked? "There is no alternative but either to let the villains escape, which is good encouragement for them to renew their aggressions, or deal with them in a summary way, which is not pleasant in all cases." He overcame his distaste. A few handfuls of flour laced with arsenic and tied in a handkerchief were left on top of a sack in his store. Two blacks died. Uhr held an inquiry. Nothing happened.

This was a time of fierce quarrels. The angriest involved Uhr. Each brawl saw the Colonial Secretary being battered with letters from all sides and give up in despair. Edgar Aldridge of the Bush Inn denounced Uhr to the Colonial Secretary for failing to take any action when one of his Chinese workmen shot a black. "Mr Uhr said it was not worth while taking any notice of the matter and that he could not afford to lose the services of the Chinaman." But this was nothing to Uhr's fight with Arthur Halloran, his fellow magistrate and the Commissioner of Crown Lands, a squabble so tangled and desperate its subplots were still being debated half a century later. Put simply: both men saw themselves as the leading citizen of the town. When the dispute broke into the open, Uhr condemned Halloran in an astonishingly pompous letter to *The Moreton Bay Courier* and petitioned for redress. The Attorney-General declined to intervene. The bench split for and against. So did the publicans and storekeepers. Through all this, the town's new paper, the *Maryborough Chronicle*, was bombarded with peppery, sarcastic and libellous letters. "We will guarantee to hold you harmless of law costs," one side assured the editor, Charles Buzacott. But the other side warned that "any further letters on the subject would necessitate his being publicly whipped". Buzacott eventually fled. "There were too few people for peacefulness," he said of Maryborough. "And they had far too little to do."

A new Governor-General arrived. Sir William Denison was Eton-schooled, military-trained and no stranger to Australia. He had been blooded in its ways as Lieutenant Governor of Van Diemen's Land, now self-governing and under the new name of Tasmania in an attempt to erase its tainted past. Denison did not share FitzRoy's enthusiasm for the Native Police and ordered its numbers be cut by half, its operations curtailed and its command be transferred to the Chief of Police in Sydney. Marshall resigned. This was not what the squatters of the north had in mind for the Native Police.

> Just as they were becoming well trained and schooled to their work, the government—actuated by a questionable spirit of

economy—disbanded them, and this step was soon followed by the most disastrous results. Taught by the semi-civilised blacks who had been attached to the force, depredations and atrocities of the foulest kind were committed; and the consciousness of the absence of any force to oppose them, emboldened the savages to an incredible extent. Tragedy followed upon tragedy, outrage succeeded outrage, until the legislature was at length aroused to a sense of its duty, and the reorganisation of the force was sanctioned.

After some months, the squatters moved in the new parliament of the Colony to hold a swift inquiry into the force. It recommended its numbers be restored to 120 men split into ten divisions, each led by a lieutenant overseen by the chief official, the Government Resident in Brisbane. Edric Norfolk Vaux Morisset, the twenty-seven-year-old son of the former military commandant of Norfolk Island, was appointed Commandant. Morisset Jr was a man of some ability and simple convictions. He had none of Walker's contradictory sympathy for the original inhabitants of the Colony. "The blacks," he said, "know very well what they are shot for—they can only understand brute force."

Uhr finally had what he had demanded for so long. As the new headquarters of the force, Morisset chose Owanyilla, 12 miles from Maryborough on the riverbank Jones once tried to claim. Though relieved in some ways, Uhr confessed to having lost faith in the force. "I would sooner see no Native Police than as it is at present," he told the select committee of the Legislative Assembly of New South Wales. "They certainly are not doing much good, and they tend to do much harm; the natives having got a contempt for them." He was not impressed by the camp – "bark and slabs of the rudest description" – nor by the sight of the troopers wandering about the town. "Some of them look rather smart, others look like hogs in armour. Their clothes sit uncomfortably on them. I suppose they make themselves as decent as their nature will allow them." He was beginning to believe the force should be reconstituted with white troopers and a few blacktrackers. "I don't think there is much perseverance in the blacks." But could white troopers handle the scrubs?

> Certainly, in the scrubs they would have a good deal of hardship and difficulty to contend with; but we have had the experience of gentlemen, going out and protecting their stations, going into the scrubs and successfully protecting themselves against the murders and outrages of the blacks. Now, if gentlemen could do this, I think paid men ought to be able to do it with blacks as trackers.

Uhr was giving evidence to the third inquiry by the Assembly into the Native Police in a little over a decade. It came after the murder of the Fraser family at Hornet Bank, the worst massacre yet of whites in the colonies.

Early on the morning of 27 October 1857, a mob of Yiman gathered at the rough Hornet Bank homestead on the Upper Dawson. The 230,000-acre run 200 miles west of Maryborough was on the remote edge of settlement. The place was all but undefended. John Fraser had died of dysentery after bringing north thousands of sheep, his wife, eight children, their tutor, four shepherds and a black servant called Bahlee, who clubbed the station dogs to death that night so the Yiman could catch their victims sleeping. They killed all the men and, it was said, raped Martha Fraser and her two eldest daughters. The only survivor was fourteen-year-old Sylvester Fraser who, battered but hiding under his bed, heard the carnage raging around him. At dawn he emerged and rode 12 miles to raise the alarm.

Why Hornet Bank? Yiman resistance to the invasion of whites and their sheep had been gathering strength for two or three years. The failure of the Native Police to bring order to this brigalow country cut with gorges and scrubs was already the subject of bitter complaints. Second Lieutenant Thomas Ross, the local commander of the force, was inexperienced and showed little vigour. All his troopers deserted after a particularly bloody engagement and their replacements were local blacks – badly mounted, badly fed and hardly trained. He led them from one makeshift camp to another. Newspapers reported him botching operations against the Yiman. He had called at Hornet Bank in June 1857 looking for the men threatening Fraser's widow. He was almost alone when he found them. Ammunition was short. He retreated and when he returned with his troopers in the morning they had vanished. *The North Australian* lectured him: "Every one acquainted with the character of the blacks knows that a retreat is generally attended with disastrous consequences." Over the next six weeks the Yiman killed six shepherds on the nearby Eurombah run. Lieutenant Ross failed every time in his pursuit of the killers. When news broke of the October slaughter at Hornet Bank, Ross was widely accused of neglect of duty, want of energy, inefficiency and a perfect inability to keep his troopers in line. But it soon emerged the Yiman had crimes to avenge. The Fraser boys were raping their women. The Colonial Secretary was told that Mrs Fraser had repeatedly asked a local constable to reprove her sons "for 'forcibly taking' the young maidens, & that in consequence she expected harm would come of it, that they were in the habit of doing so, notwithstanding her entreaties to the contrary. Several of the Working Chaps said that the Frazers were famous for the Young Gins."

In *The Cry for the Dead*, her fine, early account of the squatter invasion, the poet Judith Wright wrote of whites driven mad for revenge by Hornet Bank and by the fear that it marked the start of a general uprising:

> Arrivals from English families ... rode out beside their own stockmen and shepherds in days and nights of bloodshed which spared no Aboriginal camp. It was not ... a very long war, but it was a thorough one, though it went largely unrecorded. In scraps of reminiscence written down long

Native Police dispersing the blacks

years later, men recalled the great bottle-tree around whose trunk dozens of Aborigines were handcuffed, to be killed off at leisure; the swamps into which others were driven, the mountains where they stood at bay to be killed. Pearse Serocold and his party roped together a dozen or more men, led them into open country, and let them loose to run as moving targets for the carbines.

In those weeks, no Aborigines were arrested, none was brought to trial, and not a single inquest was held. George Pearce-Serocold of Cockatoo Creek assured his brother that they "spared none of the grownup blacks which we could find". The Colonial Secretary was happy with this open slaughter. To the Government Resident in Brisbane, he wrote: "The murder of the Fraser Family with the attendant circumstances required that the perpetrators of such monstrous enormities should be punished in the severest manner wherever they could be found." But the language of the reports perturbed him. Did Lieutenant Powell have to say that among the blacks shot were "three Gins as they were running away"?

Young George Lang joined the chase in Maryborough, believing the punishment of the blacks for Hornet Bank was a righteous cause. But on the way to the interior his eyes were opened. "I now know that nothing could have been more unworthy of human beings than the procedure both of the members of the Police Force and the white population than their horrid indiscriminate murders of the Blacks." One of his uncles was the Reverend John Dunmore Lang and another was Andrew Lang, appointed for a brief time to the New South Wales Legislative Council. On the day of his appointment, George sent him a dossier on the carnage in Wide Bay and on the Burnett, hoping that something might be done:

> I learned from various sources that a party of twelve – squatters and their confidential overseers – went out mounted and armed to the teeth and scoured the Country for blacks, away

from the scenes of the murder of the Frazers altogether, and shot upwards of eighty men women & children. Not content with scouring the scrubs & forest country they were bold enough to ride up to the Head stations and shoot down the tame blacks whom they found camping there. Ten men were shot in this way at Ross's head station on the Upper Burnett. Several at Prior's station and at Hays & Lambs several more. The party in scouring the bush perceived an old blind black-fellow upon whom they immediately fired sending a ball through his back, another through his arm which shivered the bone to pieces and a third grazed his scalp. This old man had been for a long time a harmless hanger on at the different head stations and of course could have been in no way identified with the Frazer murderers.

By Lang's count, the Native Police and vigilantes shot another seventy.

One of their acts deserves especial notice. They arrived at Humphrey's station, went to the Blacks encamped near the house, bound two of the men and led them into the scrub and deliberately shot them, the cries of the two poor wretches were heard by the superintendents family at his house. I had supposed that these things although acted with seeming openness in the far interior and with evident impunity would not be tolerated in more civilized society and that the neighbourhood of Maryborough the chief town in the District could not be disgraced by any such barbarities. I was mistaken however.

At Maryborough, the local commander, Second Lieutenant Francis Allman, led a raid that destroyed the blacks' camp between the old and new settlements. Lang recorded: "The party of whites then followed and shot a boy of twelve years of age dead—a lad well known in town as a harmless, helpless lunatic and wounded a man with a ball in the thigh, besides." Next day he watched Allman and his men destroy the camp in the old town.

> I have witnessed no actual murder but I have witnessed scenes that I considered, occurring where they did, in the heart of the town, libels on the very humanity of the people, a disgrace to its Magistrates its Storekeepers its fathers & sons and every thing British in the place. For instance the spectacle of a blackfellow endeavouring at the public wharf at eight o'clock last Sunday night, to construct a frail raft of sheets of bark to carry over a river as broad as the Hunter at Raymond Terrace and twice as rapid a child twelve months old and another but ten days old and all this because he had been chased from his fires and threatened with a ball from a carbine by a ruthless wretch wearing the queens livery.

Where, he asked, were the magistrates of Maryborough?

> I reply our magistrates are all here and they might as well be at Jericho they do not care a fig for either law or justice and in short knowing how matters stand they are as guilty of every act of cruelty as the actual perpetrators of them. They are traitors every man of them and unworthy the confidence of the people.

The Select Committee on Murders by the Aborigines on the Dawson River was not interested in knowing what provoked the slaughter of the Frasers. The members only investigated more effective ways to protect squatters' lives and property. Vigilantes were not interrogated. Commandant Morisset was not examined. Uhr gave evidence. Some witnesses were quizzed about the ferocity of the troopers but nothing the committee heard made them condemn the Native Police. It was decided to stick to black troopers; recruit them once again in the south; and increase their pay to eight pence a day. Morisset was to be given time to build a force able to keep the natives under control. Firing on gatherings of peaceful blacks, officially forbidden by Walker, was mandated by Morisset:

> It is the duty of the Officers at all time and opportunities to disperse any large assemblage of blacks; such meetings, if not prevented, invariably lead to depredations or murder; and nothing but the mistaken kindness of the Officers in command inspired the blacks with sufficient confidence to commit the late fearful outrages on the Dawson River. The Officers will therefore see the necessity of teaching the aborigines that no outrage or depredation shall be committed with impunity—but on the contrary, retributive justice shall speedily follow the Commission of crime.

After Hornet Bank, the old rhetoric of high purpose was all but stripped away. Dispersing blameless gatherings was officially blessed. Retribution was the stated purpose of the force. It would be so for as long as the Native Police lasted.

16

QUEENSLAND

Cannons barked as Sir George Bowen's steamer came up the Brisbane River. He was days late. Bunting hung limp in the heat. News that he was finally on his way brought 4000 people to the Botanic Gardens to watch his portly figure come ashore. "The cheers that were given were worthy of any company of loyal Britishers all the world over," gushed *The Moreton Bay Courier*. Sir George was a protégé of the statesman William Ewart Gladstone, sent to the far side of the world with a singular brief: to set up a colony, as he said, "full-blown from the beginning". There was little revenue and only 25,000 settlers to fill a territory three times the size of France. London picked a man in love with Empire. Bowen saw Britain's colonies circling the globe as an almost sublime manifestation of Christian civilisation. Another twenty-one guns fired as the Bowens made their way through the gardens. No colourful natives had been mustered to welcome them, though Aboriginal people in the new Colony outnumbered whites by about eight to one. As the vice-regal couple reached the steps of Government House, a nurse brought their baby out to be kissed. "Sir, that was a touch I couldn't stand," wrote a weary observer. "It would have melted the heart of a wheelbarrow."

Separation had taken so long. Queensland might have joined Victoria as it broke away from New South Wales in 1851 but there were so many squabbles to resolve. Where would the boundary be – as low as Grafton or as high as Gympie? What portion of the debts of the Colony would Queensland be responsible for? Who would have the vote? And where

THE BOWENS

would the capital be? Edmund B. Uhr joined Gayndah's hapless campaign to prevent Separation until it was done on the big squatters' terms. The name of that little village on the Burnett had become shorthand for arrogance. Money got them what they wanted. "Of all narrow-minded men, the Burnett squatters, or rather the clique round about Gayndah, is certainly the most contracted," wrote *The Sydney Morning Herald*. "It is a pity they have not travelled, or read a little more." Much as they craved Separation, they preferred to stay part of New South Wales rather than have Brisbane as their capital. Their terms were: Rockhampton or nothing. The town's fine harbour, Port Curtis, was close to their runs. Their petition to Queen Victoria was admirably frank. They did not pretend to be speaking for a "numerical majority" but as the proprietors of acres and sheep. Uhr was a signatory:

> Your petitioners possess, in the aggregate, about 700,000
> sheep, and other stock in proportion, and occupy the

principal portion of the located country to the northward
of the districts of Moreton Bay and Darling Downs ...

And your petitioners venture, most respectfully, to express their earnest hope that your Majesty, in the selection
of a site for the Metropolis of what seems destined, at no
distant day, to become a great Province, will have regard
to the interests of future tracts of country, now untenanted
save by the aborigines.

While on a losing streak, Uhr campaigned in Maryborough for
Arthur "Slippery Mac" Macalister. "Look at him, gentlemen," cried
Uhr. "Can you not see in his countenance intellect and ability?" Pitted
against Macalister was William Tooth of Widgee Widgee, whose supporters asked why anyone would vote for a squatter's attorney when
they might elect a "leviathan squatter" with 700,000 acres in his name.
And so they did. Tooth represented the town as the final decisions were
taken to separate from New South Wales. The capital would be Brisbane; the border would run south of Brisbane, along the mountains,
the Dumaresq and the Macintyre until it hit the twenty-ninth latitude.
There would be an elected Assembly and a nominated Council. New
South Wales allowed every adult male to vote in the last election before
Separation. But Queensland stripped the vote from a third of those
men, limiting the franchise to property holders and residents of many
years' standing. That was a great victory for the squatters. Better still
was the gerrymander that gave them, for decades, unchallengeable sway
in the Colony's new Assembly.

Squatters fawned on Bowen as he made a brief vice-regal progress
through the hinterland of Brisbane. He was elated to have four hundred
horsemen and a brass band escort him into Ipswich. "The numerous
cavalcades of hundreds of well-mounted horsemen, which came forth
to meet and escort the first Representative of their Sovereign, presented
spectacles such as can be exhibited in only two countries of the world, –
in England and in Australia." He watched his black subjects dance a

corroboree at Eagle Farm, a performance described thoughtfully by
The Moreton Bay Courier:

> The darkies had been well fed previously with "bullock,"
> damper, &c., the gift of his Excellency, and it may therefore
> be imagined that they were not particularly agile after their
> feast. Lazy as they appeared to be, however, they were per-
> fect in their "time," both in singing and dancing, and the
> uncouthness and variety of their gestures afforded a con-
> siderable amount of amusement to the spectators.

After only four months in his post, Bowen laid out the history of
conflict between black and white in Australia for the benefit of the
Duke of Newcastle, Secretary of State for the Colonies. Mutual provocation was inevitable. So was bloodshed. No one was to blame.

> In the early days of the occupation of each district, Colonists
> are frequently obliged to associate together, for self-defence
> against the blacks ... For many obvious reasons, it seems
> highly desirable that this border warfare, when absolutely
> unavoidable, should be carried on under some control on
> the part of the Government. The establishment of the Native
> Police has contributed much towards this end.

Bowen had inherited the whole force from New South Wales: eleven
officers and about a hundred troopers. Though he had doubts about the
discipline of the officers, he admired Edric Morisset's energy and resolution and kept him as Commandant. He also admired the skill and
courage of the troopers. The wild blacks, he told Newcastle, were no
match for them.

> The spears, boomerangs, and waddies of the former (danger-
> ous weapons as they are,) are no match at close quarters for
> the carbines and sabres, which the latter use with great skill,
> and which make amends for the disparity of numbers ...

> Your Grace will probably agree with me that men who almost instinctively become bold and skilful riders and admirable marksman must be possessed of several faculties of a higher order than it is the common fashion to ascribe to the Australian Aborigines. Galloping over the prairies of the interior on my official tours, I have more than once seen a black trooper of my escort, at the word of command, unsling his carbine, and Kill a bustard on the wing, with a single bullet, at the distance of forty or fifty yards.

Bowen larded his despatches to London with sweet rhetoric about the mercy and justice of his government. He deplored the wholesale cruelties of the past. He feared if greater kindness were not shown, the blacks were doomed to early extinction. But their land was there to be taken. Land was the new Colony's only asset and wool the only sure revenue of a nearly insolvent government. Millions of acres had already been occupied but millions more were waiting for squatters and their flocks. Bowen was hard-line: he believed Aborigines had no claim whatsoever to their country. Queensland, he said, was "territory over which these few Aboriginal tribes formerly wandered; for it would be incorrect to state that they ever in any strict sense, occupied it."

Robert Herbert came to Queensland as Bowen's secretary but emerged after the elections of April 1860 as leader of his government – effectively the Premier, though he called himself Colonial Secretary. The twenty-eight-year-old grandson of the Earl of Carnarvon, educated at Eton and Oxford, appointed his lover John Bramston to the Legislative Council.

The Speaker of the new parliament, Gilbert Eliott, was yet another son of a Scottish baronet. He held the post for a decade. This courteous, inscrutable, conservative Christian with 16,000 acres at Gayndah was elected, with the help of Edmund B. Uhr, to the seat of Wide Bay. For once, Uhr had backed a winner. His was the first signature on the petition calling on this "able, manly, and straight forward" figure to stand for parliament. Eliott's victory was celebrated in Maryborough with eating, drinking and doggerel:

> The Speaker is the foremost man of Queensland's
>   wide domain—
> Our votes thus high exalted him and gave him place
>   and gain.
>
> So we resolved to dine with him. Sixteen the table graced.
> Of bluest blood were all our chiefs (though with their
>   arms defaced.)
> Dread Blucher Uhr our chairman was, who keeps the
>   Boiling Down,
> For hides and fat tongues, lard, and pork, almighty his
>   renown ...
> Substantial were the eatables which on the board were seen;
> Our beef was rare—and, oh! ye gods, 'twas painted
>   sable green;
> A goose with onions stuffed, and sage (the oldest of
>   the town);
> Pork chops and bullock liver, all fresh from the Boiling
>   Down ...
>
> And so with song and sentiment, we made the feast
>   go down;
> We drank "Success to squatters," then "Perdition to
>   the town;"
> "Confusion to all democrats," "Gags for the bold and free;"
> "Our stations into freeholds may they quickly changed be."

Uhr was entangled with the government in other ways that would prove both useful and difficult in time. Dreary Sir Robert Ramsay Mackenzie, the Colony's first Treasurer, was married to his niece Louisa Jones. He would later be Premier. Louisa's sister Mary Australia gave five children to William Bligh John O'Connell before dying, no doubt

ROBERT HERBERT

exhausted, at the age of thirty-three. This link left Uhr connected to John O'Connell Bligh, who was about to succeed Morisset as Commandant of the Native Police. Through all his troubles, this wretched man would have the public and private support of Edmund B. Uhr JP.

*

The Blighs had come back to Australia to claim what they could of the lucrative estates Governor Bligh granted himself in his unhappy reign of New South Wales. Enriched, they stayed. Offices came their way. John O'Connell Bligh was only nineteen when Governor Fitz-Roy made him an officer of the Native Police in 1853. He proved his worth. "The fear of Bligh acts like a hangman's whip on the blacks in our quarter," wrote a squatter from the Bunya Mountains. Bligh was remembered at Baramba. "One evening, a little before sunset, Mr. Bligh, of the Native Police, and his troopers came galloping up to the station and surrounded all the blacks, male and female, also the blacks that were in constant work on the station, and handcuffed all around a large gum tree all that night." Bligh zealously guarded his reputation for never allowing his quarry to escape. "This we think is what gives to his name a magic dread amongst evil doers of the black race in our quarter."

One morning in February 1860, when he and his men were stationed at the Owanyilla camp on the outskirts of Maryborough, Bligh led his troopers into town and began to kill. Maryborough watched the slaughter. *The Moreton Bay Courier* put the story together:

> Mr. Bligh, with a party of the police ... fired several shots at a few blacks encamped near Cleary's; then came into East Maryborough, charged a camp near Mr. Melville's, drove the poor creatures from it—some through the town, some into the river—and commenced butchering them forthwith. "Darkey," who had been constantly employed in the town— who could have been apprehended at any moment, had there been any desire, or occasion, was shot down opposite Mr. Palmer's, where his body was left, and subsequently roasted.
>
> "Young Snatchem," an excellent and industrious black, was driven into the river, near the public wharf,—scores of men, women, and children stood by, and Lieut. John O'Connell Bligh stationed himself in the bow of a boat, which was in readiness, and forty or fifty shots were actually fired, five or six by Mr. Bligh himself. The boat overtook him (the black) in an exhausted state, and the "gallant hero" ... lowered his carbine, and shot the defenceless, tired, unresisting wretch, in the back.

Richard Sheridan was having breakfast when a Butchulla man dashed along his verandah, pursued by a trooper. As they ran out of sight, Sheridan heard shots. He was a magistrate and Customs officer, new to the town after working for many years on the south coast of New South Wales. There he had come to respect the blacks and deplore their persecution, for which he would become known in Maryborough as a

croaker. He rushed from his cottage and joined the crowd on the riverbank in time to see Bligh pursuing a man swimming for his life. "I saw
the Native Police officer, myself, fire four or five shots, and I eventually
saw the black man at whom he fired sink,—raise up his hand, and sink;
that was the last that was ever seen of him." Bligh killed at least one
other man that morning. In a well-sourced list of "plain questions" put
to Bligh in the *Maryborough Chronicle*, "Sword of Damocles" asked:
"Did you then capture a poor old man who also had been a constant
attendant in the town, against whom there had never been a charge;
did you, sir, capture the poor old fellow, handcuff him, march him out
of the town, and have him shot?"

In time, Bligh would produce all sorts of excuses for this rampage,
but a squalid explanation soon emerged. Bligh and his friends had been
accused by the Camp Sergeant at Owanyilla of taking indecent liberties with his wife while drunk. Bligh sacked him. But Maryborough
was on the side of the sergeant. "Heads were gravely shaken, and low
mutterings went abroad," said *The Moreton Bay Courier*. On the night
before the raid, the magistrate Arthur Halloran had ridden out to the
camp to discuss the awkward rumours. It appears the mighty display of
the Native Police in action next morning was designed to blow Bligh's
embarrassment away.

Uhr convened an inquest. Sheridan sat with him. They did not inquire into the death of Young Snatchem though dozens standing on the
riverbank watched Bligh shoot him. The principle: no body, no inquest.
They attended only to the death of Darkey, whose body had been found
by one of the town constables after following a trail of blood into the
bush. Dr Palmer gave evidence of two gunshot wounds: one in the groin
and one in the chest. The latter was the cause of death. Bligh was to be
the next witness at the inquest, but Uhr suspended proceedings in the
afternoon in order to chair a meeting that night to applaud Bligh's gallant conduct. Uhr reassured the four hundred citizens gathered at the
Court House:

Many might think, from his having taken evidence in the enquiry touching the death of "Darkie," that he was not quite with them on this occasion. Such, however, he could assure them was not the case, and he was most happy to see that Maryborough, as it always was, seemed to be unanimous on this occasion. A larger meeting he had never seen in Maryborough, and with their permission he would take the chair. (Cheers.)

The publican George "Bantam Cock" Howard had organised the gathering. A short, stout man with jet-black eyes and a sharp tongue, Howard was immediately on his feet, lashing Bligh's critics even before they had had time to emerge:

There were several in the town whom he should designate croakers, that were watching and spying to try to find some speck on which they could form a complaint, and who were ever ready with lengthened faces to cry pity for the poor blacks. (Cheers.) Some of those gentlemen should have been in Maryborough as long as he had, should have heard, seen, and felt the merciless outrages these wretches, called by the croakers "the poor blacks," had committed ... What man amongst them was there who could say but that the blacks had got anything but what they deserved? What man was there who did not feel it?

Speakers tumbled over one another to be heard. Uhr had difficulty keeping the meeting on track. Yet the argument of the night was clear: the town had been begging Bligh for help for months; he had given it in spades; and now he was to be thanked. The citizens voted to set up a fund "for the purpose of presenting Lieutenant John O'Connell Bligh with a suitable and useful present. (Loud and continued cheers.)"

The Maryborough meeting attracted cruel commentary in the colonial press. No paper was crueller than the radical Sydney *Empire*, founded by Henry Parkes, which named the four hundred at the meeting "the meanest men, individually and collectively, in all Australia", who beslimed Bligh with their adulation. Bantam Cock Howard was not surprised by the commentary. What else would you expect from naive humanitarians who knew nothing of life in the bush, nothing of the harsh realities that made it necessary to kill? The publican and his friends decided to order from the Queen's jeweller in London a ceremonial sword for Bligh "as a mark of esteem for his services in suppressing the outrages of the blacks". It was their secret until the weapon arrived a year later.

Uhr resumed the inquest a few days after the meeting. Bligh's evidence was perfunctory. He was not asked about his dealings with the Camp Sergeant's wife or his killing of Young Snatchem in plain sight of the townsfolk. He claimed to be unable to clarify the circumstances of Darkey's death. "I was on duty with the others," he said. "The only evidence I know touching the death of darky is by hear say." Uhr bundled up half a dozen depositions and sent them to the Attorney-General, Ratcliffe Pring, a volatile English barrister driven out to Australia by chronic bronchitis. Pring decided to take no action.

*

The stench of melting carcasses was proving too much for Maryborough. For nearly a decade, the land on which Uhr built his boiling-down had been designated the site of Victoria Park. He would soon have to move. But the pots were not prospering, so his mind turned once more to finding a government post. His oldest son, Ned, had already left the King's School. His next boy, Reginald Charles Heber, was still at that solemn academy in Sydney. In late 1860 Edmund wrote asking the Governor to appoint him Police Magistrate at Ipswich:

I make this request as I have a large family whom I am desirous of having located in a place possessing educational advantages.

I would beg to remark that I am not unknown to many of the old Inhabitants of Ipswich as I lived for some years on the Wivenhoe Station and used to attend the Ipswich Bench.

First, he had to pass an exam. He failed. A Maryborough storekeeper called John Purser recalled him being angry about this for the rest of his life: "He expressed a very strong opinion of the injustice done to him that after giving his services for a number of years he should be refused an appointment." Purser had not been in town for long before he was shown "a poetical effusion setting forth a raid undertaken by the Burnett squatters against the blacks. Mr. Uhr was to have taken part in the raid. The poem recites the excitement caused by his absence . . . the hero was found carefully hidden underneath his wife's petticoats." He would never escape "The Raid of the Aborigines". Uhr found 30 acres 2 miles downriver he named Woodlands. There he rebuilt the plant and immediately offered it for sale.

It didn't sell. Uhr was lumbered with Woodlands for the next five years. The local press was kind: "Mr. Uhr makes great improvements to his establishment every year, but next year he will adopt a new plan and boil down by steam power, which will greatly facilitate the operation." The mighty Mort and Co. of Sydney endorsed his tallow and hides, which "have always commanded the highest prices in this market and in London". Steam power, once installed in 1862, also drove a sawmill with "two superior Engines, Benches, and all the necessary plant and gear" to process 5000 feet a day of cedar and pine. Young Ned ran the mill. But Uhr's heart was not in his business.

More than ever, he saw himself as the leading citizen of the town. This so irked Bantam Cock Howard that one night in 1860, when Uhr had taken the chair uninvited at a meeting in the Court House, Howard called on all present to choose a chairman for themselves.

First-class Boiling-down Establishment.

Land and House facing the Mary River.

ALLOTMENTS Fronting the Queen's Wharf, Kent Street, &c., &c.

FOR PRIVATE SALE, on account of ill-health of the Proprietor, who is about to leave the district,

Woodlands Boiling-down Establishment,

Comprising a substantial DWELLING-HOUSE, containing Sitting-room. Dining-room, four large Bedrooms. Kitchen. Stable. Servants apartments, Dairy and all the out-buildings and requisites for carrying on a boiling-down establishment. lso,

FIVE ALLOTMENTS OF LAND,

on which stands the pleasantly situated and comfortable

Cottage,

now in the occupation of John Kent, Esq., P.M.; together with sundry

ALLOTMENTS FRONTING THE WHARF, KENT STREET, &c., &c., in the town of Maryborough.

A large portion of the purchase-money can remain secured on the property, at the rate of 8 per cent interest.

For further particulars apply to

EDMUND B. UHR,

Woodlands.

☞ None but principals will be dealt with.

After some show of acrimony on both sides Mr. Uhr descended from his position. It was then proposed, seconded, and carried that Mr. Uhr take the chair.

The Chairman opened the proceedings by saying that he felt much obliged to Mr. Howard for what he had said as it caused him to be placed in a much prouder position than he was in before for he was now elected by the voice of the people, and he thanked them for the honour they had conferred upon him.

Like many quarrellers, Uhr also grovelled. When Sir George and Lady Bowen made their first visit to Maryborough, he presided over the *déjeuner* on the verandah of Aldridge's Hotel to welcome the couple. His words were magnificent:

We desire to express through your Excellency our loyalty and devotion to the person of our gracious Sovereign. We regard with feelings of peculiar interest and much gratification the high honor she has bestowed upon us in naming our new colony after her own august title; and we appreciate much her having appointed as our first Governor a gentleman of your Excellency's high character and attainments. This wise choice on the part of her Majesty evinces her earnest solicitude for the welfare and prosperity of this, the youngest colony of her mighty empire.

The Bowens did not stay for lunch but left on the tide for Rockhampton.

Bligh's sword, "profusely embellished with embossed flowers and scroll work of the most exquisite design", reached Sydney in early 1861. Bantam Cock Howard soon had the weapon on view in his pub. Patrons could, if they wished, have a beer while admiring a blade capable of "passing with a single thrust through an iron plate thicker than a cuirass".* News of the sword revived the ridicule and disgust

* Armour.

that followed Bligh's deadly work in the streets of the town. "Dickey" of Wide Bay thought the gift "a blot so foul and deep-stained as will leave on this otherwise fair portion of God's earth the brand of eternal infamy". What, he asked, was the gallant act for which he earned the weapon?

> Why, in raising carbine while standing in the prow of his boat in the River Mary, and shooting at a distance of two yards or thereabouts, a naked, defenceless and terror-stricken blackfellow—shooting him dead, coward-like, in the back.

"Red Indian" mused on the chivalrous history of swords given to heroes. "I should say a butcher's knife would be a fitter gift." After being displayed at the scene of Bligh's crimes it was taken up to him in Rockhampton, from where he thanked the citizens of Maryborough for "the noble way in which they expressed their feelings in my favour, at a time when there were those in Maryborough who would have been glad to hunt me to the death for doing what I considered a simple act of duty".

*

Queensland was not much more than a year old and Bligh's sword was one of a cluster of scandals involving the Native Police. Alarm bridged town and country. Not at issue was the protection settlers said they deserved as they laboured to "reclaim the wilderness from savagedom". The agitation in young Queensland focused on the conduct of the Native Police, those "diabolical scoundrels" denounced in the Colony's newspapers as inept, expensive, brutal, out of control and counterproductive. *The Moreton Bay Courier* had abandoned the squatters. Now in the hands of Thomas Blacket Stephens, the high-minded son of a Baptist clergyman, Brisbane's chief paper gave voice to those calling for an inquiry into the force. On side was the *Maryborough Chronicle*:

DR HENRY CHALLINOR

Let all such remember that the law "Thou shalt not kill" is of world-wide force and application, and in every case— whether ignorant or educated, civilised or uncivilised, black or white, clothed or unclothed—He who created of one blood all the nations of the earth, looks upon the wilful taking away of life as *murder*.

In December 1860, Lieutenant Frederick Wheeler had led an unprovoked attack on a sleeping camp at Dugandan near Ipswich, killing two blacks and abducting at least one woman for the pleasure of the troopers. A child in arms and three men were left dangerously wounded. The thirty-year-old son of a London merchant and a Sicilian noblewoman, Wheeler was cutting a swathe through Moreton Bay. From Dugandan he took his men to John Hardie's Fassifern a few miles away, rode into the scrub, shot three old men, smashed two of their skulls and trashed their camp. Spears were broken, tomahawks beaten flat and clothes strewn about. After Wheeler's rampage, the Fassifern blacks sheltered with the station's overseer, with kind shepherds and the publican of the Bush Inn. Inquests were held into both killings by a most unusual man. Henry Challinor of Ipswich was a doctor of profound Nonconformist faith and liberal views. He didn't drink. He was not a tool of the squatters. His enemies dismissed him as wordy and tiresome, but he took the search for truth seriously. He questioned Aborigines and believed them when they told him they were fired on without warning. He wrote to the Attorney-General:

> The information of witnesses severally taken upon oath …
> will not allow me to arrive at any other finding than that
> the said aboriginals were wantonly and wilfully murdered
> on the twenty-fourth day of December last by Lieutenant
> Wheeler and the detachment of Native Police on that day
> under his command.

When Pring did nothing, Challinor published in the press his 6000-word brief of evidence and this succinct accusation of murder.

Next, in February 1861, Rudolph "Dosh" Morisset, the older brother of the Commandant of the force, led a killing spree on Manumbar station at the foot of the Bunya Mountains, where clans from miles around had gathered once again to feast. The *Maryborough Chronicle* put the deaths at "some thirty or thirty-five blacks—including men, women, and children". The Mortimers of Manumbar were not sticklers for British justice. After twelve years in the district, they approved summary execution of blacks if – but only if – they were guilty of something. The Mortimers did not hide their anger behind pseudonyms but took out advertisements in half a dozen newspapers to damn the Native Police.

> To the Officer in Command of the Party of Native Police,
> who shot and wounded some Blacks on the Station of
> Manumbar, on Sunday, the 10th instant.

SIR,—If in future you should take a fancy to bring your troopers upon the Station of Manumbar on a sporting excursion we shall feel obliged if you would either bag or bury the game which you shoot, as it is far from pleasant for us to have the decomposing remains of four or five blackfellows laying unburied within a mile or two of our head station. If you will do neither please be kind enough to remove the corpses from waterholes near the head station from which we sometimes use water for culinary purposes. As most of the blacks you left dead on our run were feeble old men, some of them apparently not less than eighty years of age, will you please to inform us whether these hoary sinners are the parties chiefly engaged in spearing bullocks and "cramming monkeys," &c.; or whether you just shoot them because the younger ones are too nimble for you. Besides the four or five you left dead on our run, you have wounded two of our station blacks, who have been in our employment during lambing, washing, and shearing, and all other busy times for the last eight or nine years, and we have never known either of them to have been charged with a crime of any kind. One of them came to the station with a bullet wound through one of his thighs, another through one of his arms, and another through one of his hands; the other had a bullet wound through one of his arms. These blacks, being in our employment, very naturally look to us for protection from such outrages, and we are of opinion that when you shoot and wound blacks in such an indiscriminate manner, you exceed your commission, and we publish this that those who employ and pay you may have some knowledge of the way in which you perform your services.

We have, &c.,

J. & A. MORTIMER.

Two hundred miles north in the hinterland of Rockhampton, squatters were dealing with a pompous and inept Native Police officer anxious to prove his mettle. Second Lieutenant Alfred March Gorsed Patrick had been only months in the force. His troopers deserted the moment he arrived. When fresh recruits turned up in the new year of 1861, Patrick set about clearing the blacks from stations on the Nogoa and Comet. The district had been largely peaceful until then, but no longer. Lieutenant Frederick Wheeler, perhaps to spread the blame, complained to the Attorney-General that Patrick's men had killed a number of working blacks on Christopher Rolleston's 163,000-acre Albinia Downs, some on his verandah and some in his kitchen, despite Rolleston's protests.

> Two blacks who had by some whim been spared were then made to bury the victims, and one Ruffian said to the other, what shall we do with the Sextons? The answer was, shoot them ... one was accordingly shot, why the other was spared I know not, possibly the supply of cartridges was running short.

News of the massacre reached Charles Dutton, "a bookish young man with a passion for justice and a generous temper", who ran nearby 209,000-acre Bauhinia Downs with his brother Henry. Charles was also a magistrate. "My blacks asked me 'what for policeman shoot him, bail blackfellow kill whitefellow, bail take monkey, bail take ration, what for shoot him? you been yabber blackfellow budgery bail policeman shoot him.'"* Dutton concluded: "The conduct of the native police was characterised by the grossest cruelty, the most oppressive and exasperating acts, inspiring a feeling of hatred, and desire of revenge." When Patrick and his troopers reached Bauhinia Downs, Dutton and his brother blocked their way. Henry drew a revolver and threatened Patrick. "In a state of maniacal excitement he cried out to his men,

---

* Why are the police shooting us? We haven't killed whites or stolen sheep or rations. Why shoot us? You're talking to good blacks. Police should not shoot us.

'Unstring your carbines, and drive them out.'" But twenty-five men, women and children – some of them lame – made it safely into the scrub. Their campsite was ransacked and their spears, waddies and boomerangs burnt. Slaughter had been averted but Dutton feared for the district. "My blacks ... have frequently told me that the Warpas (Nogoa blacks) would kill some white man in revenge for the blacks shot at Albinia Downs by Mr. Patrick."

The *Courier* and the *Maryborough Chronicle* demanded a public inquiry into the Native Police to ask whether or not "their powers for mischief and their actual atrocities over-balance the benefits which may accrue from their employment?" The squatters split between those who wanted an even more savage force and those calling for humanitarian restraint. Few of them endorsed the idea of having no force out there to protect them. *The Moreton Bay Courier* swept aside these differences, declaring: "All the difficulties which may be arrayed against the settlement of the question should be counted as nothing in presence of the gigantic evil which has been growing up in our midst, and which will only be the more difficult of eradication the longer it is nurtured." A fortnight later, in April, the Governor announced the appointment of a select committee to inquire into the organisation and management of the Native Police force.

*

Australia learned early the value of a shrewdly conducted inquiry. In the colonies' first seventy years, inquiries were held into everything agitating the settlers, from bushrangers to quarantine, from immigration to scab in sheep. But no issues had been inquired into so often as the condition of the Aborigines and then the workings of the Native Police. This would be the fourth such inquiry in five years. Each was designed to ventilate disgust and take no action. Each lowered the bar. The failure to act after so many horrors were revealed meant that each inquiry left the Aboriginal people worse off.

The 1861 inquiry was expertly hobbled. The terms of reference were vague. The committee was not directed to investigate particular officers or particular massacres, merely to examine "charges of unnecessary cruelty brought against their officers when dealing with the Natives". Sitting on the committee were seven squatters who between them held over 3.5 million acres; one was the father of an officer in the force. *The Moreton Bay Courier* asked: "What amount of impartiality in calling witnesses, taking evidence, and framing a report" could be expected from a committee composed of such men? Stung by the question, the government threatened to jail the editor for libelling the Assembly. The witness list was carefully culled. No squatters fundamentally hostile to the Native Police were called to give evidence. Charles and Henry Dutton of Bauhinia Downs were not allowed in the door. The committee questioned no Aboriginal people.

Bligh lied blind. He lied that that morning in Maryborough he was pursuing blacks from the scene of a robbery; lied that he had fresh warrants for the arrest of men he was chasing; lied that both Snatchem and Darkey had "committed many outrages" around the town; and lied that it was "perfectly impossible" for him to have captured any of the men shot that day. Rumours were circulating when the inquiry began that Commandant Morisset was about to resign and Bligh might take his place. The rumours proved true. Two days before the committee published its report – declaring him "justified in his attack on the natives in the town of Maryborough" – Bligh was gazetted acting Commandant. Haughty and vicious, he was to lead the Native Police for the next three years, a perpetrator of slaughters, scourge of settlers wishing to protect the blacks, and an uncommonly well-connected gentleman.

Feeble as it was, the committee's questioning laid bare the brutal methods of the force. The Colonial Treasurer asked Frederick Wheeler what orders he had given his men that night near Ipswich where he was accused of wilfully murdering sleeping blacks:

I told them to surround that camp ... and to disperse them.

What do you mean by dispersing?

Firing at them. I gave strict orders not to shoot any gins. It is only sometimes, when it is dark, that a gin is mistaken for a blackfellow, or might be wounded inadvertently.

Do you think it is a proper thing to fire upon the blacks in that way?

If they are the right mob, of which I had every certainty ...

Was there any necessity for such an indiscriminate slaughter upon that occasion?

I don't think there was any indiscriminate slaughter: there were only two blacks shot ...

I can understand this—if there are warrants out against certain men, and they take to the scrub, that your troopers are ordered to follow them, and, if they do not stop when called upon in the Queen's name, to fire upon them; but in this case there were no warrants out. I wish to know what induced you to give those orders?

The letters I had received from several squatters, complaining that the blacks were robbing their huts, threatening their lives, and spearing their cattle and sheep ...

Don't you consider this is a very loose way of proceeding— surrounding blacks' camps, and shooting innocent gins?

There is no other way.

Dr Challinor of Ipswich, the magistrate who declared Wheeler a murderer, had entered the Assembly earlier in the year at a by-election. The committee could not keep him out. He was one of the first witnesses, staunchly defending his inquest and speaking eloquently for the blacks:

> I think that they ought to be entitled to hunt game on the runs on which they have always done so. I think they should be allowed to procure food on the grounds on which they have been accustomed to procure it; to hunt and fish, unless the Government, in lieu of that, gave them some compensation in the way of food. I say this, because I could produce evidence of cases in which I know that quiet blacks have been molested when fishing, and also when they have been camped on alienated land. In the latter instance their dogs were shot, and blankets and opossum rugs collected and burnt; in the former, they were fishing in the Bundamba Lagoon, and were chased away by dogs and by a man or men on horseback, with stock-whips.

Even more damning, perhaps, was the critique of the force by Maurice Charles O'Connell, squatter and President of the Legislative Council:

> If the object of the Native Police is merely the destruction of the aborigines, they are a most efficient force for that purpose. If you want to destroy the blacks by wholesale slaughter, you could not find people more suited to the purpose than the Native Police.

He spoke of six men who had committed no crime whatever shot by the Native Police near Gladstone and another case of a black "taken into custody by an officer and party of Native Police, handcuffed, marched away from the station, and never delivered over to the regular police; that man is believed, from the account of the blacks, to have been shot dead at a short distance from the station". But surely, the chairman asked, recent outcries against the Native Police in the press were much exaggerated?

I believe that the horror of all right-thinking people is very
greatly excited by the knowledge that cruelty and injustice
have been committed under the guise of law, and there is
also an instinctive feeling against taking human life.

In the committee's shabby report, everything Challinor and O'Connell had to say was ignored. Bligh was exonerated. Morisset was passed
over entirely on the ground that he was no longer in the force. His
brother Rudolph escaped any censure for the killings at Manumbar.
Wheeler was heavily defended. The Attorney-General, Ratcliffe Pring,
"defied any man to say that Lieutenant Wheeler had not done his duty"
and declared he was throwing Challinor's insinuations about him "to
the dogs". No one challenged Wheeler's definition of *dispersing*. From
this point in the history of the Native Police it meant only one thing:
killing. Pring, the first law officer of Queensland, accepted without
demur that Aborigines could be killed by the Native Police with nothing to warrant their deaths but the complaints of squatters. He threw
aside the old polite language of Sydney to admit the Native Police were
not police at all:

It was useless to call the native police troopers a civil force;
they did not go out with little stumps of sticks like town
police, but with carbines and balls. Those were not given
them to play at soldiering, but to disperse the blacks, and
to show them that they were given for something. Therefore
he should call the native police force a semi-military force.

O'Connell tried to budge the government. In the Council he took
his argument against the force to a high constitutional plane:

It did seem strange to him that it never occurred to those
who took an active part in the discussion that the native
police force as at present constituted, was clearly illegal, and
in direct violation of the fundamental principles of the British constitution. The hon. Gentleman then went on to show

that, according to the Bill of Rights, the raising of a standing army in time of peace other than the regular army, was
illegal. This, in fact, was the foundation of all their rights,
as secured to them by the great constitutional measure to
which he had alluded ... The existence of such a force had
in times past proved extremely dangerous to the liberty of
the subject, and he saw no reason to doubt that, if tolerated,
it would prove so again.

He moved that the Native Police be placed on a legal footing as soon as
possible. The motion was lost. The force would never be properly established in law. How could it be? Laws to allow the killing of blacks on
suspicion, killing at random and killing for revenge would defeat the
most able parliamentary draftsman.

*The Courier** mocked the inquiry – "A more piquant farce was never
enacted" – and voices were raised in the papers to keep fighting for the
blacks: "Now it is the duty of the Press to redeem the honor of the colony." But the inquiry had done its work. The public and the subject were
exhausted. Even *The Courier* suggested it was time for Queensland to
get on with the business of being a colony – occupying and exploiting
native lands. Then came Cullin-la-ringo.

After a long journey from Victoria with his family, servants, stockmen, wagons and over 7000 thousand sheep, Horatio Wills pitched
his tents by the Nogoa River in early October 1861. Eight months earlier, "the perfect state of peace" on the Nogoa had been shattered by
Lieutenant Patrick. More violence had followed in the months since
as Patrick went about his work. On 14 July, he and his men were out
hunting sheep-stealers on Rainworth, only 20 miles from Wills' new
station. The pursuit became a bloody shambles. Several troopers were
clubbed; the Rainworth Superintendent shot Patrick in the knee; and
at least two blacks were slaughtered in the scrub. Native Police reinforcements were immediately sent to continue the operations on

---

* No longer *The Moreton Bay Courier*.

the Nogoa. Further inflaming the rage of the Gayiri was the abduction of children by two run-hunters, a crime reported in *The Sydney Morning Herald*:

> Returning homeward, they seized two boys, raised them upon their saddles, and carried them off. They were followed by about sixty men for a considerable distance, who entreated them to give up the boys ... how strongly must the moral sense of these gentlemen have been perverted to have permitted them to commit an offence against nature, one which every civilised code pronounces an atrocious crime!

The Willses were not to blame for any of this but, as the paper pointed out:

> The blacks, like their civilised invaders, confound the individual with the race; that, in common with all people, whether savage or half-civilised, they exact the penalty from the first of the adverse nation who falls into their hands. In war, this course is sometimes followed by belligerent States, professing to rank with civilised nations. Indeed, the principle of reprisals is nothing else than punishing the innocent for the guilty.

The family had been at Cullin-la-ringo for ten days when about a hundred Gayiri men and women descended on their camp and killed them all in broad daylight. Among the nineteen dead were seven children. Though they had many guns to defend themselves, the only shot fired in the attack was from Wills' revolver. His head was nearly severed. Bodies were left scattered among the tents. Absent that day, and the only survivor of the family, was their son Thomas.* News of the killings at Cullin-la-ringo broke around the world. It remains the bloodiest massacre by blacks in the history of Australia.

---

* Already a distinguished cricketer and pioneer of Australian Rules football.

"An uncontrollable desire for vengeance took possession of every heart," Bowen told the Duke of Newcastle, the Secretary of State for the Colonies. Bowen had no quarrel with such "just chastisement". All over the north, settlers and Native Police rode out to kill. Scrubs and mountains were scoured. Blacks were shot and driven over cliffs. The *Rockhampton Bulletin* reported the clashes with something like delight.

> The Native Police overtook the tribe of natives who com-
> mitted the late outrage at Nogoa, and succeeded in driving
> them into a place from whence escape was impossible. They
> then shot down sixty or seventy, and they only ceased firing
> upon them when their ammunition was expended.

Those who sought shelter in Rockhampton – "the little town of mud and dust" – were driven back out into the bush to be shot. As it was after Hornet Bank, blacks were executed hundreds of miles from the scene of the crime. Runs on the Comet, the Nogoa, the Dawson and the Mackenzie were stripped of Aborigines. About four hundred are thought to have died in the weeks after Cullin-la-ringo, but that is no more than a cautious guess. The Yiman, Wadjigu, Gayiri and Darumbal peoples were nearly wiped out.

The Native Police came back to Bauhinia Downs. Charles Dutton heard they were on their way. The troopers were led not by a novice lieutenant this time but by the new Commandant, John O'Connell Bligh. He rode up to Dutton's homestead and ordered him to expel every black from his run. "If they were not off the station by tomorrow, they might look out." Dutton remonstrated with Bligh: "I pointed out to him that such a course of procedure was manifestly unjust, and not warranted by law, he replied to the effect that he was not guided by law, he had his orders, and there were those who would support him in whatever he did."

Dutton was in no mood to cooperate. The murders at Cullin-la-ringo were the catastrophe he had been told to expect. No brake had been put on the police since he complained about young Patrick's wild behaviour earlier in the year. When the select committee's report was published, the chairman had ridiculed Dutton in parliament, spinning an "unjust and unmanly" story that he and Lieutenant Patrick had quarrelled over a black servant girl. Only days before Bligh appeared on his doorstep, Dutton had published in *The Sydney Morning Herald* all his correspondence with officials about the Native Police. Face to face with the Commandant, Dutton did more than refuse his orders. Judith Wright wrote: "Charles Dutton threw open his doors and admitted the fleeing Aborigines to his house." He barred the way. The blacks lived and Dutton was never forgiven by the squatters.

The Duke of Newcastle sharply disagreed with Bowen. As well as the Governor's account of the massacre at Cullin-la-ringo, he had read the evidence to the select committee. From Downing Street in March 1862, His Grace delivered a mighty rebuke:

> The first lesson of importance which a savage ought to learn from a civilized Government is the difference between discriminating justice and indiscriminate vengence. This lesson some of the most degraded Indians of North America have learnt from the Hudsons Bay company, and the consequence is that persons connected with that Company can travel with safety when a Known native* of the United States would be murdered, if possible, by any Indian who met him. I do not know why the Australians should be incapable of learning this lesson and I hope the Government of Queensland is not incapable of teaching it. When this is done and not till then I shall entertain some hope that the Colony under your Government may be an exception to that unhappy law which seems to prohibit the occupation of the same country by the Anglo Saxon and the Aboriginal.

* Citizen.

But it was too late for London to deliver such lectures. Intimidated from the start by the squatters and their partners at Home, British governments had taken no effective steps to protect the native peoples of Australia. With Queensland now a self-governing colony, the blacks were more than ever beyond London's help. Bowen was elegantly polite to his overlords in Downing Street, but when the fate of the Aboriginal people was at stake, he ignored them.

After Cullin-la-ringo there was no hope left of reining in the Native Police. Vengeance was blessed. No limits were set on the awful powers of the force. More than ever, the government placed the highest value on the energy of its officers and their discretion – in both meanings of that slippery word: judgement and secrecy. Nowhere would the occupation of Australia prove bloodier than here, and no instrument of state as culpable as the Native Police. Slaughter was bricked into the foundations of Queensland.

III

REG & D'ARCY

The native mounted police of Queensland ... carries out its sanguinary will without the intervention of judge, jury, or law. Practically, there is no appeal from its almighty vengeance.

"An Ex-Officer", 1879

EXPEDITION RANGE

17

PRO CHRISTO ET PATRIA

The King's School was a stone barn with a Doric portico on an unhealthy stretch of the Parramatta River. Its doors had closed once or twice. Scarlet fever one year carried off a dozen boys. The place survived by educating, safe in each other's company, the sons of squatters. A little before Reg Uhr arrived in 1859 at the age of fourteen, a new headmaster came from England with plans to open a wider world to these colonial boys. The Reverend Frederick Armitage imagined King's as a gateway to Oxford and Cambridge, to the East India Company and the learned professions. He was young and rich. He admired the German approach to schooling. "No people," he said, "equalled the Germans in the solidity of their attainments." He introduced mathematics. For a few extra guineas, boys could learn to draw and dance. But Armitage mistook his market. The school's Tory clientele had narrow ambitions for their sons. Wool, trade and the law were the careers they had in mind. Numbers dwindled. Teachers drifted off. The three years Reg spent as a dayboy at Parramatta saw Armitage's high hopes fade and die.

What survived was a new military ethos he brought to the place. Armitage was a keen member of the Parramatta Volunteer Rifles, one of hundreds of citizens' military units formed throughout the Empire at this time. In Britain they saw themselves as the last line of defence against the French. In New Zealand they fought the Māori. Their mission in Australia was far from clear, but they drilled, bickered about uniforms and had a wonderful time preparing to serve the Empire.

Armitage brought an army sergeant in to drill the senior boys. They marched to church. Reg was neither a scholar nor a sportsman. Unlike his cousin the younger Richard Jones – by this time an Anglican priest in Suffolk – he showed no interest in music or Greek. But the lanky Uhr boy was not unprepared for the future he found waiting when he returned to Maryborough at the age of seventeen at Christmas 1861.

As a businessman, Edmund Uhr did not lack courage. He thought on a big scale. He took risks. But nothing really worked. He was still trying to sell Woodlands and still trying to find a government post for himself. His oldest son, Ned, ran the sawmill at Woodlands. Reg pitched in but there was no prospect of a career for him at the boiling-down. In 1862, his father began lobbying to find Reg a place in the Native Police. The beau ideal of an officer was Frederick Walker at his best – good in the bush and good with the blacks. But most young officers found their way into the corps through connections to politicians and high colonial officials. These men were not always fit for purpose. Lady Bowen won a place for one of her relatives from Corfu though he knew neither the bush nor Aboriginal people and barely spoke English. Many officer recruits were sons or brothers of politicians. Others were new chums from Britain with letters of introduction. There was a Russian and a German who had each married local brides with clout. What the officer recruits most obviously had in common were uncertain futures and well-connected families. Patrick O'Sullivan, an Ipswich merchant, told the Legislative Assembly in 1861: "This corps was looked upon as a refuge for broken-down characters who, after having spent a fortune and ruined their prospects elsewhere, came here with a basketful of testimonials, made friends with somebody in power, and received an appointment in the native police. (Hear, hear, and laughter.)"

Jones and the Uhrs had always backed the Native Police. Vigilantes had their place, of course, but where possible the family preferred blacks to be killed professionally. They did not quarrel with the methods of the force but Edmund believed the Native Police ought to be more professional, more efficient and even more aggressive. He wondered from time to time whether black troopers were right for the job. "I think a white force with trackers would have more stability, and be more benefi- cial in the end." But only blacks were on offer and he had no doubt they were better than nothing. Edmund feared time would make the natives of Wide Bay and the Burnett even more dangerous. He was calling then for sound men to lead the force after the catastrophe of Hornet Bank. A couple of years later, he was offering his second son. Reg's qualifications were slight but he had been to King's; he could ride and handle a gun; and he knew the blacks who did odd jobs for offal at the boiling-down.

This was gentlemen's work. To be an officer of the Native Police on the frontier massacring blacks was one way of living up to the motto engraved on Edmund's signet ring: For Christ and Country Danger is Sweet. The qualities Inspector George Murray looked for in officers were sobriety, energy, bush experience and "being a young Gentle- man of good character". There was even a notion that gentlemen were particularly suited to leading black troopers because gentlemen and blacks saw eye to eye. "I believe every blackfellow is one of Nature's gentlemen, in manner and disposition," the Maryborough magistrate Richard Sheridan told the 1861 inquiry. "He dislikes coarseness in every sense of the word." All this talk of good breeding attracted its share of mockery. "Red Indian" wrote in the *Maryborough Chronicle*: "It is a farce endeavouring to throw credit over such a trade, that by a uniform and by bastard titles gentlemen can be found to carry on the trade of a butcher."

Officers who showed zeal and discretion might expect to be re- warded after four or five years' slaughter with another government post as a clerk of petty sessions or even a magistrate. There was cun- ning in this. Over the years the bench in the bush would be stacked with men who knew firsthand the lawless ways of the Native Police. But such future employment depended on the shape an officer was in after years in the field. So many ended up drunks. Drink had been Frederick Walker's downfall. Pitching camps well out of towns did little to limit drinking. "A Squatter" wrote to *The Courier* complaining of officers in the streets of Rockhampton too intoxicated to sit on a horse: "I have seen a drunken officer—a bloodthirsty ruffian upon the verge of *delirium tremens* ... boast of the slaughters he had wreaked upon blacks." Drinking followed killing. The *Maryborough Chronicle* noted "the demoralising influence which the trade of a butcher in human beings has upon the mind". The 1861 inquiry into the force took a roll call of drunken officers: Powell was an efficient officer before he took to the bottle; Murray would be fired if he didn't sober up; Irving and Fulford had been "known to be drunk at stations for days together"; Fulford died of drink.

For all the carnage it caused, the force was tiny – only about a hundred troopers at any one time led by ten to fourteen officers and half a dozen officer cadets. These posts were prized. Somehow, Edmund Uhr managed to get Robert Herbert's ear and in September 1862 he wrote from Woodlands to remind the Colonial Secretary that he had "kindly promised me a cadetship for one of my sons ... and I trust by return steamer I shall see him gazetted as the sooner he is in harness the better. His name is Reginald Charles Heber." Someone scrawled on the letter: "Do you know anything about this?" Commandant Bligh recommended the appointment in December. Bligh was indebted to Uhr for his support after the killings in Maryborough. They were also, in a complicated way, related by marriage. In the first week of 1863, Herbert's office wrote to the young man confirming his appointment. "I am to request that you will have the goodness to report yourself without delay at the Head Quarters of the Force."

*

At the age of eighteen, without any training at all, Cadet Uhr was given temporary command of the Owanyilla camp, near Maryborough. A crisis was threatening the force: for the first time in its existence, an officer was facing the gallows. Local magistrates had charged the camp commander Second Lieutenant Donald Harris with having "murdered, by shooting, or causing to be shot, one Jemmy, an aboriginal". Reg Uhr was

REG

not back in his hometown long, but time enough to watch a doomed attempt by civilised squatters with high political connections to call the Native Police to account.

Harris was a young, sporting gentleman who had been with the force for barely a year and only recently promoted to second lieutenant. One evening in April, he and three troopers cantered up to the homestead at Yenda. His men looked shabby and restive. Harris said they were out searching for deserters. Yenda was home to Gilbert Eliott, Speaker of the Legislative Assembly, who regarded the force "as a band of trained savages—whose officers travelled through the country with halters* round their necks—whose occupation was so disreputable that no man with a particle of spirit could belong to such a corps". His sons managed Yenda. When Eliott Jnr found Harris at his door that evening, he offered the usual hospitality of the road: dinner and a bed. The officer

* Nooses.

asked about the blacks round Yenda. "I replied that they were quiet and had given no trouble for a long time." Were there any about? Eliott told him he would, next day, most likely overtake a man who had often worked for him at Yenda. "Jemmy was a very quiet blackfellow." Next morning, Harris and his men shot Jemmy on the road. His body was dragged three or four hundred yards and dumped in the bed of a dry creek. Cries of grief and horror alerted Gilbert's brother Henry, working at sheepyards nearby. Harris rode over and admitted one of his troopers had, while out of sight, shot the native. "Good God, do you allow your troopers to go forward and shoot any blackfellow they come across?" asked Eliott. Harris apologised.

A cursory inquest was held in nearby Gayndah. The police magistrate did little when ordered to investigate the case further. The Executive Council took no time to signal the end of the government's interest in Jemmy's death by resolving there was "no tangible evidence to warrant any further proceedings being taken in the matter". But the Eliotts were determined to see Harris answer for killing one of their men. A gentleman on the bench in Gayndah was Berkeley Moreton, second son of the Earl of Ducie, educated at Rugby and Magdalen College, cousin of the Colonial Secretary, Robert Herbert, and joint proprietor with his brother Seymour of 73,000-acre Wetheron. Young Eliott persuaded Moreton to charge Harris with murder. A warrant was issued for his arrest.

The squatters of the Burnett were fed up with the Native Police. They wanted them gone. Whatever problems persisted in Maryborough, the bush was quiet. Furthermore, they found deserters from the force, broken in by service, made good workers. Inspector Murray begged for clear authority to round these men up, but the government was in a bind. Power lay with the squatters, and the Colonial Secretary was willing to side with them. Where the squatters wanted fighters, he would supply them. When they wanted men to wash their sheep, he would supply them too. In the year of the Harris crisis, Herbert issued a directive to the Native Police not to recapture a deserter working for the Moretons:

I hereby order you and all your subordinates to desist
from further attempts to apprehend the aboriginal
deserter Hughey alias Joey, so long as he remains constant
to the services of (my cousins) the hon Berkeley and
Seymour Moreton, of Wetheron, near Gayndah.
Signed
R. G. W. Herbert.

Later, while defending these squatters, Herbert made the astonishing admission that the Native Police was an illegal force. "The native police officers had no legal right whatever to apprehend deserters. (Hear, hear.) The force had no power, no authority whatever, to do so ... as they were a wholly irregular force, they had no legal sanction for their acts." He promised laws to fix this. They never came.

Harris spent only a night in the cells. He was released on his own recognisance by the Police Magistrate. The two men played billiards together for a week, waiting for a hearing before three magistrates to decide whether Harris should stand trial. The Attorney-General, Ratcliffe Pring, did all he could to protect the officer. He plucked out of the air a ruling that the man's correspondence with his superiors could not be admitted into evidence. That correspondence would have exposed Harris lying that he had a warrant to arrest Jemmy. And, of course, neither his troopers nor Jemmy's family could tell the magistrates what they had seen that day. It would be another dozen years – the bloodiest in the colony's history – before Queensland allowed blacks into the witness box. After half a day, with almost no evidence before them, the three Gayndah justices announced: "The bench do not require any defence, and the prisoner is discharged." Harris was sacked. After this it was clear to Native Police officers that the worst they might suffer for the random killing of any black was dismissal. The Harris case renewed their licence to kill.

Herbert announced a reorganisation of the force. Largely to save money, he decided to have the Native Police and the regular police serve side by side under the Colony's first Police Commissioner – his former aide-de-camp, the son of an Irish gentleman, David Seymour, who would hold the post almost to the turn of the century. Seymour outlasted ten premiers and sixteen governments. He would be their servant. He appointed Native Police officers at their direction. He fired them rarely for their crimes but often for embarrassing his political masters. Zeal and discretion were the Commissioner's watchwords. He fiercely defended the force from those who sided with the Aboriginal people of Queensland. He was an able bureaucrat and over time built a large force both paramilitary and civilian. Sitting the two side by side seemed incongruous to Seymour's critics. "The native police officers flog their men, shoot their deserters," wrote *The Courier*. "Under these circumstances, how can this force be classed with the Constabulary?" That didn't worry Seymour. Nor did the scandals of the next thirty years. Nothing so became the Commissioner as his way of turning a blind eye.

*

By the time Harris walked free, Cadet Uhr was at Bowen, a raw little settlement of shacks, sheds and pubs on Port Denison. The Native Police camp was on the Don River, which for most of the year is a trickle of water on a swathe of sand. The force was out there, miles from town, to keep an eye on the Yuru people who lived along the river and also to try to discourage troopers drinking. That failed. Uhr moved into the officers' quarters, a timber cottage – "fast going to decay" – which he shared with Lieutenant John Marlow, his commander and patron in the force. Two white sergeants lived in barracks of their own. Four black troopers slept in bark humpies. They were not to be called boys or blackboys. There was no greater insult to be offered to them, for from the first they were told that service in the force put them a cut above servants and stockmen. While officers were expected to be unmarried, the troopers usually had women. Very often they were booty from dispersal raids. The practice of troopers kidnapping women as they worked was endlessly provocative but excused by the authorities. "Troopers after a period of good service are entitled to wives," explained an old officer. The camps were often home to children. Archaeological digs of these sites have turned up buttons, bottles – many, many bottles – cartridges and children's toys.

The troopers were up early, fed and drilled by the sergeants. Weapons were cleaned and horses groomed. When Uhr appeared, his men sprang to their feet and saluted, addressing him as *Mamae*, Father. How officers should treat their men was a subject of much sage advice over the years. Many accounts survive of officers flogging, humiliating and even shooting their men. Old hands recommended earning the respect of the troopers by keeping your word; doing what you promise; and letting no infringement go unpunished. Uhr's men appeared to trust him. He was reproached once or twice for being too generous with rations for the troopers' women. There is no record of his men deserting.

Officers and troopers both wore *shakos* – round, peaked caps – and dark-blue jackets. The boots of the troopers reached almost to their knees and came equipped with remarkably long spurs. Officers' uniforms were decorated with stripes and braid. Uhr's dress jacket was a thing of wonder:

> Dark blue cloth, Garibaldi pattern; standing collar, rounded in front, and edged all round with round gold cord; two rows of round gold cord down the front, one quarter inch apart; Austrian knot round gold cord on sleeve; round gold cord shoulder-straps.

He carried two weapons: a six-shot revolver for close work and a double-barrel carbine for killing at a distance. The carbine came with a fine colonial pedigree: designed for hunting big game in Africa and then used by the Cape Mounted Rifles against the Khoi San. Only slightly modified, these clumsy muzzle-loaded weapons were issued to the Queensland Native Police. Hard to load on horseback and not particularly accurate, they nevertheless delivered a fat bullet a long way. Charles

Tom, a squatter on some scale in the north, suggested to the Colonial Secretary in 1864 that the Native Police might use bird shot instead of bullets to disperse gatherings of blacks.

> This, I believe, would frequently prevent murder from being committed, and would, at the same time, facilitate the attainment of the object for which the Police are retained – security from the incursions of their countrymen. The scattering of the shot would occasion the chastisement to be widely felt, while its mildness would not be so likely to arouse those feelings of rancour which the taking of life so naturally calls into existence in the friends of the deceased.

Neither Herbert nor Seymour was interested. Killing was the point. Official instructions always came with fine paragraphs about avoiding deaths wherever possible, words the Native Police knew to ignore. The consensus in the Colony was that the blacks had a lot to learn and nothing taught them better than killing.

Marlow was Uhr's teacher. He had earned a bloody reputation in the south commanding a detachment on the Maranoa River inland from the Darling Downs. This is Mandandanji country. One day as his men were building a camp, a party of blacks approached and offered to dance with them. Marlow ordered them shot instead. This pointless little slaughter was widely reported and over time metastasised into a tale of Imperial heroism:

> British soldiers could not have faced the enemy more gallantly than did these dusky troopers against a mob of warriors four to their one. It was soon a hand-to-hand fight, and as usual in such cases the combatants became mixed. The lieutenant himself was the first to fall by a severe scalp wound from a nulla, which he got from a black who had somehow got behind him, and who at the same moment seized the lieutenant's carbine by the barrel.

JOHN MARLOW

The troopers won. Marlow recovered from his wounds. When the
time came for him to leave, the Maranoa squatters were sorry to see
him go. "We are perfectly satisfied with Lieutenant Marlow, and his
mode of dealing with the blacks," wrote the occupier of 80,000-acre
Amby. Marlow was needed urgently in the Kennedy district – Bowen
and its hinterland – which by 1863 had become the bloodiest corner
of Queensland.

The problem was George Elphinstone Dalrymple, a volatile, dash-
ing, impatient Scottish adventurer. There were titles and castles back
home. He had tired of life as a coffee planter in Ceylon and come to
Queensland at the age of thirty to make his fortune. His charm was
formidable and his prose lyrical. He could sell the crudest colonial
enterprise as an adventure for settlers of pluck in a landscape of endless promise. He got men going. Dalrymple was the master of a familiar
genre in colonial Australian writing: explorer porn. In 1859, with over
a thousand pounds raised from a syndicate of investors, he set out to

explore the pastures Ludwig Leichhardt had seen a dozen years earlier on the Burdekin, Bowen and Suttor rivers. In contrast to the German, Dalrymple killed along the way. One of his companions noted: "We had seven times to fight for our lives." The grasslands were good but Dalrymple saw two things were needed before they could be settled: Native Police and a harbour. After much disappointment he settled on the shallow anchorage at Port Denison, a great bay dotted with islands. He wrote: "The whole coast country seems to swarm with blacks, whom we found here, as elsewhere, very hostile."

Dalrymple was appointed Commissioner of Crown Lands for the Kennedy and marched north with settlers, stock and fifteen Native Police who killed as they went. Two shiploads of settlers were waiting for them in Port Denison when they arrived. Blacksmiths, shopkeepers, carpenters and publicans came ashore and pitched their tents by the only reliable water: wells dug by the Giya and Yuru people. In an act of brazen flattery, Dalrymple named the settlement Bowen and told the Governor:

> It is now most deeply gratifying to me to see the British flag flying over the spot which we found a wilderness; to see a small but happy and orderly population of men, women, and children, quietly settled, where, a few days ago, the wild aboriginal held undisputed sway,—cattle and horses feeding over the rich virgin pastures, and the sounds of industry and civilisation marking the advance of another great wave of Anglo-Australian energy from South to North.

He wanted the blacks – this "race of bloodthirsty miscreants" – cleared from the coast. No attempt was made to open dialogue with them. Trouble was to be met with gunfire. In the first weeks of settlement, three men returned from the bush complaining they had been menaced – merely menaced – by the blacks. Dalrymple sent the Native Police in pursuit. Vigilantes joined the party. Hundreds of Aboriginal people eluded them by disappearing into a great swamp. Dalrymple then ordered the dispersal of warriors gathering on the beach. Their only sin was to assemble. Two were shot and the rest swam out to sea. Next morning the Native Police returned to find men on the beach again. "They were speedily put to the rout with a loss sufficient to teach them a severe, and, it is to be hoped, a useful lesson," reported the *Rockhampton Bulletin* in its very first edition. So a cycle of violence began that grew steadily bloodier. The killing of two sailors gathering oysters on Shaw Island provoked a wave of righteous anger across the Colony, but the *Maryborough Chronicle* asked readers to look at this through the eyes of the dispossessed:

> The new settlement of Port Denison, under the guidance of misrule and causeless violence, is preparing to undergo that baptism of fire and blood through which it is fondly hoped it will attain to civilization and greatness ...
>
> War has broken out between the two races; white men without any reasonable cause have been murdered by blacks they never saw before; according to established usage the Native Police will pay the Shaw Group a visit and destroy every native they can find—men, women, and children, utterly ignorant and innocent as they may be of the previous outrage; the blacks, feeling deeply aggrieved at the loss of their companions, will vow vengeance and take it out upon the first white men that visit them, kindly intentioned and innocent as they may be. Thus will the white man and the black man retaliate upon each other by successive murders—the principle of their warfare being exactly similar—until the stronger party gains the victory.

Squatters needed protection. Within a year of the first whites settling in Bowen, two million acres had been granted along the rivers of the hinterland. At the edge of settlement for a time was Biddulph Henning's 280,000-acre Exmoor on the Bowen River. In mid-1862 he was joined there by his sister Rachel, whose letters have won her a place in the literature of Australia. She was educated, fearless and found the country beautiful. She told her family the homestead Biddulph was building her had "a noble view over a wide sweep of undulating plains dotted with gum-trees and patches of scrub, like a park, beyond the thick bush and a panorama of mountains all round, peak behind peak". After the Native Police visited Exmoor in early 1863, she wrote home:

> We are likely to be well protected from the Blacks for a day or two ago a small detachment of the native police with a sergeant & Lieutenant came up here & announced that it was the intention of the Commandant at Port Denison to found a permanent station here within a couple of miles of the Exmoor head station. We considered it in the light of an awful bore. in the first place the black troopers would always be about. then the officer Mr Price is a prosy elderly man an incessant talker & always putting himself forward & he will be always coming here. we shall never keep a Black boy on the station ourselves. we are not the least afraid of Blacks & do not think there are any within 8 or 10 miles.

There were few about because, not long before her arrival at Exmoor, the Native Police cleared the Biri people from the banks of the Bowen. "I have had to disperse war parties of from 60 to 80 men," the then local commander told Dalrymple. "No gins or children to be seen, but spears & other native weapons in profusion." The Native Police came back to Exmoor to take a second look, this time led by the Commandant of the force, John O'Connell Bligh. "Rather a pleasant gentlemanly young man," Henning told her sister. They talked of places they knew in England. "Cannot you fancy Matford Terrace & the well at the corner & those beautiful elms hanging over the wall on the way to church?"

It might look a bore to the Hennings, but along the Bowen and Suttor rivers squatters vied to have Native Police camped on their runs. The prize went to one of Dalrymple's backers, an Austrian with a remarkable stutter. Philip Sellheim had tramped the bush with Dalrymple and endeared himself to the Commissioner of Crown Lands by writing to newspapers pouring scorn on city folk who, blind to "the savage character of the aborigines", were agitating for the removal of the Native Police from the Kennedy: "The pioneer settlers of the north will not tamely allow their risks and arduous labors to be undervalued by any ignorant individual, living in a well-protected township, who, to further his own private ends, perverts truth and risks the lives of his fellow-creatures." On the frantic morning Dalrymple began handing out land in the Kennedy, he gave the first block – 200,000 acres on the Bowen River – to Sellheim, who called the run Strathmore.

The Native Police set up camp there in March 1863. The first two officers to run the Strathmore camp were a disaster. Ewan Williams was a shambles, in trouble for bouncing cheques and barely attending to his duties. After only a few weeks on the Bowen, he was sent off to track down the troopers who had deserted him on the Upper Burdekin. His place was taken by Marmaduke Richardson, a known drunk, who went on a bender at a pub one night while escorting a young black prisoner to Rockhampton. He broke down a door, punched the publican and behaved, in the words of the official report, "in a most disgraceful manner". This ordinary colonial uproar might have passed unpunished but for Richardson disturbing the rest of two citizens of note: James Landsborough, brother of the explorer William, and the Reverend Thomas Jones, an Englishman about to marry Frances, the daughter of the late Richard Jones. It was not discovered until after the drunk was sacked from the force that he had shot the prisoner he was escorting to Rockhampton. An attempt to prosecute him for murder petered out. The next man Marlow sent to run the Strathmore camp was Reg Uhr.

*

John O'Connell Bligh had had no plan to promote him yet. "Cadet Uhr is not sufficiently experienced for a higher position than he holds at present, but he is a young & promising officer." But the force had run out of spare men in the north. At the age of nineteen, Reg found himself on the Bowen River, 70 miles from town, in charge of a sergeant and five troopers. He reached camp in the immediate aftermath of an attack by "a hundred fighting men, in full war paint" on the Strathbogie run 10 miles away. *The Courier* made it sound like a Wild West adventure starring the overseer and his "black boy" Charley:

> Armstrong and Charley blazed away, and several more of their bullets found a fatal billet. The overseer had, ere this, heard sufficient to satisfy him that some, at least, of the attacking party were so far advanced in civilised ways that they could use English obscene expletives. Presently the black boy shot down one of the two whom he regarded as "too much like whitefellow;" and immediately thereafter the other one rushed forward, and, throwing a spear, sang out, "Oh, you b——r, Charley." Charley's reply was another shot, which brought down his challenger ...
>
> Next day the mob was tracked by a party of people from the neighboring stations, and they got another lesson that will probably deter them from attacking a station again in a hurry. It has been estimated that about twenty-five blacks were killed.

Of the Native Police, the paper said: "The force is inadequate for the work they have to do in protecting such a large district." That was so across Queensland. The answer was to keep detachments on constant patrol, showing themselves, reminding the local inhabitants that these few men could mete out terrible punishment. Fear was the everyday weapon of the Native Police, and without shooting blacks here and there how could they keep fear alive?

Reg spent three of the next four years clearing the Biri, Yangga, Miyan and Yilba people from the hinterland of Bowen. The squatters wanted an empty landscape for sheep to graze. It was an article of faith with them – as it was with Dalrymple and Marlow – that peace was only possible if the blacks were gone. From time to time, squatters were reminded that the terms of their leases guaranteed the right of the first inhabitants of the country to continue hunting and fishing on their land. This was ignored. Already it was being taken for granted in Australia that the men of the bush could decide which laws applied to them. Stockmen and shepherds were armed and put to the task. So were the Native Police. Bowen's newspaper, *The Port Denison Times* – which first appeared in March 1864 – would look back with fury on the role of the force in the clearances:

> Where *they* "disperse" the blacks killing is no murder; no account is rendered, no inquiry held, and mystery enshrouds their deeds in distant solitude or in the dark recesses of the mangroves, where the groans of the dying reach no ears but those of the Lord of Sabaoth.* These monsters take a real pleasure in their work, and it is said of them that they have often dishonoured the widow beside the corpse of her murdered husband. We know that our own town at least had its foundations cemented in blood.

Marlow was impressed with Reg Uhr. He had cause in these years to reprimand officers who let troopers desert, horses break down, rations run out, and men get about town unkempt and drunk. But Marlow was so pleased with this young man's work at Strathmore that, in August 1864, he asked the Executive Council to promote him and backdate it to 1 January that year, "as since that date Mr Uhr has discharged the duties of a Sub Inspector, and his zeal and efficiency are fully certified". The Governor approved. The force had switched by this time from military to police ranks: second lieutenants became sub-inspectors. Reg's salary doubled to £200.

---

* The Lord of Hosts.

Rachel Henning watched the young man in action about this time as he deftly captured a band of thirteen deserters from the Native Police who turned up at Exmoor. She wrote of them:

> They each had an old shirt by way of a garment & several were carrying possums which they had caught on their way. Biddulph went over to speak to them. "Good day Sare" they all said & grinned very much & then told him they were run-away troopers from Rockingham Bay where they seemed to think they had been very badly treated in being made to work. "too much carry log" one of them said. They were on their way to Wide Bay their own country.

They were fed at the kitchen door and "made night hideous till a late hour", dancing with the station blacks. The Hennings were untroubled but some of their staff feared they had only hours to live. She continued:

> The next morning when they were peacefully eating their breakfasts up rode Mr Uhr the officer of the native police in this district. he rode straight into the camp. "Bail you run away"* he said but there was not a chance for the mounted troopers had surrounded them on all sides before they found it out. They took it very philosophically but I was quite sorry for the poor creatures some of them were very lame and footsore & three of them were gins. they must have walked nearly 1000 miles from Rockingham bay here. Mr Uhr said he only heard of it 2 days before. the whole police force of Rockingham bay had absconded leaving the settlers there in a great plight, surrounded by wild blacks.

Despite Uhr's success at Exmoor, there was growing anger among squatters on the Bowen and Suttor at the want of police protection. In October 1864, two shepherds were killed on Pentland Hills, a

---

* Don't run away.

BOWEN & SUTTOR

128,000-acre run on the Campaspe River. Gilgunyah on the Burdekin was attacked in broad daylight. "Although no lives were lost, Mr Curr's family narrowly escaped." In November, two shepherds were killed and mutilated on a corner of John Melton Black's 250,000-acre Victoria Downs. "I have had two of my shepherds Huts deliberately burnt down, a stack of sawn timber of the value of £200 deliberately fired and totally destroyed," he told Herbert. "No less than ten men under twelve months agreements bolted from their employ, leaving in many instances the sheep in the bush."

John Black had clout. The deaths on Victoria Downs – "accompanied by the atrocious brutalities which mark these scenes of savage ferocity" – provoked much reflection in the press, none of it sympathetic to the Aborigines. *The Brisbane Courier* urged those who love the "poor blacks" to acknowledge colonial reality:

> There is no need to argue in favor of our right to occupy this country—we take this to be granted. Nor, need we say a word of our duty to protect ourselves against every possible danger that we may encounter in taking possession of such a magnificent inheritance. All this must be admitted. Common humanity dictates that, as the habits and customs of the aborigines are almost wholly in violation of what Lord RUSSELL designates as "the eternal and universal laws of morality," we cannot treat them as a vanquished people and allow them to live according to their own laws.

Missionaries could not "instil into the minds of the aborigines, the virtue of non-resistance and peaceful submission to the will of man", said the paper. No. That was the work of the Native Police. But what the police were to do was left strangely vague in the press: they were to take *stringent measures*, to *act* with *firmness* and to *restrain* the blacks. The new and civilised *Port Denison Times* signalled the truth behind the blather: "The blacks having been lately menacing the Native Police Barracks at the Belyando ... were followed ... and 'dispersed' in the usual and approved manner." Soon those inverted commas were being used everywhere. Readers knew what they meant.

Squatters continued to arrive. This was no country for battlers. These men needed capital to stock their runs, build homesteads, provision little armies of workers, and wait a long, long time for their first wool cheque from London. Cuthbert "Fethers" Fetherstonhaugh* borrowed at 17.5 per cent to buy 5000 sheep to stock his 32,000 acres on the Suttor he called the Hermitage. "A pretty little run," he said, "but surrounded by scrub." Like so many men in the Colony, Fetherstonhaugh was driven to make good in Queensland by the failing fortunes of a big family. His memoir, *After Many Days*, is a tale of fine horses and handsome friends; of japes in Rockhampton, steeplechases in Melbourne and hard times on the Suttor; and the mass murder of blacks. He admired his neighbours. "It has never been my lot to meet a grander lot of men—brave, loyal, unselfish, hardy and uncomplaining. They took the ups and downs in an even spirit—cracking jokes when things were at their worst, and never admitting such a thing as 'downheartedness.'"

Fetherstonhaugh was having a hard time at the Hermitage. His run lay on the border of Yilba and Miyan country. "The heat was very great, the nights no relief, flies and mosquitoes intolerable, food rough, and a good deal of fever." The rains had failed that year and his shepherds were looking anywhere for feed, even taking their flocks deep into the scrubs. On the evening of 13 December, half the flock tended by a boy called Charley had returned without him. Next morning there was still no sign of him. Fetherstonhaugh directed Dan Smith to take the sheep out for the day while he searched for the missing boy. He did not find him. But later in the day at a spot still called Murdering Lagoon, Fetherstonhaugh came across Smith's body. His head had been smashed in and his corpse thrown on a fire. "His legs were quite burnt away." Fetherstonhaugh saw nearby a black in a tree and ordered him shot. "I was just breaking my heart to be after them to avenge these murders," he wrote in

* Pronounced *fan*-shaw.

his memoirs. He called for the Native Police. Reg Uhr and his men took a fortnight to arrive. They were busy with the blacks at Conway, where a hutkeeper had also been found roasting on a fire. When Uhr reached the Hermitage, Fetherstonhaugh and a party of vigilantes were waiting to ride with him. The chase that followed and the "prompt justice" Uhr dealt out to the blacks were reported in twenty-five newspapers across the country. In the aftermath, Uhr reported to Marlow "shooting six blacks for murder of shepherd". In his memoirs, Fetherstonhaugh put the number higher:

> We all started off on our punitive expedition. These fellows tracked the blacks with ease. They put the number down at about twenty from the tracks, including gins. We white men could not see a sign of a track till after we had been a week after them. In one place we were crossing a rocky river, and I asked a Murray black, called Capito, an old fellow, what he was following. He pointed to where a black had spit out something he had been chewing, and sure enough others had also been chewing and spitting.
>
> Our trip was quite a picnic. We did about ten miles a day, tracking all the time. Sometimes, of course, off the scent and delayed. No one watched at night, and if the blacks had been about and been game, they could have easily crept on us in the dark. I asked Uhr if this had ever happened. He said only once, and then the wild blacks were led by two runaway black troopers and they pretty well wiped out the police camp. The troopers cooked good food for us and most delicious "beggars on the coals," sort of Johnny cakes.
>
> After doing about one hundred miles on the tenth day, as Capito and I were riding in the lead in open scrub country, suddenly he leaned down on his horse and went off as hard as he could, I after him. He had sighted the "myalls." We galloped into them. They were running in all directions.

The gins lay down, one was shot by mistake. We shot down two blackfellows and got through them and turned back. A shot from one of our fellows hit my horse in the chest—no harm done. In a few minutes all the blacks, twelve of them, were shot. If one or two tried to fight they had no chance ...

We sat down, and it seemed very cold blooded that with some of the dead blacks lying close to us, and the gins scowling at us from a little distance off, we ate and enjoyed our pot of tea and our dinner.

18

VALLEY OF LAGOONS

George Elphinstone Dalrymple had another scheme. While following in Leichhardt's footsteps up the Burdekin in 1859, he found himself in high basalt country that had provoked another of the German explorer's lyrical outbursts:

> We discovered an extensive valley with large lagoons and lakes, and a most luxuriant vegetation, bounded by blue distant ranges, and forming the most picturesque landscape we had yet met with. A chain of lagoons connected by a reedy brook followed the outlines of the table land, along the foot of its steep slopes. We descended by a tolerably gentle slope into the valley, and encamped near the reedy brook … Water, grass, hills, mountains, plains, forest land; all the elements of a fine pasturing country, were here united.

Dalrymple agreed. He could see Valley of Lagoons – as Leichhardt called this place – as the heart of a mighty pastoral empire. For that he needed three things: political backing, capital and police protection. First, he persuaded the Colonial Secretary, Robert Herbert, to join him. Herbert in turn recruited an old friend from Eton and Oxford, Arthur Scott, who brought with him his brother Walter. They were the sons of a rich, fox-hunting Whig MP. It was a perfect colonial syndicate: a gallant Scot to grab the land; wealthy Englishmen to fund the project; and the leader of the government to make sure it had all they needed – beginning with a grant of 656,000 acres centred on the valley in the country

GEORGE DALRYMPLE

of the Gugu Badhun. Only one more thing was needed to guarantee success: a practical dray road from this paradise to the coast.

Dalrymple was no longer Commissioner of Crown Lands. He had been allowed to retire in 1862 after a minor scandal over the allocation of land. The Scotts arrived in Queensland early the following year and Dalrymple took Arthur Scott up to see the valley. The lagoons were thick with black swans and magpie geese. The river flows through ancient volcanic rocks "as though suddenly cooled but yesterday" and the soils were so rich Dalrymple dreamed of "the possibility of the production of wine-grapes to compete with those of southern Europe". But try as they might, the syndicate could not find a wagon track across the mountains to the sea a hundred miles away. Nevertheless, the Scotts moved into a rough homestead in the valley on a ridge between the river and Pelican Lake (Yanggarrji) and began, in the words of the Rockhampton *Morning Bulletin*, "shovelling capital into it with unparalleled liberality".

Dalrymple's role with Scott Brothers, Dalrymple & Co. might have ended soon after when he beat the Police Magistrate John Jardine in the streets of Rockhampton with the ivory handle of his hunting whip while shouting: "I have the satisfaction of telling you that you are the most damnable scoundrel in Queensland". Both men were on horseback.

WALTER JERVOISE SCOTT

Their mounts were prancing and leaping. Jardine's hat was smashed. He parried with his cane, struck the whip from Dalrymple's hand and ordered a passing constable to take the former Commissioner of Crown Lands into custody. Seventeen magistrates sat on the bench next morning to hear a charge of gross and unprovoked assault. They committed Dalrymple to trial at Quarter Sessions some months away. Herbert wrote to Walter Scott:

> By this time I feel more sorry for poor Dalrymple than anything else; he has been indiscreet, but by all accounts he is expected to see the inside of the Gaol which is a hard thing and I shall be very glad to hear that he escapes that fate.

Herbert was able to arrange that. Jardine was sent 1000 miles north to be Commissioner of Crown Lands at Port Albany on the tip of Cape York. When the case came to trial, the Attorney-General cited Jardine's inability to attend, plus "special reasons known to himself", for insisting Dalrymple be found not guilty.

*

In January 1864, a few months after horsewhipping the magistrate, Dalrymple chartered the *Policeman* to explore Rockingham Bay 230 miles north of Bowen. The aim was to find a port to service the Valley of Lagoons. On board the schooner were Arthur Scott, Philip Sellheim, a detachment of Native Police commanded by John Marlow, and an eager bunch of colonists ready to build a settlement on the bay. As an interpreter, Dalrymple had brought James Morrill, a convict who had lately emerged after living for seventeen years with the Yuru and Bindal peoples, who took him in after his boat was wrecked in the Coral Sea. Morrill had presented himself naked at a hut near Bowen in early 1863. "Do not shoot me," he called. "I am a British object." He had hoped to become an intermediary, a peacekeeper between blacks and whites, but the Queensland government was not interested. He was given a job with Customs in Bowen, from where Dalrymple borrowed him for the voyage north.

Rockingham Bay lies in Warrgamay country. To the east are the high hills of Hinchinbrook Island (Pouadai) and to the west – beyond miles of mangroves, scrub and swamp – is the Great Dividing Range. The *Policeman* fired guns and rockets to celebrate its arrival. Two days were spent exploring the bay. On the third, a dozen men appeared on the shore. Dalrymple and Morrill rowed over. Though Morrill did not speak their dialect, both sides made themselves understood. This was not a negotiation. Dalrymple laid down the law through his interpreter.

> On nearing the beach the natives stood in the water; beckoning us to come on shore. I had a conversation with them, asking where their chief camp was; they pointed along the beach to the northward. They wanted to know whether we came to have a corroboree with them, or whether we came as enemies; to which I answered that we came as friends, but as we were going inland we wished them to keep away, or if they did not we would make war.
>
> I told them that we had been surveying a creek, and asked where the big river was. They said that the creek was

worthless, and that the river lay up at the back of the ranges further north. They asked for some clothes, if we had any to spare in the boat besides what we wore, and were astonished to see the native police in their dress. We said no, as we had no wish to give them anything, thus inducing them to remain hovering about us.

I then said that they must clear out and tell others to do so, as we wished to occupy the land, and would shoot any who approached; that we were strong, and that another party would soon follow. They told us to leave and not to return, and then they went away.

Dalrymple thought these "large muscular men, with bullet-shaped heads and a ferocious, cunning and repulsive cast of features" were trying to deceive him. When he asked if there was a track through the ranges, they told him there was but far to the north. Yet Dalrymple could see behind him a gap in the range that surely offered a way to the interior. He was certain these "cunning savages were answering every question by a falsehood for their own purposes".

Everything depended on a road. "I long to hear of the exploration of a good line of road from your town site to the Valley of Lagoons," Herbert wrote to Arthur Scott. "That is all that is necessary to make the future town at Port Hinchinbrook of great importance." Dalrymple took Marlow and his troopers to explore the gap. As they left the camp, they found blacks in the scrub. Morrill reported they were "set upon suddenly by Mr. Dalrymple's men and rather cut up". Beyond the gap an immense swamp blocked their way. But on a second attempt ten days later, Dalrymple made it to the valley. It was hard, hard work. Bashing their way up the Seaview Range took a fortnight. Coming back down with three bullock drays and a mob of cattle took seven weeks. Nevertheless, Dalrymple dressed up the track to the valley as a mighty discovery. Governor Bowen named the settlement Cardwell after the latest Secretary of State for the Colonies, appointed a Police Magistrate,

CARDWELL & VALLEY OF LAGOONS

and sent up a fresh detachment of Native Police under the command of Sub-Inspector Charles Blakeney. Making this slew of appointments to little Cardwell brought ridicule on Herbert:

> The story about Dalrymple having found a practicable road from the Bay into the interior is false, no such thing has been effected. When the Minister of Lands and Works is asked to give an account to the Legislative Council for acting in this tomfoolery way, by appointing a police magistrate, etc., etc., to a place of which he knows as much as the babe unborn? I really anxiously wait for this reply. Perhaps his plausable friend, Mr. Herbert, may attempt to palm off to the House his latest *visionary* intelligence from the Valley of Lagoons!!!

Herbert pushed through the Assembly a payment of £2292 to Scott Brothers, Dalrymple and Co. to reimburse them for expenses incurred in opening Cardwell. "Our account is nevertheless in by no means a healthy condition," Herbert told Walter Scott and begged him to come to Brisbane as soon as he could. "Everything as regards the partnership is at sixes and sevens." Despite the English capital pouring into those acres, Valley of Lagoons under the management of Walter Scott was threatening the partners' ruin almost from the start.

Sub-Inspector Charles Blakeney arrived in Cardwell in August 1864 with eleven troopers. As he had in Bowen, Dalrymple was determined to clear the country around the settlement. To do otherwise, he argued, "would be to allow a multitude of armed savages to have the chance of watching and harassing, and endangering, at any weak moment, a small isolated camp of settlers in a densely wooded country". The Police Magistrate Beckwith Leefe backed Dalrymple. Blakeney had the men for the task but refused to cooperate. He explained to Leefe:

> To do so I should have to resort to violent measures which for the present would be unwise and likely to make the natives retaliate and moreover from the various Patrols I have made in and about that locality I am convinced the Natives only use that portion of the country as a passage down from the range to the Sea on fishing excursions.

That Blakeney was haughty, gutless, lazy, disobedient and a man with a few principles saved many lives in Cardwell and beyond. A cause of constant complaint, he survived for seven years in the force because his uncle was the Registrar-General of Queensland. His time in Cardwell had already been a disaster. All eleven of his troopers had deserted within weeks. These were the men Reg Uhr rounded up at Exmoor. Soon after refusing Leefe's orders, Blakeney's second troop disappeared. "The native police have again thought proper to take French leave," reported *The Port Denison Times*. "The whole body decamped last week, leaving behind an unfortunate gin, who being in an interesting situation was incapable of travel."

Blakeney was ordered back to Rockhampton. Reg Uhr was directed to take his place. But while Uhr disentangled himself from Strathmore, Inspector John Murray was sent north to give Cardwell its first taste of heavy policing. A failed squatter from the Macintyre, Murray was one of the great drinkers of the force. He had been sacked and suspended several times, but his flair for enlisting troopers always saw him taken back. He was about to leave to recruit down on the Murrumbidgee when he was diverted to Cardwell. He saw eye to eye with Leefe and Dalrymple: the blacks should be kept out and squatters who didn't clear their runs should be denounced. False humanity, he argued, always led to fresh atrocities. Murray's "indomitable perseverance, utter disregard of personal fatigue and his great practical experience" impressed the locals. But in May 1865, Sub-Inspector Uhr arrived with eight troopers – among them Bungalo, Robert, Mich and Billy Go By One – with orders to take the Native Police from Cardwell to the high country, where he was to set up camp "within four miles of Messrs Scotts Station on the Valley of Lagoons".

*

Uhr came with a reputation. As he set out for Cardwell, newspapers were still applauding the exploits of this "most indefatigable and energetic officer". The story of the Hermitage campaign reached Scotland, where the meaning of "prompt justice" had to be spelt out for readers. *The Perthshire Journal* wrote: "Prompt justice was done to them, and the blood-thirsty cannibals, one and all, bit the dust." Once in Cardwell, Uhr swiftly won the approval of *The Port Denison Times*:

> Our black brethren have been keeping quiet lately, and I
> have not heard of any depredations having been committed
> by them; no doubt they have been kept in awe from the fact
> of our gallant Sub-Inspector and his 'brave army' having
> been amongst us, preventing them from 'kicking up a row.'

Uhr and his men set up camp at Pelican Lake in Valley of Lagoons in about September 1865. In theory, he was responsible for a vast territory stretching from the Pacific to the Gulf of Carpentaria and

miles north towards Cape York. But his essential task was to police
the country seized by Herbert, Dalrymple and the Scotts. That meant
tangling with the Gugu Badhun, whose country covered about 3500
square miles running west from the Seaview Range. In Valley of
Lagoons, they hunted kangaroo, trapped fish and harvested water-lily
seeds in streams that never ran dry. It is thought that over a thousand
Gugu Badhun were on country when the invaders came. The Scotts
derided them:

> I am sure they have not as keen senses as humans higher in
> the scale of humanity. "Like beasts, with lower pleasures;
> like beasts, with lower pains". They have not the slightest
> sense of gratitude, in any kind of way; far less than a dog,
> or horse. Of course they know where they are well-treated,
> and well-fed. I believe fish, even, learn that.

The Scotts set about getting rid of them. In *Gugu Badhun: People of the
Valley of Lagoons*, it is written: "After the establishment of the pastoral stations, any Gugu Badhun person who ventured into those areas
risked being shot and killed." But their resistance was strong. The country favoured them. "Their lands ... included a good deal of rough, basalt
country unsuitable for grazing sheep or cattle, but still holding water
and food resources." In that broken landscape, horses could not give
chase to the Gugu Badhun who could hide in caves, biding their time
until they emerged to attack again.

Arthur Scott, back in England to become a fellow of All Souls, was
deeply worried about the run. At that point they had ninety white men
on the payroll. He thought perhaps it was time to stop driving the blacks
away and start putting them to work. He remarked that the Gugu Badhun had already been given a "dressing" and believed that was enough
to keep them in line.

> I am rather sorry about those blacks; I think the time has
> now come to try & be friendly with them, we are strong

> enough now to defend ourselves & they would do a lot of
> work in washing ... Certainly the best way will be to bring
> in some gins and boys & we shall soon make the others
> understand what we want. I am convinced that with our
> scrub & lava it is far more dangerous to keep them out than
> to let them in.

He knew that his brother Walter was fiercely hostile to the idea. "Do think well over about letting in the blacks in places. We may do worse by driving them to despair." But Walter stuck to his guns for the next eight or ten years. He told his brother, "I entirely despair of ever establishing satisfactory relations with the Blacks."

Economy was beyond the partners. Money flowed through Valley of Lagoons like a river in spate. Dalrymple sold out. Herbert hesitated to approach new investors, wondering "if the concern is sinking and will not recover, we ought to drag them into our ruin". Walter Scott was advised on all sides to switch to cattle. Herbert begged him "no longer to indulge in those playful woolly animals which are costing us so much of our own & other people's money". Walter wouldn't budge. Arthur had a bright idea in England: "You know the way to make a fortune is to find out a want & supply it. Now the great want of England amongst the Upper Classes is how to dispose of its sons without a great outlay of capital. This is the want which Queensland is adapted to meet." He proposed the brothers charge aristocratic new chums £2000 each to be taught the ways of the bush in the valley and then sell them a slice of their country. "Mind you send me the black fellows' arms – shields, swords & stone instruments especially," he wrote. "They will be worth anything to me as an advertisement."

The Gugu Badhun remember this time. Harry Gertz was born in about 1890 and as a little boy in the valley heard stories about the Native Police or "trackers" from an old lady who looked after goats. The children called her Grannie. Gertz told these stories to the anthropologist Peter Sutton in the 1970s.

Well, one silly fool, he went and killed a bullock. He didn't kill it to waste, everybody's eating it—cut it all up and cooked it: beef hanging everywhere. Of course, you know the old Black-trackers had to attack them now. They fired on them and chased them, couldn't catch a lot of them. Some of them got shot, some of them didn't—most of them didn't anyhow. They went out to Walters (Plains) Lake way, way out there, because that's too open country. Back that way from Walter's Lake, it's all granite country, big rocks, they're living about in them. And attacked them again, hunted them from there—they went into G.W. Swamp. All along that swamp there were big camps: oh, they chased them there, shooting them, killed a lot of natives.

One of Uhr's troopers had captured his wife on the Logan River south of the Darling Downs. After she had learned a little English, she told Uhr a story he thought might cast light on a mystery that troubled Australia: the disappearance of Ludwig Leichhardt, never seen again after his party left the Downs in 1848. Lost explorers have a special place in the mythology of the outback as the martyrs of colonisation. Leichhardt was beatified by the squatters who followed his tracks into their kingdoms of grass. But he was mourned as well by hard men who fell under his spell and for his beautiful prose. Those who paid for his explorations had had their names scattered across Queensland: the Archer, the Isaac, the Cape, Mt McConnel and the mighty Burdekin, which became a highway for their sheep and cattle into the far north. So many expensive search parties had gone out and found nothing but trees on which he had carved an elegant "L". In February 1866, Uhr told *The Port Denison Times* that his trooper's wife might be able to find Leichhardt's bones:

> About eighteen years ago, when she was quite young, a party
> of white people, the first her tribe had ever seen, came near
> to where she was taken prisoner. They had with them black

boys, horses and cattle, and the country being flooded, they
formed a camp there, put up stockyards and remained some
little time, until the blacks came down upon them at night,
surprised them and murdered the whole party. She says that
if taken to the district she can find the remains.

The papers lapped up Uhr's story. Reports were published in nearly
every city in every colony. Leichhardt search committees found a new
lease of life. Lady Bowen co-opted Uhr's mother, Amy, to raise funds
for her Brisbane Committee. *The Port Denison Times* begged that
"Lieut. Uhr with the black boy and his gin could be spared from their
duty for a short time for a purpose which might clear up all doubts as
to the fate of the unfortunate Leichhardt." Leave was not granted. The
search continues.

More was expected of "that indefatigable officer Lieut. Uhr" than
discreet slaughter. Officers were required to keep accounts, write
reports, issue stores and pay wages. Uhr's paperwork was a mess. Problems that began in Strathmore continued in Cardwell. Shopkeepers
were left unpaid. His accounts arrived at headquarters late, in a mess
and, as often as not, unsigned. He was spending too much on stores.
The deaths listed in his "very imperfect" half-yearly Return of Horses at
Cardwell suggested to headquarters "that they could not have received
fair play". Despite repeated reprimands, Uhr failed to lift his game. His
pay was stopped as punishment. Other officers were sacked for making
such a hash of their paperwork, but Uhr survived. No disasters at his
desk overshadowed his successes in the field.

*

Inspector Murray made his way back to Queensland with twenty-two
new recruits from the Murrumbidgee. How he gathered them isn't
known. Deception and kidnapping had come to play a part in renew-
ing the ranks of the Native Police. "A tremendous amount of steam" was

got up in Sydney as these big men passed through the city. Some eyed them off like slaves at market.

> Looking on the twenty-two strapping fellows, who have just entered the Queen's service, and the two comely dames that accompany them, all apparently in the enjoyment of robust health and capable of much endurance, it is difficult to believe the common doctrine, that they belong to a race which is fast wasting away through some mysterious and inevitable decree. One would think that a people with such muscular frames, good appetites, and quickness of apprehension, required only prudent guidance to become a very useful element in the colonisation of Australia.

The Empire was suggesting clearly enough that killing blacks was not the useful role it had in mind. Even before he left the south, Murray had an angry exchange with the local *Deniliquin Chronicle* when the paper accused him of taking the recruits north to mete out slaughter to any blacks they could find without proof of guilt. "Lieutenant Murray denies the possibility of this occurring, as the evidence of guilt is always sought for by means of tracks from the scene of outrage to the camping ground." Execution for footprints. *The Brisbane Courier* could see how bad it looked for Queensland for Murray to be parading these men through peaceful New South Wales on their way to kill in the north. "The Queensland Government will shortly have to do something to save itself from utter condemnation in the eyes of the obstinate but generous, though inexperienced part of the Australian censorial community, as hirers of bravos and murderers."

Murray returned to Cardwell and Uhr was posted back to Bowen. Marlow and his friends gave him a hero's welcome. In July they gathered at George's Hotel to celebrate his twenty-second birthday. The champagne was excellent. "Lieutenant Marlow proposed the health of Mr. Uhr, and commented upon the valuable service which he had given to the force. Mr. Uhr replied in a suitable manner; and the company dispersed about 10 p.m., highly satisfied with their evening's entertainment." Days later, Uhr and his men were at work. "Natives from very distant tribes both southward and westward" had been seen gathering not far from town at Euri Creek, a stream that runs along a low line of hills and into the sea. Nothing had been stolen by them. No one had been killed. But the spears in their possession suggested "they were evidently bent on mischief of some sort". *The Port Denison Times* reported:

> Mr. Sub-inspector UHR dispersed a mob of over two hundred encamped near Euri Creek ... it is evident that our sable brethren are advancing in civilisation; and they seem to be rapidly losing a portion of that dread, we may say awe, of the white man, which is so great a safeguard to us, and, we may add, to them, as without it we should be compelled to enter upon a war of extermination, or to abandon the country.

19

AT LAST A PERCH

Maddened by gout, the Sergeant-at-Arms of Queensland's parliament put a bullet through his head in September 1864. As Speaker, Gilbert Eliott – squire of Yenda and scourge of the Native Police – had the power of appointment. The time had come for him to repay Edmund B. Uhr J.P. for enlisting eighty citizens of Wide Bay to petition his nomination in the 1860 elections. After begging for so long for a government post, Edmund was appointed Sergeant-at-Arms. For a salary of £300, he was to sit in an armchair at the back of the Assembly, dressed in lace, knee breeches and silver-buckled shoes ready to enforce the orders of the Speaker. The post was rather a joke in the Colony, but the *Maryborough Chronicle* did its best to congratulate him:

> We are no great admirers of such offices merely ornamental, as they appear to us; but since they who should know better deem this one necessary for the good behaviour of legislators, and to add dignity to Parliament, inspiring vulgar outsiders with becoming reverence and awe, we submit, and congratulate Mr. Uhr on his good luck, than whom we know of no one more thoroughly fitted for the office. Mr. Uhr has been resident in the Wide Bay and Burnett upwards of fourteen years, and though we believe he has not accumulated a fortune he has earned, both as a public and private man, a larger share than ordinarily falls to the lot of one man of the good wishes and esteem of his fellow-colonists.

Not all the papers were so kind. When the new Sergeant-at-Arms arrived in Brisbane in May 1865 to be drilled in his duties, the *Rockhampton Bulletin* remarked: "Of this individual it has been truly said that his intense flunkeyism is only equalled by his despicable insincerity. *Verbum sap.*"*

The Queensland parliament met in the old convict barracks on Queen Street. The place reeked of misery. "Where the Governor enters the House formerly stood the three sisters—i.e., the triangles—where almost every morning the refractory lags got a few dozen before breakfast." Uhr's work was humdrum and occasionally mortifying. One afternoon, Eliott sent him out to deal with a rowdy menagerie pitched over the road. His failure was reported unkindly:

> The Sergeant-at-Arms was sent over, and the demeanor of
> that gentleman ... was almost sufficient to guarantee that
> no further disturbance would occur. But such was not the
> case; the lion roared and the tiger bellowed, in spite of the
> authoritative remonstrances of Mr. Uhr.

Uhr's arrival in the parliament coincided with the election of William Henry Walsh as Member for Maryborough. The superintendent of 95,000-acre Degilbo on the lower Burnett, Walsh was an uncertain friend to the Aboriginal people of Queensland but a longstanding enemy of the Native Police. He no longer hid behind the *nom de plume* "A Squatter" to attack them as a force which "inevitably taints all those who are responsible for its existence". In person he was noisy, combative and widely detested. "A horrible new member of Parliament," Herbert called him, "who makes endless speeches and bores me to death." Now Uhr found himself face to face with an intractably difficult member of the Assembly. Hitherto, the conduct of the place had been reasonably orderly. But with the arrival of Walsh it plunged into chaos, with the Sergeant-at-Arms often being directed by the Assembly to take Walsh into custody and walk him from the chamber.

* Enough said.

SERGEANT-AT-ARMS

On 1 June 1865, Walsh asked a question without notice: had the government heard that Sub-Inspector Cecil Hill had been murdered by the blacks? Herbert prevaricated. For the first time an officer of the Native Police had been killed on duty, but the government was curiously reluctant to detail the circumstances of his death. No inquest was held. Herbert continued to fob off questions as the killing drove months of rage and soul-searching across Australia. Familiar voices denounced the villainy of the blacks. Others argued that young Hill and his troopers got exactly what they deserved.

Hill was no bushman. He owed his position in the Native Police to his mother's friendship with the Bowens. After only a few months in

the force he had been rapidly promoted to Sub-Inspector. The Mackenzie River in the hinterland of Rockhampton was his first posting. On
21 May that year, 1865, he and his troopers had been called out to the
Pearl Creek run to deal with the murder of a shepherd. Hill asked to
be pointed to the nearest blacks' camp, which the detachment reached
a little before sunset. They immediately charged the mob of Gangulu.
At least one was killed. How many more is not known. The men fled
into the scrub, leaving eighty-nine women behind. "I counted them
afterwards at Mr. Hill's request," said the station overseer. That night,
Hill pitched camp close by. At about three in the morning, the Gangulu crept out of the scrub and rained spears on the police. Hill was
speared through the heart. All his troopers were killed. Historian Robert Ørsted-Jensen wrote: "It was perhaps the most successful act of
retaliation against the Native Police Force ever performed by Aboriginal people in the history of colonial Queensland."

The retribution was terrible. Native Police spent most of June shooting any blacks they could find on the Mackenzie River and in the
Expedition Range. Sub-Inspector Otto Paschen gave the government
no more than a bare list of these *dispersals*, a list first published in
late June:

> June 4th.—On the Sanders Run, near the Expedition Range.
> The blacks dispersed towards the Comet Range.
> June 5th—On the foot of the Comet Range; the
> blacks dispersed.
> June 7th.—In a scrub near the Tryphinia Vale Station; the
> blacks dispersed ...
> Early on the morning of the 10th June a collision took place
> in the Expedition Range between the four detachments Na-
> tive Mounted Police and a party of aboriginals, when the
> latter were dispersed.

Paschen's timetable of slaughter provoked horror in Australia and
London.

Gideon Lang was preparing to deliver a lecture in Melbourne on *The Aborigines of Australia: In Their Original Condition, and in Their Relations with the White Men* when Paschen's list appeared in *The Brisbane Courier*. The Lang brothers came from the heart of the squatter world. They owned famous runs in four colonies. Lang was no blind partisan of the blacks after living for so many years "in a state of active hostility or dangerous peace". But after joining a vigilante raid early on, he had decided "never to shoot a black unless in circumstances which would justify me in shooting a white". For Lang, the Paschen list was fresh evidence that killing on such a scale was "an ordinary proceeding of the native police". He added a coda to his lecture in early July, eloquently defending the blacks while attacking Hill, the Native Police and the Colony of Queensland, where "there has always been more destruction of the blacks in occupying new country than in any other colony, but within the last few years it has been wholesale and indiscriminate, and carried on with a cold-blooded cruelty".

Cecil Hill's death, Walsh's rage and Lang's lecture – widely read when published as a pamphlet – provoked a general ventilation of the *native question* in the colonies. In Queensland, the argument was narrow and hard. Dispossession was taken for granted. No one argued the conquest of their country should stop. At issue was the best way to go about it. Those who demanded more humanity and those who called for greater efficiency both blamed the Native Police. One or two newspapers contended that as the wealth of Queensland came from its soil, some benefit should flow to its original inhabitants. They were ignored. Hardly a soul argued for country to be set aside for Aboriginal people. A few clerics – backed by the Governor – still spoke of offering them, in return for their country, a chance to enter the Light of Christ. The radical *Empire*, calling on the memory of Abraham Lincoln, warned against the vengeance of the Lord:

> If the late President of America, looking sorrowfully on the
> long continuance of the mutual havoc of his countrymen,

and remembering the much longer continuance of slave-holding atrocities, was impressed with the thought that "for every drop of blood shed by the lash, GOD in His justice might have determined that a drop of blood should be shed by the sword," has not every settler in Queensland reason to fear that in some terrible manner, the blood of murdered aborigines will return upon the heads of a community who have allowed hundreds of them to be slain without even the semblance of just cause?

As the debate rolled on from August to October 1865, the Native Police found few defenders. George Dalrymple, having extracted himself from the financial catastrophe of Valley of Lagoons to become the Member for Kennedy, was almost alone in the Assembly singing anthems in praise of the force. Walsh attacked the Native Police with a ferocity the parliament had never heard before. But the master of Degilbo was no sainted humanitarian. He was an efficiency man, ruthless, but in his terms decent. To cries of outrage from the members, Walsh catalogued the crimes of the force: drunkenness, ineptitude, theft of women and cowardice:

It was a reckless force, and its only effect was the extirpation of the blacks. He admitted that when blacks committed crimes they ought to be punished, and there was only one way of punishing them, namely, shooting them down. He remembered the time when he would not have been able to leave his station for a single day, in consequence of the presence in the neighborhood of disreputable whites, but for a knowledge that he could leave everything safely in charge of his faithful blacks. How often had the blacks brought in persons who had been lost in the bush, or afforded succour to shipwrecked sailors? Why then should the Government let loose a native police force, whose recognised mission was to shoot them down?

Governor Bowen did nothing. His inaction endorsed the role of the Native Police at their worst. Once again, humanitarian outrage rebounded to Indigenous disadvantage. The Governor took an uncomfortable pleasure in the violence. He wrote at this time to the Duke of Newcastle:

> As in all other instances of colonization among savage races, occasional loss of life is inevitable among the first settlers in each new district in Queensland. But this very fact lends to the efforts of our pastoral adventurers a tinge of danger, which is of itself fascinating to many minds. As I remarked once before, there is something almost sublime in the steady, silent, flow of pastoral settlement over North Eastern Australia. Although it is difficult to ascertain exactly what progress may have been made at the end of each week and month, still at the close of every year we find that the margin of Christianity and of Civilization has been pushed forward by nearly two hundred (200) miles.

In October, His Excellency boarded the *Platypus* for an official tour of the northern ports. The steamer caught the citizens of Maryborough unprepared, their wharf not yet decorated with a welcoming display of greenery and flowers. Among those who rushed to the river when the Governor's cannon boomed was Edmund B. Uhr, still proprietor of the Woodlands boiling-down, who delivered one of half a dozen loyal addresses. At Bowen, when the *Platypus* hove into sight and fired a salute, the boats in the harbour returned volley after volley. "Guns, pistols, anvils, and in fact everything which could for the nonce be converted into ordnance, re-echoed the sounds." Under a marquee on the shore, Bowen praised – as he would up and down the coast – the heroic work of Queensland's pioneers who, in six years, had added to the British Empire territory four times the size of the United Kingdom.

Gentlemen, the triumphs of the pioneers of Christianity and of civilisation in Australia are triumphs not of war but of peace. They are conquests without injustice and without cruelty. They are triumphs not over man but over nature; not for this generation only, but for all posterity; not for England only, but for all mankind.

But Queensland's economy was falling to pieces. The rains had failed over vast swathes of the country for a couple of years. The market for wool was sliding. Business was depressed. Extravagant borrowings were proving impossible to repay. Creditors were seizing runs. The business prospects of Edmund B. Uhr had never been bleaker. Strapped for revenue, the Queensland government announced there were no government posts to be had. Citizens were warned not to bother applying. Applications were to be ignored. But in late 1865, the Sergeant-at-Arms managed to slip another son onto the payroll of the Native Police.

Wentworth D'arcy Uhr was a big, wild boy of twenty. There was no money to send him to King's. What schooling he had in Maryborough is unclear. But he was bright and he could write. He was nineteen when his crew "in very pretty blue uniform" won race after race in the Separation Day regatta on the Mary. He was fearless. For a rough and tumble life in Queensland, D'arcy was extraordinarily well equipped. But there were deep flaws in the young man. D'arcy was a liar, uncontrollable and cruel.

He and his friends made a sport of robbing blacks. In July 1865, a Butchulla man called Mellon wandered through Woodlands with ducks he had shot on the river. D'arcy and co. pounced, taking the game and his gun. It was a familiar lark but that night there was a hitch: Mellon told them that Mr Sheridan had lent him the gun and sent him out hunting. The ducks and gun belonged to one of the town magistrates. D'arcy's mate George Finnimore rushed to hand in the gun to the police but on the way ran into Sheridan, who accused him bluntly of robbing Mellon. Back at Woodlands, D'arcy concocted a letter to the *Maryborough Chronicle* in Finnimore's name. He declared Mellon a notorious scoundrel. He lied that the black was putting the lives of women and children in danger by hunting on Woodlands. He lied that he insulted him and his friends; lied that the gun was seized only after an altercation; and lied that Mellon had then run away, abandoning the ducks. The letter ended with threats: "If blacks have as much right to use firearms as white men, I consider we have no right to complain of sticking-up either of drays or men. Law in my hands is this—The next 'darkey' I catch near my residence with a gun, unless he be protected by a white man, I will do the same again, and, moreover, take him into custody." D'arcy put a pound on the table so his letter might be run as an advertisement if rejected by the editor. But it was run, and the young thugs escaped prosecution.

Three months later, D'arcy was directed by the Commissioner of Police to report with the least possible delay to the Native Police headquarters in Rockhampton and bring some recruits with him. Queensland was too broke to send anyone to the traditional hunting grounds along the Murrumbidgee. D'arcy had to forage locally. Here he had an advantage he boasted all his life: "I can speak the language of the Southern Queensland tribes quite as fluently as I can speak my mother tongue." He took three or four men from Brisbane Gaol, for the government had decided blacks might serve out their sentences with the Native Police. One of the prisoners was a powerful man well known to the Uhrs under many names: Ferriter, Sam Pootingah or Sambo. Sambo had been in and out of the Native Police – and prison – for years. He would serve D'arcy to the end. When D'arcy caught the steamer to Rockhampton in late November, he took nine men with him. The *Maryborough Chronicle* did not like what it saw: "Mr Uhr is, we believe, about twenty years of age—rather young to have charge of such a gang, engaged in such fearful work as slaying men without responsibility to any human tribunal."

D'arcy was taught the ways of the Native Police by Frederick Wheeler, one of the cruellest men who ever served in the force. Wheeler was the murderer Dr Challinor identified in 1861, the man who told the

public inquiry that year that *dispersing* was Native Police code for killing, and that a squatter's complaint was, in itself, reason to shoot a black
man. Wheeler observed that the only thing to do with badly behaved
blacks was kill them.

> I don't think they can understand anything else except shoo-
> ting them; at least, that is the case, so far as my experience goes.

> When you go to a camp, do you call upon them in the Queen's
> name, in any way, to surrender?

> No, because directly they see you they run ...

> Do you think it would be practicable to take a black prisoner
> under ordinary circumstances—for instance, if you met a
> camp of blacks in the scrub, would it be possible to take any
> of them prisoners without their consent?

> No, I don't think so, not in a scrub ... but I think, if there
> was a chance in an open plain, you might run a blackfellow
> up a tree, and you would soon get him there. You could not
> take him without shooting him, or felling the tree.

None of this stood in Wheeler's way. In 1864 he was made an inspector.
He taught cadets for fifteen years that there were no rules and regulations
in the Native Police. "An officer of police must use his own judgement."
The historian Jonathan Richards observed of the cohort of officers
Wheeler reigned over: "Each of them killed many Aboriginal people."

D'arcy's schooling was brief. A few days before Christmas 1865, he
and five troopers joined an expedition to the Gulf led by the distinguished
explorer William Landsborough. With them was a surveyor – always
key agents of colonisation – and what Landsborough called "a considerable party of men in search of employment or bound otherwise to try
their fortunes in the new district Burke at Carpentaria". Ahead of them
lay a journey of 1000 miles. Their destination was a point on the Albert
River chosen by the explorer to be the centre of administration. It was

to be called Burketown. An old pioneer recalled sorrowfully: "We were going to found a town that would be Melbourne and Singapore rolled into one, the greatest commercial port in Australia."

20

TROUBLEMAKER
IN A SHANTY TOWN

T he discovery in 1860 of the mighty grasslands he called Bowen Downs had not made William Landsborough rich. The run lay halfway across Queensland. So much money, so many sheep and cattle were needed to make a million acres of that country profitable. He found partners. They took more land. Drought followed floods. Blacks fired the grass. Ten thousand sheep were lost at one go making their way up from the south. Facing little or no return from Bowen Downs, Landsborough accepted the post of Police Magistrate in the Gulf in 1865. He knew the country from an expedition he led searching out there for Burke and Wills. Now he was returning as the one-man government of a wild territory the size of France, rapidly filling with stock and squatters. He was in great part responsible for the rush. In the journals he published of his explorations he wrote of an el dorado of grass. "He had had twenty years experience of Australia, and he had never seen better country for stock than he found on the Gulf of Carpentaria," he told the Royal Society of Victoria. But members of learned societies did not have men like Landsborough's second-in-command, George Bourne, to tell them what living in that country was like. First there were the mosquitoes:

> They get through our curtain at night: bite through two suits of clothes. People, unable to rest, are walking up and down all night. When the sun rises, and the mosquitoes retire to the shade, their watch is relieved by clouds of flies,

WILLIAM LANDSBOROUGH

which are, perhaps, even a greater torment than their fore-runners, it will not be wondered at that we lead a life of suffering, without rest or respite, from these two plagues.

As Landsborough's party made its way west in January 1866, the Chief Commissioner of Crown Lands predicted: "When fully occupied, the district will be capable of depasturing three or four millions of sheep, and at least two hundred thousand horned cattle." That the Gulf was already occupied deterred no one. There would be Native Police to deal with trouble when it came.

Landsborough went via Bowen Downs, where D'arcy staged a little rebellion. Landsborough's plan was to try to find a better way to the Gulf, one that would avoid plains of dry spinifex and poison bush on the route early settlers had taken north. D'arcy would neither go exploring with Landsborough nor guard the rest of the party waiting at Bowen Downs. He took his troopers the old way, straightaway. Bowen noted in his diary: "Monday 5th March. Mr Uhr and the native police left me and started for to go by the Flinders." After searching for two weeks without finding another way north, Landsborough turned back and followed D'arcy down the river. They arrived at the humpies and pubs of Burketown a week apart in April 1866.

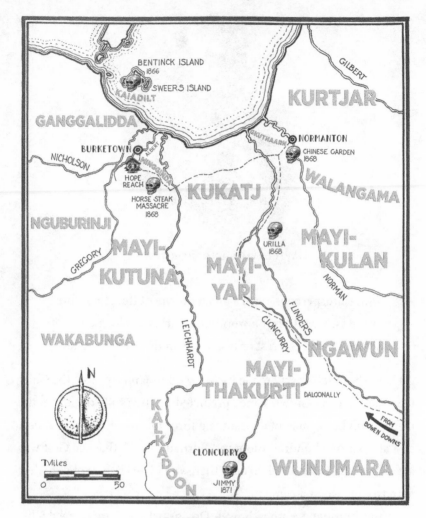

GULF COUNTRY

It was a wretched place for a port. The sea was 30 miles down a river choked with sand banks. Crocodiles prowled its waters. The settlement was surrounded by swamps. There was fever about. Many had died in the wet season just past:

> The rain came down in sheets. In places where the trodden down vegetation covered the ground, it formed a spongy rotting mass, and where the traffic was greatest this rotten grass and mud were churned into a quagmire that would have turned the stomach of any well disposed pig. Men came

out in the early morning and stood on the verandah of the new building, and the perspiration streamed from them, running down to their boots. And, looking over the plain, a fog seemed always hanging—the steam that all the thousand tons of rotting vegetation threw up. And the men drank all day and all night.

Landsborough saw his mistake at once. He ordered D'arcy to take his men 15 miles upriver to Hope Reach while he took a schooner out to investigate moving the settlement to the healthy air of Sweers Island in the Gulf.

One of D'arcy's early tasks at Hope Reach was to join yet another search for traces of Ludwig Leichhardt, missing, by this time, for nearly twenty years. A squatter called Duncan McIntyre had heard of pale children on the Gulf coast who might – just might – be the offspring of Leichhardt's men. "There is a boy and a girl, from ten to twelve years of age, almost white, with light blue eyes and red hair; and in another tribe, a girl about fifteen years of age; and in another a full-grown woman, perhaps eighteen years of age." McIntyre had persuaded a committee of Melbourne women to fund a search for these elusive youngsters living with fierce blacks who had yet to come to terms with the settlers. D'arcy and two troopers turned out to round up the tribe. "We had to make prisoners of them all before they would allow us to see them properly," reported McIntyre. But there was no sign of pale children among them. A few days after this human muster, McIntyre died of Gulf fever.

To this day, no one knows what this fever was. "Some declared it was 'yellow jack'," wrote a pioneer of the time. "Others pronounced it to be a virulent form of dengue or 'break bone.' Whatever it was it swept away a large proportion of the inhabitants and almost all who were afflicted and recovered ... fled from the place." Its source also remains a mystery. Many said a boat brought the plague from Java. Others blamed life as it was lived on the river: "There was nothing for the people to do but drink; and this they did with diligence and energy." Most days everyone retired to a rough racecourse built on the edge of town. "They had races in the morning, funerals in the afternoon, and wakes at night." There was no doctor. Men wolfed down quinine, hoping for the best. In the five months after D'arcy arrived, seventy-five whites died in and around Burketown.

Among the dead was the first Commandant of the Native Police, Frederick Walker, searching for a suitable way for the proposed telegraph line to the Gulf. After his sacking from the force, Walker and about eight former troopers, his faithful boys, offered their services to the squatters – run hunting, establishing stations from scratch, and protecting them from the blacks. When he was forced to disband his troupe, Walker reinvented himself as an explorer. He led one of the parties searching for Burke and Wills. He continued to kill. On the Leichhardt River in December 1861, men were seen approaching his camp. "They were stretching out in a half moon, in three parties," Walker noted in his diary. "This move, which my men term stock-yarding, is, I believe, peculiar to blacks throwing spears with a woomera." Walker ordered his men to charge the line. "Their right wing which was, I think, the strongest mob, got over the river and were off; but their centre and left wing suffered a heavy loss." The fever had him by the time he reached the Gulf coast in November 1866. He died near the Norman River a few days later. Walker's obituaries said nothing of the many killed at his command. That was no surprise. Remembering was not the point of death notices for colonial monsters. *The Queensland Times* painted the picture of a hero's death:

> We may surmise that he died in his tent, surrounded by some of the boys he brought from the Murray River; those boys who had known him in his days of social exaltation and humiliation. Of this, one thing, however, we are well assured, that in whatever circumstances Frederick Walker died he resigned his latest breath with that fortitude and heroism which have characterised every incident of his chequered career.

Evading the fever makes sense of D'arcy's behaviour over the next year. He was the only policeman in the Gulf, but he spent little time with his men and even less time policing the nest of criminals and drunks that was Burketown. "Men went there who had been wanted by the police for years," wrote Edward Palmer in his history of North Queensland. "Horse stealing and forging cheques were very common pastimes among the fancy, and Burketown society, in its first efforts to establish itself, was of a kind peculiarly its own." But D'arcy, abandoning most of his men at Hope Reach, sailed out into the Gulf to join Landsborough 30 miles from shore on Sweers Island. He represented this escapade as a mission of mercy, helping half a dozen sick citizens of Burketown reach Sweers in an open boat. With him, D'arcy brought troopers Jemmy and Sambo. Next morning, Landsborough took them to explore Bentinck Island, a couple of miles across the water. The Kaiadilt men who ran to meet them appeared friendly. That afternoon Landsborough left D'arcy's party to cross the island on foot.

> Before we had gone far we heard the discharge of a gun and thought it was merely discharged at some cockatoos that we could see in the distance. I was sorry to learn however from Mr Uhr that the blacks had rushed towards him with spears and he had to discharge the carbine at them.

Landsborough wrote: "I am sure Mr Uhr would not have fired upon them if he could have avoided it."

Back at Hope Reach, D'arcy found the camp turned upside down. He had been away nearly a month. His favourite trooper, Tommy Curtis, had died only hours before he reached camp. The rest of his men were too ill to walk. "I had to cook and do everything," he complained. He shifted the camp closer to town. But a few weeks later he was off again, this time to chase a couple of horse thieves to New South Wales. The cavalier pursuit of these petty criminals kept D'arcy from the Gulf for three months. Pointless as it was, the ride was an extraordinary feat of horsemanship and made D'arcy – helped by his own promotion – a celebrated outback figure of the time. At stake were two horses. D'arcy and a trooper left the district without permission. After about 800 miles he sent the trooper back. "Finding it difficult to get a supply of horses for both, I proceeded alone." One thief outran him, but he caught Matthew Duffy at Thargomindah and took him over the border to Bourke where, fortuitously, there was a newspaper correspondent he could bewitch with tales of "perseverance rarely to be met with, and under difficulties of no ordinary character", pursuing his thieves "over a country uninhabited for a great extent, or at least the stations being at a great distance of each other, the entire distance not being less, taking into account the detours, of two thousand miles, accomplished in something like forty days".

D'arcy was back in Burketown for only a few days when he sailed out to Sweers to steal children. It was not his first time. With him on that leg of the journey was Michael Bird Hall, a veteran stockman so appalled by what happened next that he pursued D'arcy for years, hoping to see him prosecuted. Hall wrote to the Colonial Secretary that on the afternoon of 23 November 1866, D'arcy took several men from Sweers over to Bentinck. They slept that night on the beach.

> Early upon the following morning they found a Blacks camp, rushed it and sequred 2 small boys between eight or ten years of age with the whole of the Implements belonging to the Blacks and conveyed them to the boat followed by the supposed parents crying for their children. Mr Uhr brought them to Swears Island also the Blacks Implements the children were ironed together to keep them from escaping or for fear the blacks might come and fetch them away. I have often seen these poor children beat for only going down to the beach opposite Bentick Island. I then let Mr Uhr know I should report the matter to the Government. Mr Landsborough ordered Uhr to take them back the Implements were taken but not the children, the Implements were thrown upon the beach at Bentick Island and left.

D'arcy named the boys Daylight and Bentinck. Back in Burketown, he handed them to settlers. Hall could not swear to the terms of the deal. "But I was informed at that time for grog."

Men everywhere in the Colony had black boys. They were often said to be *rescued* or *saved*, which meant being snatched up by Native Police after bloody dispersals. It was a custom, wrote *The Queenslander*: "The gentleman in charge will secure a terrified baby boy as a present for one of his friends." And they were sold, too. Harvesting children and women after massacres was a lucrative practice for the Native Police. That they were the worst of the kidnappers was a constant provocation to violence. Isaac Watson, a resident of the Gulf, complained to the Colonial Secretary in 1880:

> It has been customary for several years past and also up to the present time for the Sub Inspectors and their troopers to go into the Bush round up the Blacks and shoot them indiscriminately and Kidnap the Gins and little Boys and take by force either to stations or to the township of Normanton and their made slaves of and if any attempt to escape is made they are shot down like wild beast ... I think therefore it is quite time to put an end to such disgraceful proceedings.

Nothing was done. The upshot was horrific. Women were used for work and sex. So, inevitably, were the children. They were slaves – not paid, and kept hundreds of miles from their own country, captives of distance.

From the earliest days of the colonies, the kidnapping of women had been condemned, not least by the churches. But the taking of children was never denounced as vigorously. Many argued it was a godsend for a child to be plucked from savagery and given a new and civilised existence. The younger the better, said these divines. William Chatfield of Natal Downs reminded holy men that taking children to save their souls provoked the wrath of their families. "Let any 'missionary' picture to himself the exposed condition of stations with perhaps five men on them, and say 300 blacks camped round. Does he think these people are of such a mild inoffensive nature, that they are to be ill-used with impunity?"

Chatfield was a twenty-seven-year-old former army lieutenant who had come to this vast run on the Cape River a few years earlier. His nearest neighbour lived 70 miles away. The peace he had worked so hard to achieve on the run was being threatened by kidnappers. In early 1869 he had "every proof" of a kidnapping and wrote to the Police Magistrate in Bowen, to the Police Commissioner and to the Attorney-General, Charles Lilley, asking for action. He was scrupulously polite.

> Can you kindly give me your opinion as to whether the Law will protect the children of Aboriginals as it is becoming a common practice in the district to kidnap boys from the camps of quiet blacks as of course the blacks who are becoming quiet and are let in on the stations are the principal victims; if this kind of thing continues much longer the Aboriginals will naturally take revenge on us and we shall revert to the old style in this district.

The Bowen magistrate wrote to the Commissioner of Police, David Seymour: "I hardly see what either you, or the Government can do in the matter." Seymour agreed. The Solicitor-General advised Lilley that the *Slave Trade Act* of 1824 "would remedy such practices if its provisions were enforced by the bench". The act made it a crime to gather slaves – "to carry away, or remove ... Persons ... in order to their being dealt with as Slaves". Chatfield was sent that advice. He had witnesses. Nothing was done. The *Offences Against the Person Act* of 1828 also made it a crime to take "any Child under the Age of Ten Years" from their parents. This was rarely cited as a possible remedy for kidnapping in Queensland. Who, after all, could pinpoint the age of an Aboriginal child? Their mothers, of course, but blacks could still not give evidence in a court of law.

Michael Bird Hall blamed D'arcy for provoking the first violence in the Gulf. "Before the arrival of this Gentleman there was no complaints

DAVID SEYMOUR, COMMISSIONER OF POLICE

but immediately upon his arrival he commenced the trade by kidnapping a black boy upon the main land that set the example thence followed." That first child was called Victoria. "Upon the same suit numbers of Boys were stolen from their parents, and we have been and are still receiving the retribution from the blacks for their misconduct." Hall had witnesses to the Bentinck kidnappings and offered them to the Colonial Secretary so that D'arcy could be prosecuted for his crimes. "I am prepared to prove as I saw the whole transaction and the Boatmen can easily be found as I believe one is in this District the other upon Swears Island, there are 3 or 4 creditable witnesses who saw the whole transaction."

But D'arcy was not prosecuted. Truman Smith in his thesis on kidnapping in Queensland wrote that D'arcy's escape became the template. "The correspondence in that case was still being used for reference some fourteen years later." In 1882 Seymour was still throwing up his hands about kidnappings. "I do not know any way of preventing it," he told the Colonial Secretary. The Attorney-General of the day, Pope Alexander

Cooper – who was to become a notoriously severe judge – saw eye to eye with Seymour. "I don't think there is any means of punishing these men." The obvious solution to the problem – legislation in the Queensland parliament, enforced by the colonial authorities – never happened. Despite the lives ruined and blood spilt, slavery and kidnapping were everywhere and officially tolerated in Queensland.

*

Old timers' memoirs written at the turn of the century have a lot to say about D'arcy. "An exceptionally smart, plucky fellow, whose constant activity and relentless following up of black marauders helped in a large degree to make the work of the pioneers possible," recalled "A.H.", adding that D'arcy was also "foremost amongst the practical jokers of the Gulf of Carpentaria". Some remembered him as a great man with a stockwhip, a bare-knuckle fighter and a drunk in a town driven by thirst. Shearers, bullock-drivers and shepherds made good money in the Gulf and the grog shanties of Burketown were ready to strip them of every penny. The sellers were a sardonic lot. Among their shanties were Blue Ruin and The Gigantic Swindle, but D'arcy's haunt was The Dead Finish. None of these rough roadside huts were licensed but the owner of The Dead Finish was never troubled by the authorities.

> No police ever came his way, unless it was the officer in charge of the native black troopers, when returning from a "dispersing" expedition, and he was only too glad to get to the "Dead Finish," where he would make some such excuse as "knocked-up horses" in order to remain a few days enjoying Brooks's brandy. It was not his business, he would say, "to trouble as to licenses; that was the duty of the common constable. He, thank goodness, was not sunk so low as that. He was a sub-inspector in charge of native police," which

occupation he interpreted as a license to shoot down men, to capture women and children, to burn mi-mi houses*, and to destroy native property in general whenever met with.

Landsborough remained the Police Magistrate but John Sharkey had been appointed Crown Lands Commissioner over his head. Sharkey had to deal with the killing of Jemmy Ching, a crime so vicious it gnawed at the conscience of the town. D'arcy was away again when Ching went on a rampage one afternoon, riding around with a pistol drawn, threatening to shoot anyone he met, particularly any of his own people. "The Chinese mustered up," reported *The Brisbane Courier*. "After a hard run, he was captured, but not without a fearful struggle, in which two Chinamen were stabbed." Ching was chained in the morgue. His cries could be heard all night. "It is certain," wrote Sharkey, "that he was tied up and cruelly treated by his countrymen." No one intervened. Next morning, Ching was seen being taken across the river by six or seven Chinese. The leader of the party was carrying a rope. No one stopped them. Their captive was never seen again. On his return a few days later, D'arcy claimed he could find no evidence to justify an arrest. But the identity of the abductors was known; the marks of a rope were found on a tree near the river; blood spotted the bank. Sharkey had no doubt Ching had been murdered and called for an inquiry, which never came. He blamed D'arcy for failing to pursue the culprits. "Without police conversant with their duty even this will pass unnoticed." *The Brisbane Courier*'s verdict was bleak: "The Gulf country, instead of enjoying the blessings of the British Constitution, is now under the sway of Judge Lynch."

D'arcy and the town larrikins delighted in humiliating a pompous official, George Sandrock, Coroner and Sub-Inspector of Customs. One morning D'arcy set up a mock duel in the street. "Shots with blank cartridges were duly exchanged, and one of the combatants doing duty as the corpse was decorously laid out and covered with a sheet." D'arcy went

---

* A version of *mia-mia*, a temporary shelter.

up and down with a smoking gun in his hand, daring anyone to arrest him. Sandrock was called to view the corpse. "Approaching the table on which the body lay the old gentleman reverently drew the sheet aside, when the gory corpse sprang up and locked him in a wild embrace. There was a tableau." April Fools' Day that year was particularly wild. "Several people were forcibly shaved," reported *The Brisbane Courier*. Drunks then dragged the outhouse of the Crown Lands Office into the street and set it on fire, "nearly every person in town taking part in the incendiarism". Sharkey was ill. "Mr Landsborough fruitlessly remonstrated with the culprits and asked them to desist." D'arcy did nothing. Michael Bird Hall believed this bonfire was Sharkey's reward for trying to put an end to kidnappings. Watching the madness that night was Alexander Manson, skipper of the schooner *Salamander* that called often at the Albert River to collect wool. Manson had come to despair of Burketown's violence even before the night his West Indian cook was baited for hours by a drunken rabble that included one of D'arcy's troopers. Manson told the 1869 inquiry into the Colony's police:

> There was no police protection whatever there. The police were down at Sweer's Island ... and Uhr, when he was in town, was the companion of the whole of them.

> He was hail-fellow-well-met with the whole of them?

> Yes; and in horse-racing, &c.

> Do you think that Mr Landsborough knew of those proceedings in the town?

> I do not know how it could be otherwise; but, I think he would be utterly powerless to prevent anything, in the then state of affairs.

> Were you a witness to any infraction of the law?

> Yes, to the setting fire of the water-closets and so on; and

the attack on the black fellow—and fights innumerable. Then, for a week or two, the place would be as quiet and well conducted as the city of Brisbane. It was such a place that—I heard Mr. Sharkey say so—he would not act there as a magistrate.

Have you any notion why?

I think that Uhr would not assist him. Uhr was as much opposed to him as the roughest men in the place could be.

When John Williamson shot one of his customers at his shanty on the edge of town, D'arcy rode out to investigate. He found the victim, a blacksmith called Molloy, wandering about wrapped in a mosquito net caked with blood. Molloy accused Williamson of the deed and Williamson confessed "that while in the heat of passion having been struck by Charles Molloy he took the revolver and fired at him". D'arcy had Williamson taken out to join Duffy the horse thief in the only lock-up in the Gulf out on Sweers. When Molloy died of his wounds a few weeks later, Williamson faced the gallows. Both prisoners made a break for it. In the shanties of Burketown, where D'arcy admitted being "'hail fellow well met' with all of the rowdies", he heard the escapees were heading for Bowen. He set out in pursuit. Once again, the papers lapped up a wild-west epic with D'arcy riding alone, night and day, for 420 miles to recapture the men and bring them back to Burketown in chains, where they were locked up in a pub. Duffy escaped and was never heard of again.

D'arcy took Williamson on the *Salamander* for trial in Brisbane. Catching Manson's sloop was a bizarre choice. The boat was sailing via Perth. D'arcy's journey would take ten weeks – "an immense time", complained the Police Commissioner – and while he was at sea leaving Burketown without any police, the mob took control of the place. It was quiet during the day, reported the *Rockhampton Bulletin*, because the rowdies were sleeping off the night before. But when the sun went down, violence erupted again in the streets:

D'ARCY

Firing guns and revolvers, and throwing bricks on the iron roofs of houses, are favourite amusements of these gentry. A bullet whistled quite close to me a few evenings ago. There are a number of black boys in town, who get drunk almost every night, using most disgusting language; this mob is headed by one of the Native Police, and who, it is said, shot a wild blackfellow, near the race course, lately, taking two gins from the tribe.

Uhr and his prisoner did not reach Brisbane until July 1867. Williamson was committed for trial in August. At the last minute, it was decided more witnesses were needed from the Gulf. The Police Commissioner warned he had no authority to spend the money required to bring them to Brisbane. Williamson was discharged on 19 November "by order of the Court … the necessary witnesses for the prosecution not being present". The whole thing had proved a fizzer.

Uhr's future in the force may well have been in doubt. He had spent ten of the past eighteen months away from his post. When in Burke-town, he had displayed contempt for the authorities. His kidnapping of children was not secret. In the harsh economic times of the late 1860s, the Native Police were being culled. But Uhr kept his post and was pro-moted. The reason was simple: in August that year, this young renegade turned into the best-connected officer in the Native Police when Robert Ramsey Mackenzie became premier. His wife, Louisa, the daughter of Richard Jones, was D'arcy's cousin.

Power had shifted in Queensland. Extravagances at home and bank collapses in London had left the Colony on the edge of ruin. Robert Her-bert's long reign was over. Four brief governments beginning in 1866 saw Mackenzie have his turn in August 1867. In October, his Executive Council recommended D'arcy be appointed a Sub-Inspector and Justice of the Peace and "have charge of all Police (White & Black) in the Burke District". David Seymour, Commissioner of Police for nearly ten years, had, at the direction of politicians and without protest, appointed and promoted many unsuitable officers of the Native Police. But he dug in his heels at the thought of promoting D'arcy. He could hardly have been more emphatic when he wrote to Arthur Palmer, the Colonial Secretary:

> It is impossible for me, in consequence of the numerous reductions in the rank of Sub-Inspectors that will take place at the close of this year – no less than ten officers of that rank being struck off – to recommend the promotion of so junior an officer as Acting Sub Inspector Uhr; to do so would be unjust to many highly deserving officers of far longer service. Mr Uhr is a very active young officer, but inexperienced and ignorant of Police duties as yet, and will

require to be some time under the supervision of a more experienced officer before I would feel myself justified in placing him in charge of a district.

Palmer scrawled on the letter: "Mr Uhr has deserved his promotion and is to have it."

Ambition blossomed in D'arcy. The steamer taking him and eight white constables from Brisbane to Burketown called at Somerset on Cape York. Governor Bowen had planted a station there with the Imperial notion of commanding the Torres Strait. It was proving less than a success. Under the command first of John Jardine and later his son Frank, the tip of the Cape had been a site of terrible slaughters. In late January 1868, D'arcy wrote from there to Palmer offering himself as the station's next commandant. But he was told bluntly there was no vacancy. From Burketown he complained his promotion had been gazetted but not his appointment to the bench. "It is very necessary up in this part that I should be a Magistrate." He was told that only inspectors of Native Police were now made JPs. He had to be content with a salary of £245 and command of all the police in the Gulf.

*

The quiet times were over. Guerrilla resistance to the squatter invasion was intensifying among the peoples of the Gulf – the Ganggalidda or Yukulta, Mingginda, Nguburinji, Mayi-Katuna, Kukatj, Mayi-Yapi, Gkuthaarn, Mayi-Kulan, Walangama and Kurtjar. Settlers demanding more white constables to deal with town rowdies when D'arcy left for Brisbane in May 1867 were begging, by the time he returned in February 1868, for more Native Police to deal with the blacks. Hetzer and Little, partners in the 320,000-acre Urilla run in Mayi-Yapi country, wrote to the Colonial Secretary of the aggression of the blacks in the weeks before D'arcy's return:

We had the first proofs that they were not so innocent as had been supposed when they attacked at night a party of travellers on the road from Burketown to the then newly discovered Norman river settlement and so severely wounded one man that his recovery was considered doubtful for a very long time. Not long after this, they killed a traveller and wounded another, within about 100 yards of a head-station on the Cloncurry. Lower down the same river they speared a shepherd through his tent and wounded him badly in two places. To prevent similar occurrences, and to stop the innumerable robberies committed on our shepherds, we built iron huts provided with padlocks, but the blacks either broke into the sides of the huts, or wrenched the locks off and robbed all things, even such as could be of no use to them. Four miles from another head station they killed four blackboys who had come out with different parties from other parts of the Colony and had then joined to return to their homes together, and a month ago, on an opposite part of the same river they killed a shepherd, a short distance from his hut, stripped him of all his clothes and took all his and his mates things from the hut.

D'arcy went to war. His massacres in the Gulf in early 1868 have been cited ever since as evidence of the bloody cruelty of the Native Police. Worse happened in the secrecy of the bush, but D'arcy's feats were celebrated and recorded. We know the numbers. He began after several horses were speared about 10 miles from town and steaks cut from their rumps. *The Brisbane Courier* reported: "As soon as it was known, the Native Police, under Sub-inspector Uhr, went out, and, I am informed, succeeded in shooting upwards of thirty blacks."

D'arcy then took his men down to Urilla to avenge the death of Hetzer and Little's shepherd. They wrote: "Possessed of great knowledge of the habits of blacks, he was not long in finding a party of them

encamped on the Flinders, who rushed into the river, which here is deep and wide." Hetzer joined D'arcy and his troopers in the slaughter that followed, first in the river and then in the bush. At the blacks' camp, they found piles of fresh mutton, a compass and revolver that offered a grim solution to the mysterious disappearance of a man and his Chinese shepherd driving a flock of fat sheep to the Norman. "A close search down the river was made and the two bodies were found about six miles below the camp on the other side of the river, being partly in the water and about four days dead." Another round of killings followed. *The Brisbane Courier* summarised D'arcy's massacres on Urilla:

> Mr. Uhr went off immediately in that direction, and his success I hear was complete. One mob of fourteen he rounded up; another mob of nine, and a last mob of eight, he succeeded with his troopers in shooting. In the latter lot there

was one black who would not die after receiving eighteen or twenty bullets, but a trooper speedily put an end to his existence by smashing his skull . . .

In this expedition I am informed Mr. Uhr was accompanied by Mr Hetzer, who has been very kind and indulgent to the myalls for a long time, but now sees his folly. Everybody in the district is delighted with the wholesale slaughter dealt out by the native police, and thank Mr Uhr for his energy in ridding the district of fifty-nine (59) myalls.

21

NO BETTER MAN

The financial crisis of the mid-1860s cut down the northern squatters one by one. By the time Reg Uhr was back on the Suttor and Bowen in 1866, Philip Sellheim had walked off Strathmore and Cuthbert Fetherstonhaugh had lost the Hermitage to his creditors. Yet in his ruin Fethers found consolation.

> For though I had lost money, labour, and to some extent, health, I had in a most extraordinary manner in 1865, while at The Hermitage, found that which is of a thousandfold greater value than riches, success and health all put together. I had found myself, I had found my own soul, and I had found God.

So many of his sins were now clear to him. But not on the list in his memoirs was the massacre of Aborigines. Biddulph Henning was hanging on at Exmoor but his sister's sharp eyes were no longer turned on the district. She had married and gone south.

The sombre lump of Mount McConnel dominates the landscape where the Suttor and the Cape feed into the Burdekin. Uhr and his men arrived at the Native Police camp there in August 1866. "The inhabitants of the Bowen and Suttor will be much pleased to hear that their old friend, that indefatigable officer, sub-inspector Uhr, is to be again stationed amongst them," said *The Brisbane Courier*. Uhr joined forces at Mount McConnel with Sub-Inspector Frederick Murray and his men, who had arrived some months earlier and been hard at work. Another of the many unrelated Murrays in the force, he was a former bank clerk and this was his second posting since joining the Native Police a year earlier at the age of twenty-four.

As the senior of the two, Reg Uhr commanded one of the most powerful units of Native Police: two officers, one acting sub-inspector – essentially a cadet – a dozen troopers and twenty-five horses. In September they rode 80 miles to avenge the death of Henry Clark, who had been searching with his brother William for land along the Belyando. One evening, William returned to camp to find no sign of his brother other than his boots covered with blood. William found Henry's body next morning, scalped and with a spear through his heart. *The Northern Argus* reported:

> Lieutenants Uhr and Murray, two first-class officers, were quickly at the scene of the murder, and after running the tracks of the black with their troopers, came upon the camp, where the police found sundry articles of Mr. Clarke's clothing, and inflicted punishment on the savages in the usual manner.

William Clark filled in the details: blacks were found fishing in Leichhardt's Lake on Avon Downs. "On the creek bank stood a blackfellow with cockatoo feathers in his head; a long shot from a rifle reached him. With a yell the rest fled, but covered by 21 guns the result may be guessed." *The Brisbane Courier* counted the dead: "eight or ten of the blacks".

In the new year of 1867, Uhr and his men were posted east to the Sonoma run to deal with the intensified resistance of the Giya and Biri peoples. Reg was back where he had begun. Strathmore was not far away. He and his men lived under canvas and patrolled the district. Critics of the force argued that constant patrolling exhausted the Native Police, leaving them unable to respond swiftly to pleas for help. That was often true but patrolling remained their everyday work. Robert Herbert had explained to Westminster:

> It is not doubted by any person who has a knowledge of the habits and character of the Australian aborigines that the

only way to deter them from attacks upon life and property
is to convince them of the superior power of the white man
by the frequent and unexpected presence of an organized
patrol in every part of the thinly populated districts, and by
the prompt punishment of crime.

*

Richard Jones never ordered his runs cleared of blacks. Ruthless as he
was when taking country, and ready as he was to kill to keep it, Jones
never mandated the Aborigines be exiled from their land. Yuggera worked on Wivenhoe. In the jargon of the great contest that divided the
squatters, he was on the side of *letting them in*. About the time Reg took
his men over to Sonoma, his older brother Ned – no longer in the timber trade but racing horses and selling pastoral runs – helped organise
a "rather important meeting" of squatters and clergy in Bowen to challenge the consensus in the Kennedy district that the blacks must be *kept
at a distance*. Debate between the squatter factions over this had been
going on for years. *The Port Denison Times* had hitherto been hostile to
change. Six months before the meeting at Wills' hotel in January 1867,
the paper was floating the idea of legislation to keep blacks out:

> We should almost be inclined to advocate the passing of
> law which should render it punishable even for squatters
> to admit the blacks to their stations at all. *Omne ignotum
> pro mirifico** is a very true saying, and the less insight the
> blackfellows are allowed to get into the white man's habits
> the more awe they will have of him, and the more easy they
> will be to manage; the less money it will be necessary to
> spend on our side and the less blood on theirs for the pro-
> tection of our interests here.

---

* Everything unknown is wonderful.

But things were shifting. The paper now applauded the efforts of the meeting to find a way of civilising the blacks, of using their labour and allowing them back on their land in the interests of humanity and peace. "It is of course most desirable that it should be done," said *The Port Denison Times*. But it had to be done safely.

In the southern colonies, the fighting was over. Squatters no longer cleared their runs and had not for years. More recently, the squatters of the Darling Downs had opened their land to its original inhabitants. The men and women squatters once shot were now working for them. With the catastrophic fall in wool prices in the late 1860s, squatters were looking for labour that cost almost nothing. Queensland was importing Chinese, Indian and Pacific Islander workers but Aboriginal people were cheaper still. They worked for food. In return, they expected to be protected. "Pastoralists," wrote Truman Smith, "attempted to secure their land and labour force by offering sanctuary to Aboriginal people from the Native Police and kidnapping." Not for the first or last time in colonial Australia, greed and decency walked hand in hand.

The meeting at Wills' Hotel petitioned the Governor to set runs apart where the natives would be encouraged to come in. On each of these runs, four Native Police troopers and an officer would be stationed to protect life and property. Ned Uhr added a proposal: "That the Government supply such stations with a few blankets and tomahawks as an inducement to come in." This was an expensive plan that would see a great expansion of the Native Police. It was swiftly rejected by the Executive Council, not on the ground of cost but for fear it would "result in increased injury to the aborigines who might mingle more indiscriminately with the European population".

But the campaign continued. The battleground was *The Port Denison Times*, where writers reminded the squatters that – according to their leases – they could lose their runs for keeping the blacks out.

> Refusing to let the blacks come in to the rivers to fish is
> opposed to all principles of justice and humanity, as well as

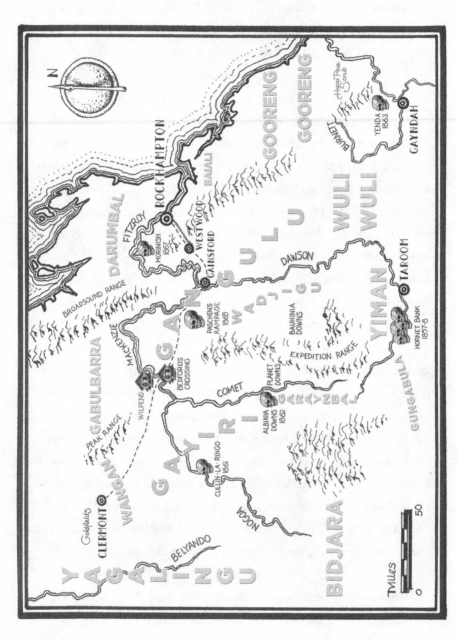

MACKENZIE & DAWSON

to one of the conditions of our leases, viz, "And we do further reserve to the aboriginal inhabitants of our said colony such free access to the said run, and to the trees and waters thereon, as will enable them to procure the animals, birds, fish and other food on which they subsist."

As usual, that argument carried no weight whatsoever. That clause had sat in the pastoral leases of New South Wales for nearly twenty years, and those of Queensland for nearly ten, without either government ever attempting to enforce it. Those fine words were known to few and feared by no one.

In late 1867, William Chatfield, the campaigner against kidnapping, let the blacks in on Natal Downs. "From the year 1864 to 1867 this run was almost untenable owing to the hostility of the Aborigines," Chatfield wrote to the Police Magistrate in Bowen. Twelve whites were killed by Miyan people on or around Natal Downs from late 1864 to early 1865. These bloody clashes ended when Chatfield let them in. "Since 67," he told the Magistrate, "they have been remarkably quiet and friendly." He accused squatters of using trouble with the blacks as an excuse for careless management.

> Every man who has neglected his cattle and got them scattered all over the country by his own negligence says, in excuse, that the niggers have been "hunting all over his cattle camps." How is he to keep them? If a *little* trouble is taken with the blacks and a good deal to make the cattle quiet and break them in properly there need be no loss from this cause.

The men who nearly forced the run to be abandoned were, by this time, employed by Chatfield. "Were it not for the work done by them the writer would be quite unable to keep sheep on Natal Downs." And there was this practical advantage: "The blacks are of the greatest use in keeping the marsupials down, and the day is not far distant when the Kennedy runholders will regret the days when the blacks wandered in mobs over the country destroying these vermin."

Within a year, Chatfield's example was being followed all over the Kennedy. Reg Uhr was enthusiastic. When he was posted south to the Mackenzie River, he wrote an impertinent letter to the Colonial Secretary:

> Sir I do myself the honor to inform you, that the Squatters
> in this district, express the highest approbation of the
> recent new Police Force, at present under my command
> it will be a great preventive of Crime by "Whites" and
> also the Natives in this district. The last named I do not
> anticipate any trouble from as they are allowed in on
> nearly all the Stations in the district.
>
> I have the honor to be Sir
> Your most Odbt Servt.
> Reginald C.H. Uhr
> Sub Inspector

The Colonial Secretary noted in the margin: "Mr Uhr should address his Superior officer not Colonial Secretary tell him so." Perhaps fame had gone to the young man's head, for at the time he wrote he was being feted for his part in solving a murder that had captured Australia's imagination and became, years later, the raw material for a mighty three-volume novel, *Lost for Gold*.

*

Half a dozen years of killing by the Native Police had brought peace of a kind to the rivers that fed the Mackenzie in the brigalow country behind Rockhampton. Two waves of retribution had swept across this landscape – first after Cullin-la-ringo on the Nogoa River and then in Otto Paschen's hunting ground around the Expedition Range. The country was soaked in blood. By the mid-1860s, the Aboriginal people of the rivers were taking refuge along the Mackenzie. "Those great scrubs were defeating the troopers," wrote Judith Wright. "Swamps, dense brush and brigalow scrubs too thick to admit horsemen protected such of the Kangulu and Kanooloo* as had taken refuge there." The mission for the Native Police was further complicated in 1861 by the discovery of gold at Clermont over the Peak Range. As well as protecting the squatters, the force was expected to support gold escorts travelling from the mines to Rockhampton. Their camp was on the river at Wilpend.

One morning in October that year, a messenger came with news that two men of the gold escort had been found murdered near the river crossing. Reg Uhr sent a young cadet, Richard Stokes, to the scene to interview witnesses while he set out to raise the alarm. "I deemed it advisable to proceed to Rockhampton, and acquaint Sub-Inspector Elliott of the circumstances ... I started from the barracks at noon on Thursday, and reached Gainsford at 9 a.m., Friday; the distance is one hundred miles." That remarkable ride became a bush legend. Fifty years later, the Brisbane *Truth* gushed: "Sub-Inspector Uhr's hundred-mile ride, with one arm in a sling, to report the murder, still figures among the greatest riding feats of Australia's intrepid horsemen." Uhr, utterly spent, gave a note to a local constable, who rode to Westwood and caught the train – the railway had opened only months earlier – to Rockhampton. But Sub-Inspector Elliott had already been told of the Bedford's Crossing murders by the Clermont Gold Commissioner, Thomas Griffin.

Elliott set off for the murder site next day with Griffin, several police, an official of the Australian Joint Stock Bank and a Rockhampton surgeon to dissect the corpses. Uhr was waiting for the party at Gainsford. Elliott was suspicious. That night, he took the precaution of scraping the detonating powder from the caps in Griffin's revolver. He told Uhr of his suspicions. Next morning, as Uhr was riding with the Gold Commissioner, Griffin began to cry. "He said he was a branded felon ... that he

---

* Gangulu.

did not care if they hung him at once, as he had no friends in the colony ... he also said if he was acquitted, he'd leave the colony, and change his name." The police party reached the decomposing bodies at midmorning. Both men had been shot in the head. The money was gone. Uhr and his troopers looked about. He later told the court:

> I have been five (going on six) years in the force; I have had some experience in tracking—it is part of my duty ... I saw the spot (the camp), and made a strict search for tracks, and found some ... I followed a track, accompanied by Sub-Inspector Elliott, until it came to a log where the person sat down ... the ground at the log was light loamy soil: there appeared to be two feet close together—that led me to suppose some one had sat down on the log—from there the track took a direction to the main road or towards the hotel ... the track was a small one, made by a boot with a round toe ... I saw prisoner leave a footprint in front of Bedford's hotel, and I measured that ... I could not be mistaken : it corresponded exactly.

At 10.30 a.m., Elliott arrested the Gold Commissioner on suspicion of murder. The news caused a sensation across Australia.

It turned out this "despotic, arbitrary, and partial" official was a gambler and broke. He bet with Chinese on the Clermont field and by mid-1867 was making good his losses by stealing gold they left in his care. They beset him in Rockhampton in mid-October demanding their money. Griffin came up with an audacious plan. A gold escort had just arrived from Clermont. Griffin withdrew £4000 from the bank for the escort to take back to the goldfield. But first, he called his creditors to the Chinese club and paid his debts. When the escort was about to leave later that day, one of the officers demanded the bag of cash be sealed. This was his right. He could have had no idea the bag was short £252. At first Griffin refused. Clearly, he wished to blame the escort for losing those hundreds of pounds along the way. But the officer continued to insist.

The bag was sealed. Griffin then ordered the escort cut from four men to two and rode out of Rockhampton with them, something he had never done before. A few nights later, when they were all camped at Bedford's Crossing, he stupefied the two young men with a narcotic and shot them.

When Griffin was convicted, Reg was showered with praise for his role in seeing the man hanged. *The Northern Argus*:

> The skill shewn by Mr. Uhr in tracking the murderer's foot-steps from the tent to the trunk of the tree—from the trunk to Bedford's, was *the* one great fact which enabled justice to lay its hand upon the guilty man; it was conclusive and damning, and at once cut every chance of escape from beneath the feet of him, who stood in the dock, denying to the last that he was the shedder of blood. The inhabitants of Brisbane have shown their appreciation of Uhr's conduct, by not only warmly applauding him, but by loading him with tokens of their appreciation. Among others, the Hon. R. Pring presented him with a handsome set of uniform belts and sword, mounted in solid silver; and the Hon. C. Lilley, with a set of legal works, which will be useful to him in his career.

Dissent came in a furious and tightly disciplined letter to the *Rockhampton Bulletin*, pointing out that Griffin's tracks had, in fact, been discovered by a trooper, Wellington, days before Uhr appeared on the scene.

> He was shown the tracks by the trooper ... who certainly, although a black trooper, is deserving of something more substantial than generally falls to the lot of sagacious, intelligent, and able native troopers. Without this man, the tracks in all probability would not have been found.

The author of the letter, "*Palmam Qui Meruit Ferat*",* knew the evidence at Griffin's trial intimately. He must have been one of the lawyers – perhaps

---

* Award the palm where it is deserved.

R.R. Mackenzie

even Griffin's defence counsel Samuel Griffith, who would be twice Premier of Queensland and the first Chief Justice of the Commonwealth. *Palmam Qui Meruit Ferat* wondered why there had been such applause for Uhr. "The secret is, R. R. M——e is his uncle. He is also applying for another appointment." He was not quite right. Though old enough to be Uhr's uncle, Premier R.R. Mackenzie was his cousin by marriage. The same hand that saw D'arcy Uhr promoted in late 1867 against the Police Commissioner's wishes was now, in April 1868, heaping honours on his brother Reg.

The Mackenzie River was so quiet by April 1869 that Uhr and his troopers were sent south on extended patrols in the Port Curtis and Burnett River districts in the hinterland of Gladstone and Maryborough, where squatters had been complaining loudly about "the inroads of the blacks". The *Rockhampton Bulletin* was much relieved:

> No better man could be found than Mr. Uhr; he is thoroughly
> acquainted with the habits and language of the aborigines, he
> is a capital horseman, a good shot, and has plenty of pluck.

On the Mackenzie he has reduced the blacks to perfect submission, and in a district where murders were once frequent
and robberies of daily occurrence, all is now quiet and orderly.
Mr. Uhr, we expect, will rise rapidly in the service, and he
thoroughly deserves promotion, let it come when it may.

Soon after his twenty-fifth birthday, Reg Uhr was appointed Police
Magistrate at St George, a tiny settlement on the Balonne deep in squatter country 300 miles west of Brisbane. A few officers hung on in the
Native Police for twenty or thirty years but killing blacks for half a dozen
years, as Reg had, wore most officers out. Those who had given satisfaction could expect another government post. His reputation for messy
paperwork might have counted against a place on the bench, but Reg
had excelled – if that is the word – in the field and still had family in
high places. His appointment to St George came three weeks before the
fall of R.R. Mackenzie's government. His promotion was praised but not
welcomed everywhere. The *Gladstone Observer* was astounded by the
appointment of another "utterly unsuitable" person to an important post:

It is not here denied that Mr. Uhr is honest and respectable; but something more is required in a Magistrate. It is not
here denied that he has rendered good service to the State
in assisting to apprehend criminals, and "punishing"—that
is the correct term, we believe—blacks; but experience of
this sort is not the only kind required by a Police Magistrate.

About a dozen officers had already been promoted to the bench. The last
thing the government needed in the bush were magistrates taking a strict
view of the law. They were expected, instead, to work hand in hand with
the Native Police. Reg Uhr understood the mission. When he left, the
Native Police camp on the Mackenzie was shut down. Inspector George
Murray made the arrangements. One tracker and as many horses as necessary were to be left behind with a few white constables. He added: "Be
particular in ascertaining if Mr. Uhr has paid all accounts."

22

BLAZE OF GLORY

D'arcy's massacre of fifty-nine *myalls* in the Gulf was reported all over Britain. From London to the remote Highlands and across Ireland, local papers told their readers how the Native Police went about their work. Never omitted from the reports was the trooper smashing the skull of the man who had taken twenty rounds but would not die. "Exterminating the Natives in Australia" was the headline in London's *Weekly Review.* "Australian Vengeance" in the *Bradford Daily Telegraph.* *The Nation* in Dublin took a broader view under the headline "Colonial Humanity and Civilisation":

> When a man because his skin happens to be black can with impunity be shot dead with a rifle for an offence punished with a few weeks' imprisonment, when committed by a European, civilization has evidently sunk to a very low degree in the individual guilty of such a deed. But when armed men in the Government employ surround and shoot down scores of unarmed and defenceless wretches, for the pettiest of larcenies, the crime becomes national and affects the character of the entire population.

The Illustrated London News put it this way:

> The savages committed certain outrages, on which the native police, under a white officer, sallied forth and made so tremendous an example in the way of shooting, that though

"everybody in the colony is delighted," we at home should be rather glad to be sure (which the story does not quite make us) that the vengeance fell not only heavily but in the right place.

Disraeli's government could not have been ignorant of this crime committed in a corner of the Empire. But would Westminster exert itself in any useful way to protect the Aboriginal people of Queensland? Royal instructions had been carried to Australia by every governor, directing them in one form of words or another, to prevent all violence and injustice which may in any manner be practised against the Native Inhabitants of the colonies. That had not turned out well. In so many ways, this is a story of Britain's failure to enforce its own instructions. That Queensland was created a self-governing colony left Westminster without the power to intervene directly but Britain could still, if it wished, wield mighty influence.

Edward Cardwell tried. By the time this Liberal reformer of immense skill was appointed Secretary of State for the Colonies in 1864, he had already brought order to the railway building boom and before his career was out he would transform the British military, turning a bolthole for aristocrats into a professional force. He was a man of determination. In early 1865 he caught Governor Bowen lying to him about massacres at Somerset on the Cape. Bowen assured him there had been no collisions with the natives. From naval sources, Cardwell knew of the slaughters by the Jardine family. He wrote to Bowen:

> I trust that great care will be taken to prevent the recurrence of such proceedings and I have no doubt that before this Despatch reaches your hands the circumstances under which this loss of life has been incurred will have been fully inquired into and reported on by you.

They were not. John Jardine's excuses were conveyed to London. In the following year, Cardwell saw Otto Paschen's list of Native Police slaughters that followed the killing of Sub-Inspector Cecil Hill, the stark list that had provoked such soul-searching in Australia. This time, Cardwell ordered Bowen to investigate. He was faultlessly polite. "I should be glad to know whether this document is authentic, and if so, whether any and what steps are taken upon it by your Government."

No inquiry was held. Queensland's leaders prepared, instead, a dossier of lies they dispatched to London in late 1866. Robert Herbert assured the Secretary of State the reprisals carried out after Hill's death were the well-considered work of the most experienced and trustworthy officers. What's more, these men had been sent to the scene of the crime with orders to avoid all collisions that might lead to bloodshed. Herbert could not have been more reassuring:

> The Imperial Government may place the fullest confidence in the determination evinced by all persons in this Colony, from the Governor downwards, to protect the aborigines from committing crime, rather than to punish them after its commission; and to extend to them in all cases that leniency and forbearance due to human beings whose deficient intellect and incapacity for civilization would render it unjust that they should be held, beyond a certain point, morally responsible for all their Acts.

The Premier, Arthur Macalister, birched London for doing so little in the early years when saving "Aborigines from destruction" was its responsibility. Now it was Queensland's. He invited Cardwell, if he objected to the ways of the Native Police, to send troops to Queensland as Britain did to New Zealand to keep down the natives. At the moment it cost London nothing. But without the Native Police it would take 2000 fighting men and half a million pounds sterling each year to protect the colonists. While rebuffing Cardwell, Macalister had a favour to ask: could the Secretary of State for the Colonies urge the missionary societies in England to put some effort into bringing Christianity and the arts of peaceful industry to the Aborigines of northern Australia, "who appear to have hitherto been more neglected by those Societies than any other heathen subjects of the British Crown"?

Lord Russell's Liberal government had fallen by the time the dossier reached London. Cardwell's place had been taken by the Conservative Earl of Carnarvon. He saw through Herbert's posturing. When he replied, his language was polite but his verdict damning: "I earnestly wish that the statements contained in these papers furnished more ground for anticipating that the natives of Queensland would escape the unhappy lot of other Aboriginal Tribes who have been brought into contact with Anglo Saxon settlers." But Carnarvon signalled neither he nor his government would lift a finger to help the Australian natives. It was an important moment. London declared itself powerless and not particularly interested: "I have little hope," Carnarvon wrote in February 1867, "that any observations of mine on this very painful subject can lead to any practical result." Carnarvon allowed himself one splendid shot at Macalister and his plea for British missionaries:

> I cannot help observing that the duty of extending Christianity to these unfortunate savages whose grounds are rapidly occupied and themselves scarcely less rapidly extinguished by the progress of the prosperous settlement of Queensland, rests in the first instance not on a Voluntary Society of Residents in Great Britain but on those for whose advantage these people are disappearing.

In early 1868, the Aborigines' Protection Society took up the cause of the blacks killed at the Morinish diggings, and there was renewed hope that these "men of high position and standing in the religious and political world of England" might be able to convince the Duke of Buckingham – the next Secretary of State for the Colonies – to use his influence to prevent barbarous slaughters of this kind.

The facts were not in dispute. Sub-Inspector Myrtil Aubin and four troopers had raided a sleeping camp at Morinish in the hinterland of Rockhampton to avenge the theft of a pound of tea from a shepherd's

hut. *The Brisbane Courier* reported that miners, woken by shots, went
to the scene.

> The camp was deserted, but around the fires nearest to the
> township lay the scanty garments of men, gins, and picca-
> ninies, many of them saturated with blood, while the track
> of the fugitives could be easily traced by the trail of blood
> leading from the fires in every direction. At the fire nearest
> to the Creek, which separates the camp from the township,
> and around which a number of blacks apparently had been
> sleeping, two pools of blood and brains showed where foul
> murder had been perpetrated.

Another puddle of blood and brains was found at a fire nearby. The first
body they found was an admired young stockman, Tommy. The next
was a naked woman half-hidden under a bush. The wounded began
to walk out of the scrub: a little boy and little girl both shot through
the leg. Diggers took up a collection to send them to hospital. Six bodies in all were found. It soon emerged the Native Police had attacked
the wrong camp. "It was a pity," said Aubin, "that it had happened in a
township so near Rockhampton, as there would be such a *blow* about it,
had it been in the bush it would never have been heard of." Buckingham
showed no enthusiasm. He would only promise to hand the society's
dossier to Major Samuel Blackall, making his way to Queensland to
replace Governor Bowen. "His attention will be called to the subject of
the outrages alleged to have been committed by the Native Mounted
Police." That would achieve nothing.

As D'arcy Uhr's 1868 Gulf killings became known in Britain, *The
Brisbane Courier* still hoped the Aborigines' Protection Society could
bring its influence to bear in Westminster.

> The attack on the camp at Morinish was a trifle, performed
> in the grey of the morning, before breakfast, and when
> there was nothing to incite the preserver, of the peace and

defenders of the lives of the colonists, but Mr. Uhr's was a regular expedition of vengeance, and a battue* of fifty-nine wild blacks is the result.

But the society had also given up. Its attention had shifted to the South Sea Islanders kidnapped or contracted to work in British Columbia, Fiji and the Queensland cane fields. Though Disraeli's government fell in December 1868, Gladstone's Liberals showed no renewed interest in the fate of Australia's Aboriginal people. Indeed, the despatches of Buckingham and his immediate successors to the governors of Queensland had nothing more to say on the subject. Aubin was sacked for failing to kill "quietly" and Paschen was dismissed from the force for having "very much exaggerated" the number of collisions with the blacks in the aftermath of Cecil Hill's death. D'arcy Uhr was untouched. Indeed, in the aftermath of his massacres, he was given further responsibilities in Burketown. This pleased *The Brisbane Courier*:

> The last *Gazette* announces that the Government has conferred on him the distinction of Inspector of Slaughter-houses for the district of Burke. It is written, "Happy is the man whom the King delighteth to honor," and though it is only a Minister, who smiles on the active Sub-Inspector, and the rewards in the hon. gentleman's bestowal are neither rich nor many, there is so much good taste, appreciativeness, and sense of fitness marking the nature of the reward, that it cannot fail to be highly valued by the recipient, and to give satisfaction to his admirers.

*

D'arcy was twenty-three, healthy and robust, a fine bushman with a sharp mind. When the mood was on him, he was good company, much

---

* The beating of woodlands to flush out game.

loved for his pranks and yarns. He was also a fearless liar, and what they called in those days a blatherskite – a bullshitter. His temper was explosive. In his veins ran the blood of two families of arrogant quarrellers, the Uhrs and Kemps. They made him a sure friend and a formidable adversary. This man was the hero of his own life. He could only work for himself. It was said when he died, "His temperament ... was such as that he could not brook 'regulations,' and he soon cut loose from official restriction and 'went on his own,' and stopped there ever since."

Unable to prevent D'arcy's promotion, Seymour the Police Commissioner sent a more senior officer to the Gulf as his Commander. Tom Coward was thirty-four, a former policeman from South Australia with four years' service in the Native Police in which he proved himself an enthusiastic killer, though admonished by the *Rockhampton Bulletin* for boasting about his kills: "If the blacks must be slaughtered, gentlemanly feeling would dictate a decorous reserve, even if there were a morbid taste for sanguinary performances." Coward was belligerent and domineering. The idea that D'arcy would obey such a man was so ludicrous it suggests Seymour sent him to the Gulf deliberately to drive Uhr from the force. When Coward and a fresh squad of troopers arrived in Burketown in July 1868, the overall command of the Gulf police so briefly enjoyed by D'arcy passed to Coward.

Hostilities between them did not begin for some months. This was the time of D'arcy's most famous prank, when a bunch of senior politicians from New South Wales and Queensland came to town and a banquet was planned in their honour at the Golden Fleece Hotel. An appeal had gone out for ducks, fowls and dainties of any description to fill the table. "The piece de resistance, however, came from a well-to-do Chinaman butcher (Ah Foo, I remember, was his name), who was the proud owner of the only sucking-pig in Carpentaria." As the politicians droned on in one room, "dusky figures might be seen flitting in and out of one of the doors of the dining-room, and to and fro across the space that separated the hotel from the native police officers' quarters". When the speeches were done, the dignitaries and citizens poured into the dining room only to find the feast gone. We're told they met the ordeal with polite smiles until Sub-Inspector Uhr rose and invited them to his quarters over the way. There the feast was waiting for them. "Great was the wrath of the landlord, the original spreader of the feast, but it passed away amidst the shouts of laughter and the clatter of knives and forks, wielded with a vigor born of hunger."

Burketown was dying. Fever, floods and that difficult river had done for the place. It would soon be almost deserted. A new settlement about a hundred miles east on the Norman River was enjoying "a somewhat wild and uproarious infancy". The air was cleaner there; the roads to the interior better, and the river far easier to navigate. It was clear Normanton would soon be the principal town on the Gulf coast. Coward split the force, leaving D'arcy with half a dozen troopers in Burketown while he set up a new headquarters on the Norman. Trouble began in November when Coward gave orders directly to Uhr's sergeant. D'arcy was deeply offended. He fired off a protest to the Police Commissioner and while waiting for Seymour's reply told Coward: "I refused to obey your orders or act under you." Coward suspended him. Seymour hoped to see him fired – first for "disobedience of orders, followed by a distinct refusal to obey any orders or do any duty under Mr. Coward". Second for the "very gross" assault and battery of a man called Dowling in Normanton.

When D'arcy began this high-handed brawl with Coward, his political connections were still strong. But about the time he went on strike, R.R. McKenzie's government fell. He was on his own. Even so, the Executive Council, "after mature consideration", decided not to sack him. His conduct was unbecoming and indeed disgraceful, but given "Mr Uhr's previous services" the council declined to "visit him with the extreme severity his actions deserve." Instead he was reduced to the rank of Acting Sub-Inspector. He was a cadet again. That provoked a further protest by D'arcy to the Colonial Secretary and, on 29 March 1869, his resignation.

I should certainly wish an inquiry into my charges that Mr
Sub Insp'r Coward may have brought against me ...

I intend coming to Brisbane in September next ensu-
ing. I shall then ask for copies of all correspondence that has
taken place between Mr Coward and myself.

With your permission I shall publish, the whole, and
also my reasons for having resigned my appointment.

For two months, the Colonial Secretary pondered the issue. He could see
no reason why an inquiry should be held into Coward's conduct. Seymour urged him to accept the resignation: "He refused to do duty and
has shown himself most insubordinate." The resignation was accepted
in early June. The issue was not over. Later in the year D'arcy wrote several times to the chair of the Select Committee on the Management and
Working of the Police, begging for justice and reinstatement. It did no
good. He was gone.

Three months later, he set about getting his revenge, denouncing
Coward to Seymour as a murderer:

About the latter end of November 1868 Thomas Coward,
Sub Insp'r of Police then in charge of this district murdered
four or five aboriginals within four miles of this Town, in
the Norman river, opposite a place known as the Chinamens
garden – Thomas Coward used a boat to get within shot
of them. it was rowed by Three europeans by his orders ...
Some Chinamen were present on the bank of the river
endeavouring to prevent them from getting up the bank.

These blacks have at no time committed any murders,
the most serious offence they are charged with is stealing a
few petty things at night from householders in the Norman.

To Frank Scarr, the new Commissioner of Crown Lands and a Justice
of the Peace, D'arcy took Johnny Ah Young, a gardener, who could
give eyewitness evidence of the killing. Scarr should have then issued a

warrant to bring Coward in for questioning. He did not, and explained to the Colonial Secretary that he knew D'arcy was pursuing a bitter quarrel with Coward and was not impressed by him posing as a protector of the blacks:

> Mr Uhr has been in the habit of annoying the blacks himself by stealing boys and gins, one young gin he brought in a few days after my arrival here, and kept her several days, but ultimately gave her up, after the mother had repeatedly come into town, offering a boy in exchange for the gin.

He thought Coward had no case to answer. "In new districts like this it is necessary the blacks should occasionally be dispersed, and that in doing so, it is well known some of them do incidentally get shot."

*

Months before his resignation was accepted, D'arcy had walked away to join a man called Travers running the Royal Hotel in Normanton. This did not work out well. He was charged with abusive language on one occasion; obscene and indecent language on another; and then two charges of resisting arrest. He escaped them all. He loved court battles and was a bush lawyer who put his father's efforts to shame. But he began to lose. In October, the magistrates made him pay £36/7/0 plus costs for wages withheld. Then Travers fled town after being charged with committing unnatural offences upon Wyndham, a Kanaka waiter. Travers was also sodomising young blacks. Uhr sold the pub on his instructions and retreated to a cottage in Normanton with Jane Hayes, who became his first wife. Their son Wentworth was born in July the following year.

By that time, D'arcy was hard at work destroying Landsborough and Scarr, brothers on the bench who were finding him guilty time after time as he continued to rage and brawl around Normanton. Landsborough fined him twice in February 1870 for assault and again for larceny in May. He refused to pay and spent forty-eight hours in the lock-up. Then he was fined £11 for illegally employing Wyndham the waiter. The authorities wanted to pry the man loose from Uhr, for they still hoped to track Travers down and make him pay for his crimes. "Uhr was thought to be a very improper person to have the control of the principal witness in that case, against his own partner," wrote Scarr. "We considered it highly probable that Wyndham might be removed beyond the reach of the police before Travers could be re-arrested."

D'arcy's first attempt to ruin Landsborough failed. He came to Scarr demanding the man's arrest for allowing someone to ride off to Cloncurry on his (D'arcy's) horse. The facts were ridiculous. Scarr turned him down flat. Peace reigned for a few weeks until D'arcy found himself back before the bench, this time for another assault. Landsborough and Scarr had lost all patience. D'arcy had faced the court sixteen times in the last eighteen months. They sentenced him to fourteen days' hard labour. He refused to work, claiming he was ill. "It was plain to anyone that this excuse was mere pretence," said Scarr. To try to bring him to heel they stripped his cell of bed and bedding. He still refused to work. The lock-up had no yard, so in the heat of the day they shackled their prisoner to a verandah post and showed him to the town.

D'arcy wrote an unsigned, sweeping attack on Landsborough's rule in the Gulf for the Brisbane papers: the best lands of the Gulf were empty; Landsborough had ruined all he lured there; squatters were taking their stock south or boiling them down; and miners were abandoning the Cloncurry field for want of food. "Almost all the diggers I saw were bare-footed and almost naked, having been without boots for nine months." Lynch law, he said, ruled the goldfields. D'arcy's raging provoked inquiries into both magistrates. The Secretary for Land had accused Scarr of being "party to an illegal act of harshness and cruelty" for his treatment of Uhr in the lock-up. The Colonial Secretary had accused Landsborough of being "guilty of culpable ignorance of the law" in his handling of the dispute over Wyndham the Kanaka. And D'arcy still had Coward in his sights. It worked. Tipped off by his father the Sergeant-at-Arms, D'arcy was soon able to tell the same Brisbane papers that Coward, Scarr and Landsborough had all been sacked.

There was an upswell of support for the men in the Gulf. Petitions were signed and representations made in Brisbane. Martin Hetzer, whose run Uhr cleared of blacks early in 1868, bumped into D'arcy in Townsville and wrote in disbelief to Scarr:

> Mr Uhr seemed to take great credit to himself for being the cause of these dismissals. I have known Mr Uhr ever since he has been in the Burke district, and have had a most favourable opinion of him as an energetic Police Officer, but since his dismissal from the N. P. force he has forfeited the good opinion of every rightminded person in the district. It seems impossible that he, who has been convicted of larceny and … who generally bears such a bad character, should be able to bring such influence to bear as to cause the dismissal of two Magistrates from the bench, for a slight error (if there is one).

Hetzer hoped the men might yet be saved, but he overlooked the Uhr family's place in the Brisbane political establishment. Mackenzie's government had fallen but they had friends where friends were needed. Petitions were ignored. Landsborough went to Brisbane to argue his case and lobby for an inquiry. He was ignored. Fresh allegations about D'arcy's kidnappings in the Gulf were reaching the Colonial Secretary. They were also ignored.

D'arcy celebrated his victory by posting around Normanton a spoof newspaper, *The Norman Snorter*, that thrashed Scarr ("fat boy Frank") and Landsborough ("Billy Intelligent") all over again for the wretched injustices they had done to him. The handwritten parody was a little masterpiece of bile. The *Snorter* had all the usual sections of a newspaper of the time: commercial and shipping news, letters to the editor and late reports just to hand:

By
ELECTRIC
TELIGRAPH
Brisbane Sep 17/79
Landsborough
Scarr
and
Coward
dismissed from
their Billets
Sep 18/70
no good
prosecuting
Landsborough
for damages as he
no means
I will go at
him criminally

Coward was suspended from the force for only a few weeks. Scarr was restored to the magistracy in early 1872 and got on with his life. But D'arcy ruined Landsborough. He had recently lost his share of Bowen Downs after running up debts of £50,000 with the company. A job surveying a new line of road to Cunnamulla ended unhappily when he was accused of overpaying his men. He was a tin miner for years until he was finally restored to the magistracy in 1877.

*

The Native Police got back to work in the Gulf under the command of Inspector Aulaire Liddiard Morisset, another of the brothers of that family. The Kurtjar people called the years that followed the *nokotink* or "no good times". Old women told the stories to young boys like Rolly Gilbert, who passed them on in the 1970s:

> They drove us away from our soak at re·ktřañc, or Skull Hole, so that their cattle could have the water. They shot many of our people there, and you could still see the bones in recent years, before the last flood.* The white men or the Native Police also shot up whole camps of our people at such places as Impertñ, řokmpak, ñomokŋktat and Inṭetř. Butcher Pallew's father was shot at Inṭetř, but by playing dead he was able to later escape and tell us what happened. Sometimes white people left poisoned flour for our people to take, and some of our people died from that too.

Bad as the experience of the Kurtjar was under the Native Police, Gilbert thought the neighbouring tribes worse off. "There seem to be fewer of these people left today."

D'arcy lent a hand in the killing. In September 1871, he turned up at Donald McIntyre's million-acre Dalgonally and volunteered his services tracking two blacks accused of murdering a stockman. A runaway trooper called Charley had appeared at the station and lured one of McIntyre's black boys, Billy, into the bush. They were accused of killing cattle. The evidence for this was thin. After a time, McIntyre sent one of his men, Archibald McLeod, and a "couple of civilised aborigines" to find the runaways. They did. But one night on their way back to Dalgonally, the boys seized their firearms and shot McLeod and one of his men before disappearing into the bush. The Cloncurry police were alerted but according to *The Brisbane Courier*, "Mr. Wentworth d'Arcy Uhr, who was formerly connected with the police in the Burke district",

---

* About 1974.

had already set out in pursuit. D'arcy chased them for a hundred miles without success and returned to Dalgonally for provisions.

D'arcy was a boaster. He sought out the press. The only source for *The Brisbane Courier*'s account of what followed could have been him. It's a fine yarn. He is, of course, the hero. And D'arcy knew, as good storytellers do, when to stop. He told the paper that, hearing a rumour the fugitives were now in the hills behind Cloncurry, he set off there with three companions. One was Dillon Cox, a squatter he would soon be droving with in the western Gulf. After riding for a few days, D'arcy and his vigilantes surrounded a small high hill near Cloncurry where Billy, Charley and several women were camped. *The Brisbane Courier*'s account of the attack next morning is vivid and incomplete:

> Dogs barking, gins howling, partial darkness, and smoke in any quantity, created some confusion. The first glimpse revealed the camp, the gins, and their collection of spoil. The blackfellows were at the base of the hill, springing from rock to rock. A general chase took place. Mr. Uhr, the fastest runner in these parts, would have soon captured the trooper, had it not been for the difficulty of rapidly descending the rocks. All gave the chase up as useless and returned to the camp, from which they brought into the town the double-barrelled carbine, revolver, saddles, pouch, &c., formerly the property of Archibald McLeod.

The police arrived at D'arcy's camp. Constable George Johnston asked where Billy and Charley were. "But the[y] would give him No satisfactory answer." The police began to search. They found Billy's body 200 yards away. "It had a bullet wound in the belly about one Inch above the navel, the head was Greatly Disfigured and covered with blood." D'arcy's talk convinced Johnson he was responsible for the death, and that evening Johnson arrested him "on suspicion of murder from alusions he maid the Day previous". D'arcy arrived under arrest at Normanton on 23 August. The local magistrate wrote next day to Seymour:

The evidence appears to be purely circumstantial and consequently uncertain. Uhr, however by the Constables Statement to me, made himself very conspicuous in connexion with the affair, by his conduct on the day previous to, and on the day of the alleged outrage.

Martin Hetzer was brought to town to sit on the bench. He had lost all regard for D'arcy as a decent policeman, but this was the man whose slaughter brought peace to Little and Hetzer's run. The magistrates dropped the charges. D'arcy was free to look for another life.

23

THE REAPER

General decay was given as the cause of Edmund B. Uhr's death. Though ailing for years, he managed to do his chores in parliament and sit occasionally on the Brisbane bench. In March 1874 he was given three months' leave and he died in July. The few obituaries were tactful. Forgotten were his quarrels and pompous striving. He was remembered in *The Brisbane Courier* as an honourable but persistently unlucky gentleman.

> Mr. Uhr had a very eventful career, having met in his time with even more of the "ups and downs" than usually attend the lives of colonists. He was a large squatter when squatting was by no means the easy life that it now is, but when the pastoral farmers of Australia were in reality the pioneers of civilisation, and when it was almost a constant struggle against the aborigines for very existence.

The paper blamed his departure from Tent Hill on the blacks. No doubt this was the story Edmund had told for years to cover the catastrophe of Richard Jones' bankruptcy.

> He migrated to the Burnett district ... His ill-luck, however, seemed to follow him, for the catarrh attacked his sheep and destroyed the greater number of them. With the remnant of his fortune, about £1,000, he went to Maryborough, and started the first boiling-down establishment in

the district, and was moderately successful.

On the day of his death, the Colonial Secretary regretted the House was too busy to adjourn in his memory. Amy Uhr was awarded £300.

His son Reg had spent four years on the St George bench by this time and appeared to enjoy the humdrum work. A typical day in the courthouse would see him and a couple of gentleman JPs deciding what to do about a bashing, a theft, workers who wouldn't work, squatters arguing over a bullock, and the occasional murderer they sent for trial in Brisbane. Reg proved hasty, tough and still poor at paperwork. Judges complained of it. Reg was liked in the town but everywhere he went in his time as a magistrate he was dogged by small scandals. He had not escaped the usual fate of Native Police officers. In July 1873, a sad advertisement appeared in the local paper. While asleep on a sofa at the Royal Hotel, Reg had been robbed of his watch, a fob chain and a Prussian eagle dated 1752 from the reign of Frederick the Great. A reward of five pounds was offered for their recovery. He could not have been sober.

When the election for the Member for Balonne in 1873 ended in a dead heat – fifty-two votes each – Reg, as Police Magistrate, had the casting vote. He chose the local mail contractor. The man's opponent, with 133,000 acres on the Macintyre and another 356,000 on the Maranoa, was not one to be jockeyed out of a seat. Reg soon found himself attacked on all sides for his conduct of the poll. *The Dalby Herald* stood by him:

> The upright and honorable character maintained by Mr. Uhr, during a residence of over four years, is quite sufficient guarantee for his impartiality, and amply refutes the innuendoes of malignant scribblers who would attribute to honorable men the same grovelling ideas that permeate through their own miserable brain pans.

He was birched by a parliamentary committee and the seat went to the squatter. Six weeks later, he was posted to Taroom, 220 miles north,

where about a hundred settlers lived on a dusty intersection on the
Dawson River, a place where the Premier admitted "there was not very
much to do".

Reg brought with him a wife. At the age of thirty he had married
Mary (Minnie) Mackenzie. She was twenty, the daughter of a government sheep inspector, and a great horsewoman said to be always eager
to "scamper after the wily kangaroo". The Uhrs were in Taroom for
three years. Like his father, he chaired all town meetings. He gave the
Queensland Museum a most interesting specimen of a large predatory
fish the locals called a *barramundi*. He campaigned for the native bauhinia – which grew around Taroom – to be used as street trees in the
towns of Queensland: "For beauty and shade they are not surpassed by
any tree in this colony." In 1875, he recruited a dozen young men for service with the Native Police. "They are the pick of the tribe," reported *The
Brisbane Courier*. And he fathered two daughters. Mary, born in 1875,
became Mrs Gerald Allen of Mahratta, a mighty house on Sydney's
North Shore. Ethel, born in 1877, was matron of Townsville Hospital
before dying in the wreck of the *Yongala*, which came to grief on the
Queensland coast in a tropical cyclone in 1911.

His reputation restored after a blameless time in Taroom, Reg was
posted in 1878 to Hughenden and Cloncurry. For five years he rode
back and forth 250 miles between the two towns – Cloncurry, a hive of
prospectors and gold panners, and Hughenden, not much more than a
pub and a courthouse on a grid of empty streets by the Flinders River.
His third daughter, Maud – my great-grandmother – was among the
first children christened in Hughenden. When the town was given its
own Police Magistrate in 1883, the Uhrs departed for Cloncurry with
the good wishes of the town, a purse of gold sovereigns and a ball held
in their honour at the courthouse.

Once in Cloncurry, Reg devoted himself to his duties as Mining
Warden. He discovered his brother D'arcy's passion for prospecting.
Gold was being washed in the rivers – when it rained – and copper
was turning up in the hills. Reg and his boy Brisbane rode out with

prospectors to certify their finds. He thundered for the field, predicting Cloncurry would become "the premier mineral producing locality of Australasia, if not the world". Geoffrey Blainey, in his 1960 history of the Cloncurry and Mount Isa mines, called Reg Uhr the "archpriest of the copper field".

The district's Native Police were camped at a waterhole 3 miles from town. The detachment was large: two sub-inspectors, a constable and ten troopers. The officers, Frederick Clerk and Alfred Smart, were both drunks. Clerk said Smart was "often not in his right mind, in consequence of having taken too much to drink and frequently threatened to shoot himself". When Clerk was drunk he flogged his troopers viciously and got about the camp naked. After Smart heard two prospectors had been killed by blacks on the Leichhardt in August 1883, he took troopers north and shot several Kalkadoon* camping peacefully on the Coolullah run. The prospectors turned up alive. News of the killings reached the Police Commissioner, who did nothing for months until Ernest Henry made an odd appearance in *The Brisbane Courier*. Henry wished to deny being the source of the story that those prospectors had died at the hands of the blacks. "The only tragedy he has lately heard of in that neighbourhood was perpetrated by the native police."

Henry could not be ignored. He was a big figure on the Cloncurry field and a friend to the Kalkadoon, in whose country he had discovered great lodes of copper. They had led him to deposits he was soon to mine at Argylla and Mount Oxide. Police Commissioner Seymour telegraphed: "Will you kindly tell me what tragedy you refer to." He also telegraphed Smart: "Have information of what took place short time back at Coloolah from two persons now in town, if correct you had better resign at once unless you wish for enquiry." Seymour directed Uhr to investigate the allegations. "Ernest Henry can give you information about it." And he ordered Cloncurry's only policeman: "Do all you can

* Or Kalkatungu.

to get to the bottom of the case and report to me soon as possible if you can get sufficient grounds to lay information." But neither the constable nor the magistrate gathered any useful information. Two landowners failed to answer their enquiries. Whether much effort was put into their search or if they faced the silence of the bush is not clear. Perhaps both. A few days before Christmas, the policeman told the Commissioner he had "made all possible inquiries and up to the present can find no evidence to support an Information".

Reg Uhr played it by the book. This was why men like him were put on the bench. They understood the problems. Charging Smart with murder was inconceivable. At the same time, he had to be dispensed with to guard the reputation of the force. Reg managed the exits with tact. He held an inquiry into housekeeping at the Native Police camp and recommended both Smart and Clerk be dismissed. They went. But embarrassment was not avoided. Three months after their departure in May 1884, a Melbourne newspaper published a letter by "Drover" who was camped by the Leichhardt the afternoon Smart and his men turned up looking for blacks.

> They crossed, full gallop, and at the unfortunates they went. The moment the natives saw them they jumped up from their camp fires and plunged into the large water hole they were camped by. The police surrounded the hole and shot every one of them except four women and I think four children. After the battle was over the women were divided as follows:—one to a stockman who came up, one taken to a man on the Dougal, one claimed by the police, and the fourth, being old and ugly, after being knocked down by the sub-inspector of police with the butt end of his rifle, was sent with the children into the ranges to fare the best way they could. The police then came over the river, and camped for the night near me. Next morning they went off (as the sub-inspector informed me) to inquire into the reported

killing of the two whites. So ended the earthly career of these unfortunate blacks, dying, they knew not what for, and dying with a most damning opinion of the white men.

Drover had already reported Smart. Now he denounced "the conduct of the Government that allows such wholesale murders to be committed by its officers". The inquiry into the Coolullah massacre was not reopened.

*

Reg Uhr had fallen out with Jack Low of the Palace Hotel, who denounced him in April 1886 to the Colonial Secretary for showing "gross partiality on the Bench, habitual drunkenness, making unseemly quarrels and disturbances and fighting in public places". At this distance, it is impossible to sift the rights and wrongs of these allegations. The claims of misbehaviour on the bench look trivial but Low's detailed indictment of citizen Uhr went back years: drunk, quarrelling and using foul language on the racecourse in Hughenden in 1883; drunk at a race club ball in that town; so drunk one night in Low's Cloncurry pub that he "broke up the ball in a disgraceful manner" when someone asked Mrs Uhr to dance; drunk and brawling in the street one night at three a.m.; and very drunk in January 1886 when he sat "fooling" with Mrs Reilly in the coffee room of the Palace before disappearing for forty-five minutes to her room. Low accused Uhr next day of making a "whore shop" of his premises. "I do not want to be mixed up with a divorce case."

Reg denied everything. A few days after sending a long defence to the Colonial Secretary, he applied for twelve months' leave. He wrote:

> I have drifted into pecuniary difficulties (only Temporary) through no fault of my own caused principally by the dull times, expensive rate of living here, over speculation and depreciation in the value of property. Owing to

the protracted drought it would mean ruin to me at the present time, were I forced to dispose of my property ...

I may here inform the Honourable The Colonial Secretary that should my request be considered favourably it is my intention to occupy my time in exploring & prospecting the Auriferous Ranges* in this locality as I am convinced there are some rich finds yet to be discovered.

Permission was given. Low kept complaining.

Mr Uhr, the Police Magistrate, has been distinguishing himself again. On Friday, the 20th August, at Peter Cardley's "Royal Hotel" he was drunk & struck an old gentleman, a Mr Henry, one of the pioneers & founders of Cloncurry, cutting his eye open; he then issued challenges to anyone in the room to take Mr Henry's part. He afterwards harangued the mob on the subject of the impartiality of his decisions from the bench, saying, "that we would all be sorry when poor old Uhr was gone."

According to Low, the night was not over.

The landlord came into the room & Mr Uhr started to call him "a bloody loafer" "a damned young rogue" and other magisterial flowers of speech. Reggie Phillips the landlord told Uhr to be quiet, & that this was a free country. Uhr then struck him, but Phillips got the better of him, knocking him down & then slinging him off the verandah. I may mention that Phillips is less than half the size of Mr Uhr.

The Colonial Secretary scrawled on the letter: "Mr Uhr to explain." Reg left to go prospecting in October. But after only three months in the field he was ordered to return. A Police Magistrate had been dispatched to Cloncurry to enquire into Low's complaints, which had

---

* Gold-bearing rock.

REG UHR, PROSPECTOR

broadened to include not only Reg but the whole Cloncurry bench, the staff of the court and the local police. Evidence was heard for three days in January 1887. Reg produced a petition from about 170 miners, tradesmen and hotel-keepers expressing regret that he faced these unfounded charges and declaring that they "could not obtain a better or more just Warden and Police Magistrate than R. C. H. Uhr Esq". He travelled to Brisbane for the verdict. At some point he gave an interview to *The Queensland Figaro and Punch:*

The bronzed face and kindly eyes of Reginald Uhr, Police Magistrate at Cloncurry, have been beaming upon Brisbane this week, and I, of course, could not resist the temptation of having a long "pitch" with him about the old days.

He was still spruiking for the Cloncurry field:

"The prospects, as a goldfield, of the Cloncurry and surrounding districts," asseverated Reginald Uhr, without hesitancy, "look better now than they have done for the last ten years. There is more gold coming in. My opinion, which is the opinion of most old diggers who have visited the Cloncurry, is that it will be a goldfield for years and years after other fields are worked out."

He told the paper he was on twelve months' leave to use "in a manner dear to his heart" – prospecting for gold, perhaps as far afield as the Kimberley goldfields in Western Australia.

But his leave was over. Though cleared of all charges, Reg was banished to the little settlement of Springsure near the Mackenzie River. He begged for four months' salary in advance. "Otherwise I shall be compelled to allow some of my Life Assurance Policies now due to lapse." He battled his way back to Cloncurry through floods in March and then refused to budge for weeks, effectively going on strike. The floods had so damaged the roads, he told the Commissioner, that his family could not travel until May: "Cobb & Co would not guarantee passage." The Springsure appointment was cancelled and Reg was told to proceed instead to Blackall, on the empty plains west of Springsure. He arrived in late May 1887. The archpriest of the copper field had fallen a long way.

He lasted a little over a year. He was ill and desperate. In July 1888, he begged the Premier, Sir Thomas McIlwraith, for a promotion that would bring him south. "I do not ask so much for myself as I do for wife & family. My wife has been over three months in bed since we came here." A fortnight later, his mother went knocking on the door of the

Colonial Secretary. When he refused to see her, she wrote:

> The purport of my visit was, to ask you to remember my son
> should a vacancy occur South ... he has been over twenty
> years in the far North. He has never had an inside billet, –
> his wife has suffered very much from the intense heat and
> his health is now beginning to give way, in his last letter
> which I received a few days ago he mentioned he had some-
> thing the matter with one of his eyes, he has three children
> whom he is anxious to have Educated but he cannot afford
> to send them down here to school, so I do earnestly trust
> you will have him removed as soon as opportunity offers
> for my sake as well as his.

Reg died of a stroke a few days later in August 1888 while he was out
shopping. He was forty-four. The obituaries were generous. A veil was
drawn over his service with the Native Police except for his glorious
part in the Griffin case. He was otherwise remembered for his efforts
on the goldfields and his active part in racing matters. *The Western
Champion* wondered if, after his exertions in Cloncurry, having hardly
anything to do in Blackall might have undermined his naturally robust
condition. The paper observed: "He was a white man in every sense."

24

D'ARCY IN HIS PRIME

T he Northern Territory was the next frontier. The Gulf was proving hard and unprofitable for squatters. They heard of better pasture in the Top End and a more bearable climate. Like every frontier on the continent, this would start from scratch. Everything would happen all over again – the same pretence the land was there to be taken, and the inevitable violence when its Aboriginal custodians resisted the invasion of squatters and cattle. Stocking the north was the first great challenge the settlers faced. The road from South Australia – administrator of the Territory until 1911 – was long and dangerous. D'arcy Uhr pioneered the track from Queensland and earned a tactful entry in the *Australian Dictionary of Biography* as "a fearless and competent bushman who had little sympathy for the natives".

D'arcy's client on the pioneering journey of 1872 was Dillon Cox, last seen chasing blacks with him in Cloncurry. Cox was an Englishman with capital whose dream – shared by many Top End squatters – was to sell beef and horses to India and the Dutch East Indies. On a visit to Port Darwin he staked out 115,000 acres of Larrakia land on what is now the Cox Peninsula. His optimism was colossal. Despite all the dangers and difficulties in the Territory, he imagined within a year "thousands of stock where now there is scarcely a hoof". In February 1872 – six months after D'arcy sidestepped the murder charge in Cloncurry – he and Cox set off together from Charters Towers with a mob of unbroken horses and a hundred fat cattle bought at Bowen Downs. This was a trial run. Once the track was found, thousands of head would follow.

When they reached Burketown in March, D'arcy disappeared to Normanton for a few weeks to marry the mother of his son Wentworth. They did not regroup until late May to push on towards Port Darwin. Cox was in charge of the horses and D'arcy the cattle. But D'arcy led the way. The two men were a volatile mix: D'arcy hated direction and Cox's temper was at least as explosive. Five men were with them. Each carried a Westley Richards carbine on his saddle and a revolver in his belt. But D'arcy had a Martini-Henry, lately adopted by the British Army, a rifle that fired big bullets rapidly and with perfect accuracy for nearly 1000 yards. Ahead of them lay a dozen rivers, swamps, tracts of spinifex and the country of seven or eight Indigenous peoples. They had a track to follow, an Aboriginal trade route Leichhardt found in 1845 which ran parallel to the coast for about 400 miles. Whether it could take Cox and Uhr's mobs of cattle and horses had yet to be discovered. They made about four or five miles a day.

One night they camped in Ganggalidda country close to the Territory border. "Just as the four men were remounting their horses to look for the best patch of grassed country to put the horses on for the night, Mr. Uhr heard the blacks sing out down the creek," wrote James Barry, a member of the expedition who wrote an account of the drove in the third person, its candour almost unique in the records of the northern frontier.

> Mr. Uhr and Barry moved down the creek to face the blacks, and prevent them from coming among the horses. With this view they proceeded to cross the creek, but hardly had they mounted the opposite bank when all hopes of diplomacy were destroyed by a boomerang which came buzzing close by Barry's head. Plunging his spurs into the mare he rode, he dashed at his assailant, but was quickly recalled by the shouts of Mr. Uhr, causing him to notice that the blacks were trooping up from the bed of the creek in mobs.

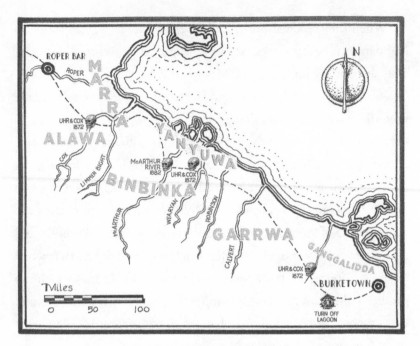

DARCY'S GULF TRACK

The boomerang thrower was shot. The blacks tried to encircle the camp. "Being, however, promptly followed up, a brief struggle sufficed to drive them back down the creek, and to secure a prisoner from among their number." They kept the man hostage for two days. "His comrades hovered around the little party in great force, burning the grass ahead of them, and continually signalling to the neighbouring tribes, but carefully keeping out of range of the rifle."

They entered the country of the Garrwa people, who were "naturally of a more peaceful disposition", but about a fortnight later they crossed the Wearyan River into the lands of the Yanyuwa people, whose territory includes nearby islands in the Gulf. The Yanyuwa had had centuries of contact with foreigners – Macassans, the Dutch and the English. "They were renowned for their no-nonsense approach to perceived ill-treatment by visitors," Tony Roberts wrote. D'arcy unwisely captured a young boy to be their guide. They called him Pilot. On they went until, one morning, the cattle turned and rushed back on the drovers. The men who went to investigate were showered with spears.

"Quickly unslinging their rifles, they retaliated with a brisk fire, the Westley-Richards telling with deadly effect even at 350 and 400 yards. Still the blacks showed a bold front, and were not driven back without an obstinate resistance." D'arcy's men found their camp and destroyed all their weapons. Pilot disappears from the narrative.

The party crossed next into Binbinka country. Gifts were exchanged. The drovers were given another black boy as a guide. His people kept an eye on him. "This tribe followed up the camps of the party during several days, as if convoying them off their territory." They followed the Limmen Bight River inland and crossed a tongue of Alawa country to the river given Cox's name. The following day was Sunday, a day of rest. The men went shooting and three friendly blacks joined them for a feast of wild goose. They'd scarcely finished when the drovers were surprised to see the horses galloping towards the camp. "The cloud of dust which they created at first prevented any view of what might be behind them." Stampeding the horses were about 130 blacks.

> These were now seen to be in regular war costume, being beautifully painted in a martial fashion, and with feathers and down of all kinds of birds tufted on their breasts and oil over their bodies.

This suggested war paint to the drovers. It's more likely the drovers had disturbed a ceremonial gathering. The blacks advanced. "On grasping the situation, the plucky leader, Mr. Uhr, ordered every man to arms without a moment's delay." Uhr went forward alone to try to broker a peace.

> It is supposed that the sight of so insignificant a number opposed to them hardened the natives against all attempts at accommodation. Instead of returning the friendly signs of the leader, they began the combat by discharging a flight of spears at him, which he had great difficulty in evading. Then the Martigny rifle made its voice heard, and they halted in astonishment to pick up their comrade, who

NAWAKIN, A YANYUWA MAN
OF THE WUYALIYA CLAN

seemed stricken down by magic. The check lasted, however, only for a moment, and they were not to be denied, but steadily pressed forward again.

Matters now began to look very serious; spears and boomerangs were travelling through the air, and the slightest sign of unsteadiness on the part of the explorers would have been their certain destruction. But Mr. Uhr was equal to the occasion. Posting his men to the best advantage he made them fire by files at the word of command. No man fired out of his turn, and thus there were never more than two barrels empty at a time, and each man took deliberate aim before firing.

For a short space all appeared useless, the blacks continued to advance, and their spears and boomerangs whizzed and buzzed every moment in more dangerous proximity to the defenders' persons. If the natives had shown desperate determination up to this point, the attitude of their white foes was now no less resolute. With teeth hard set and frowning brows they kept up a continuous rattle of rifle shots, few of their bullets being allowed to speed in vain.

At length, after a fearfully anxious period, savage doggedness found its limit. Their advance was checked, but yet for nearly a full half-hour they held their ground in the face of strange weapons, of whose deadliness they received momentarily fearful proofs in the numbers of their comrades who writhed or lay forever motionless among them.

The three friendly blacks negotiated a surrender. D'arcy made his foes give up bundles of spears, nulla-nullas and boomerangs which were then burnt.

Meanwhile the blacks engaged in attending to their wounded. Some tore from the tea-trees strips of bark for bandages, while others came up to the fire and got pieces of broken spears to serve as splints for the shattered limbs of the sufferers.

Uhr drove the stock past the camp of dead and wounded on his way to the Overland Telegraph depot at Roper Bar, which he reached about a week later. He had made history: at the cost of an untold number of black lives, a stock route had been found which with a few nips and tucks over the next fifteen years would carry about 200,000 head of cattle from Queensland into the Territory, the animals laying waste to the country and the streams along the way. History of a kind was also made when Cox sued D'arcy for assault in the first legal action of its kind in the Territory. Somewhere along the track, they had a row. Why, no one knows. But D'arcy exploded. Cox told the magistrates gathered in the telegraph workers' mess tent: "Uhr rushed upon him, knocked him down, and tore a large handful of hair out of his (Mr. Cox's) beard. Mr. Cox then dismissed Uhr, but that individual refused to resign his charge of the cattle unless he were paid, or received a promise that he should be paid, full wages up to the time the cattle arrived at Port Darwin." In the end, D'arcy settled for £100 in wages and a month's provisions to get him to the goldfields.

*

Goldfields suited D'arcy. He would go droving and run city pubs but for the rest of his life he was drawn back to rough mining towns. Maybe he caught the bug in Burketown, where he could be anything he wanted: hail-fellow-well-met with the rowdies one day and a gallant captor of horse thieves the next. Goldfields were made for men who couldn't take direction. He found backers on the goldfields but not bosses. He got what he needed with threats and charm, by spinning yarns and heady plans to make fortunes. He always needed money. A thousand pounds could be gone in a few months. He bet and drank. Then he disappeared to the next big opportunity. They said of D'arcy Uhr that he had "go".

Gold had been discovered at Yam Creek near Darwin in 1870 by crews digging post holes for the telegraph line across the Territory. Diggers were soon crawling up and down all the creeks nearby. For over a year, diggers had been washing for gold in Pine Creek before D'arcy arrived from his long drove, jumped a claim and came across a reef of gold-bearing quartz. For this he is remembered on a plaque as the man who found the first payable gold on the field. He quickly sold out for £1000 and left for a wild time in Palmerston, the name then given to the town on Port Darwin. His brother Ned was in town. Both were soon in trouble. Ned was fined for bashing an auctioneer he was playing billiards with one night and D'arcy escaped a forgery charge a few days later. They left the Territory. Gold had been discovered 900 miles across the Gulf at the Palmer River on Cape York. "A great rush set in," wrote James Venture Mulligan, the authority on the field. "Darcy Uhr followed with a mob of fat cattle killing as required by the crowd." His brothers Ned and Leslie – a bank clerk who threw in his job to find gold – joined him selling meat to miners at Uhr's Camp on the Palmer. Leslie died of fever the following year at the age of twenty-four. Ned went blind but with the help of two Kanaka men went on working in D'arcy's several rough butcher's shops on the diggings.

The Yanga people had already shut down the Gilbert River field, which had boasted seven pubs and a hospital. By the time the Uhrs arrived on the Palmer in 1873, at least twenty-four miners had met their deaths at the hands of the Kuku Yalanji. The dynamics of black resistance were so different on the goldfields. Pastoralists arrived on black lands in small numbers with many sheep. Miners came by the tens of thousands. They brought famine with them. The native peoples of the Cape were faced with immediate disaster. "The country is not fertile, is poorly stocked with game, and the whites have taken possession of all the main watercourses," reported *The Queenslander*. "The white men occupy their only hunting-grounds, and in default of the fish, roots, and game of the water holes and creek 'bottoms,' they are in a manner compelled to eat horses and bullocks." Yet the rugged country suited the blacks. So did the miners' way of shifting about from creek to creek and keeping as secret as possible their next destination. Two or three whites alone in the bush were an easy target. Newcomers, often city folk who had never handled a gun in their lives, were warned by old hands:

> The miners must protect themselves, and treat the aborigines like other destructive inhabitants of the bush. A breech-loading rifle should form an item in every northern-bound digger's outfit, for revolvers, although useful in close quarters, are not efficient at the long ranges from which boomerangs and spears are thrown by dexterous savages.

No serious attempt was made to reach an accommodation with the peoples of the Cape. The fighting on the goldfields would not be over for twenty-five years, and the original proprietors of these wild lands were soon regarded as the most hostile blacks in Queensland.

Native Police were stationed on the Palmer in strength. But still the miners cried for more. D'arcy wrote to the papers: "Were the Government officials as energetic in pursuit of the blacks as they are in enforcing the gold-fields regulations with regard to miners' rights, things would be in a different position than they are now, and life and property would be far more secure." Commissioner Seymour warned the Palmer River miners he could only do so much:

> In a wild unsettled country it would not be possible for ten detachments of police to protect from the blacks solitary travellers or persons out prospecting who do not take ordinary precaution and who frequently keep as a close secret the direction they intend taking.

Yet the Native Police killed continually on the goldfields. In October 1874, the commander of the force on the Palmer – D'arcy's nemesis Tom Coward – took his troopers and a contingent of miners out to avenge the killing of three members of the Straher family. A brief report in the Queensland papers used inverted commas to make its meaning clear: "A day or so after the murders had been committed, Mr. Inspector Coward with Sub-Inspectors Townshend and Douglas came upon the black vagabonds and 'quietly dispersed' them." They called the place Skull Camp.

On the Palmer diggings, Chinese miners far outnumbered whites. At first they came from other goldfields, but in 1875 they began to arrive in large numbers from China. Nothing on this scale had been seen in Australia before. There were soon 17,000 Chinese on the Palmer and only a few thousand whites. D'arcy came to despise the men he called, in the slang of the time, *Celestials*. They were rarely armed. They had no horses. Many were killed on the hundred-mile walk from Cooktown. Many died at the diggings. One morning, in June 1875, some Chinese came to D'arcy with a request: would he kill the blacks who had just murdered one of their party?

He rode out that afternoon with four armed companions and arrived in no time at the Chinese camp, looted of everything but their gold cradle. The body was nowhere to be seen. In his *Cooktown Courier*'s account of the next twenty-four hours, D'arcy gave himself the usual standing ovation for pluck and energy, strategic nous, and an intimate understanding of the Aboriginal people. As usual, he did not say everything:

> We pushed on to find the missing man; went to where he was last heard working at the river; found only a jacket and hat saturated with blood. We pushed on on their tracks, seeing that they had carried the Chinaman with them— we could track them by the spots of blood. In half-a-mile a fearful sight came before us—a pool of blood (about two quarts) lying in a bason of the rocks, together with some entrails, were here; a long-handled shovel was lying here covered with blood (with this they had evidently cut the man up in small pieces); the rocks are fearfully stained with blood for some distance round. I suppose, by the blood, the man had been cut up half an hour previous to our arrival.

They walked. The country was too rough for horses. After about a mile they found greasy cooking stones and – according to D'arcy – part of the miner's foot "left behind, roasted". They clambered all night through "the roughest country I have ever seen in any colony" and found themselves at dawn on the edge of a ravine. From the blacks' camp below, a spear was thrown that fell at D'arcy's feet. "As long as I have been amongst blacks, I never saw a spear thrown up hill so far." He stayed above keeping watch while his companions fought their way down into the camp, where one of them discovered "the head and neck together with part of the back bone of the Chinaman were stuck on a stump partially eaten". As the vigilantes were gathering stolen property and burning spears, about 150 men appeared on the cliffs above and "showered down volleys of spears". D'arcy ordered a retreat.

I deemed discretion the better valour; but how to get away
was no simple matter, for as soon as we commenced to
descend, they would shower spears at us ... I suppose I have
had more experience amongst blacks than any other man of
my age in the colony, and never have I yet witnessed such
a lot as the ones above referred to; I should not think it any
good for a detachment of police to go after them in the country they are now in with any less than twelve black troopers.

Yarning at his shop some days after his return, D'arcy gave his
friend Arthur Ashwin details of the expedition that appeared only fifty
years later in Ashwin's memoirs, *From Gold to Grass*, memoirs in which
D'arcy and his exploits appear many times. The vigilante attack on the
Palmer was a business proposition, D'arcy told him. The Chinese had
given him £50 to find and kill the blacks. And he told Ashwin of the
carnage on the retreat from the blacks' camp:

After a couple of volleys were fired a big mob of niggers came
down the creek to a rocky waterfall and Uhr then fired on
them but they were game and showed fight and threw spears.
Uhr kept firing on the leaders and started to get back to their
horses, the niggers after them. Darcy Uhr and his mate were
dead shots and kept dropping the leaders. He came down to
the last cartridge when they got to their horses. Uhr reckoned he never saw such a game lot of niggers.

Archibald Meston would be an influential critic of the Native Police
one day and have a hand in shaping Queensland's dealings with the
Aboriginal people of the Colony. But at this point, he was a twenty-four-
year-old journalist with a sharp eye for the ridiculous, who mocked
Uhr's story in the *Cooktown Courier* for making the feats of Richard
Coeur de Lion seem "mere amusement in comparison with the heroic
daring of the self-devoted band who charged the retreating savage!"
Meston also noted something missing:

He does not say whether any of the blacks fell under his deadly aim or not, but possibly he was seized at the time with a fit of shaking ague so prevalent in that pernicious climate, and unable [to] keep his "Martini" steady. Still I am under the impression that two breech-loading rifles should have persuaded a few savages to join their forefathers, especially if in the hands of men who know how to use them!

D'arcy replied, "I am sure I never shot a black in my life … I merely fire over their heads."

*

When the miners moved to new fields, D'arcy abandoned the Palmer and set up shop on the edge of Cairns. "Darcy made a few thousands on the Palmer," wrote Ashwin, "and got through it horse racing and other ways." Cairns suited him. He lived with his wife and son for about a year until they split up. It seems he never saw his son again. Done with Cairns, D'arcy went droving again. This "picaresque and sinister" man, as Judith Wright called him, lost 200 head of her family's cattle. "Uhr was a careless drover". He selected land for the Wrights behind the Atherton Tableland, land that was "steep, rough and barren", infested with poisonous plants and heavily defended. Wright wrote:

> The Aborigines of the region were trapped between the seething goldfields below, and the guns of the new settlers on the tableland above; unable to reach the coast, where timber-getters and prospectors occupied the forests, or the lower part of the rivers, they were cut off from their main food supplies. The redoubtable Uhr probably disposed of many, but his cousin, herding the cattle on Corunna run, was badly speared, and the cattle were harassed and could not settle.

His cousin was George Uhr, son of the Sheriff of New South Wales. He was speared in the groin but lived. The Wrights abandoned the run.

D'arcy drove cattle to runs north of the Palmer fields. He logged the Mulgrave River south of Cairns, where angry blacks "spear horses and cattle, and rob the farmers and cedar-getters week after week". He drove horses to Port Darwin in October 1880, defending himself against claims by others to have discovered the Gulf track. "I am the pioneer of the road to Port Darwin." Before Christmas that year he opened a pub on the Yam Creek goldfields: "One of the best and most complete hotels in the country," promised *The Northern Territory Times*. He kept it for a year. He raced horses. Some won. The Protector of Aborigines took him to court for beating his boy Leichhardt. "The assault was merely a box on the face with open hand," declared the bench. "Case dismissed." He went back to butchering, this time at the Bridge Creek rush south of Port Darwin. He slaughtered a bullock a day, he boasted to *The Northern Territory Times*. "This place you can safely put down as a permanency." He had a partner in the business. They ended up in court. D'arcy won £21 plus costs, the pigs, plants, and book debts. He was known well enough in the Territory to be the subject of a quip in the *Times*.

> Darcy (indignantly, to Chinese customer): "You're a big liar!"
> Heathen Chinese, in reply: "You're another!"—"Uhr"
> another—(do you see the joke?)

He went back to droving. In 1883 he set out from Cloncurry with over a thousand cattle to drive to Newcastle Waters in the heart of the Territory. This, his third time on the Gulf track, was the drove from hell. "The present season is the driest I ever knew," he reported. "Creeks and lagoons are quite dry that I always thought were permanent and everlasting." He sat with his cattle for months on Batten Creek, waiting for rain. Wild stories appeared across Australia that he and his party had been slaughtered by blacks. It was rather the other way round. D'arcy led a reprisal raid on the Macarthur River in October after two men with another droving party were killed and five of his own horses speared: "Some of my best hacks." D'arcy set out with two young blacks to find the perpetrators. After three days they confronted a dozen heavily armed warriors. "They had one hundred and forty spears and eight two-handed clubs. One native threw a spear pointed with a knife at me, but missed." D'arcy never said what followed. But the son of a stockman travelling with Uhr at that time wrote years later that D'arcy "eagerly undertook the congenial job of 'dispersing' the black criminals. This he did with his usual severity, and so effective was the lesson that his name had a fearful memory among those blacks for years afterwards."

Supplies were short. When the cattle reached the Cox River in December, D'arcy's second-in-command, Henry Mant, asked what he was doing to get food for the drovers. The explosion that followed was supercharged by D'arcy's irritation that Mant was travelling with an Aboriginal woman:

> He called me a "white-livered cur," and told me he would get me flour; he also said that he would ram his fist down the throat of the first man he caught giving my nigger flour; told him I would give the nigger some while there was any in the camp, and he then said "Alright, you can go, and I won't settle with you … I was leaving the tent when he jumped up and followed me out; he caught hold of my beard, asked me what I meant, and then threw me on the ground; he then got hold of me by the trousers and said, "You b——r, I'll put you on the fire;" he attempted to lift me off the ground, but my trousers broke; he then let me go and I rose on my feet; I was going to start home when he took my horse away and said I'd have to walk; I said "All right," and started off, but when I got a short distance away he called me back and gave me my horse; he then asked me to put up my hands and fight him; I held my hands to my face and told him I was a cripple and not to hit me.

D'arcy had agreed to hand over to another droving party about 150 stray cattle he'd picked up along the way. Mant left with them a few days before Christmas, telling D'arcy: "I do not consider myself safe alone with you." D'arcy refused him his wages. Mant decided to see him jailed. He persuaded the owners of the stray cattle – Fisher and Lyons of the 1.5-million-acre Glencoe on the Adelaide River – to have D'arcy charged with theft for failing to hand over calves worth £24.

The arrest was news but the trial in March 1884 was a fiasco. The prisoner was his own lawyer, a role he always loved – quizzing witnesses and brawling with the prosecution. In another life, D'arcy might have been a swashbuckling barrister. He was as beguiling at the bar table as he had proved, again and again, in the dock. Mant had nothing to back his allegations. After making "a fluent statement in support of his innocence", D'arcy was acquitted. Mant's action to win his wages also failed. With his credit in tatters, the prosecution decided to drop another charge he had brought against D'arcy: killing with intent to steal. "It would be useless to proceed."

D'arcy told the world he planned to sue Fisher and Lyons for £5000 for the damage done to his reputation by having this blameless citizen arrested and charged. The press lapped it up. *The North Australian* was "certain all reasonable readers of this journal will be happy to hear that his action for damages will turn up trumps". He left to engage lawyers in Adelaide. Uhr was taking on mighty figures. Since buying Glencoe, Fisher and Lyons had bought the adjoining run Victoria Downs, 10 million acres stocked with 30,000 cattle. At the time it was thought to be the largest pastoral holding in the world. The case took a year to reach court. Only the best lawyers were employed: Uhr had the Solicitor-General as his counsel and his opponent engaged the Attorney-General. On the bench was the Chief Justice. The jury took an hour to decide that D'arcy Uhr had, indeed, been defamed and was due £2000 for the loss of his droving business and another £1000 for damage to his character. The losers appealed. Over a year later, the jury's verdict was upheld. There were mutterings from Fisher and Lyons that a last appeal would be made to the

Privy Council in London. It didn't happen. D'arcy's victory was secure.

Long before these legal shenanigans were done, D'arcy had become a loud voice in Adelaide condemning the blacks. For all his talk of knowing the Aboriginal people intimately, D'arcy despised them. As he grew older – he turned forty during his battles with Fisher and Lyons – he took it upon himself to scold "the black-protecting class" for its ignorance. He was in Adelaide in September 1884 when news arrived that four copper miners at Daly River had been killed by blacks. The city was enraged. D'arcy joined the clamour. "The poor unfortunate blacks! God gave them, I may say, all Australia. What for? God only knows, as they are a useless race of savages."

D'arcy was one of a delegation of Northern Territory gentlemen in Adelaide who went to see the Minister for Justice days later to argue for a Native Police force in the Territory. D'arcy's argument was as old as the invasion of Australia: pioneer settlers are entitled to protection; blacks attack whites without reason; they grow more dangerous when left unpunished; imprisonment holds no fears for them; chastisement must be swift to be effective:

> I do not hold with shooting or molesting the natives without just cause, but I certainly think, and from my experience of aboriginals, which is more than that of most men, to keep savages in subjection you must have them afraid of their superiors.

D'arcy delivered three blasts in the press in five days. A clergyman needed to be shouted down for pointing out, "We have stolen the land from the blacks". D'arcy finished with some advice to the government on the sort of men needed to lead native police: "You don't want to send noblemen's sons or new chums just out from England to officer a detachment of black troopers. No; he requires to be a thorough bushman used to hardships and privations." A man like D'arcy Uhr.

South Australia established a force later that year, 1884. Bill Wilson, in his thesis on the Northern Territory Native Police, called the fifteen

years that followed a time of institutionalised violence. Senior officials –
police and civilians – knew what was happening and they did nothing.

> Despite this knowledge, the native police, particularly in
> Central Australia, operated with only minimal controls.
> Police records were brief and sometimes written up from
> memory. The native police were brutal and operated out-
> side the law when they wantonly killed other Aboriginal
> people. Police violence was at the extreme coercive end of
> the violence continuum and remained there until the native
> police were disbanded.

The Commander for much of that time was William Willshire, a ruthless man repeatedly denounced by the Hermannsburg missionaries
for his brutal killings. Willshire was eventually charged with murder
but acquitted. D'arcy wrote: "My sympathies are and have been with
M.C. Willshire."*

Adelaide's mood shifted in mid-1885 as rumours spread about the
revenge exacted by police after the Daly River killings. Seventy or more
blacks were said to have been slaughtered. Nothing was known officially
but some of the constables were being indiscreet. "Their deeds were
the subject of common conversation," remarked James Foster Smith, a
former policeman. He heard one of the police, a poor shot, had "cut fourteen notches on the butt of his carbine, being the tally of those whom he
knew he had himself killed". Smith learned that the Commander of the
police, Corporal George Montagu, had written an official report of the
operation. This was denied by the government, which mocked rumours
of carnage. But when that government fell later that year, a radical member of parliament, Rowland Rees, persuaded the new ministers to table
Montagu's report. When the details were revealed, *The South Australian Register* wrote:

---

* Mounted Constable.

We have no hesitation in saying that the cold-blooded manner in which Corporal Montagu and his associates murdered these unhappy wretches is a disgrace to him, a disgrace to the community, and an outrage upon the civilization about which we boast.

Montagu's report revealed his men shot any blacks who tried to flee from them. The police fossicked among the corpses and in their camps to find anything – tins of baking powder, for instance – that could be deemed stolen goods. Montagu took his men well north of Daly River, destroying camps as they went. On the McKinlay River, they drove thirty armed men into the water. Montagu reported:

> One of them while in shallow water was in the act of throwing a double wooden spear at Constable McDonald, and it was only McDonald's quickness in firing that saved his life. A spear passed through the top of Constable Cox's singlet and grazed his neck ... None of those who took to the water were known to have got away.

As the press denounced Montagu's work with almost a single voice, D'arcy was back in Darwin calling for a "monster meeting" to be convened so the public might give thanks for the actions of the police. He called Smith a malicious and wilful liar, and as one "well acquainted with the whole circumstances of the Daly murders" he assured Territorians those whom Montagu killed 70 miles from Daly River were, being of the same tribe that murdered the miners, fit to be punished.

> Had these men been Europeans, and suspected of the same atrocious crime, and done the same as the blacks did, the police would have been quite justified in shooting them, and the verdict would have been justifiable homicide; but because

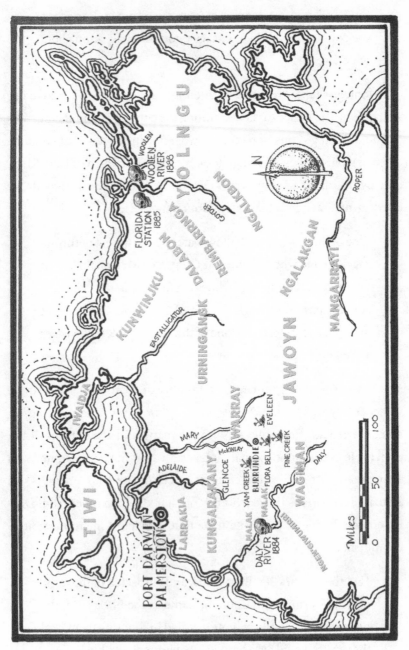

TOP END

they tire* at these useless savages—a race of men about as good as themselves—say the police ought to be hung.

Even by colonial standards, the inquiry held in Palmerston into the Montagu rampage was lame. The chairman had ridden on vigilante parties himself. Smith was not called as a witness. Not a single policeman testified to seeing anyone shot. Montagu was criticised for writing an exaggerated report but otherwise unanimously absolved of any wrongdoing. The board came to the view that the blacks had been treated leniently after the Daly River murders. The Protector of Aborigines protested and was sacked. When D'arcy applauded the findings in the press, he found himself under attack from newspapers, preachers, retired police and James Foster Smith. "Psalm-singing hypocrites", D'arcy called them and returned fire:

> These men, Mr. Editor, speak without experience, speak as their mind guides them; such is the case now in the moral city of Adelaide. Morality amongst the wild tribes is not known. I thoroughly endorse Mr. Alfred Giles's** sentiments, and say that all the tribes that I have met with—and I have made the acquaintance of a few—nearly always try to force you to take their women as a peace offering, or decoy to get a good opportunity of attack ... I could, Mr. Editor, relate dozens of instances where men have been murdered without any cause.

The Montagu inquiry had the usual consequences – Aboriginal people were left more exposed than ever. Would anyone be punished for abusing and killing them if Montagu and his men escaped without penalty of any kind? In the words of the historian Gordon Reid, the inquiry's verdict "meant that police and settlers in the Territory could now take the law into their own hands with impunity, provided that they acted discreetly."

---

* Fire a broadside.

** Explorer.

*

Back in the Top End, D'arcy spent £1000 on the Exchange Hotel. "The Hotel has been thoroughly renovated, and is now second to none in Palmerston," he assured patrons in February 1885. "Every attention is paid to the catering, and the public can rely on a good meal. The Bedrooms are under the supervision of Females, NOT CHINESE." In March, without bothering to divorce, he married Essie Thompson, whom he had met in Adelaide. He called himself a widower. They had five children but only one survived, their daughter Gladys, born in Adelaide the following year. By that time, D'arcy had left town for the Eveleen silver field where he was supplying charcoal to smelters. After losing the contract to a band of Chinese – cue further harangues against Celestials – he set up again as a butcher. He and two mates had a mine of their own, the Flora Bell. In the end, the mine yielded more litigation than silver and was abandoned. In 1887 D'arcy contracted to supply 100,000 feet of cypress pine to builders on the field, and early in the new year he took a steamer north with machinery and men to cut down trees on Florida Station in Arnhem Land.

For the four years of its existence, Florida's 650,000 acres had been a site of violence. Resistance by the Yolngu was stubborn and the brutality of the whites extreme. The first manager of the station mounted a swivel cannon on the homestead verandah to keep the blacks at bay. Richard Trudgen, the distinguished scholar of the Yolngu, records a poisoning on the station in 1885.

> The pastoralists came with one of their wagons, offering horsemeat to many of the clans ... That evening they ate, thanking the pastoralists for their good gifts. It was only when some of the people became violently ill that the Yolŋu realised the Balanda had tricked them with some strange sorcery ...
>
> Members of many clans died that day ... Yolŋu struck back, fighting with spears against muskets and carbines.

D'arcy's plan two years later was to log the Goyder River. Everything went wrong. Instead of the Goyder, they sailed into the Woolen where his crew and machinery were unloaded on a rocky ledge about 6 miles upstream. Without waiting to see if all was well, the steamer left for the coast. That afternoon, D'arcy could find nothing but "stunted pines, quite useless for our purpose". He had to find another river. All he had was a cutter – a big rowing boat – to haul the machinery back to the sea. One trip was made. Three of the crew – two Malays, Ali and Salem, plus an Aboriginal called Larrikin – were sent back to collect the rest while D'arcy and a few men slogged across country to the Florida homestead. He wrote: "What with the dangers from blacks, buffaloes, crocodiles, and snakes, and the minor annoyances of wading waist deep through leeches, mosquitoes, and sandflies, a traveller's life on the north coast of Australia is not a happy one." They were welcomed at the house on a bald ridge by a horseshoe lagoon. The garden was flourishing. After breakfast they set off searching for timber, returning to the homestead six days later to find Larrikin waiting with grim news: Ali and Salem had been lured ashore by the blacks, and killed. He had abandoned the cutter, swum ashore and saved his life.

Once more, D'arcy was on the warpath. With him was the Sub-Collector of Customs for the Territory, Alfred Searcy. He and D'arcy wrote an account of all this for *The Northern Territory Times* which was, as usual, filled with vivid detail until they found their quarry, at which point the usual curtain of euphemism fell. They never found the bodies of Ali and Salem. The logging machinery was untouched on the rocks. The cutter was found in the mangroves and D'arcy set to work to make it seaworthy. He was not on the river when three Yolngu beckoned Searcy and his men ashore. "We did so." Why, but to kill? "Their conduct looked very suspicious, and as it was a splendid place for an ambush, we speedily cleared them out." The number killed is unknown. D'arcy cut no pine. The bloodletting continued on Florida Station for a further five years until, in a great victory for the Yolngu, the place was abandoned.

25

THE LAST CHAPTER

D'arcy put the Territory behind him in 1889. He was a forty-five-year-old man of the frontier with two wives, two children and no fortune. After showering praise on the place for so long, he now delivered a sour evaluation of the Territory in the pages of *The Sydney Morning Herald*: "Considering that some 14 to 16 years have elapsed since the first stocking of country within 400 miles of Port Darwin took place, no one can reasonably and fairly dispute the failure to prove it a success. Without a doubt it has proved a disastrous failure to its owners." Mining, however bright its future might be, had also failed. "Much money has been thrown away on the mines." And then there were the Chinese. Whites can work in the climate, he said, "but they cannot compete with the Mongolian labour; the Mongolian will work for one-third what you have to pay a European, therefore, all employers of labour will employ the cheapest".

Sadly, rumours that he rode in a wild west show at this time appear to be untrue. He was back droving in 1890, bringing a mob of cattle a thousand miles from the Diamantina to Echuca in Victoria. He took up the licence of the handsome Botanic Hotel on Adelaide's North Terrace, but six months later was back in Sydney buying and selling pubs in the city. He was, of course, soon in trouble. When the police raided the Castlereagh in Woollahra one Sunday they found "two glasses on the counter containing fresh beer, and there were also in the bar two pewter measures half-full of fresh beer. The counter was wet, apparently with beer." D'arcy fought the charge of Sunday selling all the way to the Supreme

Court before paying a £30 fine. Along the way, he claimed he had never before in his life been summoned to court, forgetting, for the moment, his latest charge of assault five months earlier. He was fined £1. Restless and probably broke, he persuaded three wealthy men in Sydney – railway builders and a mine manager – to pay his way to Western Australia to join the last great Australian gold rush. Flush with other people's money, D'arcy Uhr was setting out once more to make his fortune. By the time he arrived in Coolgardie in 1894, the town had three dirt streets, a few shops and tents pitched for miles out into miserable country, a landscape of rubble stripped of timber. Afghan camel trains added some colour to the confusion. But there was nothing left for D'arcy there.

COOLGARDIE, 1893

> Some hundreds of leases are pegged around Coolgardie. Most of them appear to me to be taken up purely and solely for speculative purposes. If there are ten out of every hundred claims pegged payable when a battery starts then I will be agreeably surprised.

He decided to chase the rush to Mount Margaret, a hill on the edge of a shallow salt lake 200 miles north. The field was unknown to him and his record for finding gold was thin at best, but he charged new chums £50 each to go with him into the wilds and learn to make their fortune. He also found black guides to take him to promising outcrops of quartz – in the pidgin of the field, "big pheller yerilla". Tents also filled the gullies around Mount Margaret. Three hundred miners had beaten them to the field. D'arcy and his Babes in the Woods explored reefs to the west and north of the mountain and found nothing. This is Wangkatha, Djalgandi and Kuwarra country. Out near Hawks Nest, D'arcy's party came across a notice posted by the prospector and explorer William Carr-Boyd:

> BEWARE OF THE BLACKS.
> Niggers mustered here in force.
> Tackled us yesterday.
> Saved by our dog.
> Signed, W. J. Carr-Boyd.

Arthur Ashwin had joined D'arcy's party and mentioned the same sign in his memoirs. "Darcy Uhr proposed tracking the nigger tracks up so we run them till they split up about four miles. There was a big muster of blacks by the tracks, we could not see one but the tracks were quite fresh." When they returned to the camp that night, D'arcy announced he was so hungry, "he reckoned he could eat a bit of a blackfellow". Ashwin shot a pigeon. "We split it in half and cooked it on the coals, it tasted very moreish."

D'arcy returned empty-handed to Coolgardie, paused for a few weeks and set out for Mount Margaret with two prospectors, George Alexander and Michael Galway, and two fresh new chums. Perrin was particularly troublesome. He kept getting lost. At one point he went missing for days and when they found him at last, under a bush half mad with thirst, D'arcy hung a horse bell round his neck. "Now you wear that day and night while you're with me," he ordered. "If I ever catch you without it, I'll shoot you like a ——dingo." Perrin still went missing. They were on the road when they heard that a prospector called Phil Mack had been killed by blacks at Black Gin Soak about ten days before. Only soaks and wells made travel possible in that country.

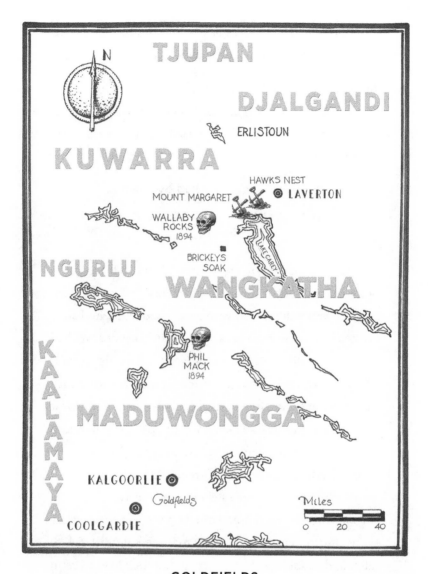

GOLDFIELDS

Mack's death was on D'arcy's mind when his party camped one morning at a soak near Mount Margaret called Wallaby Rocks. D'arcy wrote:

> We had only turned our horses out for about an hour, when a blackfellow hailed us from the granite. We had taken the precaution to camp on open clear ground. I made signs to the blackfellow to go away. As this was 30 miles from the spot where the young man, P. Mack, was tomahawked on

the 7th July, I considered I was dealing with the same tribe. We heard or saw no more until about 3 p.m.

Over the years, D'arcy had written many accounts of his clashes. This one in *The Coolgardie Miner* is among his most polished: a brief tale of resolute bravery, of savage blacks confronted, of duty done, restraint shown and lives saved:

Mr. Darcy Uhr Attacked by Blacks.

THE NATIVES FIGHT AND REFUSE TO RETREAT.

… When we were all in camp some thirty to forty blacks came rushing out from the rocks about 200 yards from us; they were fully armed with spears and clubs, and were assisted by their women in carrying spare weapons. We had only two small revolvers; Alexander took as his weapon a half axe, and we advanced to meet them, thinking they would retreat; but they made one bold rush, and threw spears at all of us. Galway narrowly escaped getting struck. I had no alternative left but to fire to try and make them retreat, but this they stubbornly refused to do.

Finding that they were surrounding our camp, we beat our way through the ring and caught our horses. They made every effort to cut us off, but we managed at great risk to catch and saddle our hacks. Seeing that our lives were in danger, and knowing that a party of six men were camped one mile and a half away, Galway galloped down and asked them to assist us or lend a rifle. The latter request was complied with, and some of the men went out to muster their horses. The natives were still fighting to gain possession of our camp. When Galway returned I managed to make them retreat, using no more violence than was actually necessary to defend life and property.

Perhaps the Commissioner of Police in Perth was not used to finding such stories in the local press. In Queensland they were commonplace. He scribbled on a clipping: "Who is this gentleman?" Constable Douglas Saunders knew the Wangkatha people of Mount Margaret. He had no doubt a clash had taken place at Wallaby Rocks, but he called Uhr's claim that the Wangkatha were unprovoked a fairy tale.

> From information corroborated by many during my journey to Mt Margaret, I heard; that a party of white men ... went down to this Creek – for water, & on reaching the spot, found some natives there – chiefly women & children. The whites at once commenced to hunt them away; although the aboriginals shewed them that they also wanted water. They called out "Gabé me"? "Gabé me"? and no doubt made a great noise over it although their meaning was simply – "Give me water"? or something to that effect.
>
> It transpired that the whites 7 in number assumed the offensive, and fired on the Aboriginals with revolvers – and whether they were rank bad shots or did not wish to harm their opponents is hard to say anyhow – it simply made the Blacks "form up" into Battle array, and placing the children in the foreground and the women in the centre they took up themselves a position to the immediate rear – with weapons poised for action.
>
> Spears were thrown and during this somewhat ill-assorted "melée" one of the party of whites, ran for a rifle.

The accounts of the slaughter at Wallaby Rocks all share this detail: as the Wangkatha began to surround the whites, Uhr sent Galway to fetch a powerful rifle from prospectors camped nearby. He posted Perrin as a decoy:

> If you had seen the barbarous way he acted when we were attacked by natives at the Wallaby Rocks, you would scarcely

wonder at my dread of him. When I thought it was all over with us and spears were bounding against the rocks, we were sheltering behind, he actually shoved me outside into the open, and told me to stay there and draw their fire, said it was all I was fit for.

Galway roused the men at a nearby camp and borrowed a Winchester. "When our Winchester rifle was requisitioned the fun became fast and furious," recalled one of the miners who rode back with him. "The result was that nine niggers bit the dust. A few years afterwards, I passed that way and the skeletons were still bleaching in the sun."

Killing did its work over the next couple of years, particularly around Mount Margaret. "That locality has been almost depopulated of its dark-skinned inhabitants through violence and fear of violence," *The Coolgardie Miner* wrote in 1896. "One may travel all over that portion of the territory and not see half-a-dozen aborigines." The paper was backing the Mayor of Coolgardie's appeal to the Premier for a few hundred pounds to care for Aborigines who, driven from their land, were hanging about settlements and towns hoping for work, shelter and food.

> Up to the present moment nothing has been done ... for the original denizens of the wilderness, now so widely peopled by men whom the blacks might justly call intruders upon their domains ... They shiver with cold in their scant and filthy rags, and are suffering from complaints of various kinds which bid fair to almost exterminate them. They have no proper food or clothing, no shelter from the inclemency of the weather, no medical remedies for their ailments.

D'arcy replied that they were doing just fine:

> It would appear to those ignorant of the manners of the blacks, that we, as the pioneers of Coolgardie, had deprived the natives of their homes and their means of earning a

livelihood. Before we came here the natives, who are at present around Coolgardie had to exist on what? On an occasional lizard and a few grubs, getting just enough to keep them from starving. As to clothing and covering for shelter they had none, not even an oppossum skin.

Now they have more provisions than they can use, as down at the slaughter yards they can get more than would supply four times as many as there are around Coolgardie, and food that many poor European families would be glad to get.

As to clothing and house accommodation this shows that the writer of the leading article knows but little of the manners and habits of the Australian blacks. It is a well-known and established fact to all Australians that aboriginals always prefer their camp fire to sleeping in any dwelling. It is as natural to them to lie out in the dirt as for us to lie in a bed, and equally as natural to be without clothing as for us to have it. Clothing worn only occasionally by blacks is the primary cause of most of their sickness.

Much as I like to see them well-treated I do hope the Government, appealed to by our Mayor, will not grant any sum of money to erect a building that will not be used.

*

D'arcy ended his life as a butcher. His last days as a prospector came with the usual little catastrophes: lawsuits and the high hopes of investors vanishing into the air. Floated in 1895 with a nominal capital of £6000, the D'arcy Uhr Goldmining Co. disappeared along with most of the £7.5 million raised in London to dig mines in Western Australia. Despite his failures on the field, D'arcy's opinions were quoted in prospectuses in Europe. It amused *The Northern Territory Times*: "The Alligator Rivers country is said to have been floated in London on the strength of reports made by Messrs. D. Uhr and H. Stockdale; whereat we smile."

Back in the butchering business at the age of fifty-two, D'arcy Uhr
seemed again on the threshold of success. From early 1896, in partnership with Charles Kidman, D'arcy built up the biggest butchering
business on the goldfields. By late the following year they were droving cattle from the Kimberley, shipping stock from the eastern colonies
and slaughtering 200 bullocks, 2000 sheep and fifty pigs a month.
Newspapers praised the sparkling cleanliness of the shops and their
extravagant window displays: "Notable ... were a shoulder of mutton
so arranged as to resemble a duck setting, oxtails presenting human
faces, and saddles of mutton dressed to justify their designation." As
Kidman and Uhr opened more shops, D'arcy cheerfully admitted the
firm was in collusion with every other butcher about the place to keep
prices high. He was loathed for this. After his election to the Coolgardie Council, they cried "Meat ring" every time he stood to speak. After
six months on the Council he walked away saying he was too busy to
attend. But he sat on many sporting committees – cricket, polo and,
most important, the Coolgardie Racing Club.

He supported Federation. A few days before the vote, there was a
noisy street meeting in the town. On the platform was one of the best-
known men in the Colony, Frederick Vosper, a radical MP and owner
and editor of Perth's *Sunday Times*. Vosper wanted the Colony in the
Federation but was demanding better terms. D'arcy interjected:

> A Voice: I earn my money by working—that's more than
> you do, Vosper.
>
> Mr Vosper: Yes, working as the tool of that monopoly.
> I should be ashamed to show my face at a public meeting if
> I stood in Mr Uhr's place.
>
> Considerable uproar here took place, and Mr Uhr pro-
> mptly accepted Mr Vosper's challenge to come up on the
> platform. He then characterised Mr Vosper's comments on
> the Bill, which had been drafted by the combined genius
> of Australia, as a piece of impertinence.—Loud applause.

For years he had known Mr Vosper as a strong Federalist, his present attitude was that of a turncoat.—Cheers. He (Mr Vosper) had never been anything but a noisy agitator—Cheers.—He (Mr Uhr) trusted all would be unanimous on Tuesday and vote for Federation—Cheers ... Mr Uhr then resumed his seat in the audience.

Vosper hadn't finished with Uhr. "The meat ring, he said, was the most unscrupulous gang of sharks to be found." Loud applause.

Kidman left and his place was taken by Tom Butcher. He looked after the shops while D'arcy took charge of the stock, land and slaughter yards. They proposed saving a fortune by raising cattle and sheep near the goldfields rather than shipping them from the east. For this they accumulated nearly two million acres around Laverton on the edge of the desert. It was a last great land grab by a family that had been seizing country for eighty years, since Richard Jones crawled to Lord Bathurst for his first Hunter Valley acres. Every generation of Uhrs had believed the land was there for the taking. That was once a question passionately debated, but the fact that Butcher & Uhr was taking this country from the Djalgandi, Kuwarra and Tjupan peoples without compensation of any kind was not thought the least remarkable.

But Laverton found Butcher & Uhr's enthusiasm for the waste of sand and saltbush around the town rather a joke. D'arcy gave an interview in full boasting mode to *The Coolgardie Miner* in 1904: on their run was pasture as fine as any in the state, horse-breeding country as good as any in Australia, and water everywhere. "There is no danger of stock running short." It was explorer porn delivered by a lifetime exponent of this frontier genre. In reply, the Kalgoorlie *Sun* ran a spoof interview of George Washington conducted apparently by the great hoaxer of the time, Louis de Rougemont. The subject was the pastoral prospects of Mr Washington's Laverton acres:

"Of course there is no grass whatever there, but salmon gums, granite rocks, ant beds, spinifex and mirages are to be found in abundance, on which bungurras, lizards, carpet snakes, and other stocks are said to thrive splendidly." I believe there is a plant called parrakelia that grows there which contains a great amount of moisture? "Oh yes," was the reply: "in one small patch I extracted water with my little hatchet sufficient to supply a private distillery for five years, and in addition to that, I captured 245½lb. of Murray cod." "But with regard to cattle, how does the country suit them?" asked the scribe. "Splendidly," replied George. "I hold a stretch of country under a pastoral lease 316 miles long by 276 miles wide; three weeks ago I placed 940 bullocks on it, and they have done so well that the mirage fodder has led them away." "Have you seen horses reared there Mr. Washington?" "Oh yes; I have seen horses bred there which, in proportion to their frames had the largest curbs and splits I have seen on any horses in Australia. My father was engaged in cab-driving all his life in Queensland, and as I have been connected with cab horses as long as I can remember, I should be a judge of curbs." In reply to a question as to the water supply for grazing purposes, Mr. Washington said that there was ample water to be obtained by sinking; an unfailing supply of beautiful salt water may be had at depths varying from 95ft. to 360ft. The advantage of fattening cattle on salt water must be apparent to every butcher as it saves 75 per cent. of salt in curing the beef. After thanking Mr. Washington for his information I withdrew, just as he commenced to speak of wild oats which he had found at an old roadside camp, where carriers had been feeding horses.—Yours, etc.

Louis de Rougemont

There was time for one last jape. In May 1904, D'arcy and two accomplices paid £90 for a fine trotter in Victoria called Hark and shipped her to Western Australia as an unknown mare called Belle. "I know I could get her on the course and command a market of £10 to £1," he told his two mates. Word got out that D'arcy had an expensive horse in Coolgardie, so he directed his trainer to run her last in Kalgoorlie, "to deceive the public and get her a bad name, and this he did". Pay day was to be a meeting in October in the little town of Northam, near Perth. Belle was backed "with good gold in a very solid manner", but at the last minute so much money was put on a horse called Bob that the bookies closed their books. Bob won by half a mile. Belle came third. Anyone else but D'arcy might have quietly licked their wounds. But he entered a protest. Without much effort the stewards at the Northam track discovered the horses running first, second and third were *all* ring-ins. Bob and Snowdrift were disqualified and their owners banned for life. But as he had so often before, D'arcy talked his way out of it. "Mr. Uhr spoke at some length and said he had not the slightest knowledge of any previous performance on the part of Belle." *The Coolgardie Miner* lathered him in praise:

A TURF INQUIRY.

THREE HORSES DISQUALIFIED

MR D'ARCY UHR EXONERATED.

D'arcy touted himself as a champion of honest racing and claimed – falsely – to have himself discovered the evidence the stewards used to uncover the fraud. All went well until one Sunday in January 1905 when Vosper's paper published this:

> My goldfields correspondent tells that the self-styled turf cleanser, D'Arcy Uhr, has arrived back from his Eastern trip, blowing like a whale. Wonder if he has brought along with him any more trotters of the Belle and Thelma type to

ring-in on the gullible W.A. public! By the way Northam folk have at last seen through the nice little part which Uhr played in the Bobs-Snowdrift-Belle fiasco, and he'll get a cool reception when he again swaggers into that quiet country settlement. The case mentioned exposed Uhr as an unmitigated schemer, whose friends at court alone saved him from disqualification along with his mare, and sportsmen will go to no pains to show their contempt for him on sight.

D'arcy sued for £2000. *The Sunday Times* had huge fun at his expense. They printed the libel all over again on the front page under a bank of headlines:

HIS GOOD NAME.

"Who steals my purse steals trash."—D'Arcy Uhr.

A Goldfields Butcher Sport.—Who Proposes to Make—A Chopping Block—Of the Public.—Takes Exception to Fair Criticism—And Talks Libel Law.—Bobs—Snowdrift—Belle—Thelma.

"An honest sport's the scarcest work of God."—Revised version.

D'arcy was always falling out with his accomplices. One of them had provided the paper with copies of all their correspondence setting up the sting. "He was our butcher's meat from the start," crowed the paper. On the day set down for the hearing of *D'Arcy Uhr v. The Sunday Times* in the Supreme Court in Perth, the plaintiff made no appearance. Judgement was entered for the paper with costs.

D'arcy was suddenly in charge at Butcher & Uhr. Tom Butcher sold out and the financial director left soon after. Despite these departures, *The Coolgardie Miner* reminded the public that the company – "in which Mr. Uhr naturally holds a large interest" – had seventeen shops, thousands of cattle in the field, thousands more on their way from the north, new cool rooms being built in Boulder, etc. "These facts show plainly what a big industry is controlled by Messrs Butcher and Uhr in catering for the meat supply of the goldfields." D'arcy was dead a few weeks later at the age of sixty-two.

After meting out so many savage deaths, the old liar was carried off by a domestic affliction: appendicitis. On 10 February 1907 he complained of feeling unwell; his doctor advised against an operation; in hospital he rallied for a while; but on the afternoon of 18 February, he signed his will, and went to his reward. After a lifetime of killings and quarrels and litigation; after years in the saddle, herding cattle through wild country; after all his new beginnings and triumphs in the courts, his estate was worth £1238. He could not have had more than a handful of shares in Butcher & Uhr and, despite his boasts, his name was not on a single acre of the millions they had lately taken. Flags were lowered here and there in Coolgardie. A crowd mustered for his funeral. Thirty butchers walked in front of the hearse. The Uhrs' phaeton was laden with wreaths. Buggies carried civic dignitaries to the graveside. Quarrels were forgotten. The chairman of the Coolgardie Racing Club was a pallbearer. Vosper's old paper gave D'arcy an elegant farewell:

> There were some who avowed that a good heart lay at the bottom of his sometime sporting eccentricities and personal bounderisms. What this paper said of him at the time was fully deserved, but Death is an eternal Truce to our terrestrial antagonisms. So, Vale! to an old enemy.

*

D'arcy almost outlived the Native Police. As the frontier moved up Cape York and west towards the Territory, the last camps in Queensland closed one by one. Despite all the rage and disgust that swept the Colony over the years, the force was allowed to go quietly out of existence. For half a century decency and money had faced off in Queensland. Money always won. The Native Police survived so long because they did their job so well. The force was, in the words of its chronicler Jonathan Richards, "an armed, mobile wing of government" that protected settlers from the people whose country they were invading, "the enemy within – the Indigenous owners of 'vacant' land". Slaughters would continue in Western Australia and the Northern Territory into the 1930s, but Queensland was conquered. Only one camp remained – on the outskirts of Coen in gold-mining country on Cape York, a site of prolonged resistance by the Kaantju or Kaanju people. That camp survived until 1929.

While David Seymour remained Commissioner, the operations of the Native Police barely changed from decade to decade. One change mattered: soon after Reg and D'arcy left the force in the late 1860s, troopers were issued with new weapons. "It was this breech-loading Snider carbine, more than any other single item, which was responsible for tearing Aboriginal resistance into shreds," wrote Ray Evans, Kay Saunders and Kathryn Cronin in *Race Relations in Colonial Queensland*. "The Snider, never particularly accurate, would, at close quarters, simply tear apart anyone or anything it hit." The Martini-Henry replaced the Snider in the 1880s, as destructive but over a far greater range. As the frontier retreated, Seymour had begun in the 1870s to distribute troopers to civilian police stations with a view, he said, "to the gradual disembodying of the Native Police". The troopers were rebranded trackers. Inspectors became constables. But killing continued until the end and so did opposition to that bloodshed – vocal, decent and ineffective.

In May 1880, Carl Feilberg – a journalist born in Denmark, educated in Scotland and writing for a decade in the Australian press – began a series in the weekly *Queenslander* denouncing "the sickening and brutal war of races that is carried on in our outside settlements". Feilberg is forgotten but the series, with the sardonic title "The Way We Civilise", is famous because here, the barbarity of the system was laid bare in unforgettable detail. Feilberg's opening salvo has been celebrated ever since:

> This, in plain language, is how we deal with the aborigines: On occupying new territory the aboriginal inhabitants are treated in exactly the same way as the wild beasts or

birds the settlers may find there. Their lives and their property, the nets, canoes, and weapons which represent as much labor to them as the stock and buildings of the white settler, are held by the Europeans as being at their absolute disposal. Their goods are taken, their children forcibly stolen, their women carried away, entirely at the caprice of the white men. The least show of resistance is answered by a rifle bullet; in fact, the first introduction between blacks and whites is often marked by the unprovoked murder of some of the former—in order to make a commencement of the work of "civilising" them ...

A few have always protested in the name of humanity against such treatment of human beings, however degraded. But the protests of the minority have been disregarded by the people of the settled districts; the majority of outsiders who take no part in the outrages have been either apathetic or inclined to shield their companions, and the white brutes who fancied the amusement, have murdered, ravished, and robbed the blacks without let or hindrance. Not only have they been unchecked, but the Government of the Colony has been always at hand to save them from the consequences of their crime.

The most lasting impact of "The Way We Civilise" was to convince the Imperial government that Queensland was not fit to annex Papua New Guinea. It also provoked the last and most candid public debate on the Native Police in the Colony. Squatters argued for the inevitability of violence on the frontier. They freely confessed – under *noms de plume* – to their part in mass killings. They spoke of colonisation as good but inescapably grim. That Queensland might have been occupied more peacefully, without such bloodshed, was a notion few entertained. This is "Never Never" answering Feilberg:

Hide it as you will, our policy towards the black is bad, but it is only the game we played all over the world; and it starts with the original occupation of the country, and any other policy would be equally outrageous that entailed the taking of the land from the blacks ... The unanswerable fact remains that by overrunning this or any other country we expose the natives to the chances of suffering the rigors of guerrilla warfare—always the cruellest and worst—and, knowing that, we come here and take up our quarters with our eyes open; by our very presence in the land justifying the act of every white ruffian in the outside country.

We are all savages; look beneath the thin veneer of our civilisation and we are very identical with the blacks; but we have this one thing not in common—we, the invading race, have a principle hard to define, and harder to name... We work for posterity, we have a history, and we have been surrounded by its tales and legends since infancy. We look upon the heroes of this history as familiar friends, and in all our breasts there is a whisper that we too by some strange chance may be known to posterity. This brings us here to wrest the lands of a weaker race from their feeble grasp, and build up a country that our children shall inherit; and this feeling is unknown to the native of Australia. He has a short history, but it is more a matter of gossip than any-thing else, and only goes back one generation. He has no thought of the future, because he never knew of anyone being remembered more than a lifetime, therefore he has no interest but to pass through life as easily as possible, and he never seeks to improve land for those who will come after him. This justifies our presence here; this is the only plea we have in justification of it, and having once admitted it we must go the whole length, and say that the sooner we clear the weak useless race away the better.

"The Way We Civilise" ran until July 1880. In October, John Douglas, recently and briefly Premier, made a last call for a royal commission into the Native Police – if only to explain what the £318,278 spent on the force since Separation had achieved. Douglas conceded settlers in the remote stretches of Queensland still needed protection. "The blacks were entrenched in the natural fortresses of their scrubs and inaccessible country, and it would be many years before they could be brought successfully within the direct influence of the white people." But he thought something more useful might be done than simply killing them. "That," he said, "was the sole function of the native police." So little had changed that Douglas might have been speaking in one of the debates in Governor Bowen's time. He complained that the force continued to operate outside "either military or civil law"; he deplored kidnappings, "a practice which might very well be put a stop to by the Government"; he raised the old, old problem of hiring officers who were no more than "young inexperienced new chums, mere boys, who have no recommendation except an unusual amount of bounce and the influence of an M.L.A at their back."* He laid before the house fresh horrors from the frontier. The Colonial Secretary, Arthur Palmer, shut down the debate. The proprietor of 576,000-acre Beaufort run on the Belyando accused Douglas of relying on witnesses "completely stuffed with camp-fire lies".

Seymour retired at last in 1895. By this time only seven Native Police camps were still operating – all on Cape York except one at Turn Off Lagoon in the Gulf, at the start of the cattle track D'arcy pioneered to the Territory. Augustus Glissan of nearby Rocklands Station asked the Native Police to find him a black boy. Favours of this kind were still being done by the force. Oscar was brought from Cooktown in 1887 with a fresh draft of troopers for Turn Off Lagoon. He was nine or ten years old. How the boy fell into the hands of the police on the Palmer River is unknown. He couldn't ride but he could draw. When Oscar was

* Member of the Legislative Assembly.

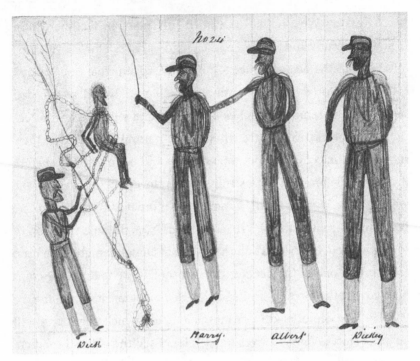

Police boys doing duty (Lynch law)

about seventeen Glissan gave him a notebook, in which he drew scenes from his childhood and awkward, haunting images of the Native Police still at work in the Gulf at the very end of the century. He dictated the captions to Glissan: "Police boys doing duty (Lynch law)", "Dispersing usual way, some good shooting", "Murderer hoppled to tree".

With Seymour gone, the government decided in 1896 to take a fresh look at the Native Question. Archibald Meston was appointed a Special Commissioner and sent north to report on "the nature and causes of the troubles between the wild tribes and the settlers in the Cape York Peninsula, and the general condition of the Northern aboriginals". The man who once mocked D'arcy after his killing spree on the Palmer River had become a writer, politician, crocodile hunter, athlete and showman, whose awful plan to take a troupe of Aboriginal performers to the Chicago exposition of 1893 had come to a messy end. Bankruptcy had claimed Meston more than once. As a Special Commissioner, he travelled for four months around the Cape with Gnootaringwan, an interpreter from Coen, as his only companion. He boasted to the Home Secretary: "My travels have brought me in contact with about 2,000 members of sixty-five different tribes, speaking thirty different dialects, and extending over 9 degrees of latitude."

They told him terrible things. He found tribes living in the wild, untouched by whites, and tribes decimated by contact with settlers. On the beach at Albatross Bay men showed him bullet wounds inflicted by the Native Police. He heard of *bêche-de-mer* fishermen and pearl fishers who lured Aboriginal men onto their boats, treated them like dogs and abandoned them on faraway coasts. Meston took this to be proof "of the utter unfitness of civilised men to be allowed an unfettered and irresponsible control over a savage race". He regretted the money spent on the Native Police. "One-third of that cost expended for the friendly benefit of the blacks would have been immeasurably more effective in promoting peace, and have left an infinitely nobler record behind." He found a cohort of its officers unfit to be given "any voice or power of action or any business whatever with the aboriginals either in peace or war", for they lacked "the finer feelings of humanity and the sense of justice necessary in dealing with a wild race to whom the administration of our law, and the law itself, is a hopeless conundrum." He called for the earliest possible abolition of the force. So alarmed was the new Commissioner of Police by Meston's recommendations and the "*ex parte* aboriginal testimony" on which the Special Commissioner relied, that he immediately took a steamer for the Cape. "Spare of flesh, but hard as nails", William Parry-Okeden was an Australian-born Police Magistrate who had risen to the top of the public service in Queensland. He travelled the Cape, not with an interpreter but an escort of Native Police, speaking to those "whose evidence is really of value". He came away convinced the Native Police should not only survive but be strengthened.

> So long as bushmen, pioneers, prospectors of our own race
> require protection, or lost persons and criminals, white

or black, are to be tracked in the wilds of the bush, and so
long as we have wild uncivilised blacks to control, punish,
or in any way look after, deal with, or even feed in their
native haunts, I consider strong native police detachments
a necessity.

He called once more for the reforms officials had promised for decades.
Nothing was done. The Native Police were allowed, killing by killing,
camp by camp, to disappear.

By the time Parry-Okeden returned to Brisbane, politicians had en-
thusiastically embraced the big recommendation Meston brought back
from the Cape. There was another side to this man. He brought a sharp
eye to the failings of the Native Police and a kind eye to the condition
of the Aboriginal people, but he believed the races must live separate
lives. His solution to the Aboriginal question was to introduce to
Queensland a version of the reserves for native peoples of the United
States and Canada.

To keep our aboriginals away from contact with the whites,
or that section with which they unfortunately mingle, is
the most beneficial act of friendship within our power to
bestow. It is also the only possible method of saving any
part of the race from extinction.

Meston was offering the government a way to keep the blacks under
control now that they were all but beaten. The Home Secretary, Hor-
ace Tozer, brought a bill to parliament that would give officials, police
and magistrates the power to compel Aborigines to live their lives on
reserves. Tozer was lyrical.

The bill proposed to make reserves ... as attractive as possible to the aboriginals. He would like to see the blacks have
the same freedom, consistent with the protection of the
whites, as they had before the whites came to Australia.

The Brisbane Courier had its doubts:

> So much power is asked for that everything will depend
> upon the administration whether liberty is real or a mock-
> ery. Reserves are to be made, into which aboriginals may be
> drafted—like sheep … and when there they may be impris-
> oned for breaches of discipline or summarily punished by
> the Protector appointed to look after them. Regulations may
> be drafted which will place them absolutely at the mercy of
> the white man in authority …
>
>   Let the aboriginals be amply protected, but see that they
> do not find in protection something to stir up feelings of
> more intense bitterness against those who seek to help them
> against themselves.

The bill was carried on the voices. For fifty years, the Native Police had
operated without the intervention of judge, jury or the law as it went
about its work. For the next seventy, Aboriginal people in Queensland
would be subjected to total, arbitrary control. Execution at will made
way for imprisonment at will. The mission was the same: to keep down
the blacks. Aspects of this regime lasted into the 1970s.

We will never know how many died at the hands of the Native
Police. The core records of the force have disappeared, presumed destroyed. But scholars have lately found in odd corners of the archives
about 100 reports officers sent to headquarters every month recording
dispersals, collisions and deaths. Cautious interpretation of these frag-
ments has seen estimates of the numbers killed since Frederick Walker
led his rogues up the Barka rise from 10,000 to 20,000 and now to more
than 40,000. The figure is neither precise nor final. Work continues in
the archives. Though too soon to carve the death count into stone, it's
past time to commemorate the Native Police in the national capital. The
Australian War Memorial Act already includes them in its wide embrace
as a "military force of the Crown raised in Australia before the establishment of the Commonwealth", a force entitled to be commemorated

in the memorial for its part in "wars and warlike operations". There is space in those sad halls to stand two Australian figures in bronze, a white officer and a black trooper, and engrave on the plinth beneath:

THE
NATIVE POLICE
IN THE CONQUEST OF THIS COUNTRY
KILLED
UNTOLD THOUSANDS.

WE REMEMBER THEM.

FAMILY BUSINESS

The maths is indisputable: we each have sixteen great-great-grandparents. Reg Uhr was one of mine. I don't believe he's tainted my blood. I don't believe I am responsible for his crimes. But when I learned what he had done, my sense of myself and my family shifted. I grew up in a tribe of engineers. We celebrate a blacksmith who came from Scotland and became an iron founder. Marrs made iron in Sydney for a century. We were never very curious about who else might be up in the tree. Occasional discoveries were a source of amusement. My mother was disturbed – and we were delighted – to find convicts lurking up there. But the past mattered only so much to us. We grew up knowing we had to make our own lives.

My mother's family was good at secrets. I was about eighteen when I asked my grandmother about a photograph on her mantlepiece of a young man in Air Force uniform. "That's my brother, Don," she said. I had never heard of him. Don came back from World War II a wreck, tried to kill himself and was, by the time I asked about him in the 1960s, a gardener at a convent in Sydney. Another mystery: though I never saw my great-grandmother Maud after I was about eight, she lived until I was in my early twenties. Why did she disappear? No one left alive can explain. I don't know if Maud ever told anyone her father rode with the Native Police, but the news hadn't reached her grandson Jim Graham, who asked me in 2019 to find what I could about her life. This book is the result.

We can be proud of our families for things done generations ago. We can also be ashamed. I feel no guilt for what Reg did. But I can't argue away the shame that overcame me when I first saw that photograph of Sub-Inspector Uhr in his pompous uniform. I checked with Wikipedia. The Native Police were exactly who I thought they were. Wikipedia even had thumbnail accounts of Reg's and D'arcy's massacres. I pulled from my shelves everything I had on the frontier wars. The brothers were there but I hadn't made the connection. It embarrasses me now to have been reporting race and politics in this country for so long without it ever crossing my mind that my family might have played a part in the frontier wars. My blindness was so Australian.

There are many of us descendants of the Native Police. The 442 officers and 927 troopers who served in its ranks over half a century bred many hundreds of families. Because I made no secret of what I was writing over the last few years, people have told me of their own murdering ancestors. Some were in the Native Police. Others were squatters. One was a magistrate. The great-great-grandfather of a colleague of mine poisoned two dozen men and women on the Clarence River in New South Wales in the 1840s. She will tell that story one day.

I have been asked how I could bear to write this book. It is an act of atonement, of penance by storytelling. But I wasn't wallowing in my own shame. None of us are free of this past. James Boyce told me: "Men like D'arcy become a part of the story that we are ALL implicated in. His deeds are our responsibility, his legacy belongs to us all." My links to the Uhr brothers made the obligation to come to grips with this past personal. For a man of my trade, the outcome was obvious – I had to write their story.

What began as an account of the bloody exploits of the brothers turned into a history of an invasion in which they were foot soldiers. I was drawn into the worlds of sheep, money, merchants, the press, the church, the law and London's imperial cowardice. I was intrigued by the shadowy forms of today's politics emerging from the frontier wars – particularly the still potent belief in many quarters that the Aboriginal people deserve nothing for the continent they lost. Polls show hostility is strongest where most blood was shed. Despising those we have wronged is another way we humans have of dealing with our shame.

But these investigations always led me back to the killings and the uncountable victims of the Uhr boys from Maryborough to the Cape, across the Gulf, into the Territory and down to the West Australian goldfields. There were days at my desk I was ambushed by dread and disgust. I tried as best I could to stick to the promise I made myself at the start – no excuses.

I feel for my family. There are Uhrs – good people I'd not met until I began writing – who have a different view of our ancestors. I fear they will not welcome this. My siblings were ambivalent at best when I began work. I've embarrassed them often enough over the years, but this time they would be more than spectators to my antics. This involves them. By the end they all agreed the story had to be told. "This was a long time ago in our family," said my sister Jane. "The shame we carry for this is the shame every white Australian should share." Our sister Annabel added: "But I still hate the fact that our family is involved." She spoke for Australia.

This is a white man's view of this history. I've drawn on rich Indigenous resources to write the bloody tale of Mr Jones and the Uhrs, but I found it was not my place to give the Aboriginal view of this tangled history. I asked Lyndall Ryan, veteran of so many academic battles on the frontier, which Indigenous scholars I should read. Indigenous scholars, she said, research particular incidents in their country. "But they don't work on the frontier wars. The topic is whitefella business." An Indigenous colleague I've known for years put it this way: "You mob wrote down the colonial records, the diaries and newspapers. You do the work. You tell that story. It's your story."

Indigenous Australians are, of course, alive to the past, telling their own stories of the wars in their own way, most powerfully through painting, dance and film. These men and women are the heirs of young

Oscar in the Gulf, looking at the horrors of that time – and times since – through their own eyes. Some see their work as retaliation. Jack Green is a Garrwa painter born in the country D'arcy Uhr first drove cattle through in the 1870s. "They used the bullet to shoot us down," he said recently. "We are using our art like a bullet to fire back at people, to speak like a tongue, to get people to understand what they done to us and how they keep destroying our land."

One afternoon in Brisbane when I had just begun writing, I spent time with another descendant of a Native Police officer. This shrewd man of business urged me not to focus too much on the plight of the blacks. Australia was going to be colonised, he said. Their land had to be taken. A guerrilla war had to be fought in Australia just as it had been in South Africa. "To bring twenty-first-century thinking to the Queensland frontier is a great mistake. We were different then."

No. Times change, not people. After all these centuries, Homer still makes sense. On a good night, Shakespeare moves us profoundly. When he was reading Manning Clark's great histories, Patrick White wrote to friends: "What is so amazing is that Australians have changed so little; we are the same arrogant plutocrats, larrikins, and Irish rabble as we were then." He might have added that the good among us are much the same as they have always been. They listened to the Aboriginal people. They called the killings murder as they happened. Journalists were the most persistent voices. But lawyers, missionaries, stockmen, a few magistrates, and a cohort of decent squatters also argued from the start that the conquest of this country, though inevitable, did not need to be so savage – the most brutal colonial invasion in the nineteenth-century Empire. So many were slaughtered. Kidnapping never ceased. Every acre was taken. None of the huge wealth earned on their country flowed back to its original owners. Laws counted for nothing. No treaties were made. And when the fighting was over, we set about forgetting how Australia was won.

The Uluru Statement from the Heart calls not only for a Voice in the Constitution but truth-telling about our history. Books can't change the past but facing the truth together can change the future. *Killing for Country* went to press as the political struggle over the Voice was unresolved. At this uncertain moment, I offer a bloody family saga from the frontier in the hope of us one day reaching the ultimate goal set at Uluru: the coming together after struggle, *Makarrata*.

ACKNOWLEDGEMENTS

Once my ancient uncle set me on the trail, I borrowed *The Petersons and the Uhrs* by John Steele, where I discovered my connection to the Native Police. The book, erratic but valuable, was beside me all the way. By June 2019 I was in contact with two Uhr cousins. Frank Uhr in Brisbane has spent years researching and writing about frontier conflict and the family's history in Queensland. Anne Stockton in Canberra is a supremely skilled family researcher. We shared our findings. Though we didn't always see eye to eye, Frank and Anne were fundamental to the whole project.

Next, I turned to my colleague Lorena Allam, the Gamilaraay and Yuwaalaraay woman who is Indigenous affairs editor of *The Guardian*. In early 2019 she produced *The Killing Times*, an interactive map and analysis of data collected by the Colonial Frontier Massacres project led by Professor Lyndall Ryan at the University of Newcastle. *The Killing Times* was a first in Australia. She and Ryan have since updated it twice. Lorena briefed me on the lie of the land in massacre studies – a not always happy terrain. She read the manuscript and advised me on cultural issues raised in the text. I take full responsibility for what I've written here while being deeply grateful for her guidance over the last four years.

When I began, Heather Burke and Lynley Wallis had not yet allowed public access to their database *Frontier Conflict and the Native Mounted Police in Queensland*. They let me in early. From mid-2019 I was continuously exploring their mighty collection of documents and archaeological evidence from the frontier. My gratitude to them and their team of researchers, contributors, transcribers and IT managers is deep. The site continues to grow.

In March 2020, when Covid shut the archives, I began asking my partner, Sebastian Tesoriero, to hunt for material online. He has a lawyer's mind and a hunger for facts. I knew he was a skilled internet sleuth. Trove opened its riches to him. As the year went by, we began working closely together and continued doing so to the end. He proved a fine – at times, savage – editor. We had many disagreements. Not all are resolved. His extraordinary discoveries and his interrogation of my work have been crucial to the book.

The archives reopened. Until she was called away to Cambridge, Dr Meg Foster researched for us in the NSW archives. Her place was taken by Dr Selena Williams in mid-2021, a veteran with supreme mastery of the files. She never failed. Jill Beard of Griffith University began work for the project in the Queensland archives before handing the task to Dr Lisa Durnian of Griffith University. She became our companion in the project; she understood what we were doing; her patience was endless; she brought order to the process; and deep in the papers she found gold. And my thanks to the staff of the archives, the Mitchell and the John Oxley libraries.

Scholars have been working in this field for nearly half a century. My debts to their work are even deeper than the hundreds of references in the book suggest. I particularly thank Henry Reynolds, the man who changed our minds about this country's past when he published *The Other Side of the Frontier* in 1981. I want to remember, also, the pioneering work of the poet Judith Wright. In *The Cry for the Dead*, she was the first to make sense of this history through family memoir. As well as mining the work of today's historians, I turned for help to Ray Kerkhove, Tim Bottoms, Truman Smith, Mina Murray, Heather Burke, Lynley Wallis and Lyndall Ryan. Particularly generous to me was Jonathan Richards. I thank all of them for their help all over again.

Mark Dunn, author of the beautiful *Convict Valley*, read my pages on the Hunter. I took his advice. The splendid James Boyce read the whole manuscript – some of it more than once – and somehow managed to be, at the same time, tough and fiercely supportive. His advice was superb and his orders always the same: this matters, keep writing. James, thank you.

Thank God for local historians who know their territory in such fine detail. On the Liverpool Plains, we were helped by Kay Pittman of the Quirindi and District Historical Society. In Armidale, by Bill Oates of the University of New England Regional Archives. In Toowoomba, by Dr Mark Copland of the Friends of Multuggerah. In Brisbane, by Janet Prowse of the Queensland Parliamentary Library and by Jenny Steadman of the Queensland Women's Historical Association. In Cardwell, Stephanie Berger and Thea Ormonde of the Cardwell and District Historical Society came to our rescue. In the far north and at the last minute, I called on the help of Dr Sandi Robb of the Cairns Historical Society and her ally Dr Jan Wegner. My thanks to all of them.

I'm especially indebted to the custodians of Maryborough's history. The first to help me make sense of the place were Ian Scougall and Kym Walker of the Maryborough and Wide Bay Burnett Historical Society. Merv Hopton offered me documents. Then Wayne Boldery and Tony Clift took me down into the murky past of the town to a depth I'd thought impossible. I am grateful to them all.

The filmmaker Rachel Perkins, who knows this field so intimately, was a great support when I was struggling to find my way to the end of the book. Her work and the paintings of Judy Watson, both superb interpreters of the horrors of the frontier, convinced me that today's Indigenous response to the Native Police was not my story to tell. I leave it in better hands.

It's impossible to thank everyone who helped over the last four years. But thank you, Bob Cameron of Bolwarra House; Janette Holcomb, a.k.a. Jan Mallyon, author of *Early Merchant Families of Sydney*; Max Lambert and Jake Spear, who recorded William Uhr's hit ditty

"She Loves Me Not"; Saliha Belmessous of the University of NSW, who deciphered and translated the diary of Edmond de Boissieu; Jack Latimore of *The Age* and Carly Williams of the ABC for their advice; Paul Memmott of the University of Queensland; Margaret Ker, scholar of the Ker family; my blunt legal team of retired judges; Marcelle Burns of the Myall Creek commemorations; churchmen Paul Collins, Russell Powell and Fr Frank Brennan; Dr Nicole Sutton of UTS; Tony Pagels, weapons expert; Patsy Withycombe from my law days, now an authority on Myall Creek; Kim Eberhard of the Westpac Group Archives; Lyn Tranter of Australian Literary Management, who has been looking after my affairs forever; Charles Ovadia, Peter Youssef, Robyn McGregor and Nitya Patanjali, who got me through some tough times; 212 Blue of Australia Street, Newtown for keeping me amused and caffeinated every day; Catherine Bishop, Mark McKenna and Chip Van Dyk, who tried and failed to decipher the blurred word in that Donaldson letter; and Leonie Jones, who solved the riddle – the word was "immense".

Survivors from from The *National Times* days still grab the chance to work together. Neil Moore drew the fine illustrations and worked with Sebastian Tesoriero on the maps. Neil arrived on a visit to Australia just in time to rescue us. He did weeks of work. His seated troopers – trapped and haunted men – are among the most compelling images I've seen of the Native Police. Lorrie Graham took yet another author pic. She did her best.

Chris Feik is a hard editor to thank because he leaves barely a trace behind. He works inside your head. Every time I've written for him in the last fifteen or so years, his engagement with the project has been sympathetic, deep and quiet. He reads along. Useful books and papers arrive unbidden. He knows an early draft when he reads one. He doesn't panic. He lets the text grow. Only when the time is right do terse suggestions arrive from Melbourne – for a nick here, a new phrase there and a deep slash to the text in the name of "pace". Months of work vanish in a moment. He's usually right. Where he must, Feik takes defeats well:

this book is two years late. He is a fine man to have on your side from start to (eventual) finish. My gratitude to him is endless.

Working with him on this project were his scrupulous lieutenants at Black Inc. Rebecca Bauert and Denise O'Dea. Mary Callahan gave us the superb cover. The designer Beau Lowenstern worked for weeks with me and Sebastian as we fiddled with the maps and illustrations. He was a model of creative patience. Kate Nash and I find ourselves on the road again flogging the product. And somewhere, hovering over it all, is Black Inc.'s founder Morry Schwartz. My thanks to his whole crew.

I never stop talking. Some of my best writing is done as I'm sounding off. It's tiresome for everyone. Luckily, my friends agreed the murderous Uhrs were worth pursuing. My nephew, the Walkley Award–winning water engineer Tom Patterson, treated my early drafts with kindness bordering on insolence. Filmmaker Penny Chapman lectured me – usefully – on POV. Lindy Bourke lent me books that failed, I'm afraid, to convince me Sir Richard did much good for his Aboriginal subjects. Greg Bearup says I couldn't have done it without him. Sandy Gordon was my sounding board on ancient squatting matters. Despite my best efforts, I failed to implicate his family in the murdering business. My friend Rae de Teliga, ninety-five, who has proofread my work for decades, said when she finished this: "It's ghastly." I think she meant the story. Mary Vallentine has announced: "David, none of us has another book in you."

IMAGE CREDITS

REFERENCES

ABBREVIATIONS

AJCP	Australian Joint Copying Project
CO	Colonial Office
HoC	House of Commons
HRA	*Historical Records of Australia*
HRV	*Historical Records of Victoria*
JOL	John Oxley Library
ML	Mitchell Library
NLA	National Library of Australia
NSWLA	Legislative Assembly of New South Wales
NSWLC	Legislative Council of New South Wales
NSWSA	New South Wales State Archives
QLA	Legislative Assembly of Queensland
QSA	Queensland State Archives
QSL	Queensland State Library
SLQ	State Library of Queensland

I   MR JONES

1   "No man": Niel Gunson (ed.), *Australian Reminiscences and Papers of L.E. Threlkeld: Missionary to the Aborigines, 1824–1859*, Australian Aboriginal Studies no. 40, Ethnohistory Series No. 2, Australian Institute of Aboriginal Studies, Canberra, 1974, p. 213.

1   CROSS-BREEDING

2   "But I" & following: *The Maitland Mercury*, 5 January 1860, p. 3.

3   "Big fellow water": William Telfer, *The Wallabadah Manuscript: Recollections of the Early Days*, edited by Roger Milliss, New South Wales University Press, Sydney, 1980, p. 54.

3   "small country" & "Papa was sent": *Early Reminiscences of R. Jones*, written by his third daughter, Elizabeth, 1899 in Papers Relating to Richard Jones 1833–1899, (ML), p. 1.

4   "Very bad indeed" & following: *Report from the Select Committee on the State of Gaols*, 1819, (HoC), p. 138.

5   "the dissentions": *The Sydney Gazette*, 7 January 1810, p. 2.

5   "You are to endeavour": George III's instructions to Governor Phillip, 25 April 1787, issued to each succeeding governor until Darling, *HRA*, series I, vol. I, The Library Committee of the Commonwealth Parliament, 1914, pp. 13–14.

6   "While they entertained": David Collins, *An Account of the English Colony in New South Wales*, vol. I, printed for T. Cadell Jun. and W. Davies, London, 1798, p. 147.

6   "unite in": *The Sydney Gazette*, 11 August 1810, p. 1.

7   "I entertained": Gunson (ed.), *Australian Reminiscences and Papers of L.E. Threlkeld*, p. 347.

7   "The first was": Samuel Marsden, *An Answer to Certain Calumnies in the Late Governor Macquarie's Pamphlet*, J. Hatchard & Son, London, 1826, p. 68.

8   "Educating, and bringing": Macquarie to Bathurst, 8 October 1814, *HRA*, series I, vol. VIII, p. 369.

8   "Several of the little": *The Sydney Gazette*, 4 January 1817, p. 2.

8   "Black Natives": Macquarie to Captain Shaw, 9 April 1816, Colonial Secretary's Papers, 1788–1825, 4/1734, p. 149. "You must fire": pp. 163–4.

9   "the pure doctrines": *The Sydney Gazette*, 4 January 1817, p. 3.

9   "I believe that the London": Judge-Advocate's report on the criminal trial of J.T. Campbell, 20 March 1821, *HRA*, series I, vol. X, pp. 461–2.

11   "It renders": Macquarie to Bathurst, 1 March 1819, *HRA*, series I, vol. X, p. 18. "at once on": p. 20.

11   "The more I view": Jones to Marsden, 6 July 1819, Samuel Marsden papers, Letters, 1794–1837, vol. I, A1992, (ML), pp. 251–2.

12   "his cheerful": *The Sydney Gazette*, 26 September 1818, p. 3.

13   "German wools": Stephen Roberts, *History of Australian Land Settlement*, Macmillan and Co. Ltd in association with Melbourne University Press, Melbourne, 1924, p. 154.

13   "the principal": *Report of the Commissioner of Inquiry, on the State of Agriculture and Trade in the Colony of New South Wales*, 13 March 1823, (HoC), p. 18; "As an unfettered": p. 83.

14   "I trust your Lordship": Jones to Bathurst, 19 October 1824, Records of the Colonial Office (as filmed by the AJCP), Fonds Series CO 201, File 159, Settlers, A-L, 1824, (NLA), pp. 570–1.

14   "And therefore": Strathallan to Murray, 24 November 1829, *HRA*, series I, vol. XV, p. 402.

14–15   "I am the first": *The Sydney Monitor*, 28 March 1835, p. 4.

15   "most nobly": John Ker, *The Breach of Promise; or, Mis-led Nobleman, by Artful Teachers; or, Honor Sold for the Sake of a Trifle*, W. Lewis, London, 1814, p. 15. "I am informed": p. 27.

16   "There is a man": Anne Ker, *Edric, the Forester: or, The Mysteries of the Haunted Chamber*, vol. I, self-published, London, 1817, p. 1.

18   "having lately": Anne Ker to the Royal Literary Fund, 24 August 1820 in *Cardiff Corvey, Reading the Romantic Text*, issue 11, December 2003, p. 97.

2 LORDS OF THE SOIL

18   "Badly Watered": annotation on Henry Dangar's *Map of the Hunter River, and Its Branches*, engraved and published by J. Cross, 1 August 1828.

18 "I have invested": Jones to Colonial Secretary, 7 April 1828, Letters Received from Individuals Relating to Land, 1826–c. 1860, 28/2903, (ML).

18-19 "swimming hither": *The Maitland Mercury*, 11 August 1877, p. 9. "You ugly" & "your hair": 4 August 1877, p. 3. "the voices": 25 August 1877, p. 10. "The aromatic cedar": 1 September 1877, p. 10.

19-20 "He was directed": Gunson (ed.), *Australian Reminiscences and Papers of L.E. Threlkeld*, p. 49.

20 "In the Aboriginal": Grace Karskens, *People of the River: Lost Worlds of Early Australia*, Allen & Unwin, Sydney, 2020, p. 132.

20 "Plenty shake hands": Henry Reynolds, *The Other Side of the Frontier*, Penguin Books, Melbourne, 1990, p. 76. "For the groups": p. 78.

20 "testy, talented": Smith's one-time editor William Watt in *The Sydney Gazette*, 23 July 1833, p. 2.

20-1 "If the blacks": *The Monitor* (Sydney), 1 September 1826, p. 125.

22 "Treat them": *The Australian*, 9 September 1826, p. 3.

22 "A hot conflict": *The Australian*, 23 September 1826, p. 3.

22 "prevent and restrain": George IV's instructions to Governor Darling, 17 July 1825, *HRA*, series I, vol. XII, p. 125.

22 "Vigorous measures": Darling to the Landholders at Hunter's River, 5 September 1826, *HRA*, series I, vol. XII, p. 577.

23 "The numerous": *The Australian*, 23 May 1827, p. 4.

23 "It is the general": *Report from the Select Committee on the State of Gaols*, 1819, (HoC), p. 147.

23 "inconsistencies": *The Moreton Bay Courier*, 26 October 1850, p. 3.

23 "Mr. Jones": *The Sydney Monitor*, 27 March 1839, p. 2.

23 "The purchasers all admit": John Macarthur to his son John, 1 August 1827, Macarthur family papers, series I, vol. III, (ML), A 2899 (Safe 1/395), p. 173b.

23 "A strange mixture": Elizabeth Macarthur to her son Edward, 4 March 1827, Macarthur family papers, 1789–1936, First Collection, series 3, vol. X, (ML).

24 "On the evening": *The Sydney Gazette*, 7 June 1826, p. 2.

24 "He is a very steady": Jones to Donaldson snr, 2 July 1829, Sir Stuart Alexander Donaldson correspondence, 14 October 1823–24 April 1840, (ML), p. 26.

25 "Johnstone went close": *The Sydney Monitor*, 8 October 1831, p. 2.

25 "The climate has": *The Sydney Morning Herald*, 22 December 1842, p. 4.

26 "Lords of the Soil": Scott Family Papers Vol. 4, Correspondence of Robert Scott, 1820–1843, A 2263, microfilm CY Reel 2178, (ML).

26 "There are several": *The Sydney Monitor*, 6 March 1833, p. 1.

27 "It is not excelled": Jones to Davidson, 14 January 1834, in *W.S. Davidson's Narrative of His Business Connexion with His Nephew Patrick Leslie*, privately printed, 1844, p. 5.

27 "Mr D's": Jones to Donaldson snr, 2 July 1829, Donaldson correspondence, p. 26.

28 "Mr Jones, as one": *The Sydney Gazette*, 20 May 1826, p. 2.

28 "It has been": Address of the Landed Proprietors and Merchants of New South Wales to His Excellency Lieutenant General Ralph Darling, 7 July 1829, *HRA*, series I, vol. XV, p. 71.

29 "the old poisonous": *The Sydney Monitor*, 13 February 1830, p. 2.

29   "Not a stooper": Manning Clark, *A History of Australia*, vol. II, Melbourne University Press, Melbourne, 1968, p. 231.

30   "All the Sheep": Jones to Riley, 16 January 1834, Donaldson correspondence, pp. 67–8.

3 RACE AND FAITH

31   "Natural and much more": *The Sydney Gazette*, 4 February 1830, p. 2.

32   "I think he acted": *Report from the Select Committee on the State of Gaols*, p. 146.

32   "one of the great": James Boyce, *1835: The Founding of Melbourne and the Conquest of Australia*, Black Inc. Books, Melbourne, 2011, p. 136.

32   "wanton and savage": *Committee for the Care and Treatment of Captured Aborigines: Minutes*, 1830–33, Tasmanian Archives, p. 57. "As Men": p. 71. "dread of the effect": p. 67. "They venture": p. 80.

33   "the obstinate superstition": William Grant Broughton, *A Charge, Delivered to the Clergy of the Archdeaconry of New South Wales*, printed by R. Mansfield, for the executors of R. Howe, Sydney, 1830, pp. 29–30.

33   "Mr Jones' assistance": *The Sydney Gazette*, 7 October 1830, p. 3. "the advantages which": p. 2.

33–4   "They seem to me": *Report from the Select Committee on Aborigines (British Settlements)*, 5 August 1836, (HoC), *Minutes of Evidence*, p. 17. "Any attempt": p. 16. "With a very": p. 14. "They are not of a dull": p. 14. "They have a conception": p. 19.

34–5   "starving, insulting": *The Sydney Gazette*, 30 September 1826, p. 2.

35   "Oh! William" & "The fishing": *The Sydney Gazette*, 2 February 1829, p. 2.

35   "One of the party": *The Sydney Monitor*, 2 February 1829, p. 8.

35   "After listening": Royal Australian Historical Society, *Journal and Proceedings*, vol. XI, part 5, Sydney, 1925, p. 303.

36   "An effective, unpolitical": *The Sydney Gazette*, 20 October 1832, p. 2.

36   "The scholar who travels": in Keith Sinclair, "Laplace at Hobart Town and Sydney Town in 1831: The Humanism of a French Naval Captain", Australian Academy of the Humanities, *Proceedings 13*, 1984–1986, p. 97.

36–7   "The only businessman" & "The Story": translation of Edmond de Boissieu, manuscript written on board *La Favorite* on the LaPlace voyage, detailing Sydney society, c. 1831, MSS 9913, (ML). Transcribed & translated by Associate Professor Saliha Belmessous, University of New South Wales.

38   "Thus prematurely closed" & following: Jones to Donaldson snr, 2 July 1829, Donaldson correspondence, p. 13.

38   "As he had always": *Australasian Chronicle*, 11 June 1840, p. 3.

39   "Think of the annoyance": *The Sydney Herald*, 21 April 1842, p. 2.

39   "as little exclusive": *The Sydney Gazette*, 26 January 1830, p. 2.

39–40   "The inheritors": Lloyd Waddy, *The Kings School, 1831–1981*, Council of The King's School, Parramatta, 1981, p. 17.

41   "The less we have": Jones to Darling, 29 September 1830, *HRA*, series 1, vol. XV, p. 786.

41   "AUDACIOUS FORGERY": *The Sydney Monitor*, 22 October 1831, pp. 2–3.

42   "the most ruinous": *The Sydney Gazette*, 29 October 1831, p. 4.

42   "The character of": *The Sydney Gazette*, 14 November 1829, p. 2.

42   "to graze stock": Jill Ker, 'The Wool Industry in New South Wales 1803–1830, Part II', *Business Archives and History*, 1962, vol. 2, issue 1, p. 47.

4 BREAKOUT

43 "would seem a perverse": Bourke to Glenelg, 10 October 1835, *HRA*, series I, vol. XVIII, p. 156.

44 "A flock of sheep": *The Hobart Town Courier*, 27 October 1827, p. 3.

44 "Scotch twill" & following: Telfer, *The Wallabadah Manuscript*, p. 90.

46 "This part of the Mokai": John Gould, *The Birds of Australia, 1840–1842*, vol. VI, printed for John Gould, London, 1848, plate 24. "This lovely little": vol. V, plate 44.

46 "His stature is immense" & following: Mrs David Milson, *Kamilaroi Vocabulary and Aboriginal Songs*, 1840, NSW State Library, FL 380928. Her mother, Eliza Dunlop collected the words, p. 9. "What are you" & following: pp. 10 and 12.

47 "One man": Sadleir to Archdeacon Scott, 14 January 1828, *Report from the Committee on the Aborigines Question with Minutes of Evidence*, Sydney, 12 October 1838, Appendix E to Sadleir's evidence given 21 September 1838, (NSWLC), pp. 40–41.

47–8 "While conflict": Reynolds, *The Other Side of the Frontier*, p. 65.

48 "We care not" & following: *The Sydney Gazette*, 18 January 1834, p. 2.

49–50 "There was an erroneous": *The Sydney Monitor*, 18 November 1835, p. 3.

50 "the melancholy state": Gunson (ed.), *Australian Reminiscences and Papers of L.E. Threlkeld*, p. 138.

50 "If Gentlemen Farmers": *The Sydney Monitor*, 18 November 1835, p. 3.

51 "Sir Richard's career": *The Sydney Herald*, 19 October 1835, p. 2.

51 "His great passion": Manning Clark, *A History of Australia*, vol. III, Melbourne University Press, Melbourne, 1973, p. 145.

52 "varied according": Bourke to Stanley, 15 January 1834, *HRA*, series I, vol. XVII, p. 324.

52 "1. Dennis McDonald": *Report from the Select Committee on Transportation*, 1837, (HoC), p. 236.

53 "But when I see": Jones to Donaldson, 18 February 1834, Donaldson correspondence.

54 "You villain": *The Sydney Herald*, 16 December 1833, p. 2.

54 "I had the misfortune": *The Sydney Monitor*, 11 December 1833, p. 2.

55 "exhibit their": Roger Therry, *Reminiscences of Thirty Years' Residence in New South Wales and Victoria*, Sampson Low, Son and Co., London, 1863, p. 169.

55 "obtained in a very": Bourke to Stanley, 20 September 1834, *HRA*, series I, vol. XVII, pp. 542–3.

56 "I have been acquainted": James Mudie, *The Felonry of NSW*, printed for James Mudie, London, 1837, p. 349.

56 "hasty, unnecessary" & following: Bourke to Stanley, Enclosure, 19 September 1834, *HRA*, series I, vol. XVII, pp. 540–1.

5 BOTANY BAY TACTICS

57 "I do not consider": *The Sydney Herald*, 7 March 1836, p. 2.

57 "What possible interest" & following: *The Sydney Gazette*, 3 August 1833, p. 2.

58 "had a hand": *The Colonist*, 3 September 1835, p. 4.

58 "The *Gazette*, yielding": *The Sydney Gazette*, 22 October 1833, p. 2.

58 "Mr. O'Shaughnessy depended": Charles B. Gibson, *Life Among the Convicts*, Hurst and Blackett, London 1862, vol. 2, pp. 222–3.

58   "Mr. E. W. O'Shaughnessy": Emigrant of 1821 (aka William Watt or "Humanitas"),
          *Party Politics Exposed in a Letter Addressed to the Right Honorable the Secretary of
          State for the Colonies: Containing Comments on Convict Discipline in New South
          Wales*, printed by Anne Howe at the *Gazette* office, Sydney, 1834, p. 67.

58   "a government based": *The Sydney Gazette*, 8 April 1834, p. 2.

59   "In consequence": *The Colonist*, 10 September 1835, pp. 5–6.

59   "We are bound": *The Sydney Gazette*, 28 June 1834, p. 2.

59   "HUMANITAS": *The Sydney Gazette*, 26 June 1834, p. 4.

60   "A mere cypher": Emigrant of 1821, *Party Politics Exposed*, pp. 65–6. "The whole
          of": p. 66. "Mr Richard Jones": p. 67.

60   "Observations on": Roger Therry (aka "An Unpaid Magistrate"), *Observations
          on the "Hole and Corner Petition", in a Letter to the Right Honorable Edward G.
          Stanley ... for the Colonial Department*, printed by Anne Howe, Sydney, 1834,
          p. 1. "arrogate to themselves": p. 37.

60   "containing a refutation": Bourke to Stanley, 19 September 1834, *HRA*, series I,
          vol. XVII, p. 541.

61   "a piece of useless": *The Sydney Gazette*, 20 August 1835, p. 3.

61   "a notorious liar" & following: *The Colonist*, 3 September 1835, pp. 4–5.

62   "Watt had assumed": Therry, *Reminiscences of Thirty Years' Residence in New
          South Wales and Victoria*, p. 172.

63   "Having called a Cabinet": *The Australian*, 7 February 1837, p. 2.

63   "I told him": Volume VI: Sir Richard Bourke papers, letters from Sir Richard
          Bourke to his son, 1834–1837, A 1733, 30 November 1835, (ML), pp. 103–4.

63   "Letters of pressing": *The Australian*, 7 February 1837, p. 2.

63   "I shall feel": Jones to William Riley, 31 October 1835, Alexander Riley papers,
          vol. I, 1804–c.1836, ML A106, CYReel820.

64   "found continually": *The Sydney Gazette*, 23 February 1837, p. 2.

64   "He only disgraces": Bourke to Bourke jnr, 26 December 1835, vol. VI: Bourke
          papers, (ML), pp. 122–3.

64   "I cannot with": Bourke to Glenelg, 2 December 1835, *HRA*, Series I, vol. XVIII,
          pp. 224.

64   "As extraordinary things": Bourke to Bourke jnr, 30 November 1835, vol. VI:
          Bourke papers, (ML), p. 108.

64   "meddling or": injunction, 18 January 1836, NRS 13504-32, Supreme Court of
          New South Wales in Equity, Jones and Ors vs A. Howe (now Watt), [3/3926],
          no. 132, (NSWSA), p. 7. "persons of the lowest": Bill of complaint, 31 December
          1835, p. 5. "Jones only wants": Affidavit of Anne Watt, 12 July 1837, p. 2.

65   "pliant and obsequious": *The Australian*, 16 September 1836, p. 3.

65   "For the life": *The Sydney Gazette*, 1 April 1837, p. 2.

6 DEATHS AND ARRANGEMENTS

66   "far from the utterly": Richard Keynes (ed.), *Charles Darwin's Beagle Diary*,
          Cambridge University Press, Cambridge, 1988, p. 398. "The whole community":
          p. 405–6. "The capital of": p. 406.

67   "inevitable president": Nehemiah Bartley & J.J. Knight, *Australian Pioneers and
          Reminiscences*, Gordon & Gotch, Brisbane, 1896, p. 13.

67   "I will receive": Jones to Donaldson snr, 18 February 1834, Donaldson
          correspondence, pp. 70–1.

67   "I have had your": Donaldson mother to son, 19 November 1835, Donaldson correspondence, p. 91.

68   "They are excessively": Patrick Leslie to W.S. Davidson, 13 May 1835, Leslie Family Papers, OM71-43, (JOL), p. 3 of letter 39.

68   "It is quite": Patrick Leslie to his parents, 2 August 1835, Leslie Family Papers, p. 3 of letter 42.

68   "Those with": Leslie to Davidson, 13 May 1835, Leslie Family Papers, p. 3 of letter 39.

68   "If you do": Patrick Leslie to his parents, 12 June 1836, Leslie Family Papers, p. 2 of letter 52.

68   "There being about" & following: *Sydney Times*, 14 November 1834, p. 2.

68   "Aunt Ferriter": Evelyn R. Bancroft, *The Colonial Diaries: Recording the Strength of Family and Faith of the Jones Women*, Queensland Women's Historical Association, Bowen Hills, 2000, p. 2.

70   "Many a fond": *The Moreton Bay Courier*, 31 March 1855, p. 4.

70   "It is a fact": George Augustus Robinson, Journal, Port Phillip Protectorate, 18 January–2 February 1840, A 7036/1, (ML), p. 64.

70-1   "There was no possibility": Boyce, *1835*, p. 57.

71   "private adventurers": Glenelg to Bourke, 13 April 1836, *HRA*, series I, vol. XVIII, p. 379.

71-2   "the desirableness" & "It is scarcely": Backhouse to Bourke, 25 April 1837, *Extracts from the Letters of James Backhouse Whilst Engaged in a Religious Visit to Van Diemen's Land, New South Wales and South Africa Accompanied by George Washington Walker*, Part 5, Harvey and Darton, London, 1841, pp. 50–1. "to whatever extent": p. 53. "in order to": p. 52.

72-3   "lynx-eyed" & "Attacked simultaneously": Extract from Minute No. 29 of the proceedings of the Executive Council, dated 16 December 1836, in *NSW Government Gazette*, 21 January 1837, p. 59.

73   "humbugging maniacs" & "If nothing": *The Sydney Herald*, 26 December 1836, p. 1.

73   "The fact is": *The Sydney Gazette*, 14 January 1837, p. 2.

73   "Is there any thing": *The Sydney Gazette*, 17 January 1837, p. 2.

74   "came upon": Threlkeld's 8th annual report to the Colonial Secretary in Gunson, *Australian Reminiscences and Papers of L.E. Threlkeld*, p. 145.

74   "If Government": Threlkeld's 7th annual report to the Colonial Secretary, Gunson, vol. I, p. 139.

75   "The inhabitants": *The Sydney Gazette*, 28 October 1837, p. 2.

75   "a felon mob": *The Sydney Gazette*, 7 December 1837, p. 2.

7   THE CREEKS

76   "THE POOR BLACKS": *The Sydney Herald*, 7 December 1837, p. 2.

76   "You are to act": Deposition of J.W. Nunn at Merton, 4 April 1839, *HRA*, series I, vol. XX, p. 250.

76   "[p]opping off": Gunson, *Australian Reminiscences and Papers of L.E. Threlkeld*, vol. II, p. 275. The death count is taken from Telfer's *Wallabadah Manuscript*, p. 67.

77   "Sir George Gipps desires" & "In order that": *The Sydney Gazette*, 30 June 1838, p. 2.

77   "As I reside": Foot to Thomson, 4 July 1838, from Roger Milliss, *Waterloo Creek: The Australia Day Massacre of 1838*, Sydney, 1992, p. 317.

78   "of the most shocking": *The Colonist*, 18 July 1838, p. 3.

78-9   "Too often" & "In order that": *Report from the Select Committee on Aborigines (British Settlements)*, 26 June 1837, (HoC), pp. 5-6. "Whatever may": p. 83. "To carry civilization": p. 76.

79   "choking rigidity": *Commercial Journal*, 2 October 1839, p. 2.

79   "spoke too low": *The Australian*, 10 August 1842, p. 2.

80   "So long as": *Select Committee on Aborigines (British Settlements)*, 1837, p. 83.

80   "The subscribers", "Mr Jones said", "extremely hazardous" & "As to saddling": *The Australian*, 14 August 1838, p. 2.

81   "humbug": *The Sydney Gazette*, 11 July 1840, p. 2.

81   "The rankest" & "the protectors of the Esquimaux": *The Sydney Gazette*, 18 February 1841, p. 3.

81   "Let them send": *The Sydney Gazette*, 3 September 1840, p. 2.

81   "We think it is about": *The Sydney Gazette*, 10 June 1841, p. 2.

82   "A person": *The Sydney Herald*, 23 September 1839, supplement p. 1.

83   "to protect": *The Southern Australian*, 3 November 1838, p. 3.

83   "The two public": *The Colonist*, 24 October 1838, p. 2.

83-4   "By fraud" & following: *The Australian Aborigines' Protection Society: Instituted 1838*, printed by James Spilsbury, Sydney, 1838, p. 6.

85   "the wailers", "Theorists", "Philanthropists" & "weep over": *The Sydney Herald*, 26 December 1836, supplement p. 1. "It is quite evident": 14 September 1838, p. 2. "most glaring" & "Hordes of Aboriginal": 19 September 1838, p. 4.

86   "We sincerely hope": *The Sydney Gazette*, 20 December 1838, p. 2.

388-88   "One thing of lasting": John N. Molony, *An Architect of Freedom: John Hubert Plunkett in New South Wales 1832-1869*, Australian National University Press, Canberra, 1973, p. 147.

86   "the very *words*" & following: *The Sydney Monitor*, 24 December 1838, p. 2.

86   "the outrages which": *The Australian*, 16 February 1839, p. 2.

87   "in open day": *The Sydney Gazette*, 12 December 1840, p. 2. .

87   "cash and orders": *The Sydney Gazette*, 18 August 1838, p. 2.

88   "religious instruction": *The Sydney Gazette*, 19 March 1839, p. 2.

88   "Little time was left": L.F. Skinner, *Police of the Pastoral Frontier: Native Police 1849-1859*, University of Queensland Press, St. Lucia, 1975, p. 18.

88   "Nothing but summary": *The Sydney Gazette*, 7 June 1838, p. 2.

8   HIS GIMLET EYE

89   "1837 1838": Telfer, *The Wallabadah Manuscript*, p. 110.

89   "Because the ground": Jeremiah 14, King James Version, verses 4 to 7.

89   "They are still": *The Colonist*, 29 December 1838, p. 4.

90   "Rain has descended": *The Colonist*, 1 May 1839, p. 3.

90   "I spoke to Mr Uhr": Nowland to the Committee of the Hawkesbury Benevolent Society, 6 December 1838, A 624, microfilm CY 762, (ML), p. 123.

90   "great losses": *The Australian*, 16 February 1840, p. 2.

91   "Let us unite": *The Tasmanian*, 31 December 1830, p. 4.

91   "A most amiable": *The Hobart Town Courier*, 7 July 1837, p. 3.

92   "The business most": Jones to Donaldson snr, 18 February 1834, Donaldson correspondence, p. 26.

92   "in a very small": *Early Reminiscences of R. Jones*, written by his third daughter, Elizabeth, 1899 in Papers Relating to Richard Jones 1833–1899, (ML), p. 4.

92   "A losing concern" & following: Patrick Leslie to his father, 4 December 1835, Leslie Family Papers, OM71-43, (JOL), p. 7 of letter 47.

93   "first rate advisers": Patrick Leslie to Davidson, 8 June 1835, Leslie Family Papers, p. 1 of letter 41.

93   "the greatest scoundrels", "I have seen" & "Mr Jones gives": *W.S. Davidson's Narrative of* His Business Connexion with His Nephew, Patrick Leslie, 1844–1846, (ML), p. 13.

93   "an evil hour": *Davidson's Narrative*, p. 1.

93-4   "precisely the same" & "I think you will": Davidson to William Leslie, 23 August 1839, *Davidson's Narrative*, p. 80.

94   "From this moment": *Davidson's Narrative*, p. 1.

94   "flattering approbation": Davidson to Patrick Leslie, 11 June 1838, *Davidson's Narrative*, p. 40.

94   "Be assured": Mrs H. Macarthur to Mrs W. Leslie, 13 March 1839, *Davidson's Narrative*, p. 78.

95   "this vast pretended": Davidson to William Leslie snr, 20 February 1841, *Davidson's Narrative*, p. 126.

95   "Jones grows" & "Jones handed": Donaldson jnr to snr, 9 May 1839, File 4: Stuart Alexander Donaldson letterbook, 13 April 1836–May 1841, A728, (ML), p. 5. "Between you and me": Donaldson jnr to snr, 28 April 1838.

96   "So important": *The Sydney Gazette*, 14 November 1839, p. 2.

96-7   "It is this fact": *The Sydney Herald*, 1 April 1839, p. 2.

97   "were killed under": Archibald Meston, *Report on the Aboriginals of Queensland*, Brisbane, 1896, p. 5.

97   "I have ... heard": Threlkeld to Saxe Bannister, 5 December 1825, Gunson, *Australian Reminiscences and Papers of L.E. Threlkeld*, p. 91.

97   "make your blood": Ullathorne's evidence to the Molesworth Committee, *The Australian*, 15 January 1839, p. 2.

98   "a dapper little": *The Sydney Gazette*, 12 July 1838, p. 2.

98   "Are unnatural crimes": *The Australian*, 15 January 1839, p. 2.

99-100   "I consider them": *Report from the Committee on Immigration*, 13 August 1841, (NSWLC), *Minutes of Evidence*, p. 47. "Kindness and justness": *Minutes*, p. 38. "The assigned servants": *Minutes*, p. 36. "They invariably resume": *Minutes*, p. 41. "But after having": *Minutes*, p. 46. "They frequent": *Minutes*, p. 39. "without leave": p. 6.

100   "come to this beautiful": *The Sydney Monitor*, 2 September 1839, p. 2.

101   "We much fear": *The Port Phillip Patriot*, 18 November 1839, supplement p. 4.

101   "First would come": *The Monitor*, 27 March 1839, p. 2.

101   "foolish appropriation" & following: *The Australian*, 5 September 1839, p. 2.

101   "the namby-pamby" & following: *Australasian Chronicle*, 3 September 1839, p. 1.

102   "Where is the cold-blooded": *The Australian*, 17 September 1839, p. 2.

102   "unworthy of this": *The Colonist*, 18 August 1836, p. 6.

102   "for the Sons": Bourke to Stanley, 10 March 1834, *HRA*, Series I, vol. XVII, p. 393.

103 "That it is an object": *The Sydney Gazette*, 8 October 1839, p. 1.

103 "His Excellency had": *Australasian Chronicle*, 3 September 1839, p. 2.

104 "November 3", Graham Abbott & Geoffrey Little (eds), *The Respectable Sydney Merchant: A.B. Spark of Tempe*, Sydney University Press, Sydney, 1976, p. 127.

104 "eighteen of the leading": *The Austral-Asiatic Review*, 31 December 1839, p. 4.

104 "He never saw": *The Australian*, 11 May 1841, p. 2.

104 "with such an immense": *The Australian*, 16 March 1841, p. 3.

105 "I have nothing to fear": *The Australian*, 29 May 1841, p. 2.

9 MOVING NORTH

106-7 "I entered on": Thomas A. Darragh and Roderick J. Fensham (eds), *The Leichhardt Diaries: Early Travels in Australia during 1842-1844*, Vol. 7 (1), Queensland Museum, Brisbane, 2013, p. 420.

107 "Deep ravines": James Demarr, *Adventures in Australia Fifty Years Ago*, Swan Sonnenschein & Co., London, 1893, p. 204.

107-8 "I had known" & following: John Campbell, *The Early Settlement of Queensland and Other Articles*, printed at the *Ipswich Observer* office, Ipswich, 1875, pp. 7-9.

108 "I consider that": Hodgson to Colonial Secretary, 27 October 1841, 41/9744, NSW Colonial Secretary – Letters relating to Moreton Bay and Queensland, QSL Reel A2.12, (JOL), p. 115.

108 "Such country": Charles Archer to his father William, 23-28 November 1844, Archer Family Correspondence, OM80-10, (SLQ), p. 5 of letter 78.

109 "throw open": *The Sydney Herald*, 3 September 1841, p. 2.

110 "A more formidable": *Colonial Times* (Hobart), 24 May 1850 p. 4.

112 "under the necessity": Balfour to Gorman, 6 October 1841, 41/9745, NSW Colonial Secretary – Letters relating to Moreton Bay and Queensland, QSL Reel A2.12, (JOL), p. 123.

112 "together, able": David McConnel to Henry McConnel, 22 November 1841, McConnel Family Papers, Fryer Library Manuscripts, University of Queensland, p. 3 of Item 44.

113 "There has been" & "Many of us think": David McConnel to William McConnel, 22 May 1844, McConnel Family Papers, p. 4 of Item 36.

113 "In every district": David McConnel to James McConnel, 18 October 1843, McConnel Family Papers, p. 6 of Item 32.

113 "That prince": *The Darling Downs Gazette*, 24 December 1875, supplement p. 1.

113 "in a state of uproar" & following: Brown's deposition to Hodgson, 23 October 1841, *Book of Trials Held at Moreton Bay, 1835-1842*, Item ID 869682 – Part 3, (QSA), pp. 284-6.

114 "brutally murdered" & "money scattered": Hodgson to Colonial Secretary, 27 October 1841, 41/4244, (NSWSA), pp. 2 and 3.

115 "Some half-dozen" & following: Campbell, *The Early Settlement of Queensland*, pp. 10 and 11.

116 "The Natives had" & "I cannot": Hodgson to Colonial Secretary, 27 October 1841, pp. 1-2 and 4.

116 "It is manifest" & following: Roger Therry to Owen Gorman, 23 December 1841, Copies of letters sent to Magistrates, 4/6658, (NSWSA), pp. 478-80.

117 "The poor Doctor" & "So the whole thing": Campbell, *The Early Settlement of Queensland*, pp. 14 & 15.

117 "He came close up": Gorman to Private Secretary Parker, 14 April 1842, New South Wales – Colonial Secretary Letters Received 1826–1934, 42/1627/2, QSL Reel A2.12, (JOL), p. 711.

118 "Land at nine" & following: 17 March 1842, Business and social diary of William Fanning, 1841–42, London Guildhall Library collection relating to Australia, 1834–1925, M1336, Series MS 11891, (NLA).

119 "I think you are extremely": Patrick Leslie to William Leslie, 26 August 1842, Leslie Family Papers, (JOL), p. 2 of letter 94.

119 "insane craving": *The Sydney Monitor*, 1 November 1841, p. 2.

119 "No less than" & following: *The Sydney Herald*, 10 December 1841, p. 2.

120 "The sheep are much": Daniel Peterson to John Uhr, Uhr Family Correspondence 1843–1873, MSS 946, (ML).

120 "It seems like a flattering": *The Sydney Morning Herald*, 24 June 1843, p. 2.

120 "Let only those": *The Sydney Morning Herald*, 17 June 1843, p. 3.

120 "Sydney became": Therry, *Reminiscences of Thirty Years' Residence in New South Wales and Victoria*, notes p. 228.

121 "He had every": *The Australian*, 9 September 1841, p. 2.

121 "They had been well known": *The Australian*, 12 August 1842, p. 2.

121 "Those who have": *The Sydney Monitor*, 8 October 1841, p. 2.

II EDMUND B. UHR

123 "The Colonial Treasurer": *Select Committee Report on the Native Police Force*, 17 July 1861, (QLA), p. 17.

10 VALLEY OF THE SHADOW

124 "murdered, by these": *The Sydney Gazette*, 19 March 1842, p. 3.

125 "labouring under an aberration": 12 February 1837, 38/1576, 4/2405.3, Colonial Secretary Main series of letters received, 1838 Miscellaneous Persons J, (NSWSA).

125 "Unless Mr. William": *The Sydney Herald*, 16 May 1842, p. 3.

126 "Don't you think": *Select Committee Report on the Native Police Force*, 17 July 1861, (QLA), *Minutes of Evidence* p. 71.

126 "The first pangs": Henry Stuart Russell, *The Genesis of Queensland*, Turner and Henderson, Sydney, 1888, p. 280.

126 "The … District of Moreton Bay": *NSW Government Gazette*, 11 February 1842, p. 249.

126 "first brought here" & "From the remarkable": Simpson to Colonial Secretary, 30 May 1842, *Commissioner's Letterbook*, Item ID 272324, (QSA).

127 "With the incidence": Olga Miller, *Companion to Legends of Our Lands*, Fryer Manuscripts, p. 5, from Kerkhove and Uhr, *The Battle of One Tree Hill*, Boolarong Press, Brisbane, 2019, p. 103.

127 "Some seven": Kerkhove and Uhr, *The Battle of One Tree Hill*, p. 118.

128 "These Tribes vowed": Simpson to Colonial Secretary, 30 May 1842, *Commissioner's Letterbook*.

128 "The Stations to the North": Simpson to Colonial Secretary, 13 July 1842, *Commissioner's Letterbook*.

128 "A large number": *The Colonial Observer*, 3 December 1842, p. 3.

129   "Not only have we" & "vampire of hell": *The Colonist*, 29 December 1838, p. 4.

129   "stir up": John Dunmore Lang, *Cooksland in North-Eastern Australia*, Longmans, Brown, Green and Longmans, London, 1847, p. 277.

129   "We have no words": *Australasian Chronicle*, 6 December 1842, p. 2.

129   "If so foul" & "It will not be difficult": *The Sydney Morning Herald*, 5 December 1842, p. 2.

130   "It is very evident": Simpson to Colonial Secretary, 20 January 1843, British Parliamentary Papers [Colonies Australia], vol. VIII, pp. 297–8.

130   "indispensable to the protection": Stanley to Gipps, 20 December 1842, *HRA*, series I, vol. XXII, p. 439.

130   "It would be": *The Sydney Morning Herald*, 21 June 1844, p. 3.

131   "On the blacks" & "They are determined": *The Sydney Gazette*, 27 August 1842, p. 3.

131–2   "They never show" & "They became desperate": David McConnel to Henry McConnel, 3 July 1842, McConnel Family Papers, MSS 3271, (JOL), pp. 2–3 of Item 24.

132   "Davie ... considers": Charles Archer to his father William, 29 April 1845, OM80-10 Archer Family Correspondence, (SLQ), pp. 2–3 of letter 85.

133   "too rich": Thomas Archer to his father William, 22 March 1846, Archer Family Correspondence, p. 5 of letter 103.

133   "He is therefore no" & "But their misfortunes": Thomas Archer to his father William, 24 March 1845, Archer Family Correspondence, p. 3 of letter 82.

133   "A very influential": *The North Australian*, 11 January 1861, p. 4.

133–4   "On the 1st of September": Simpson to Colonial Secretary, 3 October 1843, Simpson Special Letters, 43/7448, QSL Reel A2.16, (JOL), pp. 192–3.

134   "A tall black man" & following: *The Sydney Morning Herald*, 20 March 1844, p. 4.

134   "He does not keep": Daniel Peterson to John Uhr, postmarked 27 July 1843, Uhr Family Correspondence 1843–1873, MSS 946, (ML).

134–5   "Mr. and Mrs. Uhr" & following: *The World's News*, 8 August 1908, p. 10.

136   "It was to be war" & following: Campbell, *The Early Settlement of Queensland*, p. 18. "When the scrub": p. 14. "The blacks robbed": p. 21.

137   "This was a fatal": Kerkhove and Uhr, *The Battle of One Tree Hill*, p. 148. "undoubtedly the biggest": p. 164.

137   "The dunghill cock" & following: John Wilkes, "The Raid of the Aborigines", *Bell's Life in Sydney and Sporting Reviewer*, 4 and 11 January 1845, p. 4.

139   "An immense number" & following: *The Sydney Morning Herald*, 12 October 1843, p. 3.

139   "no small number": William Coote, *History of the Colony of Queensland from 1770 to the Close of the Year 1881*, William Thorne, Brisbane, 1882, p. 44.

139–40 "Then on a sorry" & following: Wilkes, "The Raid of the Aborigines".

140   "to assist in": Commissioner Simpson to Colonial Secretary, undated, *Quarterly Report of the Employment of Each Man of the Border Police at Moreton Bay from the 1st of October to the 31st of December 1843*, 4/7203, NSW Colonial Secretary – Letters relating to Moreton Bay and Queensland, QSL Reel A2.13, (JOL), p. 765.

141   "This period of military": *The Brisbane Courier*, 25 April 1892, p. 7.

142   "Each squatters": Telfer, *The Wallabadah Manuscript*, p. 62.

142   "very beautiful and valuable": *The Sydney Morning Herald*, 24 February 1845, p. 4.

142   "being probably, without exception": *The Sydney Morning Herald*, 23 April 1845, p. 4.

142   "He held out": Abbott and Little (eds), *The Respectable Sydney Merchant*, p. 163.

143   "There is neither": Donaldson to Henry Parkes, *Sir Henry Parkes: Autograph Letters of Public Men of Australia*, 20 March 1856, A68, CY Reel 822, (ML), p. 30.

143   "All passed for ever" & following: *Early Reminiscences of R. Jones*, written by his third daughter Elizabeth, 1899 in Papers Relating to Richard Jones 1833–1899, (ML), pp. 4–6.

144   "Mr. Edmund Blucher Uhr": Jones to Colonial Secretary, 1 July 1845, 45/5703, NSW Colonial Secretary – Letters relating to Moreton Bay and Queensland, QSL Reel A2.15, (JOL), p. 251.

11 KILLERS OF MR UHR

145   "The younger pert": Charles Archer to Kate Jorgensen, 21 December 1845, Archer Family Correspondence, OM80-10, (SLQ), p. 4 of letter 97.

145   "I stayed at the station": Thomas Archer to his father, 3 January 1845, Archer Family Correspondence, p. 3 of letter 80.

145   "Cranky Uhr": George Leslie to his brother William, 24 May 1845, Leslie Family Papers 1833–1860, OM71-43, (JOL), p. 5 of letter 218.

145   "They no longer": Simpson to Colonial Secretary, 31 December 1845, *Commissioner's Letterbook*, Item ID 272324, (QSA).

146   "with the greatest": *The Sydney Morning Herald*, 14 January 1846, p. 3.

146   "presenting innumerable": *The Star*, 17 January 1846, p. 1.

146   "into the greatest": *The Sydney Morning Herald*, 14 January 1846, p. 3.

146   "I certainly do not": Simpson to Colonial Secretary, 8 January 1846, *Commissioner's Letterbook*.

147   "blacks unknown": Libby Connors, *Warrior*, Allen & Unwin, Sydney, 2015, p. 117.

148   "He is no bushman": David McConnel to James McConnel, 5 May 1846, McConnel Family Papers, MSS 3271, (JOL), p. 4 of Item 55.

148   "We ascended the ranges": David McConnel to Annie McConnel, 5 April 1846, McConnel Family Papers, p. 4 of Item 54.

150   "The former I soon": Thomas Archer to his father, 17 August 1846 continued 25 August, Archer Family Correspondence, p. 5 of letter 112.

150-1   "Before another quarter" & "How much better": *The Sydney Morning Herald*, 8 February 1849, p. 3.

151   "supposed murderers": *The Moreton Bay Courier*, 5 September 1846, p. 2.

151   "the principal": *The Moreton Bay Courier*, 28 November 1846, p. 1.

151   "Shall a handful": *The Moreton Bay Courier*, 21 November 1846, p. 2.

152   "I then told him": *The Moreton Bay Courier*, 6 February 1847, p. 3.

152-3   "that no undue violence": *The Sydney Morning Herald*, 23 February 1847, p. 2.

153   "A very bad specimen": Thomas Archer to his father William, 24 March 1845, Archer Family Correspondence, p. 2 of letter 82.

153   "White fellows had fired": *The Moreton Bay Courier*, 13 February 1847, p. 2.

154   "enthusiasm has warped": *The Moreton Bay Courier*, 16 January 1847, p. 3.

12 TROUBLESOME BUSH LAWYER

155   "The head and mouth": *Melbourne Daily News*, 24 December 1849, p. 4.

155   "Those sheep had": Record of Proceedings (Hansard), 26 August 1869, (QLA), p. 799.

155   "There were 25,000": *Maryborough Chronicle*, 5 June 1907, p. 3

156   "The untameable": *The Sydney Morning Herald*, 12 October 1843, p. 3.

156   "From my own experience": *The Moreton Bay Courier*, 4 December 1847, p. 2.

157   "I shall never forget": writing under the name Theophrastus Secundus, *The Daily Northern Argus*, 9 May 1891, p. 3.

158   "easy and safe": *The Moreton Bay Courier*, 11 March 1848, p. 2.

158   "We laid in": *The Daily Northern Argus*, 16 May 1891, p. 4

159   "For safety sake": Labatt to Mitchell, posted 27 September 1850, 5/5526 under 58/3765, NRS 13751, Letters received [Surveyor General], (NSWSA), p. 2.

159   "We cannot offer": *The Moreton Bay Courier*, 9 December 1848, p. 3.

160   "Mr Uhr's brother": Mary McConnel, *Memories of Days Long Gone By*, self-published, Brisbane, 1905, p. 18.

160   "By administering": *The Sydney Morning Herald*, 27 June 1849, p. 3.

160   "I am glad": *The Sydney Morning Herald*, 8 November 1849, p. 3.

161   "In a very short time": *The Daily Northern Argus*, 20 June 1891, p. 4.

161   "Violent assaults": Memorial of the Inhabitants of Maryborough to FitzRoy, 15 October 1849, New South Wales – Colonial Secretary Letters Received 1826-1934, 49/11511, QSL Reel A2.23, (JOL), p. 212.

162   "It became obligatory": *The Daily Northern Argus*, 2 May 1891, p. 3.

162   "I am sorry to inform": *The Sydney Morning Herald*, 28 May 1849, p. 5.

162   "the blacks were shown": Arthur Laurie, "Early Gin Gin and the Blaxland Tragedy", *Journal of the Royal Historical Society of Queensland*, vol. IV, issue 5, 1952, p. 712.

162   "Over sixty years": Arthur Laurie, "The Black War in Queensland", *Journal of the Royal Historical Society of Queensland*, vol. VI, issue 1, 1959, p. 160.

163   "I believe I am": George E. Loyau, *The History of Maryborough and Wide Bay and Burnett Districts from the Year 1850 to 1895*, Pole, Outridge & Co., Brisbane, 1897, p. 3.

164   "as regard Law": Bidwill to Chief Commissioner of Crown Lands, 1 November 1849, New South Wales – Colonial Secretary Letters Received 1826–1934, CCCL 49/4718 under 49/11511, QSL Reel A2.23, (JOL), p. 214.

164   "That is the man" & following: Edward Armitage, *Maryborough Chronicle*, 31 January 1922, p. 3.

164   "I managed to fling": Bidwill to Chief Commissioner of Crown Lands, 16 October 1849, New South Wales – Colonial Secretary Letters Received 1826–1934, CCCL 49/4565 under 49/10971, QSL Reel A2.18, (JOL), p. 310.

164   "Mr. Bidwell was determined": *Maryborough Chronicle*, 4 June 1907, p. 4.

165   "It could not be" & following: Labatt to Mitchell, posted 27 September 1850, 5/5526 under 58/3765, NRS 13751, Letters received [Surveyor General], (NSWSA), pp. 3, 5 and 6.

165   "upwards of three hundred": Uhr's Memorial to FitzRoy, 5 March 1851, 51/3749, NRS 905, [4/2932], Colonial Secretary Main Series of Letters Received, (NSWSA), p. 1.

165   "Rent": note on report of the Assistant Commissioner of Crown Lands, 2 December 1851, 51/3749, NRS 905, [4/2932], Colonial Secretary Main Series of Letters Received, (NSWSA), p. 1.

165   "Uhr, of boiling-down fame": Loyau, *The History of Maryborough and Wide Bay and Burnett Districts*, p. 148.

165   "Mr. Uhr's boiling place": *The Moreton Bay Courier*, 15 June 1852, p. 1.

166   "After we crossed": *Maryborough Chronicle*, 4 June 1907, p. 4.

166–5 "The Boppleites had": *Maryborough Chronicle*, 31 January 1895, p. 2.

13 MY ROGUES

168   "led to a degree": Roberts, *History of Australian Land Settlement*, p. 179.

168   "The word *resistance*": *The Australian*, 23 December 1845, p. 3.

169   "These Leases": Grey to FitzRoy, 11 February 1848, *HRA*, series I, vol. XXVI, p. 225.

169   "Unless suitable reserves": Report of Robinson to Colonial Office, enclosed in FitzRoy to Grey, 17 May 1847, Despatch 107, Records of the Colonial Office (as filmed by the AJCP), Fonds Series CO 201, File 382, Despatches, pp. 104–5.

170   "I think it has been generally": Grey to FitzRoy, 11 February 1848, p. 225. "A distinct understanding": pp. 225–6.

171   "in the clearest": FitzRoy to Grey, 11 October 1848, *HRA*, series I, vol. XXVI, p. 633.

171   "Such a broad": Murdoch and Rogers of Colonial Land and Emigration Office to Merivale, 17 April 1849, Records of the Colonial Office (as filmed by the AJCP), Fonds Series CO 201, File 422, Part 3 Offices: Colonial Land & Emigration Board, p. 168.

171   "We do further": *Progress Report from the Select Committee on Crown Lands*, 29 November 1854, (NSWLC), *Minutes of Evidence*, p. 80.

172   "from their superior": *The Sydney Herald*, 28 June 1838, p. 4.

172   "the formation": *Votes & Proceedings*, 8 June 1848, (NSWLC), p. 113.

172   "a tall, handsome": *The Queensland Times*, 22 December 1866, p. 4.

172–3 "At that period" & "his old friend": *The Empire*, 6 February 1865, p. 3.

173   "in form and gait": *The Queensland Times*, 12 September 1865, p. 3.

173   "No blacks ought": Walker's Report of the Proceedings of the Sydney Native Police, 10 March 1851, 51/3266, NSW Colonial Secretary – Letters relating to Moreton Bay and Queensland, QSL Reel A2.37, (JOL), p. 37.

174   "would have amounted": Walker to Colonial Secretary, 25 January 1853, 53/1383, NSW –Typescript copies of correspondence of the Colonial Secretary's Department, Item ID 2969636, (QSA), 24_41.

174   "Victims don't make": Mina Murray to author, 9 February 2003.

175   "It would greatly": Walker to Colonial Secretary, 22 July 1848, 48/8306 with 49/11933, 15 December 1849, [4/2865].

175   "creates a famine": Jones to Colonial Secretary, 2 September 1851, 51/9055, NSW Colonial Secretary – Letters relating to Moreton Bay and Queensland, QSL Reel A2.21, (JOL), p. 45.

175   "my rogues": Skinner, *Police of the Pastoral Frontier*, p. 54.

175   "They have left": Walker to the Colonial Secretary, 6 October 1850, 50/9783.

175   "Mr. Walker had the rare": *The Queensland Times*, 22 December 1866, p. 4.

176   "I want you to shew" & following: Skinner, *Police of the Pastoral Frontier*, pp. 53–4.

176   "Luckily myself": Walker to Colonial Secretary, 23 March 1849, 49/3355, NSW Colonial Secretary – Letters relating to Moreton Bay and Queensland, QSL Reel A2.19, (JOL), p. 356.

176   "During the last" & "The whole party": *The Maitland Mercury*, 9 May 1849, p. 2.

177 "These despised denizens": *The Sydney Morning Herald*, 21 June 1850, p. 2.

178 "I found the Condamine": *The Moreton Bay Courier*, 29 June 1850, p. 4.

178 "This Report of the Commandant": Walker to Colonial Secretary, 26 May 1849, 49/5554, NSW Colonial Secretary – Letters relating to Moreton Bay and Queensland, QSL Reel A2.19, (JOL), p. 325.

178 "Just at daybreak": Telfer, *The Wallabadah Manuscript*, p. 41.

179 "As every black" & "I cannot authorise": Walker to Colonial Secretary, 26 May 1849, NSW – Typescript copies of correspondence of the Colonial Secretary's Department, 49/5553, Item ID 2969630, (QSA), 18_60.

179 "indefatigable exertions": *The Moreton Bay Courier*, 20 October 1849, p. 3.

179 "Where but a year": *The Sydney Morning Herald*, 10 January 1850, p. 2.

180 "My party accordingly": Walker to Colonial Secretary, 12 July 1849, 49/7305, NSW Colonial Secretary – Letters relating to Moreton Bay and Queensland, QSL Reel A2.19, (JOL), p. 319– 21. "for the maintenance": p. 316.

181 "In no case" & "It is impossible": Walker to Colonial Secretary, 16 October 1849, NSW – Typescript copies of correspondence of the Colonial Secretary's Department, 49/10488, Item ID 2969630, (QSA), 18_54.

182 "The fact is": Walker to Colonial Secretary, 6 October 1850, 50/9783.

182 "It was almost impossible": *Select Committee Report on the Native Police Force*, 28 January 1857, (NSWLA), *Minutes of Evidence*, p. 17.

182 "'Entre nous'": Morris to Walker, 11 May 1850, General correspondence records of the Native Police, Item ID 86134, microfilm 2435, (QSA).

182 "The new recruits": Walker to Colonial Secretary, 15 June 1850, 50/6325, NSW Colonial Secretary – Letters relating to Moreton Bay and Queensland, QSL Reel A2.52, (JOL), p. 859.

182 "Take care of yourselves": Skinner, *Police of the Pastoral Frontier*, p. 54.

183 "one of the greatest difficulties" & "Sheep are stolen": Walker to Colonial Secretary, 7 November 1850, NSW – Typescript copies of correspondence of the Colonial Secretary's Department, Item ID 2969649, (QSA), 37_107.

183 "The duty thus": 3 December 1850, Plunkett and the Solicitor-General to the Colonial Secretary forwarded to Walker, 15/50, item 86133, (QSA).

183 "It cannot be": Plunkett to Colonial Secretary, 9 November 1850, in letters on Native Police matters Government Resident, Moreton Bay, enclosed with letter 58/3614 dated 22 October 1858, Item ID 17618, (QSA).

183 "No measure of law": Skinner's *Police of the Pastoral Frontier*, p. 26.

184 "But in consequence", "Whenever opportunity" & "Our curses": Jones to Colonial Secretary, *The Moreton Bay Courier*, 14 December 1850, p. 2.

185 "They average": Walker to Colonial Secretary, 7 November 1850, 50/11402, NSW Colonial Secretary – Letters relating to Moreton Bay and Queensland, QSL Reel A2.19, (JOL), p. 301.

185 "The blacks dispersed": *The Moreton Bay Courier*, 23 December 1850, supplement, p. 1.

185 "The blacks immediately": *The Sydney Morning Herald*, 3 February 1851, p. 2.

185–6 "He was addicted": *Select Committee Report on the Native Police Force*, 17 July 1861, (QLA), *Minutes of Evidence*, p. 11.

186 "This Force never": Walker to Colonial Secretary, 1 March 1852, in *The Sydney Morning Herald*, 16 June 1852, supplement, p. 1.

186-7   "It was very curious": *Manchester Evening News*, 16 June 1874, p. 4.

187   "very natty" & following: *Report from the Select Committee on Murders by the Aborigines on the Dawson River*, 3 August 1858, (NSWLA), *Minutes of Evidence*, p. 53.

187-8   "the lives and property": Walker to Colonial Secretary, 18 February 1851, enclosing a resolution of the magistrates of Wide Bay, 19 February 1851, 51/2577, NSW Colonial Secretary – Letters relating to Moreton Bay and Queensland, QSL Reel A2.23, (JOL), p. 848. "'Neddy' : p. 847. "The Native Police": p. 843. "A large number": p. 845.

14 TO THE ISLAND

189   "It is fresh": *The Sydney Morning Herald*, 8 February 1849, p. 3.

189   "He was totally": *The Moreton Bay Courier*, 17 November 1849, p. 2.

190   "Old Dickey": *The Freeman's Journal*, 17 October 1850, p. 6.

190   "numerous inconsistencies": *The Moreton Bay Courier*, 26 October 1850, p. 3.

190   "squatting lords" & "My impression": *The Moreton Bay Courier*, 11 January 1851, p. 3.

190   "He was a squatter": *The Moreton Bay Courier*, 1 December 1849, p. 2.

190   "Glaring and improper": *The Sydney Morning Herald*, 27 September 1850, p. 3.

191   "The sound of the Gospel": *The Sydney Morning Herald*, 8 March 1850, p. 2.

191   "coarse and underserved": *The Moreton Bay Courier*, 14 December 1850, p. 2.

191   "They would not be men": *The Sydney Morning Herald*, 26 December 1850, p. 2.

191   "Being under": *The Sydney Morning Herald*, 20 November 1851, p. 3.

192   "Mostly inaudible": *The Empire*, 12 April 1851, p. 5.

192   "Totally inaudible": *The Maitland Mercury*, 16 April 1851, p. 4.

192   "The lands thus": *The Moreton Bay Courier*, 2 August 1851, p. 1.

193   "Why, magistrates": *The Moreton Bay Courier*, 7 June 1851, p. 3.

193   "the poor man's" & "NO CONVICTS": *The Moreton Bay Courier*, 24 May 1851.

193   "It can scarcely": *Moreton Bay Free Press*, 11 September 1851, p. 3, clipping located in Jones to Colonial Secretary, 51/10262, NRS 905, Colonial Secretary Main Series of Letters Received, (NSWSA), p. 526.

193   "mass of scandalous": *The Moreton Bay Courier*, 3 January 1852, p. 2.

194   "Great services" & following: Jones to Colonial Secretary, 2 September 1851, 51/9055, NSW Colonial Secretary – Letters relating to Moreton Bay and Queensland, QSL Reel A2.21, (JOL), pp. 44-5.

194   "As long as he": note on Walker to Colonial Secretary, 22 October 1851, 51/10967, NRS 905, Colonial Secretary Main Series of Letters Received, (NSWSA), p. 1.

194   "The aborigines of the north": *The Sydney Morning Herald*, 20 November 1851, p. 3.

195   "to keep up a constant": *The Moreton Bay Courier*, 10 November 1851, supplement, p. 1.

195   "It must, unhappily" & following: Attorney-General Plunkett to Colonial Secretary, 1 April 1851, 51/3313, NRS 905, Colonial Secretary Main Series of Letters Received, (NSWSA), pp. 837-9.

195-6   "The town was full" & following: *The Moreton Bay Courier*, 20 November 1852, p. 4.

197   "I informed Mr Walker": Uhr to Colonial Secretary, 26 December 1851, 52/751, NRS 905, Colonial Secretary Main Series of Letters Received, (NSWSA).

197   "Mr Duncan Cameron was ready": Walker & Leith Hay to Colonial Secretary, 1 January 1852, 52/717, NRS 905, Colonial Secretary Main Series of Letters Received, (NSWSA).

197   "Great preparations": *The Sydney Morning Herald*, 4 June 1852, p. 2.

197   "Having engaged": Walker to Colonial Secretary, 5 January 1852, 52/715, NSW Colonial Secretary – Letters relating to Moreton Bay and Queensland, QSL Reel A2.23, (JOL), p. 820.

198   "essential to the protection" & following: *The Sydney Morning Herald*, 24 January 1852, p. 2.

199-200 "The Police fired": Walker to Colonial Secretary, 5 January 1852, p. 823. "Two troopers jumped" & "The Blacks made frequent": p. 824. "But it was too late" & "I started with the remaining": pp. 825-6. "It is needless": p. 830. "It is difficult": pp. 828-9. "The Native Serjeants" & "They followed them": p. 827. "I was too footsore": p. 828.

200   "He was a good": Skinner, *Police of the Pastoral Frontier*, p. 167.

200   "A lot of our people" & "All's I know": Anna Weisse and Anne Ross, "Managing a Contested Cultural Heritage Place on K'gari (Fraser Island), Queensland, Australia", *Archaeology in Oceania*, vol. 52, no. 3, 2017, p. 155.

200   "So much secrecy": *The Sydney Morning Herald*, 4 June 1852, p. 2.

200   "Frequent allusions": *The Moreton Bay Courier*, 18 September 1852, p. 2.

201   "In future we cannot": Walker and Leith Hay to Colonial Secretary, 1 January 1852, 52/717, NRS 905, Colonial Secretary Main Series of Letters Received, (NSWSA).

201   "I have had the honor": Uhr to Colonial Secretary, 26 December 1851, 52/751, NRS 905, Colonial Secretary Main Series of Letters Received, (NSWSA).

201   "One half of the Police": Walker to Colonial Secretary, 5 January 1852, p. 829. "The Commandant's movements": p. 820.

202   "very insufficient": *The Sydney Morning Herald*, 12 June 1852, supplement, p. 2.

15 RETRIBUTION ALONE

204   "every lady's": *The Sydney Morning Herald*, 8 August 1853, p. 5.

205   "becoming aware" & "The remains of the deceased": *The Moreton Bay Courier*, 13 November 1852, p. 2.

205-6   "the things that are behind" & following: *Early Reminiscences of R. Jones*, written by his third daughter Elizabeth, 1899, in Papers Relating to Richard Jones 1833–1899, (ML), pp. 6–7.

206   "every description": *The Moreton Bay Courier*, 6 December 1856, p. 1.

206   "Various schemes": *Maryborough Chronicle*, 25 February 1935, p. 4.

206   "He has left me": Uhr to Colonial Secretary, 17 March 1853, 53/2850, NSW Colonial Secretary – Letters relating to Moreton Bay and Queensland, QSL Reel A2.29, (JOL), pp. 677–8.

207   "I have accomplished": Uhr to Colonial Secretary, 21 April 1853, 53/4171, NSW Colonial Secretary – Letters relating to Moreton Bay and Queensland, QSL Reel A2.29, (JOL), pp. 682–3.

207   "In no part": Preface to John Herbert Plunkett, *The Australian Magistrate*, printed by Anne Howe at the *Gazette* office, Sydney, 1835. "Murder is the killing" & following: pp. 231–9.

209   "Having heard of the loss": *The Moreton Bay Courier*, 6 November 1852, p. 2.

209-10 "Drunken orgies": *The Moreton Bay Courier*, 5 June 1852, p. 2.

210   "once more turned": *The Moreton Bay Courier*, 28 May 1853, p. 2.

210   "Mr. Furber seems" & following: *The Moreton Bay Courier*, 29 December 1855, p. 3.

211   "Ill or well": *The Sydney Morning Herald*, 11 May 1853, supplement, p. 2.

212   "inert, inexplicable" & following: *The Moreton Bay Courier*, 29 May 1852, p. 2.

212   "Are we poor devils": *The Sydney Morning Herald*, 27 May 1852, p. 3.

212-13   "I lost no" & following: *The Sydney Morning Herald*, 16 June 1852, supplement, p. 1.

214   "the calumnious" & following: Fourteen Burnett squatters to Colonial Secretary in *The Sydney Morning Herald*, 11 September 1852, p. 3.

214   "such free access": *Progress Report from the Select Committee on Crown Lands*, 29 November 1854, (NSWLC), *Minutes of Evidence*, p. 80.

214   "His intellect was keen": *The Queensland Times*, 22 December 1866, p. 4.

215   "That terrible failing": Morris to Walker, 6 September 1854, General Correspondence records of the Native Police, Series ID 14733, Item ID 86134, (QSA).

215   "irregularities, drunkenness": *Select Committee Report on the Native Police Force*, 28 January 1857, (NSWLA), *Minutes of Evidence*, p. 17.

215   "Should Mr. Walker": Marshall to Colonial Secretary, 25 November 1854, NSW – Typescript copies of correspondence of the Colonial Secretary's Department, 54/10704, Item ID 2969642, (QSA), 30_21.

215-16   "DEAR NED": Walker to Trooper Ned, undated 1854, NSW – Typescript copies of correspondence of the Colonial Secretary's Department, Item ID 2969666, (QSA), 56_118.

216   "Mr. Walker took his seat": *The Moreton Bay Courier*, 5 January 1856, p. 2.

216   "Civilization always": *Report from the Select Committee on Murders by the Aborigines on the Dawson River*, 3 August 1858, (NSWLA), *Minutes of Evidence*, p. 52.

216-17   "There is no": *The Sydney Morning Herald*, 10 November 1854, p. 2.

217   "Mr Uhr said": Aldridge to Colonial Secretary, 10 July 1856, 56/6062 under 56/6915, NRS 905, [4/3334], Colonial Secretary Main Series of Letters Received, (NSWSA).

217   "We will guarantee" & following: *Maryborough Chronicle*, 5 March 1907, p. 4.

218   "Just as they": Theophilus Pugh, *Moreton Bay Almanac for the Year 1859*, self-published, Brisbane, p. 76.

218   "The blacks": *Report from the Select Committee on the Native Police Force*, 17 July 1861, (QLA), p. 150.

218   "I would sooner" & "They certainly": *Select Committee Report on Murders by the Aborigines on the Dawson River, Minutes of Evidence*, p. 54. "bark and slabs": p. 52. "Some of them": p. 53. "I don't think" & "Certainly, in the scrubs": p. 52.

220   "Every one acquainted": *The North Australian*, 1 September 1857, p. 3.

220   "for 'forcibly taking'": Remarks of J.D. Wood dated 12 March 1862 under Cowper to Colonial Secretary, 10 April 1862, Inwards Correspondence, 62/1118, Item ID 3682020, (QSA), p. 3.

222   "Arrivals from English": Judith Wright, *The Cry for the Dead*, Oxford University Press, Melbourne, 1981, p. 90.

222   "spared none": George Pearce-Serocold to Charles Serocold, 31 December 1857, George Edward Pearce-Serocold Papers 1842–1951, (JOL) from Jonathan Richards, *The Secret War*, University of Queensland Press, St Lucia, 2017, p. 64.

222   "The murder of" & "three Gins": Colonial Secretary to Wickham, 15 March 1858, cited by Skinner, *Police of the Pastoral Frontier*, p. 278.

222   "I now know" & following: George Lang to his uncle Andrew Lang, 31 March 1858, Letters, documents and autograph books, 1718–1895, George Dunmore Lang, A63, (ML), pp. 176–9.

225   "It is the duty": *Select Committee on the Native Police Force*, 1861, Appendix A, p. 152.

16 QUEENSLAND

226   "The cheers that were given": *The Moreton Bay Courier*, 13 December 1859, p. 2.

226   "full-blown": Bowen to Carnarvon, 12 November 1866, Despatch 61, Records of the Colonial Office (as filmed by the AJCP), Fonds Series CO 234, File 16, AJCP Reel No: 1915, Despatches, p. 277.

226   "Sir, that was": *The Moreton Bay Courier*, 24 December 1859, p. 4.

227   "Of all narrow-minded": *The Sydney Morning Herald*, 11 May 1853, supplement, p.2.

227-28 "numerical majority" & "Your petitioners": petition to HM Queen Victoria, *The Moreton Bay Courier*, 14 January 1854, p. 4.

228   "Look at him": *The North Australian*, 23 February 1858, p. 3.

228   "leviathan squatter": *The Moreton Bay Courier*, 17 March 1858, p. 2.

228   "The numerous cavalcades": Bowen to Newcastle, 7 April 1860, Despatch 32, Records of the Colonial Office (as filmed by the AJCP), Fonds Series CO 234, File 1, AJCP Reel No: 998–999, Despatches, pp. 374–5.

229   "The darkies had": *The Moreton Bay Courier*, 3 January 1860, p. 2.

229   "In the early days": Bowen to Newcastle, 10 April 1860, Despatch 33, Records of the Colonial Office (as filmed by the AJCP), Fonds Series CO 234, File 1, Despatches, pp. 402–3.

229-30 "The spears": Bowen to Newcastle, 16 December 1861, Despatch 74, Records of the Colonial Office (as filmed by the AJCP), Fonds Series CO 234, File 5, AJCP Reel No: 1908, Despatches, pp. 197–9. "territory over which": p. 204.

230   "able, manly": *The Moreton Bay Courier*, 7 February 1860, p. 3.

231-32 "The Speaker is": *Maryborough Chronicle*, 14 March 1861, p. 3.

232   "The fear of Bligh" & following: *The Courier* (Brisbane), 4 June 1861, p. 2.

232   "One evening": *Maryborough Chronicle*, 5 June 1907, p. 3.

233   "Mr. Bligh, with a party": *The Moreton Bay Courier*, 25 April 1861, p. 2.

233-34 "I saw the Native": *Report from the Select Committee on the Native Police Force*, 17 July 1861, (QLA), p. 24.

234   "plain questions": *Maryborough Chronicle*, 21 March 1861, p. 2.

234   "Heads were gravely": *The Moreton Bay Courier*, 25 April 1861, p. 2.

234   "Many might think" & further references to the meeting: *The Moreton Bay Courier*, 21 February 1860, p. 4.

235   "the meanest" & following: *The Empire*, 3 March 1860, p. 5.

236   "as a mark": *The Sydney Morning Herald*, 10 January 1861, p. 5.

236   "I was on duty": Evidence of John O'Connell Bligh, 8 February 1860, Coronial Files (Inquests and No Inquests), Darkey [Aboriginal], Item ID 2720136, (QSA).

236-37 "I make this request": Uhr to Colonial Secretary, 30 November 1860, 60/2210 and 60/2242, Item 846738, (QSA).

237   "He expressed a very": *Maryborough Chronicle*, 27 September 1905, p. 2.

237   "First-class Boiling-down": *Maryborough Chronicle*, 28 November 1861, p. 3.

238   "Mr. Uhr makes great": *Maryborough Chronicle*, 24 July 1862, p. 2.

238   "have always commanded": *Maryborough Chronicle*, 27 November 1862, p. 3.

238   "two superior Engines": *The Brisbane Courier*, 24 September 1864, p. 1.

238   "After some show": *Wide Bay and Burnett Times*, 6 March 1860, p. 2.

238–39 "We desire": *The Moreton Bay Courier*, 20 October 1860, p. 3.

239   "profusely embellished": *The Sydney Morning Herald*, 10 January 1861, p. 5.

239   "passing with a single": *Maryborough Chronicle*, 28 February 1861, p. 3.

239   "a blot so foul": *Maryborough Chronicle*, 7 March 1861, pp. 2–3.

239   "I should say": *Maryborough Chronicle*, 28 February 1861, p. 3.

239–40 "the noble way": *Maryborough Chronicle*, 18 April 1861, p. 3.

240   "reclaim the wilderness": *Moreton Bay Courier*, 16 April 1861, p. 5.

240   "diabolical scoundrels": *Maryborough Chronicle*, 9 January 1861, p. 2.

240   "Let all such": *Maryborough Chronicle*, 14 March 1861, p. 2.

241   "The information of witnesses": *The North Australian*, 19 February 1861, p. 4.

242   "some thirty": *Maryborough Chronicle*, 4 April 1861, p. 4.

242   "To the Officer": *The Moreton Bay Courier*, 16 March 1861, p. 3.

243   "Two blacks": Walker to Attorney-General, 10 July 1861, Inwards Correspondence, 61/1909, Item ID 3682003, (QSA).

244   "a bookish young man": Wright, *The Cry for the Dead*, p. 100.

244   "My blacks asked" & following: *The Sydney Morning Herald*, 3 February 1862, p. 8.

244   "In a state": *The North Australian*, 15 November 1861, p. 3.

244   "My blacks": *The North Australian*, 13 December 1861, p. 3.

244   "their powers for mischief": *Maryborough Chronicle*, 14 March 1861, p. 2.

244   "All the difficulties": *The Moreton Bay Courier*, 16 April 1861, p. 2.

245   "charges of unnecessary": *Report from the Select Committee on the Native Police Force*, 17 July 1861, (QLA), p. 2.

245   "What amount of impartiality": *The Moreton Bay Courier*, 7 May 1861, p. 2.

246–48 "committed many outrages" & "perfectly impossible": *Report on the Native Police Force*, 1861, *Minutes of Evidence*, pp. 154–5. "justified in his attack": p. 4. "I told them to surround": *Minutes of Evidence*, p. 17. "I think that they": *Minutes*, p. 4. "If the object" & following: *Minutes*, p. 83.

248   "defied any man" & following: *The Courier* (Brisbane), 27 July 1861, p. 5.

248   "It did seem strange": *The Courier* (Brisbane), 31 July 1861, p. 2.

249   "A more piquant": *The Courier* (Brisbane), 25 July 1861, p. 2.

249–50 "Now it is": *The Courier* (Brisbane), 5 August 1861, p. 2.

250   "the perfect state": Walker to Colonial Secretary, 3 April 1861, Inwards Correspondence, 61/944 under 61/2545, Item ID 846751 – Part 2, (QSA).

250   "Returning homeward" & following: *The Sydney Morning Herald*, 12 December 1861, p. 5.

251   "an uncontrolled desire": Bowen to Newcastle, 16 December 1861, Despatch 74, Records of the Colonial Office (as filmed by the AJCP), Fonds Series CO 234, File 5, AJCP Reel No: 1908, Despatches, pp. 196. "just chastisement": p. 200.

251   "The Native Police overtook": *Rockhampton Bulletin*, 30 November 1861, p. 2.

251   "the little town": Wright, *The Cry for the Dead*, p. 121.

252   "If they were not": *The North Australian*, 13 December 1861, p. 3.

252   "unjust and unmanly": *The North Australian*, 15 November 1861, p. 3.

252   "Charles Dutton threw": Wright, *The Cry for the Dead*, p. 116.

252–53 "The first lesson": Newcastle to Bowen, 8 March 1862, Despatch No. 7, Despatches from the Secretary of State for the Colonies: Vol. 3, Item ID 17699, (QSA).

III REG & D'ARCY

255   "The native mounted": *Australian Town and Country Journal*, 15 March 1879, p. 31.

17 PRO CHRISTO ET PATRIA

256   "No people": *The Sydney Morning Herald*, 24 May 1859, p. 3.

257   "This corps was looked": *The North Australian*, 3 May 1861, p. 3.

258   "I think a white": *Report from the Select Committee on Murders by the Aborigines on the Dawson River*, 1858, *Minutes of Evidence*, p. 52.

258   "being a young": Murray to Colonial Secretary, 27 February 1863, Inwards Correspondence, 63/511, Item ID 846768 – Part 1, (QSA).

258   "I believe every blackfellow": *Report from the Select Committee on the Native Police Force*, 17 July 1861, (QLA), *Minutes of Evidence*, p. 26.

258   "It is a farce": *Maryborough Chronicle*, 28 February 1861, p. 3.

259   "I have seen": *The Courier* (Brisbane), 25 June 1861, p. 2.

259   "the demoralising influence": *Maryborough Chronicle*, 11 April 1861, p. 2.

259   "known to be drunk": *Select Committee Report on the Native Police Force*, 1861, *Minutes of Evidence*, p. 145. "the inefficiency": p. 2.

259   "kindly promised": Uhr to Colonial Secretary, 11 September 1862, Correspondence received – Lands and Works Department, 62/877, Item ID 22038, (QSA).

259   "I am to request": Manning to R.C.H. Uhr, 2 January 1863, 1863/7, *Letterbook*, Item ID 861037 – Part 1, (QSA), p. 166.

259   "murdered, by shooting": *The Courier* (Brisbane), 17 August 1863, p. 2.

260   "as a band of trained savages": *Maryborough Chronicle*, 10 September 1863, p. 2.

261   "I replied that" & following: *The Courier* (Brisbane), 17 August 1863, p. 2.

262   "I hereby order": *Maryborough Chronicle*, 13 August 1863, p. 3.

262   "The native police officers had": *The Courier* (Brisbane), 21 August 1863, p. 3.

262   "The bench do not require": *The Courier* (Brisbane), 17 August 1863, p. 2.

263   "The native police officers": *The Courier* (Brisbane), 26 June 1865, p. 2.

264   "fast going to decay": Marlow to Colonial Secretary, 6 April 1863, Inwards Correspondence, 63/747, Item ID 846768 – Part 6, (QSA).

264   "Troopers after a period": *Australian Town and Country Journal*, 22 March 1879, p. 31.

265   "Dark blue cloth": Rules for the general government and discipline of the Native Mounted Police Force, *Queensland Government Gazette*, 10 March 1866, vol. VII, no. 28, p. 261.

265   "This, I believe": Charles Tom to Colonial Secretary, undated 1864, Inwards Correspondence, 64/1765, Item ID 846786 – Part 1, (QSA).

266   "British soldiers could": *The Queenslander*, 17 June 1899, p. 1119.

267   "We are perfectly": *The Courier* (Brisbane), 5 August 1862, p. 2.

267   "We had seven": *The Courier* (Brisbane), 5 March 1862, p. 3.

267   "The whole coast": *Report of the Proceedings of the Queensland Government Schooner "Spitfire"*, Brisbane, 1860, p. 25.

268   "It is now": *The North Australian*, 7 June 1861, p. 4.

268   "race of bloodthirsty miscreants": Dalrymple to Colonial Secretary, 10 October 1861, Inwards Correspondence, 61/2787, Item ID 846752 – Part 1, (QSA).

268   "They were speedily": *Rockhampton Bulletin*, 9 July 1861, p. 3.

268-67 "The new settlement": *Maryborough Chronicle*, 10 October 1861, p. 2.

269   "a noble view": David Adams (ed.), *The Letters of Rachel Henning*, Penguin Books, Sydney, 1963, p. 111.

269   "We are likely": Henning to her sister Etta, May 1863, Rachel Henning letters, MLMSS 342/2, CY Reel 1098, frames 295-6, (ML).

270   "I have had": Powell to Dalrymple, 9 December 1861, Inwards Correspondence, under 61/3151, Item ID 846753, (QSA).

270   "Rather a pleasant": Henning to her sister Etta, 29 June 1863, Rachel Henning letters, frame 297.

270   "the savage character" & following: *The Courier* (Brisbane), 5 March 1862, p. 3.

271   "in a most": William Bayley to Rudolf Morisset, 17 September 1863, Inwards Correspondence, 63/2215 under 63/2231, Item ID 846774 – Part 5, (QSA).

271   "Cadet Uhr is not": Monthly Return of the Queensland Native Police Force, October 1863, Inwards Correspondence, 63/2329, Item ID 846775 – Part 2, (QSA).

271-72 "Armstrong and Charley": *The Courier* (Brisbane), 10 November 1863, p. 2.

272-74 "Where *they* 'disperse'": *The Port Denison Times*, 1 May 1869, p. 2.

274   "as since that date": Executive Council Minute, 16 September 1864, Executive Council minutes and despatches 1864/50, Item ID 16944, (QSA).

274   "They each had" & following: Henning to T.W. Boyce, 27 November 1864, Rachel Henning letters, frames 408-9.

275   "Although no lives": Pinnock to Colonial Secretary, 17 November 1864, Inwards Correspondence, 64/3322 under 64/3412, Item ID 846792 – Part 2, (QSA).

275   "I have had two": Black to Colonial Secretary, 5 December 1864, Inwards Correspondence, 64/3415, Item ID 846792 – Part 2, (QSA).

275   "accompanied by the atrocious": *The Brisbane Courier*, 3 December 1864, p. 5.

276   "There is no need": *The Brisbane Courier*, 8 December 1864, p. 2.

276   "The blacks having been lately": *The Port Denison Times*, 7 January 1865, p. 2.

276   "A pretty little": Cuthbert Fetherstonhaugh, *After Many Days*, E.W. Cole, Melbourne, 1917, p. 267. "It has never been": p. 193. "The heat was very": p. 268. "His legs were": p. 271. "I was just": p. 272.

277   "prompt justice": *Maryborough Chronicle*, 1 April 1865, p. 2.

277   "shooting six blacks": George Murray to Seymour, 23 January 1865, *Letterbook – Springsure Police Station*, Item ID 2368964, (QSA).

277-79 "We all started off": Fetherstonhaugh, *After Many Days*, pp. 273-4.

18 VALLEY OF LAGOONS

280   "We discovered": Ludwig Leichhardt, *Journal of an Overland Expedition in Australia*, T. & W. Boone, London, 1847, pp. 241-2.

281   "as though suddenly": *The Brisbane Courier*, 6 August 1864, p. 5.

281   "shovelling capital": *The Morning Bulletin* (Rockhampton), 17 February 1896, p. 6.

281   "I have the satisfaction": *Rockhampton Bulletin*, 14 November 1863, p. 2.

281   "By this time": Herbert to Walter Scott, 9 January 1864, Valley of Lagoons Station deposit, Noel Butlin Archives Centre, AU NBAC M27.

282   "special reasons": *Rockhampton Bulletin*, 11 October 1864, p. 2.

282   "Do not shoot me,": James Morrill, *Sketch of a Residence Among the Aboriginals of Northern Queensland for Seventeen Years*, Brisbane, 1863, p. 16.

283–84 "On nearing the beach": *Maryborough Chronicle*, 21 April 1864, p. 1.

284   "large muscular men" & "cunning savages": *The Brisbane Courier*, 6 August 1864, p. 5.

284   "I long to hear": Bowen to Arthur Scott, 31 March 1864, Valley of Lagoons Station deposit.

284   "set upon suddenly": *Maryborough Chronicle*, 21 April 1864, p. 1.

286   "The story about": *The North Australian* (Brisbane), 5 July 1864, p. 3.

286   "Our account is nevertheless": Herbert to Walter Scott, 3 October 1865, Valley of Lagoons Station deposit.

286   "would be to allow": *The Brisbane Courier*, 6 August 1864, p. 5.

286–87 "To do so I should": Blakeney to Leefe, 16 January 1865, Inwards Correspondence, 65/352 No. 6, Item ID 846794 – Part 1, (QSA).

287   "The native police": *The Port Denison Times*, 18 February 1865, p. 3.

287   "indomitable perseverance": Inhabitants of Cardwell to Colonial Secretary, 8 May 1865, Inwards correspondence, 65/1269, Item ID 846797 – Part 3, (QSA).

287   "within four miles": George Murray to Seymour, 4 May 1865, *Letterbook – Springsure Police Station*, Item ID 2368964, (QSA).

288   "most indefatigable": *Maryborough Chronicle*, 1 April 1865, p. 2.

288   "Prompt justice": *The Perthshire Journal and Constitutional*, 27 July 1865, p. 3.

288   "Our black brethren": *The Port Denison Times*, 29 July 1865, p. 2.

288   "I am sure": Walter to Mrs James Scott, 29 May 1872, Valley of Lagoons Station deposit.

289   "After the establishment": Yvonne Cadet-James, Robert Andrew James, Sue McGinty, Russell McGregor, *Gugu Badhun: People of the Valley of Lagoons*, Australian Institute of Aboriginal and Torres Strait Island Studies, Canberra, 2017, p. 24.

289   "dressing", "I am rather sorry" & "Do think well": Arthur to Walter Scott, 21 March 1866, Valley of Lagoons Station deposit. "I entirely": Walter to Arthur Scott, 22 May 1874. "if the concern": Herbert to Tommy Ashburton, 18 November 1864. "no longer to indulge": Robert Herbert to Walter Scott, 31 October 1865. "You know the way": Arthur to Charles Scott, 31 October 1865. "Mind you send": Arthur Scott to his brothers, 22 February 1865.

290   "Well, one silly fool": Cadet-James et al, *Gugu Badhun*, p. 26.

291   "About eighteen years" & "Lieutenant Uhr": *The Port Denison Times*, 2 February 1866, p. 2.

292   "that indefatigable": *The Port Denison Times*, 2 May 1866, p. 2.

292   "<u>very</u> imperfect" & "they could": George Murray to John Murray, 29 April 1866, *Letterbook – Springsure Police Station*, 137/66, Item ID 2368964, (QSA).

292   "A tremendous amount": *The Brisbane Courier*, 9 September 1865, p. 5.

292   "Looking on the twenty-two": *The Empire*, 5 September 1865, p. 4.

293   "Lieutenant Murray denies": republished in *The Brisbane Courier*, 16 August 1865, p. 4.

293   "The Queensland Government": *The Brisbane Courier*, 9 September 1865, p. 5.

293   "Lieutenant Marlow proposed": *The Port Denison Times*, 11 July 1866, p. 2.

293   "Natives from very" & following: *The Port Denison Times*, 21 July 1866, p. 2.

19 AT LAST A PERCH

294   "We are no great": *Maryborough Chronicle*, 28 September 1864, p. 2.

295   "Of this individual": *Rockhampton Bulletin*, 9 May 1865, p. 2.

295   "Where the Governor": *The Perthshire Journal and Constitutional*, 17 August 1865, p. 3.

295   "The Sergeant-at-Arms": *The Brisbane Courier*, 11 September 1865, p. 2.

295   "inevitably taints": *Maryborough Chronicle*, 13 August 1863, p. 3.

295   "A horrible new": *Australian Dictionary of Biography*, vol. 6, Melbourne, 1976, p. 348.

296-97 "I counted them": *The Queensland Times*, 29 June 1865, p. 4.

297   "It was perhaps": Robert Ørsted-Jensen, *Frontier History Revisited*, Lux Mundi, Brisbane, 2011, p. 68.

297   "June 4th": *The Brisbane Courier*, 26 June 1865, p. 1.

297   "in a state": Gideon Lang, *The Aborigines of Australia*, Wilson and MacKinnon, Melbourne, 1865, p. 77. "an ordinary proceeding": p. 80. "there has always": pp. 45–6.

298   "If the late": *The Empire*, 4 August 1865, p. 4.

299   "It was a reckless": *The Brisbane Courier*, 5 August 1865, p. 5.

299   "As in all": Bowen to Cardwell, 5 April 1864, Dispatch 15, Records of the Colonial Office (as filmed by the AJCP), Fonds Series CO 234, File 10 Reel No: 1912, Dispatches, p. 121.

300   "Guns, pistols" & "Gentlemen, the triumph": *The Queensland Times*, 24 October 1865, p. 3.

301   "in very pretty": *Maryborough Chronicle*, 14 December 1864, p. 2.

301   "If blacks have": *Maryborough Chronicle*, 8 July 1865, p. 3.

302   "I can speak": *The Northern Territory Times*, 13 March 1886, p. 3.

302   "Mr Uhr is, we believe": *Maryborough Chronicle*, 2 December 1865, p. 2.

302-3   "I don't think they can understand": *Select Committee Report on the Native Police Force*, 17 July 1861, (QLA), *Minutes of Evidence*, pp. 29–30.

304   "An officer must" & "Each of them": Richards, *The Secret War*, pp. 94–5.

304   "a considerable party": William Landsborough Papers, Series 1: Diaries (21 February–26 April 1866), OM69-17/340, (SLQ), introduction.

304   "We were going": *The Telegraph* (Brisbane), 25 December 1878, p. 2.

20 TROUBLEMAKER IN A SHANTY TOWN

305   "He had had twenty": *The Courier* (Brisbane), 1 September 1862, p. 3.

305   "They get through": *Bourne's Journal of Landsborough's expedition from Carpentaria in Search of Burke and Wills*, H.T. Dwight, Melbourne, 1862, p. 22.

306   "When fully occupied": Report of Edward Lamb, Chief Commissioner of Crown Lands, *The Brisbane Courier*, 17 January 1866, p. 5.

306   "Monday 5th March": William Landsborough Papers, Series 1: Diaries
(21 February–26 April 1866), OM69-17/340, (SLQ), 5 March 1866.

307   "The rain came down": *The Telegraph* (Brisbane), 25 December 1878, p. 2.

308   "There is a boy": "Last Letter of Mr Duncan McIntyre, Leader of the Leichhardt
Search Expedition, and an Account of His Death", *Proceedings of the Royal
Geographical Society of London*, 1866–1867, vol. 11, no. 1, p. 43.

308   "Some declared" & "They had races": *The World's News*, 12 May 1906, p. 7.

309   "They were stretching": *The Courier* (Brisbane), 29 April 1862, p. 4.

309   "We may surmise": *The Queensland Times*, 22 December 1866, p. 4.

310   "Men went there": Edward Palmer, *Early Days in North Queensland*, Angus &
Robertson, Sydney, 1903, p. 179.

310   "Before we had gone": William Landsborough Papers, Series 1: Diaries
(27 April–17 July 1866), OM69-17/341, (SLQ), 14 May 1866.

310   "I had to cook" & "Finding it difficult": *The Brisbane Courier*, 10 May 1870, p. 3.

311   "perseverance rarely" & following: *The Empire*, 10 October 1866, p. 2.

311   "Early upon the following" & following: Michael Hall to Colonial Secretary,
10 October 1870, Inwards Correspondence, 70/3098, Item ID 846880 – Part 4,
(QSA).

312   "The gentleman in charge": *The Queenslander*, 8 December 1877, p. 16.

312   "It has been customary": Watson to Colonial Secretary, 18 June 1880, Inwards
Correspondence, 80/3823 under 80/4815, Item ID 847029 – Part 1, (QSA).

312   "Let any 'missionary'": *The Port Denison Times*, 12 June 1869, p. 2.

313   "every proof": Chatfield to Police Magistrate, Bowen, 14 January 1869. "Can
you kindly": Chatfield to the Attorney-General, 6 January 1869. "I hardly see":
Police Magistrate, Bowen, to Commissioner of Police, 30 March 1869. "would
remedy": Undated note of Under Colonial Secretary Robert Gray, all in 69/1483,
item 846851 (QSA).

313   "to carry away": *Slave Trade Act*, 1824 (UK), section 2.

313   "any Child under": *Offences Against the Person Act*, 1828 (UK), section 21.

313   "Before the arrival" & following: Michael Bird Hall to Colonial Secretary,
10 October 1870, 70/3098, Item ID 846880 – Part 4, (QSA).

314   "the correspondence": Truman Smith, "The Kidnapping of Aboriginal People in
Colonial Queensland 1859–1897: Labour, Violence and Government Inaction",
University of Newcastle thesis, May 2022, p. 156.

314   "I do not know": Note on letter from Cooktown Police Office to Commissioner
of Police, 2 March 1882, Inwards Correspondence, 82/1304 under 82/1385,
Item ID 847064 – Part 2, (QSA).

314   "I don't think": Note on telegraph from Cooktown Police Office to Colonial
Secretary, 1 March 1882, Inwards Correspondence, 82/1069 under 82/1385,
Item ID 847064 – Part 2, (QSA).

314   "An exceptionally smart": *The World's News*, 18 July 1908, p. 7.

315   "No police ever": *The Queenslander*, 3 February 1883, p. 169.

315   "The Chinese mustered" & "The Gulf country": *The Brisbane Courier*, 19 April
1867, p. 3.

315–16   "It is certain" & "Without police conversant": Sharkey to Colonial Secretary,
6 September 1867, Inwards Correspondence, 67/2639 under 67/2846, Item ID
846827 – Part 3, (QSA).

316   "Shots with blank": *The World's News*, 12 May 1906, p. 7.

316   "Several people" & following: *The Brisbane Courier*, 11 July 1867, p. 2.

316   "Mr Landsborough fruitlessly": Sharkey to Colonial Secretary, 6 September 1867, Inwards Correspondence, 67/2639 under 67/2846, Item ID 846827 – Part 3, (QSA).

317   "There was no police": *Minutes of Evidence Taken Before the Select Committee on the Management and Working of the Police Force*, 1869, Item ID 282459, (QLA), pp. 26–7.

317   "that while in the heat": Deposition of D'arcy Uhr, 18 December 1866, Briefs, depositions and associated papers in criminal cases heard, Item ID 95535, (QSA).

318   "hail fellow well met": *The Brisbane Courier*, 10 May 1870, p. 3.

318   "an immense time": *Minutes of Evidence Taken Before the Select Committee on the Management and Working of the Police Force*, p. 11.

318   "Firing guns": *Rockhampton Bulletin*, 2 July 1867, p. 3.

318   "by order": *The Brisbane Courier*, 20 November 1867, p. 2.

320   "have charge": Cabinet decision, Inwards Correspondence, 67/57 under 67/2846, Item ID 846827 – Part 3, (QSA).

320   "It is impossible for me" & "Mr Uhr has deserved": Seymour to Colonial Secretary, 27 November 1867, Inwards Correspondence, 67/3065 under 69/2159, Item ID 846855 – Part 3, (QSA).

320   "It is very necessary": D'arcy Uhr to Colonial Secretary, 14 March 1868, Inwards Correspondence, 68/1354, Item ID 846835, (QSA).

321   "We had the first" & "Possessed of great": Hetzer & Little to Colonial Secretary, 18 April 1868, 68/1720, Item ID 846836 (QSA).

322   "As soon as" & following: *The Brisbane Courier*, 9 June 1868, p. 3.

21 NO BETTER MAN

324   "For though I had": Fetherstonhaugh, *After Many Days*, pp. 280–1.

324   "The inhabitants": *The Brisbane Courier*, 28 July 1866, p. 6.

325   "Lieutenants Uhr": *The Northern Argus*, 7 November 1866, p. 3.

325   "On the creek bank": *The Gympie Times and Mary River Mining Gazette*, 19 December 1903, p. 12.

325   "eight or ten": *The Brisbane Courier*, 2 November 1866. p. 2.

326   "It is not doubted": Memorandum of Herbert, 20 June 1866, Enclosure 2 to Despatch 61 of 1866, Letterbook of despatches to the Secretary of State for the Colonies, Item ID 17672, (QSA), p.634.

326   "rather important": *The Port Denison Times*, 23 January 1867, p. 2.

326   "We should almost": *The Port Denison Times*, 21 July 1866, p. 2.

328   "It is of course": *The Port Denison Times*, 23 January 1867, p. 2.

328   "attempted to secure": Truman Smith, "The Kidnapping of Aboriginal People in Colonial Queensland 1859-1897: Labour, Violence and Government Inaction", University of Newcastle thesis, May 2022, p. 207.

328   "That the Government": *The Port Denison Times*, 23 January 1867, p. 2.

328   "result in increased" & "Refusing to let": *The Port Denison Times*, 13 April 1867, p. 2.

329   "From the year 1864": Chatfield to Police Magistrate in Bowen, 14 January 1869 enclosed in Colonial Secretary, 69/1483, Item ID 846851, (QSA).

329   "Every man who" & following: *The Port Denison Times*, 5 March 1881, p. 2.

330   "Sir I do myself": Reginald Uhr to Colonial Secretary, 23 June 1868, Inwards
        Correspondence, 68/2021, Item ID 846838 – Part 1, (QSA).

331   "Those great scrubs": Wright, *The Cry for the Dead*, p. 120.

331   "I deemed it advisable": *Rockhampton Bulletin*, 23 November 1867, p. 2.

331   "Sub-Inspector Uhr's hundred": *Truth* (Brisbane), 28 December 1924, p. 13.

332   "He said he was branded": *Rockhampton Bulletin*, 3 December 1867, p. 2.

332   "I have been five": *Rockhampton Bulletin*, 24 March 1868, p. 2.

332   "despotic, arbitrary": *Rockhampton Bulletin*, 1 October 1867, p. 2.

333   "The skill shewn": *The Northern Argus*, 13 May 1868, p. 2.

333   "He was shown" & following: *Rockhampton Bulletin*, 26 May 1868, p. 3.

334–35 "the inroads" & "No better man": republished in *Maryborough Chronicle*, 6 April
        1869, p. 3.

335   "utterly unsuitable" & "It is not here": republished in *Rockhampton Bulletin*,
        2 December 1869, p. 2.

335   "Be particular": Murray to Wheeler, 24 November 1869, Letterbook of letters
        sent by the Inspector's Office, Northern District, Springsure, 182/69, Item ID
        282366 – Part 2, (QSA).

22 BLAZE OF GLORY

336   "Exterminating the Natives": *Weekly Review* (London), 12 September 1868,
        p. 901.

336   "Australian Vengeance": *Bradford Daily Telegraph*, 9 September 1868, p. 3.

336   "Colonial Humanity" & following: *Freeman's Journal*, 27 June 1868, p. 8 and
        The Nation (Dublin), 29 August 1868, p. 19.

336–37 "The savages committed": *The Illustrated London News*, 12 September 1868,
        p. 239.

337   "I trust that great": Cardwell to Bowen, 27 March 1865, Despatch 20, Original
        despatches, Item ID 294399, (QSA).

338   "I should be glad": Cardwell to Bowen, 26 March 1866, Despatch 18, Original
        despatches, Item ID 294400, (QSA), p. 155.

338   "The Imperial Government": Memorandum by Herbert, 20 June 1866,
        Enclosure 2 to Despatch 61 of 1866, Letterbook of despatches to the Secretary of
        State for the Colonies, Item ID 17672, (QSA), p. 635.

338   "Aborigines from destruction" & "Who appear": Executive Council Minute,
        7 November 1866, 1866/64, Executive Council Minute outlining options for
        protection of the Colony, Item ID 3682040, (QSA).

339   "I earnestly wish" & following: Carnarvon to Bowen, 6 February 1867, Despatch
        6, Original despatches, Item ID 294401, (QSA).

339   "men of high": *The Brisbane Courier*, 16 June 1868, p. 2.

340   "The camp": *Rockhampton Bulletin*, 15 June 1867, p. 3.

340   "It was a pity": *Maryborough Chronicle*, 17 July 1867, p. 3.

340   "His attention": *The Brisbane Courier*, 16 June 1868, p. 3.

340–41 "The attack on the camp": *The Brisbane Courier*, 16 June 1868, p. 2.

341   "quietly": Murray to Seymour, 13 July 1867, Letterbook of letters sent by the
        Inspector's Office, Northern District, 113/67, Item ID 282366 – Part 1, (QSA).

341   "very much exaggerated": Seymour to Bowen, 15 June 1866, Enclosure 3 to
        Despatch 61 of 1866, Letterbook of despatches to the Secretary of State for the
        Colonies, Item ID 17672, (QSA), p. 637.

341　"The last *Gazette*": *The Brisbane Courier*, 16 June 1868, p. 2.

342　"His temperament": *The Kalgoorlie Miner*, 19 February 1907, p. 4.

342　"If the blacks": *Rockhampton Bulletin*, 20 December 1864, p. 1.

342　"The piece de resistance" & following: *The World News*, 22 August 1908, p. 10.

343　"a somewhat wild": *The World's News*, 12 May 1906, p. 7.

343　"I refused to obey": W.D. Uhr to Coward, 23 November 1868, *Minutes of Evidence Taken Before the Select Committee on the Management and Working of the Police Force*, 1869, from Queensland Votes and Proceedings, 1869, vol. 1, Item ID 282459, (QLA), p. 126.

343　"disobedience of orders": Seymour to Colonial Secretary, 25 January 1869, Inwards Correspondence, 69/286 under 69/2159, Item ID 846855 – Part 3, (QSA).

343　"very gross": Extracts from the Police Charge Sheet – Norman, Inwards Correspondence, 71/449, Item ID 846882 – Part 8, (QSA).

343　"after mature" & following: Colonial Secretary to Seymour, 18 February 1869, Letterbook of letters to other departments, 69/135, Item ID 861252 – Part 2, (QSA).

344　"I should certainly" & "He refused": W.D. Uhr to Police Commissioner, 29 March 1869, 69/2159, Item ID 846855 – Part 3, (QSA).

344　"About the latter": W.D. Uhr to Police Commissioner, 12 November 1869, Inwards Correspondence, under 69/4532, Item ID 846865 – Part 3, (QSA).

345　"Mr Uhr has been" & "In new districts": Scarr to Colonial Secretary, 15 November 1869, 69/4532, Item ID 846865 – Part 3, (QSA).

346　"Uhr was thought": Scarr to Secretary of Lands, 15 November 1870, Inwards Correspondence, 71/449, Item ID 846882 – Part 8, (QSA), pp. 17–18. "It was plain": p. 5.

346　"Almost all": *The Brisbane Courier*, 3 September 1870, p. 6.

346　"party to an illegal": Scarr to Secretary for Lands, 15 November 1870, p. 1.

346　"guilty of culpable": Landsborough to Colonial Secretary, 3 December 1870, Inwards Correspondence, 71/114 under 71/449, Item ID 846882 – Part 8, (QSA).

347　"Mr Uhr seemed": Hetzer to Scarr, 25 November 1870, Inwards Correspondence, 71/449, Item ID 846882 – Part 8, (QSA).

347　"fat boy", "Billy Intelligent" & "By ELECTRIC": *Norman Snorter*, enclosure to Landsborough to Colonial Secretary, 18 October 1870, Inwards Correspondence, 70/3427 under 71/449, Item ID 846882 – Part 8, (QSA).

349　"They drove us": "About Kurtjar Land, A Statement by the Kurtjar People of Normanton, Queensland", Australian Institute of Aboriginal [and Torres Strait Islander] Studies, 1980, p. 2.

349　"couple of civilised" & "Mr. Wentworth": *The Brisbane Courier*, 12 October 1871, p. 3.

350　"Dogs barking": *The Brisbane Courier*, 13 October 1871, p. 3.

350　"But the[y] would" & following: Johnston to Inspector of Police – Burke District, 12 August 1871, Inwards Correspondence, 71/2267, Item ID 846890 – Part 2, (QSA).

350–51　"The evidence appears": Morisset to Seymour, 24 August 1871, Inwards Correspondence, 71/2267, Item ID 846890 – Part 2, (QSA).

23 THE REAPER

352   "Mr. Uhr had a very" & following: *The Brisbane Courier*, 14 July 1874, p. 2.

354   "there was not": Record of Proceedings (Hansard), 3 July 1878, (QLA), p. 699.

354   "scamper after": Robert Gray, *Reminiscences of India and North Queensland*, Constable, London, 1913, p. 219.

354   "For beauty and shade": *The Queenslander*, 19 May 1877, p. 24.

354   "They are the pick": *The Brisbane Courier*, 12 June 1875, p. 3.

355   "the premier": *The Week* (Brisbane), 29 March 1884, p. 9.

355   "archpriest": Geoffrey Blainey, *Mines in the Spinifex: The Story of Mount Isa Mines*, Angus & Robertson, Sydney, 1962, p. 26.

355   "often not": Clerk to Seymour, 10 May 1884, CLERK, Frederick M., Item ID 563142, (QSA).

355   "The only tragedy": *The Brisbane Courier*, 24 October 1883, p. 2.

355   "Will you kindly" & "Have information": Seymour notes, 24 October 1883, SMART, Alfred, Item ID 564448, (QSA).

355   "Ernest Henry can" & "Do all you can": Seymour notes, 25 October 1883, SMART, Alfred, Item ID 564448, (QSA).

356   "made all possible": Lacey to Seymour, 20 December 1883, SMART, Alfred, Item ID 564448, (QSA).

356   "They crossed, full gallop": *The Leader* (Melbourne), 30 August 1884, p. 35.

357   "gross partiality": Low to Colonial Secretary, 15 April 1886, Colonial Secretary, Inward Correspondence, 87/5174, Item ID 847237 – Part 1, (QSA), p. 137. "broke up the ball" & "fooling": Low's report on Habitual Drunkenness, p. 140. "whore shop" & "I do not want": Low to Uhr, 24 January 1886, p. 139. "Mr Uhr, the Police", "The landlord came" & "Mr Uhr to explain": Low to Colonial Secretary, 4 September 1886, p. 104. "could not obtain": Testimonial, 13 January 1887, p. 62.

357-58 "I have drifted": Uhr to Colonial Secretary, 14 July 1886, Inwards Correspondence, 87/3111, Item ID 847228 – Part 2, (QSA).

359   "The bronzed face" & following: *The Queensland Figaro and Punch*, 12 February 1887, p. 5.

360   "Otherwise I shall": Uhr to Colonial Secretary, 8 February 1887, Inwards Correspondence, Item ID 847220 – Part 1, 87/1096, (QSA).

360   "Cobb & Co": Uhr to Colonial Secretary, 22 April 1887, Inwards Correspondence, 87/3276, Item ID 847229 – Part 1, (QSA).

360   "I do not ask": Uhr to McIlwraith, 14 July 1888, Inwards Correspondence, 88/6393, Item ID 847283 – Part 2, (QSA).

360-61 "The purport of my visit": Amy Uhr to Colonial Secretary, 4 August 1888, Inwards Correspondence, 88/7019, Item ID 847286 – Part 2, (QSA).

361   "He was a white": *The Western Champion* (Blackall), 21 August 1888, p. 2.

24 D'ARCY IN HIS PRIME

362   "a fearless": F.H. Bauer, *Australian Dictionary of Biography*, Volume 6 1851–1890, p. 321.

362   "thousands of stock": *The Evening Journal* (South Australia), 15 July 1871, p. 3.

363   "Just as the four" & following: *The Brisbane Courier*, 27 October 1874, p. 3.

364   "They were renowned" & following: Tony Roberts, *Frontier Justice: A History of the Gulf Country to 1900*, University of Queensland Press, 2005, p. 19.

367 "Uhr rushed": *The South Australian Advertiser*, 12 November 1872, p. 2.

368 "A great rush": *The Northern Mining Register*, 25 May 1892, p. 21

369 "The country is not": *The Queenslander*, 8 December 1877, p. 16.

369 "The miners must": *The Queenslander*, 20 February 1875, p. 10.

369–70 "Were the Government ": *The Brisbane Courier*, 6 October 1875, p. 3.

370 "In a wild unsettled": Seymour to Colonial Secretary, 30 April 1874, Inwards Correspondence, under 74/2913, Item ID 846933 – Part 3, (QSA).

370 "A day or so": *The Brisbane Courier*, 3 November 1874, p. 3.

371 "We pushed on" & following: *The Telegraph* (Brisbane), 26 June 1875, p. 5.

372 "After a couple": *Gold to Grass: The Reminiscences of Arthur C. Ashwin, 1850–1930, Prospector and Pastoralist*, Hesperian Press, Carlisle, Western Australia, 2002, p. 109.

372 "mere amusement" & "He does not say": *The Telegraph* (Brisbane), 3 July 1875, p. 5.

373 "I am sure": *Cooktown Courier*, 1 September 1875, p. 3.

373 "Darcy made a few": Ashwin, *Gold to Grass*, p. 119.

373 "picaresque": Wright, *The Cry for the Dead*, p. 209. "Uhr was a careless" & following: pp. 212–13.

373 "spear horses": *The Brisbane Courier*, 6 August 1879, p. 6.

374 "I am the pioneer": *The Northern Territory Times*, 16 October 1880, p. 2.

374 "One of the best": *The Northern Territory Times*, 18 December 1880, p. 2.

374 "The assault was": *The North Australian*, 29 July 1886, p. 2.

374 "This place": *The Northern Territory Times*, 11 June 1881, p. 2.

374 "Darcy (indignantly)": *The Northern Territory Times*, 2 July 1881, p. 2.

374 "The present season" & following: *The North Australian, 11 January 1884, p. 3.*

375 "eagerly undertook": *The Sydney Stock and Station Journal*, 10 March 1922, p. 4.

375 "He called me" & "I do not consider": *The North Australian*, 4 April 1884, p. 3.

376 "a fluent statement": *The North Australian*, 21 March 1884, p. 3.

376 "It would be useless": *The Northern Territory Times*, 21 March 1884, p. 3.

376 "certain all": *The North Australian*, 2 May 1884, pp. 2–3.

376 "the black-protecting": *The South Australian Register*, 13 September 1884, p. 6.

377 "I do not hold": *The South Australian Register*, 9 September 1884, p. 7.

377 "We have stolen": *The South Australian Register*, 11 September 1884, p. 1.

377–78 "Despite this knowledge": W.R. (Bill) Wilson, "A Force Apart? A History of the Northern Territory Police Force 1870–1926", Northern Territory University thesis, 1 July 2000, pp. 327–8.

378 "My sympathies": W.D. Uhr as "Yarraman", *The Advertiser* (Adelaide), 18 August 1891, p. 7.

378 "Their deeds": *The South Australian Register*, 6 February 1886, p. 7.

378 "cut fourteen notches": *The South Australian Register*, 28 November 1885, p. 6.

378 "We have no hesitation": *The South Australian Register*, 14 November 1885, p. 4.

379 "One of them": *The South Australian Register*, 13 November 1885, p. 6.

379 "well acquainted" & "Had these men": *The Northern Territory Times*, 9 January 1886, p. 3.

380 "Psalm-singing" & "These men": *The Northern Territory Times*, 13 March 1886, p. 3.

380   "meant that police": Gordon Reid, *A Picnic with the Natives: Aboriginal–European Relations in the Northern Territory to 1910*, Melbourne University Press, Melbourne, 1990, p. 112.

380   "The Hotel has": *The North Australian*, 13 February 1885, p. 2.

382   "The pastoralists came": Richard Trudgen, *Why Warriors Lie Down and Die: Djambatj Mala*, Why Warriors Pty Ltd, Nhulunbuy, 2010, pp. 19–20.

383   "stunted pines" & "What with the dangers": *The Northern Territory Times*, 25 February 1888, p. 3.

383   "We did so": *The Northern Territory Times*, 3 March 1888, p. 3.

25 THE LAST CHAPTER

384   "Considering that some" & following: *The Sydney Morning Herald*, 16 September 1889, p. 9.

384   "two glasses": *The Sydney Morning Herald*, 20 September 1893, p. 4.

385   "Some hundreds: *The Adelaide Observer*, 11 August 1894, p. 43.

386   "big pheller yerilla": *The Western Mail* (Perth), 12 May 1938, p. 11.

386   "BEWARE OF": *The Coolgardie Miner*, 21 July 1894, p. 3.

386   "Darcy Uhr proposed" & following: Ashwin, *Gold to Grass*, p. 158.

386   "Now you wear": *Smith's Weekly*, 19 February 1927, p. 21.

387–88   "We had only" & following: *The Coolgardie Miner*, 18 August 1894, p. 4.

389   "Who is this": Commissioner of Police to Sub-Inspector Daniel O'Connell, 28 August 1894, Eastern District, York Sub-district, Coolgardie Police Station, Information on a Mr Darcy Uhr, AU WA S76 cons430 1894/1810, State Records Office of Western Australia.

389   "From information": Saunders to Stokes, 3 September 1894, Eastern District, York Sub-district, Coolgardie Police Station, Information on a Mr Darcy Uhr, AU WA S76 cons430 1894/1810, State Records Office of Western Australia.

389–90   "If you had seen": N.K. Sligo, *Mates and Gold: Reminiscences of the Early Westralian Goldfields 1890–1896*, Hesperian Press, Victoria Park, Western Australia, 1980, p. 82.

390   "When our Winchester": *The Eastern Recorder* (Kellerberrin), 25 April 1924, p. 7.

390   "That locality" & following": *The Coolgardie Miner*, 18 July 1896, p. 4.

390–91   "It would appear": *The Western Australian Goldfields Courier*, 1 August 1896, p. 27.

391   "The Alligator Rivers": *The Northern Territory Times*, 27 March 1896, p. 3.

392   "Notable ... were": *The Coolgardie Miner*, 25 June 1898, p. 4.

392   "Meat ring": *The Coolgardie Miner*, 15 March 1899, p. 6.

392   "A Voice": *The Coolgardie Miner*, 30 July 1900, p. 6.

393   "There is no": *The Coolgardie Miner*, 29 September 1904, p. 3.

394   "Of course there": *The Sun* (Kalgoorlie), 8 January 1905, p. 6.

395   "I know I could" & "to deceive": *The Sunday Times* (Perth), 6 August 1905, p. 3.

395   "with good gold" & "Mr. Uhr spoke": *The West Australian*, 30 November 1904, p. 8.

395   "A TURF INQUIRY": *The Coolgardie Miner*, 2 November 1904, p. 3.

395   "My goldfields correspondent": *The Sunday Times* (Perth), 22 January 1905, p. 10.

396   "HIS GOOD NAME": *The Sunday Times* (Perth), 12 February 1905, p. 1.

396   "He was our butcher's": *The Sunday Times* (Perth), 2 April 1905, p. 5.

396   "in which Mr. Uhr": *The Coolgardie Miner*, 12 January 1907, p. 4.

397   "There were some": *The Sunday Times* (Perth), 24 February 1907, p. 9.

398   "an armed, mobile": Richards, *The Secret War*, p. 92.

398   "It was this breech-loading": Ray Evans, Kay Saunders & Kathryn Cronin, *Race Relations in Colonial Queensland: A History of Exclusion, Exploitation and Extermination*, University of Queensland Press, St Lucia, 1993, p. 57.

398   "to the gradual": Report of the Commissioner of Police for the Year 1879, Journals of the Legislative Council, Queensland, 1880, vol. XXIX, Part 1, p. 331.

399   "the sickening" & "This, in plain language": *The Way We Civilise; Black and White; The Native Police: A Series of Articles and Letters Reprinted from the Queenslander*, G. and J. Black, Brisbane, 1880, p. 3. "Hide it as you will", p. 28.

401   "The blacks were entrenched" & following: Record of Proceedings (Hansard), 21 October 1880, (QLA), p. 1132–6. "The best liars" & "completely stuffed": p. 1137.

403   "the nature and causes" & "My travels": Archibald Meston, *Report on the Aboriginals of Queensland*, Brisbane, 1896, p. 1; "One-third": p. 4.

404   "*ex parte* aboriginal": *Report on the North Queensland Aborigines and the Native Police*, Brisbane, 1897, p. 7. "whose evidence is" & "So long as bushmen": p. 15.

404   "Spare of flesh": Geoffrey Searle (ed.), *Australian Dictionary of Biography*, vol. 11, Melbourne University Press, Melbourne, 1988, p. 147.

404   "To keep our": Meston, *Report on the Aboriginals of Queensland*, p. 14.

405   "The bill proposed": *The Brisbane Courier*, 16 November 1897, p. 7. "So much power": p. 4.

406   "military force": *Australian War Memorial Act*, 1980 (Aus.), section 3.

AFTERWORD: FAMILY BUSINESS

410   "They used the bullet": Jack Green, *Lead in My Grandmother's Belly*, Borroloola, 2020, https://www.leadinmygrandmothersbody.com/paintings

410   "What is so amazing": White to Geoff and Ninette Dutton, 28 December 1973, David Marr (ed.), *Patrick White Letters*, Random House, Sydney, 1994, p. 428.

INDEX